5

(Si

by

<---- **Rebbe Nachman of Breslev** ---->

Unabridged and with *Rimzei haMa`asiyoth* and Many Appendices

W hich we have been privileged to hear from the mouth of Rabbeinu Hakadosh, the Hidden and Concealed Light, *Nachal Nove`a Mekor Chokhmah*/ The Gushing Stream, The Source of Wisdom[1], HaRav Rebbe **NACHMAN** *ztzuk"l* of Breslev, great grandson of the **Ba`al Shem Tov** Hakadosh and composer of the books **Likutei Moharan** and several other compendiums.

G o out and see the might of your Master[2] Who has illumina-ted heavenly Torah for us to enliven us as [sure as] it is this day[3], for the everlasting world[4]; and our God has not forsaken us in our servitude but has extended kindness to us[5] in each and every generation and has sent us deliverers and rabbis and *tzaddikei yesodei `olam*/ righteous ones, foundation of the world[6] to teach us the way. His first [mercies] have come to pass[7] and yet His mercies have not ceased[8] at any period or any time. And He has performed kindness for us, drawing water from the wellsprings of salvation[9], towering things, things that are the secrets of the universe[10], un-der wonderful and awesome clothings.

S ee and understand and look at his wonderful and awesome way, which is an inheritance to us from our holy forefathers who were during ancient times in Yisrael. For such is the way of the upper holy ones[11], harvesters of the field[12], who raised their hands and hearts to God, clothing and concealing the King's troves within story tales ac-cording to the generation and according to the times. "Knowers of dis-cerning the times, to know what Yisrael should do" [1 Chron. 12:33] un-til [Mashiach] arises and delivers Tziyon and returns to build the ruins of Ariel. "Now Ya`akov and Yisrael are told what God has done."[13]

In the year *[5]575* (1815 C.E.)

English translation edited by Nissim Kaufmann, PhD   Albany, NY   2016

regarding this edition

As there had been a need for an accurate, freely distributable translation of *Sipurei Ma`asiyoth* into English, draft translations by several friends of BreslovBooks.com were carefully edited in accord with the original texts and compiled here. This translation's text is now available under the CC-BY-SA 3.0 copyleft at the following url: http://en.wikisource.org/wiki/Portal:Breslov

Thanks to R' Yaakov Siegel n"y of Far Rockaway, NY for invaluable answers and help.

Visit *www.BreslovBooks.com*
for all of Rebbe Nachman's books at non-profit prices and for free download
♦♦

The story sub-section headings that appear in brackets have been added by the editor as an aid for navigation and study and are not part of the original text. The original printing did not have story titles either; the stories were only headed *"Ma`aseh* א*," "Ma`aseh* ב*,"* etc.

The 1815 Yiddish/Hebrew first print of *Sipurei Ma`asiyoth* is available as a DjVu scanned image file from the JNUL Digitized Book Repository (Document Record Number **001124825**) at

http://aleph.nli.org.il/nnl/dig/books/bk001124825.html

and text files are available at the Hebrew and Yiddish Wikisource websites. In the 1815 edition, the tales were followed by the texts that are known today as *Shivchei haRan* (but with header *"Sipurei Ma`asiyoth"* there), *Sichoth haRan* (only through #110 and with header *"Likutei Moharan"* there), as well as omissions from and corrections to *Likutei Moharan* I.

The end of the preface and the beginning of Tale 1 from the 1815 printing.

TABLE OF CONTENTS

Foreword

Lehithvada` Ul'higaloth/ Let it Be Known and Revealed...

Foreword in Yiddish from the 1ˢᵗ printing, 5575/1815, <u>Ostroh</u>:
...that the stories in this book contain great secrets of the Torah; they contain very great things. There is no trivial word in them and even simple folk can take great *mussar* [practical life guidance] from the stories. For these stories have a great power to awaken all people from sleep so that a person should not, Heaven forbid, sleep through his days for nothing. And whoever will look into the stories with an honest eye can see and understand a little of God's greatness; even simple folk can also get some glimpse of hints of mussar. So one should take a good look around, what the purpose of the world is; so one should not rely only on this world. And one should pray day and night, and one should be saved from the foolishness of the world, and one should merit to be as Hashem Yithbarakh desires. And furthermore there are hidden things available in the stories that one cannot write or tell of, that it would be good if he could know [even] just a bit of them. And because we once heard from his mouth saying that he had great yearning that the stories should be printed with Hebrew above and Yiddish below, therefore we have fulfilled his holy desire and we have printed it so, because common folk also need to be acquainted with the stories; even if they understand scant little of what they mean and where the stories reach, a great benefit is derived for him toward the ultimate [life] purpose if he will look into them with an honest eye, because they have a great power to awaken [a person] to the Almighty, as mentioned, for the stories are not empty things, Heaven forbid. And the Rebbe, rest in peace, would each time after most of the stories confirm each sentence and each thing; so people should know that he did not say any wasted words, Heaven forbid. He slightly indicated only a little of where the stories reach unto, for all these stories are secrets of the Torah through and through.

Foreword in Yiddish from the 2ⁿᵈ printing, 5610/1850, <u>Lemberg (Lviv)</u>:
...that every word that stands here in this holy book is holy of holies; a great deal of the Torah's secrets. One should not think that they are simple tales, for the stories that stand in this book were told by the great tzaddik, the highest saint, the holy rabbi, Rabbi **NACHMAN**, memory of the Tzaddik bring blessing; may his merit stand up for us. His intention was to teach us how to serve the Almighty. And if only we would understand the great secrets and lessons that are put in these stories, we would be devout Jews like we ought to be. And Hashem Yithbarakh should send us the Righteous Redeemer now in our times, quickly in our days, Amen.

Preface

*M*ah shehayah kevar nikra shemo venoda` shehu adam/ [His greatness] in the past, his fame has long since been declared, and it is known that he was a [great] man[14]. *Vezoth torath ha'adam/* And this is the Torah of a great man[15] of holiness, who merited to complete the image of man, *ki-zeh kol-ha'adam/* for this is the entire [purpose] of man[16]. Is it not his honor, our lord, our master, and our rabbi, crown of our glory, pride of our strength, the holy and the awesome Rav, the major luminary, the upper light, the honorable and holy light, of holy renown, our master Rav **NACHMAN**, mention of the righteous and holy bring blessing, great grandson and nephew of the holy and awesome Rav the Godly Baal Shem Tov, mention of the righteous and holy bring blessing, whose light Yisrael have already enjoyed in his holy and wonderful compositions which have already come to light. Many are they who have seen and rejoiced, and the upright who have been gladdened[17]; the truth will make itself known.

*A*nd behold, see what else is in our sack[18]: wonderful and awesome story tales, which we have been privileged to hear directly from his holy mouth, who balanced, probed and established many similes, clothing and concealing lofty and awesome perceptions in story tales in very wonderful and awesome ways. Because so was [the custom] long ago in Yisrael, regarding redemption and regarding exchanging[19], that when they wanted to speak of the hidden things of God, they would talk in the manner of riddles and similes, and they clothed Torah's hidden things, the King's troves, in many, many different clothings and garments, as it is conveyed after the tale of the King's Son and Maid's Son [#11 in this book], where Rabbeinu z"l said then, that in the early days, when the friends would talk and speak Kabbalah, they would speak in such language, because until Rashbi they would not speak Kabbalah openly etc. And for the most part after several stories he would reveal a little bit, a drop in the sea of some clues where the things reach to, as the things and the clues which he told after each and every story are explained below in their places. And behold, until now these things were hidden with us, but only because many have said to our souls, *"Mi yir'enu tov/ Who can show us anything good?"*[20] — for they are many who are with us, fellow believers as us, whose souls have hoped and been consumed to constantly hear the words of the Living God which came out of the mouth from Rabbeinu Hakadosh z"l, and particularly these stories he told, which they had not yet merited that they reach them except in handwritten copies via various copiers through which the errors multiplied greatly and the meaning was spoiled — and therefore their great desire compelled us and their strong hope pressed us, until we were forced to fulfill their wishes and bring them to the printhouse. And also because there was a disclosure from the mouth of our great Rabbi z"l, as one time he revealed his mind that he wanted to print story tales — and he declared it in these words before several people: "I have in mind to print a book of story tales, and it should be written above in the holy tongue [Hebrew] and below in the common tongue [Yiddish];" and he said, "Really, what can the world say against this, for anyways are they not nice stories to tell?!" etc. — such words were heard from his holy mouth explicitly, and this is what has moved us to bring them to the printhouse.

And if we would have indeed known, and had it not been hidden from our eyes, that many had arisen against him — nevertheless the truth is witness for itself, and we are obligated to do his will, and Hashem will do what is good; the one who hears will hear and who refrains will refrain. And also because, praise God, until now His mercies have helped us, for his holy compendiums have spread out within the Holy People, in the community, the assembly and Yisrael, and his words have been joy and happiness to them, and have been sweet as honey in their mouths. All will be satiated and delight from his goodness; their souls shall be satisfied as with grease and fat, and with shouting lips their mouths shall praise. And they are more who are with us than those who argue against the truth, speaking arrogantly against the Tzaddik in arrogance and spite, who have fabricated from their hearts things that were not on his mind; but we need not belabor and talk about this, for it is a thing of Hashem's concern. And several worlds have been turned over because of that person, because of the great controversy, which has increased in our days between the chakhamim and the tzaddikim. But who can criticize the King for what is already done?

But let this be known, that our whole intention in printing these story tales is only for *anshei shlomeinu*/ our own people, who take refuge in his holy shade, who crave and hope and yearn to hear his holy words [Translator's note: It is clear that Rabbi Nachman wanted these tales available to everybody. Rather, there was great opposition to the printing of the stories, including the fact that some tzaddikim considered the stories too high for public consumption. This comment, and others, were included so as to assuage the opposition.] And if actually the words are printed in a book, it is as if they were said before a great assembly. On the other hand, we have already seen that the words have already begun to spread in writing via many copies, and there is no difference between writing and print, and also from the start they did not speak secretly, because whoever has eyes will see, and whoever has a heart will understand, *"ki lo-davar reik hu, mikem/* for it is no empty thing [unless it seems empty] due to you"* [Deut. 32:47], because these words stand at the heights of the very heights. And we heard from his holy mouth explicitly saying that each and every utterance in these stories has astounding intentions, and whoever changes one utterance from these stories from the way he himself told them, causes much to be lacking from the story. And he said that these stories are very, very wonderful and awesome novelties, containing very extraordinarily deep ways and secrets, and they are fit to be spoken before an audience, to stand in a synagogue and tell a story from these tales, because they are very, very high and awesome novelties.

Also he whose heart is whole and who is expert in the books of holiness, and particularly in the books of the holy Zohar and writings of the Arizal, of blessed memory [obm], can understand and know a little bit of the hints in some stories if he puts his heart and mind to them very well.

They also have very wonderful and astounding arousal of life lessons in most places. An intelligent man will understand them on his own, because virtually all of them arouse and pull the heart very much to Hashem Yithbarakh, to return to Hashem Yithbarakh in truth for truth's sake, to delve only in Torah and devotions constantly, and to turn his face away from vanities of the world completely, as one who sees will see with the eyes of his intellect if he gazes into them in truth. However, the ultimate aim of the intentions in these stories is much too far from the knowledge of mortals. *"Ve`amok `amok, mi yimtzaenu/* And deep-deep, who can find it out?"[21] And the praise of the splendor of greatness of these stories ought not be prolonged, because they are exalted above our knowledge, and whoever additionally speaks in praise of their greatness and depth, detracts; we have only spoken in order to somewhat alert the heart of those of our faith in order that they not forget their wonder which he showed them from afar, like one who shows with a pointer how far these things reach, via a few hints which he revealed to our eyes after telling each and every story. For although truly some of the hints were recorded which were heard from his holy mouth, nonetheless it is clear to any intelligent person that one who hears from the mouth of a *chakham/* sage himself is not like someone who sees the things in a book. And all the more so, regarding the ways of clues like this which are not understandable except by movement of the limbs, by nodding the head, squinting the eye, tilting the hand and so forth as these, through which specifically the understanding person can understand a little bit and be stymied at the sight and his eyes from afar see the greatness of Hashem and the greatness of His holy Torah which has been clothed in several different clothings as explained in all the books of holiness.

Up to here have reached a few words which encourage much. Our hearts shall "ponder in awe: Where is he that counted, where is he that weighed?"[22] "From where will our help come?"[23] "Who among us shall dwell with the devouring fire?"[24] "Who will stand for us?" Let us lift our hearts with our hands to the Almighty who is in the heavens.[25] Into His hands let us commit our spirits.[26] To You, Hashem, let us raise our souls. Your mercies have helped us until here. Our help is none but You, our Support. And let the pleasantness of Hashem our God be upon us. Until the *moreh tzedek/* Teacher of Righteousness come to our congregation and build our glory the Holy Temple. "Look upon Tziyon, the city of our solemn gatherings"[27] "Your eyes shall see the king in his beauty"[28]. Soon in our days, Amen. These are the words of the writer, arranger, and copier, to be eaten to satisfaction and for lasting clothing.[29] Written by the insignificant

Nathan, son of my lord my father our teacher the rav Rabbi **Naftali Hertz** *y"tzv* from the capital Nemryov, son in law of the rav, the genius the charitable the famous in all corners of the land, his holiness the rav Rabbi **David Tzvi**, memory of the righteous bring blessing, for life of the coming world, who was *av beith din* of the holy community Kreminitz and its environs and of the holy community Sharigrad and of the holy community Mohyliv and its environs.

◆ ◆

B efore he told the first story in this book he spoke up and said: In the story tales that the world tells, there are many hidden things and very lofty matters — but the stories have been spoiled because much is lacking from them and they are also mixed up, and they do not tell them according to the order, telling at the end what belongs in the beginning and vice-versa and so on. But really in the stories that the world tells there are very lofty concealed matters. And the Baal Shem Tov, memory of the righteous bring blessing, was able via a story tale to perform *yichudim/* unifications. When he would see that the upper channels were spoiled and it was not possible to repair them via prayer he would repair them and unify them via a story tale. And more did Rabbeinu of blessed memory speak of this, and afterwards he began to tell the story tale that is on the next page, saying, "On the way I told a story" etc.

A nd know, the stories that Rabbeinu told, virtually all of them are completely new stories that were never before heard; only he himself told them from his heart and his holy knowledge according to the lofty perceptions that he attained in his spirit of holiness, clothing that perception in that story, the story itself being an awesome sight and very lofty perception that he attained, and seeing the place that he saw. And also sometimes he told a story from the stories the world tells but he added much to them, exchanging and repairing the order until the story was completely changed from what the world tells, as mentioned. But from those stories were not written in this book except one or two, and all the rest of the stories are completely new, never before heard.

A t the time when Rabbeinu of blessed memory began involving himself in telling stories, he stated explicitly in these words: "Now I'm going to start telling story tales (*Ikh vil shoyn anheyben maysiyos dertseylen*)," and the intentions of his words were as if to say, "Since it has not been effective for you to return to Hashem Yithbarakh via my holy Toroth and talks and so forth" — which he busied with in great toils all his days to return us to Hashem Yithbarakh in truth for truth's sake, and since all these have not been effective — therefore he begins to involve himself with story tales. And then at that same time he said the torah that begins "*Pathach Rabbi Shim`on ve'amar `eth la`asoth laShem heferu Torathekha*/ Rabbi Shimon opened and said, 'It is time to do for Hashem's sake; they have made void Your law.'" etc. — *da oraitha de`atika*/ this is the Torah of the Ancient of Days, etc. printed in the first book [*Likutei Moharan*] on daf 157 [#60], where he explains at the end of the essay a little of the matter of story tales, that via story tales of the true Tzaddik, people are awoken from sleep who are sunk in sleep and who slumber through their years etc., see there; and [that] there are tales that are within [the context of human experience and] years, and there are stories of "Ancient Character" which have the character of the `Atik*/ the Ancient of Days etc. Take a good look there and understand and be enlightened a little from what has gone forth, how far the words of these stories reach, and what his holy intention was in them. And in truth in these stories there is very, very great arousal to Hashem Yithbarakh in most places, even according to their simple meaning, aside from the hidden things, because they are all awesome secrets and they have great power to awaken everyone to Hashem Yithbarakh. ***Chazak*/ Be strong!**

Second Preface

While we were involved in the first printing of the stories, a voice of tumult we did hear, saying it is not proper to print such story tales. And to repeat their words would be only superfluous, for did we not preempt [this] in the [previous] preface with the words of Rabbeinu of blessed memory, who said that his will was to print story tales, and, "What can the world say about this, for are they anyway not wonderful story tales?" And already many, many story tales have been printed in the world, too many to count, and nobody opens his mouth chirping. Especially since most of the stories of our Admor of blessed memory tell explicitly of very wonderful arousal of mussar, for example the tale of the Prayer Leader, and the tale of the Seven Beggars. Similarly in most stories we find in them explicitly words of wisdom and mussar aside from the hidden things in them, and similarly with several stories there have already been printed remarks and small portions of wonderful and awesome clues that Rabbeinu z"l himself revealed, as explained above. On top of all this, I have decided to make a few more notes [as to] how far the stories hint, according to my frail knowledge, and whoever wishes to add, let him add.

I t is known in all the books of the Zohar and the Tikkunim and in all the writings of the Ari ztz"l that "the king's daughter" is an alias for the *Shekhinah*/ Divine presence and the assembly of Yisrael, as it were, and permission to speak in these terms has already been given to us from the forerunners before us, from whose mouths we receive life. And also Dawidh haMelekh a"h and Shelomoh his son used these terms very much, as it is written, *"Kol kevudah bath melekh penimah*/ All-glorious is the King's Daughter, who is within" [Ps. 45:13], and many other such cases. And the whole book of Song of Songs which is holy of holies, which the whole world is not worthy of, is founded on this *sod* [secret or hidden meaning]. And all the writings of the Ari z"l and the books of the Zohar are filled with this, as explained there, "He who slays the serpent is given the king's daughter, which is prayer." And in particular in the discourse of *Saba deMishpatim* [The Old Man in *Parashath Mishpatim*], where he tells of "*ulimtha shapirtha deleith lah `einin*/ the beautiful maiden who has no eyes," and many such instances, too numerous to count. And in the *Yehi ratzon*/ May-it-be-Your-will recited before *Tehilim*/ Psalms: "...and to join the bride of youth with her lover" etc. And likewise in the *Leshem yichud*/ For-the-sake-of-the-unification before laying tefillin that is printed in *Sha`arei Tziyon*, we say "the groom" etc., see there.

A nd whoever looks a little in the writings of the Ari ztz"l will see there explicitly the whole foundation of the kabbalah is in this way, to unite the aspect of the groom and bride, male and female. And all the holy names and sefirot and all the down-chain of the worlds are explained there according to the likeness and image of the male profile, etc.; and explained there in detail are all their limbs and all the matters of unification, relations, impregnation, birth, nursing, and growth of a baby [lit. "little one"] and a baby girl until they become grown etc. etc.. And this is explained in great detail throughout the `Etz Chayim and the Peri `Etz Chayim. And also the Idra Raba to [Zohar] Nasso and Ha'azinu speaks by this way of remez. And also the whole book of Shir HaShirim/ Song of Songs is full of this, as it specifies all the limbs of the groom as the bride praises him, and likewise specifies the members of the bride as the groom praises her. And also our Rabbis obm in the Midrashim likened mathan Torah/ the giving of the Torah to a wedding, as they said, "beyom chathunotho/ on the day of his espousals [Song 3:11] — this is mathan Torah" etc., and they said regarding the verse, "Likrath ha'Elohim/ to meet God [Ex. 19:17] — like a groom going out to meet his bride," since the holy Shabbath is called kalah/ bride and malketha/ queen, as it is written, "Lekha dodi likrath kalah... Bo'i kala/ Go, my Beloved, to greet the Bride... Enter, Bride" etc. So it is evident that all our Rabbis obm called the inclusion and the connection of the worlds into their root, by the terminology of groom and bride, for in the image of God He made man, and all the limbs of the male and female are all the image of God, as written, "wayivra Elohim eth ha'adam betzalmo, betzelem Elohim bara otho, zakhar unkevah bara otham/ And God created the man in His image; in the image of God He created him, male and female He created them" [Gen. 1:27]. And as we say in the benediction at a marriage, "asher bara eth ha'adam betzalmo, betzelem demuth tavnitho, vehithkin mimenu binyan `adei `ad/ Who has created the man in His image, in the image of likeness of His construction, and established from him an everlasting construction," etc.

Because the man — האיש והאשה, ha'iYsh veha'ishaH/ the man and the woman — are an actual piece of God on high, and in them are included the Shem Havayah [Y-H-V-H] Barukh Hu, and if they merit, the Shekhinah dwells amidst them, for he has the Yud and she has the Hei, and all these are simple things and evident to everyone, and already the early ones have used these terms to describe Yisrael's drawing near to their Father in Heaven in terms of the connection of man and wife, because all our work, in its upper root, alludes to the joining of the Supernal Groom and Bride which is the aspect of *yichud Kudsha Berikh Hu uSh'khinteh* as all the books of the holy Zohar and the writings of the Ari z"l are full of this, and also on Tish`a be'Av in the *kinoth* that we lament on the exile of the Shekhinah and *kenesseth Yisrael*, we say, "Then when [Yirmiyahu] went... he found a beautiful woman, disgraced"[30] And similarly in the *tikkun*-prayer of the three night-watches which is from the *Zohar Chadash*, there similar terms are used, "like a woman keening over her husband" etc., see there.

From all this, and more than this, it is evident to the eyes the exile of the Shekhinah and assembly of Yisrael is an aspect of the loss of the King's Daughter and her estrangement from her Lover etc. And look in the book of the *Bahir* [and] in the sections omitted from the *Zohar* on *Bereishith* for what is written there regarding, "Come my beloved, let us go out to the field," etc.: a parable of a king who was sitting in rooms within rooms etc. and she was both wed and given to him as a present, and sometimes out of love he calls her "my sister," because he is from the same place, and sometimes he calls her "my daughter," because she is his daughter, and sometimes he calls her "my mother," and thus our Rabbis obm said regarding the verse, "...upon the crown with which his mother crowned him.."[31] — he loved her to the point that he called her "my daughter" etc., and similarly throughout the book of Proverbs he calls the faith and the holy Torah by the name "good woman, woman of valor" and the deceitful beliefs and apostasy by the name "evil woman, promiscuous woman," as explained in Rashi's commentary and all the words of our Rabbis obm. And there has already been printed the story of the Baal Shem Tov obm, at the end of the book *Toledoth Ya`akov Yosef*, of the trader and his wife who were at sea, etc., which is founded on this predicate that the "woman who fears Hashem" is the assembly of Yisrael.

Now that Hashem has informed us of all this, through our early prophets and tzaddikim and sages, according to these words the understanding reader who wants to gaze into these stories with the honest eye for its own sake can easily understand and be enlightened by them, to find wonderful awesome things. And even if it is indeed impossible to reach their character, to understand the story's connection from beginning to end, nevertheless he will understand a little bit of them and it will please his soul greatly.

AND BEHOLD, THE FIRST STORY...

And behold, the first story, of the king's daughter who was lost — it is clear that this is the *sod*/secret of the *Shekhinah*/ Divine Presence in exile. Because the exile of the Shekhinah began before the creation the world, in the secret of "the breaking of the vessels," in the secret of "and these are the kings that reigned" etc. [Gen. 36:31]. And as soon as Adam the first man was created he needed to repair this, to raise up all the worlds to their place, to reveal His blessed kingship, immediately at the time of creation of the world, just as His kingship will soon be revealed at the coming of our Mashiach; may he come speedily in our days. However he was not vigilant against eating from the Tree of Knowledge and so forth, which corresponds to what is written in this story, that the viceroy [lit. second in the kingship] did not stand up to his test and ate the apple, and through this he damaged all the worlds, and the Shekhinah again fell down and descended amongst the *Sitra Achra*/ Other Side, as is known. And afterwards Noach came, and he wanted to repair; but he did not repair, because he drank and got drunk, in the secret of, "And he drank of the wine, and was drunken" etc. [Gen. 9:21]; as taught in the [kabbalistic] books, that this is the aspect of "what is man" etc. [Ps. 8:4], his having not withstood his trial and having drank from the wine, as it is written there. And from then onwards, all the tzaddikim in all the generations have been involved in this repair, until our Mashiach comes, soon in our days, when the repair will be complete.

And this story is about every man and at all times, for even in each individual man almost this whole entire story passes over him, for each member of Yisrael needs to be involved in this repair, to raise the Shekhinah from the exile, "*le'ukma shekhintha me`afra*/ to raise the Shekhinah out of the dirt," to take the *malkhuth dikdushah*/ kingship of holiness out from amongst the idolaters and the Sitra Achra where it has been going around. For this is the secret of all our work and all the mitzvot, good deeds and Torah occupation that we do all the days of our lives, which are all founded on this pole, as explained in the [kabbalistic] writings. And even completely simple people and the masses who do not know their right and left, nonetheless they too if they are privileged to go on the straight path according to their determination, namely to shun evil and do good — because even a completely simple person knows that the Torah forbade, and if his eyes look straight ahead to shun evil and choose good — then all the repairs in the upper worlds are accomplished automatically through him, and he merits to establish the Shekhinah from its fall, in proportion with how much he merits to sanctify and purify himself.

Hence each member of Yisrael is involved in seeking and asking for the King's Daughter, to return her to her Father so that she may return to Him as in her youth in the secret of [Lev. 22:13], "and is returned to her father's house as in her youth; she may eat of her father's bread." For Yisrael as a whole are an aspect of the viceroy, because they rule over the world: just as He revives the dead and heals the sick, so do Yisrael; as they said, "Do not read it `ami/ My people but `imi/ with Me [Isa. 51:16]: 'Just as I created the heavens and earth with my speech, so do you'" etc.; and there are many more of the like. And each person, to the extent that he merits to delve into His service, whereby he delves as it were in seeking and requesting the Shekhinah and the assembly of Yisrael, to take it out from the exile, to that extent it — as it were, the Shekhinah — is revealed to him, as it were, from out of the grip of its exile, and hides and conceals itself and comes to him in secret and reveals to him its place and dwelling and what to do for it so that he be privileged to find it. [Which] this corresponds to the king's daughter's revealing to the viceroy by what means he can take her out. And the means explained there are very explicitly clear according to their simple meaning (for so was the way of Rabbeinu z"l, in most of the stories, that within the connections of the stories he tells words of mussar in the simple sense, as will be clear to one who looks into them).

For, a person must choose for himself a place, and ordain for himself repentance and fasting, and constantly yearn and constantly long for Him, Blessed-be-He, that he be privileged to recognize Him; that His kingship be revealed in the world; "and let every [man who has been] made know that it is You who have made him, and let every [man who has been] formed know that it is You who have formed him, and let all that has breath in its nose say, '...And His kingship rules over all,'" which is the main point of erecting the Shekhinah out of the exile, when people merit to recognize His kingship in complete faith in truth, and everyone knows Him, Blessed-be-He, from little to great, "and the kingship will be Hashem's" etc. And when a man begins to delve in this and chooses for himself a place to be alone [in meditation and conversation with God, *hithbodeduth*] and delve in the service of Hashem and hope and long for Him, Blessed-be-He, and sometimes merits that it continues for some time — then however when he is very close to arrive at his request, that a revelation of His kingship, Blessed-be-He, be revealed to him according to his station — then on the last day a test is summoned for him according to his station, and then on that day upon which everything depends, then the Prosecutor with all his forces fortifies himself against him in a very great surge, and enters into discussion with him and draws him to himself, and he sees that "it is a delight to the eyes, and desirable" etc. [Gen. 3] and he takes from the fruit and eats, God forbid, and he does not withstand his test in which he is required to be tried and purified then at that time. And then sleep immediately falls upon him, and sleep is the absence of the brains, when his mind and wisdom are removed from him, which enlighten his face, in the secret of "and his face fell," and it is written, "Why is your face fallen?" [Gen. 4:5]. Look regarding this at the lesson which begins "*Pathach Rabbi Shim`on*" [#60 in *Likutei Moharan*]. There it speaks of this, that through the blemish of the craving of eating, a person loses his face which is the intellect, and then he falls into the aspect of sleep; take a good look there and you will understand, for there it speaks at length concerning story tales, through which people are awakened from sleep; see there.

And at these times, when a man is in the aspect of sleep, God forbid, what happens to him happens, which corresponds to all the troops who passed over the viceroy when he was asleep. And later he woke up and became aware that he slept so long, and he went again to the place of the king's daughter, and she informed him how much pity there is upon him and her, that because of one day he lost what he lost, and she lightened the prohibition for him, that he need not fast, but only refrain from drinking wine, so that he should not come to sleep. And he again yearned for some long time in service of Hashem in order to take out the king's daughter, but on the last day also did not endure the easier test, for he saw a spring of wine and inclined himself and began to be drawn to it and said to the attendant, "Have you seen? This is a spring, and how does wine come here!?" — and meanwhile he went and took a little and tasted from the wine and immediately sleep fell upon him and he slept very long. For so is the way of the Prosecutor and the cravings: when he wants to incite a kosher man who wants to distance himself from the cravings, that is when he inclines him little by little so that he should wonder and be amazed in his mind at the interest of the thing that he craves after, and as soon as he enters into discussion over the object of desire, the Prosecutor prevails over him until he makes him stumble in it, as explained in the Torah regarding the Tree of Knowledge, how the serpent spoke with the woman, "Did God verily say...? And she saw the tree was good for food, and that it was a delight to the eyes etc." Look and you will find that this is the matter in all the cravings and trials.

And whoever is truly intelligent and has mercy on his soul in truth, to rescue his soul from destruction, and wants to endure the trial — he needs to overcome will all his valor, to distract himself completely and not enter into arguments and counterarguments with the cravings at all, and not speak of, contemplate, wonder at, or be amazed at them at all, and his ideas should not alarm him at all, as written in the Alef-Beth Book [aka *Sefer HaMidoth*], "Do not enter in to argument and counterargument with those who wish to fool you" etc., see there, but just to divert his attention from them completely and make his mind clear with words of Torah or commerce or conversation and so forth, until he escapes from what needs to escape from. And later, such thoughts and ideas return and arise to him, and he needs to again prevail over them, distracting his mind from them, and to do this many, many times; and he needs to be very stubborn until he wins the war.

A nd behold, since the second time too he did not endure the test and tasted from the wine, again a long sleep fell on him and he slept very long, namely seventy years. And the concept of sleeping the whole seventy years is clear from the instruction-lesson *Pathach Rabbi Shim`on/* Rabbi Shim`on in the chapter #60 mentioned above, that there are people who fall away from all the seventy faces of the Torah, which correspond to seventy years, etc. — see there; that it is impossible to arouse and awaken them except via story tales of Ancient Years etc.; take a good look there.

A nd the king's daughter, who is the root of this soul, when she passes by him and sees him fall into sleep many days and years, such a long time, she weeps very much, because there is great pity on him and on her, and then she let him know her place, that now she is not in the first place but in a different place, namely on a golden mountain etc. And the hint is clear, that even though he did what he did and fell how he fell such a very long time, nonetheless the Shekhinah arouses him each time, and each time hints to him new advices how he should seek and ask for the root of his holiness, which corresponds to the king's daughter.

A nd this viceroy, even though he did not endure the test two times and fell into so much sleep and all that passed over him passed over, and after such hard and extraordinary toils, travels, travails and afflictions that had passed upon him in order to find the king's daughter, and then because of one day lost everything — and so he stumbled two times, as mentioned — despite this he did not let himself despair altogether, God forbid, but only went to seek and request the golden mountain and the castle. And after he had many more hard toils and travels and sought the mountain and castle, he found a giant man with a big tree, etc. and this man dissuaded him that surely the mountain and castle do not exist, and wanted to incite him and dissuade him so that he should go back. But the viceroy did not listen to the obstacles and discouragements and said that the mountain and castle surely exist, until the big man was forced to call and assemble all the animals etc., but they all answered that it does not exist. And then he (the big man to the viceroy) said, "Look and see with your eyes that it does not exist; and for what do you exert so much for nothing? If you will listen to my words, go back." But he did not pay attention to this and said that it surely exists, and then the big man answered him that he should go to his brother who is appointed over the birds, and he went and exerted himself and sought him until he found him. And then the second one also dissuaded him and incited him to return, that the mountain and castle surely do not exist. But he did not listen to his words of dissuasion either, and the second one was forced to call and assemble all the birds, but they all answered that the mountain and castle do not exist in the world. And then this second one told him similarly, "See with your eyes that you toil for nothing. Go back." But he did not give ear to the words of the second one either, and said that he was strong in his faith that it surely exists. And then the second one informed him that he should go to his brother who was appointed over the winds. And this one also dissuaded him very much, as before, and afterwards called and assembled all the winds and they all replied that it does not exist. And then this third one said to him, "Now look and see that you have toiled for nothing, because you will certainly no longer find it. Go back." And then he saw that all the ends had been exhausted, and he did not know whether to veer right or left, in order to find her, but in himself he was strong in his mind that the mountain and castle certainly exist, where the king's daughter was captured, and then out of his great pain and bitterness of heart he began to cry very much, and at that moment Hashem Yithbarakh had compassion on him and at the same time another wind came and informed him that it itself had carried the king's daughter to the mountain and castle. And then he gave him a vessel from which he would get money, that he would not have hindrance due to money, and then he went there and made effort with strategies until he took her out. Fortunate is he!

And whoever reads this with an honest eye will thoroughly understand just how much a person needs to make himself valiant in the service of Hashem, and how and to what extent he needs to be very stubborn in service of Hashem: without bounds, limit, and number, each and every man according to his level and his ascents and declines, and even if what has happened with him has happened. See and understand and inspect this story, how much effort the viceroy exerted and how many travails he toiled and then fell very low by not enduring the easy test two times, until he fell into the aspect of sleep many, many years, until he pertained to the slumber of the whole seventy years, as mentioned. But despite this he did not despair, and he made these toils afterwards and did not listen to any obstacle or discouragement which they wanted to dissuade him to not seek and request her any more. And the more he strengthened himself and did not listen to the voice of dissuasions of those people, immediately it turned around, that those people were of help, for each one assembled for him the animals or the birds that he was appointed over, and if afterwards they again dissuaded him and said to him, "See, it does not exist," and despite this he did not listen to their dissuasions, then they assisted him and each one informed him of his brother, until he came to this one who was appointee over the winds, through whom he arrived at his object of request. And this one too dissuaded him extremely much, but since he was strong in his mind and never did despair in any case, then within an easy moment the thing reversed, and the obstacles were reversed to assistances and salvations, and one wind came and informed him that he had personally carried the king's daughter to the mountain and castle, and afterwards this very wind carried him there too, as mentioned.

See, understand and gaze on each detail of the story and understand clues and wonderful arousal, how much one needs to strengthen himself to seek, look for and request the service of Hashem constantly, as written, "*Bakeshu panaw tamid/* Seek His face always" [Ps. 105:4], etc. for if indeed the essence of the story is beyond our knowledge and we do not know at all what are the golden mountain with the castle of pearls and so forth, or the rest of the concepts whether in general or in particular — nonetheless all the clues are true and made clear to an honest eye within the story, and more clues and wonderful arousals beyond these can each person get out of them if he desires. "The wise man will listen, and increase learning" [Prov. 1:5]. And similarly in the rest of the stories. (The concept of the golden mountain with the castle of pearls hints to a wonderful affluence on the side of holiness, which one needs for [a certain level of] contemplation of Torah etc. as explained in the lesson *Pathach Rabbi Shim`on*, #60 in *Likutei Moharan*; take a very good look there, for this lesson is an explanation of this story, as we understood from him z"l).

L et us go from one topic to the next and give a little attention to the story of the Sophisticate and the Simpleton [#9]. There you will see the point a bit clarified in that story, that the main purpose is to go in simplicity without any sophistries, so take a good look there at each and every utterance and find wonderful clues for strengthening yourself in the ways of simplicity, which is the main goodly purpose even in this world; all the more so in the coming world.

A nd similarly in the story of the Exchanged Sons [#11] and in the story of the Prayer Leader [#12], and beyond so and all the more so in the story of the Seven Beggars [#13], that by each and every of the seven, wonderful and awesome mussar beyond compare are elucidated, for each one glories in how superbly far he is from this world in the uttermost, for this one glories that he is completely blind to this world and does not look at this world at all, for the whole world does not count by him as much as an eye-blink and so forth; and the deaf one glories in that he is completely deaf to hearing any sounds of this world, which are all due to things that are lacking, for the whole world is not worth hearing the sounds of its lackings and so forth; and one glories that he does not speak any utterance that does not praise Hashem Yithbarakh, and therefore he was completely mute from the speech of this world; and similarly one glories that he does not want to spend any breath on this world, and similarly the rest; take a good look there and if you will look with an honest eye you will stand still, quake and be dumbfounded and see the wonderful marvel of the mussar and the awesome arousal to Hashem Yithbarakh in this story which is beyond compare.

A nd see our words in the book *Likutei Halakhoth* in several places for what Hashem has shined on my eyes and various clues to several of the stories. See *Hilkhoth Tefillin/* laws of tefillin in relation to the story of the Seven Beggars: The first [beggar] who was blind [corresponds to a level beyond the eight partitions of the tefillin], etc.; see there in *Hilkhoth Birkhoth Hashachar/* laws of morning blessings in relation to the story of the Exchanged Sons; and in *Hilkhoth Tefilah/* laws of prayer in relation to the story of the Prayer Leader; and in *Yoreh De`ah* in *Hilkhoth Tola`yim/* laws regarding worms in relation to the story of the Sixth Beggar who had no hands who tells the story of the king's daughter who fled to the castle of water and so forth; and in *Even ha`Ezer* in *Hilkhoth [P"U] Ishuth/* laws regarding marriage in relation to that story, regarding that it is written there that the healing of the king's daughter is through ten kinds of music; and several other places. See there and find satisfaction with the help of Hashem Yithbarakh. And look in *Hilkhoth Nedarim/* laws of vows in relation to the story of the Fourth Bay regarding the two birds; and in *Hilkhoth Tzedakah/* laws of charity in relation to the story of the Third Day regarding the mute one and the spring that is above time and the heart of the world. May Hashem Yithbarakh show us the wonders of His Torah, that we may be privileged to continue to perceive true hints in all the stories and talk which we have been privileged to hear from this light.

Zoth Matzanu/This We Found

T his we found in a sack of writings, and its subject is an explanation of him [Rabbi Nathan] of blessed memory, having written story tales in such common language, and here it is:

[Rabbi Nathan wrote:] Furthermore I saw fit to alert the hearts of the readers of this book of tales, that they should not grudge him [Rabbi Nachman] that sometimes crude expressions come from his mouth in the book of Story Tales, for instance, "and he got upset at her" [lit. and he became in anger at her] in the first story, and, "he started drinking" [lit. he took himself to the drink] in the story of the exchanged children, and more in other places. Let them just judge him favorably, for this was "like an error that proceeds from a ruler" [Eccl. 10:5] under great necessity because... (up to here is what we have found, and I have copied his words, obm, letter for letter):

A nd behold, it is plainly clear that his holy desire was to write a reason for this, but apparently he stopped in the middle due to some force, and we were never again privileged that Hashem Yithbarakh cause things to happen that he should write it himself. Praise God that we have been privileged in His great mercies that these words have been written, because for each and every utterance that he wanted to write so that it be revealed in the world, there were many obstacles against them, and because of this he was very, very rushed in his writing, as we saw with our eyes, for he was accustomed to always tells us that if he did not hurry himself to break the obstacles and write immediately, he did not know if more will be written, due to several reasons held secret by him. And now since I have heard an expression of intention from him z"l that his desire when they be printed again was to write a reason for this, I decided not to hide from print one of the many reasons that were hidden and held secret by him z"l, and this is what I heard from him z"l: That our lord, master and rebbe, Moharan, memory of the righteous and holy bring blessing, told the stories in the Yiddish that was customary in our country, and our master the rav Rabbi Nathan ztz"l the chief of his dear disciples z"l copied them in the holy tongue [Hebrew] and brought himself down intentionally into simple language in order that the concepts not deviate, for those who read them in the holy tongue, away from what he z"l told in the Yiddish that was customary among us. And this is the reason why we hear from his holy tongue such simple language as this in several places. This reason is according to what I heard from him z"l, according to the simple meaning, aside from him having secret reasons which I was not privileged to hear from him z"l. And it is proper to believe that he had additional, secret reasons, for it is known from his holy books that he was superbly eloquent, yet here he brought himself down to simple language; therefore it is proper to believe that he had a profound intention in this; and a man of faith will abound with blessings[32], Amen, so be His will.

Tale 1: The Lost Princess

On the way[1331] I told [such] a story that whoever heard it had a thought of *teshuvah*, return. And this is the story.

[The Princess Is Lost]

Once, there was a king. The king had six sons and one daughter. The daughter was very dear to him, and he would cherish (in other words, love) her exceedingly and play with her very much.

One time, while he was together with her on a certain day he became angry with her and the words, "Let the Not-Good take you away!" escaped from his mouth. At night she went to her room; in the morning no one knew where she was. Her father (the king) was very afflicted and went here and there looking for her. The viceroy [lit. second in kingship] arose because he saw the king was very distressed, and asked to be given an attendant, a horse and money for expenses, and he went to search for her. He searched hard for her, for a very long time, until he found her. (Now he tells how he searched for her until he found her.)

[The Viceroy Seeks Her a Long Time, Until He Finds Her]

He went a long time, in deserts, fields and forests, and was seeking her quite a long time. He was going around in desert area and saw a way from the side. He decided, "Since I have been going for such a long time in the wilderness and cannot find her, I will follow this path; maybe I will reach a settled area." He went for a long time.

Later on he saw a castle and many soldiers standing around it. The castle was very beautiful, with the soldiers standing around it in fine order. He was afraid of the soldiers lest they not let him enter. He decided, "I will go and try," and he left the horse and went to the castle. They let him [enter], and did not hinder him at all, so he went from room to room, and they did not stop him. He came to a palace and saw the king sitting there with a crown and many soldiers standing around him. And many were playing on instruments for him and it was very pleasant and beautiful there. And [neither] the king nor any of them asked the viceroy a thing. And he saw there delicacies and good foods, and he went and ate, and went and lay down in a corner to see what would be done there.

He saw that the king called for the queen to be brought, and they went to bring her. And there was a great commotion and a great celebration, and the musicians played and sang vigorously because they were bringing the queen. And they placed a throne for her and seated her next to him. And she was the king's daughter, and he (the viceroy) saw her and recognized her. Later, the queen glanced and saw someone lying in a corner. She recognized him and rose from her throne, went to him, touched him and asked him, "Do you recognize me?" And he answered her, "Yes, I know you. You are the king's daughter who was lost."

[The Princess's Advice; the Viceroy Fails]

He asked her, "How is it that you've come here?" She answered him: because that utterance slipped out from her father (namely, that "the Not-Good should take you"), and here, this is the place that is Not-Good." He told her that her father was very distressed, and that he had been searching for many years. And he asked her, "How can I take you out?" She answered him, "You cannot take me out unless you choose for yourself a place and remain there for one year; and the entire year you must yearn for me, to take me out; and whenever you have free time you must only yearn, ask and hope expectantly to take me out, and you must fast. And on the last day of the year you must fast and you must not sleep the entire twenty-four hour period [lit. from period to period]." He went and did so, and at the end of the year on the last day he fasted and did not sleep, and he arose and went there (that is, to the king's daughter, to take her out). He beheld a tree; on this tree grew very beautiful apples. He had a big craving for it and he went and ate from them. As soon as he ate the apple, he fell down and sleep overtook him, and he slept a very long time. His attendant tried to wake him, but he could not be awakened at all.

Later he awoke from his sleep and asked the attendant, "Where am I in the world?" He [the attendant] told him the whole story. "You have been sleeping a very long time. It is already several years. And I have sustained myself from the fruit." He [the viceroy] agonized very much, and went there and found her there (that is, the king's daughter). She lamented to him very much. "If you would have just come on that day you would have taken me out of here, and because of one day you lost. (In other words, because you could not restrain yourself one day and you ate the apple, because of that you lost.) In truth, not to eat is a very difficult thing, especially on the last day, when the evil inclination becomes very strong. (That is, the king's daughter said to him that now she would make the prohibition more lenient, and he would not be forbidden to eat, because it is a hard thing to abide by, etc.) Therefore choose for yourself a place again, and also stay there a year, as before, and on the last day you will be permitted to eat — only, do not sleep, and do not drink wine so that you will not sleep, because the main thing is sleep." He went and did so.

On the last day he was going there, and he saw a running spring, and its color was red and the smell was of wine. He asked the servant, "Have you seen? This is a spring, and there ought to be water in it, but its color is red and the smell is of wine!" And he went and tasted from the spring. He immediately fell down and slept many years, until seventy years. There were many troops going along, with their trains that follow behind them, and the servant hid himself because of the soldiers. After that went a carriage and covered wagons, and there sat the king's daughter. She stood next to him, went down and sat next to him and recognized him. And she tried very much to wake him, but he could not be woken. She started to lament over him, that "so many, so many great efforts and toils you tortuously made these many, many years in order to take me out, and for one day, when you could have taken me out, you completely lost," and she cried very much about this. She said, "It is a great pity on you and on me, that I am here such a long time and cannot go out," etc. Afterwards she took the scarf off her head, and wrote on it with her tears and laid it down next to him, and stood up and sat in her carriage and rode away.

[The Princess's Lament; How She Can Yet Be Found]

Afterwards he awoke and asked the attendant, "Where am I in the world?" He told him the whole story, and that many troops passed through there, and that the carriage was here, and that she [the king's daughter] screamed, "It is a great pity on you and on me" etc. as before. Meanwhile, he glanced and noticed the scarf lying next to him. He asked, "Who is this from?" He answered him, "She left it behind and wrote on it with her tears." He took the scarf and raised it up against the sun and began to see the letters. He read what was written there: her lamentation and her cries, as mentioned; and (it was written there) that now, she is no longer in the castle; he should just search for a golden mountain and a pearl castle; "There, you will find me." He left the attendant behind and went alone to seek her. And he went and sought her for many years. He decided that in a settled area there cannot be a golden mountain and a pearl castle, because he was an expert in the world map [which is called *kroinikes*/a chronicle]. "Therefore I will go in the deserts." He went searching for her in deserts for many years.

Afterwards he noticed a very large man whose largeness was beyond human bounds and he was carrying a large tree, so large that in a settled area such a large tree would not exist, and he [the giant] asked him, "Who are you?" He answered him, "I am a man." He was amazed and said, "I have been in the wilderness such a long time now, and I have never seen a man." He told him the whole story mentioned above and that he's looking for a golden mountain and a pearl castle. He replied to him, "It certainly does not exist." And he dissuaded him and said to him, "They have convinced you with nonsense, because it certainly does not exist." He started to weep very much (the viceroy cried very much and said), "With certainty it does exist, in some place." But he dissuaded him and said, "Certainly they have convinced you with nonsense." He said, "Certainly it exists somewhere!" He said to him, "In my opinion it is nonsense, but because you are so stubborn, look — I am the appointee over all the animals. I will act for your sake and summon all the animals. Since they run all over the world, maybe one of them will know of that mountain and that castle." He summoned all the animals from small to large, all sorts of animals, and asked them. They all replied that they had not seen. He said to him, "See, they have talked nonsense into you. If you want to listen to me, turn back, because certainly you will not find [it], because it does not exist in the world." But he pressed him very much and said, "It must surely indeed be!" He said to him, "Look, I have a brother in the wilderness and he is the appointee over all the birds. Maybe they will know, since they fly high in the air. Maybe they have seen this mountain and the castle. Go to him, and tell him that I've sent you to him."

He went many, many years seeking him [the appointee over the animals] and again found a very large man, as before, and he also carried a large tree and also questioned him as before. He answered him with the whole story and that his brother had sent him to him, and he too dissuaded him [the viceroy] since, "This certainly does not exist;" and the viceroy also disputed with him, "It certainly does exist!" He told him (this man told the viceroy), "I am the appointee over all the birds; I will summon them; maybe they will know." He called up all the birds and asked all of them, from small to large. They answered him that they do not know of the mountain and the castle. He told him, "Don't you see it is certainly not here in the world? If you will listen to me, turn back, because it certainly is not here." And he pressed him and said, "It certainly is here in the world!" He told him, "Further in the wilderness is my brother; he is appointee over all the winds and they run over the whole world; perhaps they know."

He went many, many years seeking him and again found a large man, as before, who was also carrying a large tree and also questioned him, as before. He also answered him with the whole story, as before. He also dissuaded him, and the viceroy implored him likewise. He said to him (this third man to the viceroy) that he would act for his sake and summon the winds and ask them. He called them and all the winds came and he asked all of them. Not one of them knew of the mountain and the castle. He said to him (the third man to the viceroy), "Don't you see that you have been told nonsense?" The viceroy began to cry very much and said, "I know it surely does exist!"

Just then, he saw that another wind had arrived. The appointee became angry with him. "Why have you so delayed in coming? Didn't I decree that all the winds should come? Why didn't you come with them?!" He answered him, "I was delayed because I had to carry a king's daughter to a golden mountain with a pearl castle." He was overjoyed (the viceroy was very happy that he now merited hearing what he desired.) The appointee asked the wind, "What is valuable there?" (That is, "What things are precious and important there?") He said to him, "There, everything is very dear."

The appointee over the winds replied to the viceroy, "Since it is such a long time that you have been searching for her, and you have spent so much effort, and perhaps you will now have a hindrance due to money, therefore I will give you a vessel, [such] that when you put your hand into it, you will get money from there." And he summoned the wind to carry him there. The storm wind came and carried him there and brought him to the gate, and standing there were soldiers who did not let him enter the city. He put his hand into the vessel and took out money and bribed them and went into the city. It was a beautiful city. And he went to a man of means and rented food and lodging for himself, for one must remain there, for one needs to see with wisdom and intellect in order to take her out. (And how he took her out, he did not tell.) (But) in the end, he took her out. Amen, Selah.

Tale 2: The Emperor and the King

[Introduction; the Betrothal]

A tale. Once there was an emperor [*keisar*, Caesar]. The emperor had no children. And there was also one king; the king also had no children. The emperor let himself wander the earth searching: perhaps he would find some solution or treatment so that he would have children. The king also let himself travel the world. The two of them came together at one inn and they did not recognize each other. The emperor recognized in the king that he had royal mannerisms and he asked him, and he acknowledged to him that he was a king. The king also recognized in the emperor that he had royal customs, and he also acknowledged it to him. They told each other that they were traveling for children. They enacted between them that if they would come home and their wives would bear one a boy and one a girl, they would match them. The emperor traveled home and had a daughter and the king traveled home and had a son — and the match was forgotten by them. The emperor sent his daughter to study. The king also sent his son to study. They both arrived at the same teacher; they liked each other very much. They agreed between themselves to marry each other. The prince took a ring and placed it on her hand; they were espoused.

[The Separation]

A fterwards, the emperor sent for his daughter and brought her home. The king also sent for his son and also brought him home. Matches were suggested for the emperor's daughter, but she was not interested in any match on account of the bond she had already made with the king's son. The king's son yearned for her greatly, and the emperor's daughter was also constantly sad. The emperor would walk her through his courtyards and palace, showing her her greatness, but she was always sad. The king's son yearned for her so much that he became ill, and no matter how much he was asked, "Why are you ill?" he did not want to say. They asked the one who served him, "Maybe you can clarify by him?" He answered them, "I know," because the one who served him was with him there where he learned. He told them (that is, the servant told them why he was sick). The king remembered that he had already long ago made a match with the emperor, so he went and wrote to the emperor that he should prepare himself for the wedding, for the match had indeed been made long ago, as mentioned. And the emperor no longer wanted the match, but he could not brazenly refuse. The emperor wrote that the king should send his son to him, in order for him to see if he could rule countries; then he would give him his daughter. The king sent his son to him. The emperor sat him down in a room and gave him papers of government matters in order to see if he could lead a country. The king's son was deeply yearning to see her, but he could not see her.

[The Elopement]

Once time, while he was walking along a wall of mirror, he saw her and fainted. She came to him and roused him, and she told him that she does not want any other match because of the bond she already had with him. He said to her, "What can we do? Your father does not want it." She said, "Nevertheless;" she would save herself just for him. Then they took counsel: they would let themselves go by sea. So they rented a ship and set out on the sea; they traveled on the sea. Afterwards they wanted to come ashore, and they came ashore. There was a forest there, and they went into it. The emperor's daughter took the ring and gave it to him, and she lay down to sleep. Afterwards, the king's son saw that she would soon get up, so he put the ring next to her. Then they went to the ship.

[The Couple Get Lost]

Meanwhile, she remembered that they had forgotten the ring there, so she sent him after the ring. He went there, but could not find the place. He went further and still could not find the ring. He went seeking the ring from one place to another place, until he got lost and was unable to return. She went looking for him and she too got lost. He was going along and getting further and further astray. Then he saw a path and he entered a settled area. He had nothing to do, so he became a servant. She too went and got lost. She decided she would sit by the sea. She went to the shore of the sea, and there were fruit trees there. She settled there, and during the day she would go along the sea; perhaps she would find some passersby. And she sustained herself on the fruit, and at night she would climb up a tree to be protected from wild beasts.

[The Merchant's Son Finds the Emperor's Daughter]

The day came to pass, when there was a big merchant — a very big merchant — who had commerce throughout the entire world. And he had an only son. And the merchant was now old. Once the son said to his father, "Being that you are already old and I am still very young and your trustees do not supervise me whatsoever, what will happen? — You will die, and I will be left alone; I will not at all know what to do. So give me a ship with wares so that I can set out to sea in order to be experienced in commerce." The father gave him a ship with wares, and he went to countries and sold the wares and purchased other wares and was very successful. While he was at sea he noticed the trees where the emperor's daughter was dwelling. They thought that it was a settlement; they wanted to go there. When they came near, they saw that they were trees; they wanted to go back.

Meanwhile, the merchant's son looked in the sea and saw a tree there upon which was the appearance of a human being. He thought that perhaps he was misleading himself, so he told the other men who were there. They too looked and also saw the appearance of a human on the tree. They decided to draw near there. They sent a man with a small boat, and they looked in the sea in order to guide the scout so that he could hit the tree. The emissary went there and saw that sitting there was a human, and he told them. He himself [the merchant's son] went there and saw her sitting there (that is, the emperor's daughter) and he told her to come down. She said to him that she does not want to enter the ship unless he promises that he will not touch her until he arrives home and marries her lawfully. He promised her, and she entered with him into the ship. He saw that she could play musical instruments and speak several languages, and he rejoiced that she chanced upon him.

Afterwards as they began drawing near his house she said to him that the proper thing would be that he goes home and informs his father, relatives, and good friends, that since he is bringing such a precious woman they should all come out to greet her, and after that he would know who she is. (Because previously she had also made a condition with him that he should not ask her who she is until after the wedding, at which time he would know who she is.) He agreed to this. Further she said to him, "The proper thing is also that you should inebriate all the mariners who operate the ship, to let them know that their merchant is getting wed with such a woman," and he accorded with her. So he took very fine wine that he had on board the ship and gave it to them; they got very drunk, and he went home to inform his father and friends. And the sailors were drunk and went out from the ship and they fell and lay drunk.

[The Emperor's Daughter Flees From the Merchant's Son]

While they were preparing themselves to go greet her with the entire family, she went and untied the ship from the shore, spread the sails and was away with the ship. And the entire family came to the ship and found nothing. The merchant was enraged at his son, and the son cried out, "Believe me! I brought a ship with wares!" etc. — but they see nothing. He said to him, "Ask the sailors!" So he went to ask them, but they lay drunk. Afterwards the sailors got up, and he asked them, but they knew nothing at all about what happened to them. They only knew that they had brought a ship with all the aforementioned, but they don't know where it is. The merchant was very angry at his son and banished the son from his home so that he should not appear before him. The son went away wandering about. And she (that is, the emperor's daughter) was going on the sea.

[The King by the Sea Finds the Emperor's Daughter]

The day came to pass when there was a king who had built himself a palace by the sea, for it pleased him there because of the sea air and because the ships go there. And the emperor's daughter was going on the sea and came near to this palace of the king. The king took a look and he saw the ship going without a crew and no one was there. He thought he was deceiving himself. He ordered his men to look, and they also saw. And she came closer to the palace. She decided: what does she need this palace for? — and she started to turn around. The king sent and brought her back [from her ship which she had turned around] and brought her into his home. Now, this king did not have any wife, because he could not choose for himself, because whoever he wanted did not want him and vice versa. When the emperor's daughter came to him she told him to swear to her that he would not touch her until he legally marries her, and he swore to her. She told him that it would be right to not open her ship and to not touch it; to just let it stand like that in the sea until the wedding, in order that everyone would then see the vast wares she had brought, so that they should not say that he had taken a woman from the market. He promised her so.

So the king wrote to all the countries to all come to the wedding. And he built a palace for her sake, and she commanded that they bring her eleven daughters of nobility to be with her. The king ordered, and they sent her eleven daughters of very high noblemen, and they built each one an individual palace, and she also had an individual palace. They would gather unto her; they would play musical instruments and play with her.

Once, she told them she would go with them on the sea. They went with her and were playing there. She told them she would honor them with good wine that she had. She gave them from the wine that was in the ship; they became drunk, fell down and remained lying. She went and unbound the ship, spread out the sails and fled with the ship. The king and his people took a look and saw that the ship was not there, and they were very panicked. The king said, "See to it that you do not tell her suddenly, for she would have great distress (for, the king did not know that she herself had fled with the ship; he thought she was in her room), and she might think that the king had given the ship to someone. Rather, they should send her one of the young noblewomen to tell her tactfully. They went to one room and found no one. And likewise in another room they also did not find anybody, and so on in all eleven rooms they also found nobody. They decided (the king and his people) to send her an elderly noblewoman at night to tell her. They came to her room and also found nobody, and they were very terrified. Meanwhile, the fathers of the young noblewomen saw they were not having letters from their daughters; they were sending letters and got no letters back. They personally got up and all went to them, and did not find any of their daughters. They were enraged and wanted to send the king to his death, for they were the royal ministers. However, they came to the decision, "What is the king guilty of that he should be sent to death? — the king transgressed as a victim of circumstance." They agreed to remove him from kingship and drive him out. They deposed him and exiled him; he went on his way.

And the emperor's daughter who had fled was faring with the ship. Later, the young noblewomen awoke and began to play with her again as before, for they were not aware that the ship had already departed from the shore. Then they said to her, "Let's go back home!" She answered them, "Let's stay here a bit longer." Afterwards there arose a storm wind and they said, "Let's go back home!" She informed them that the ship had already long left from the shore. They asked her, "Why have you done this?" She told them she was afraid the ship might be wrecked because of the storm wind; therefore she had to do so. They were faring on the sea, the emperor's daughter with the eleven noblewomen, and were playing musical instruments, and they came across a palace. The daughters of nobility said to her, "Let's approach the palace!" But she did not want to; she said that she also regretted having approached the previous palace (of the king who wanted to marry her).

[The Emperor's Daughter Meets Twelve Pirates]

Later, they saw some kind of island in the sea, and they drew near there. There were twelve pirates there; the pirates wanted to kill them. She asked, "Who is the superior amongst you?" They showed her. She said to him, "What do you do?" He told her they were robbers. She said to him, "We too are robbers. Only, you rob with your might, and we rob with shrewdness, for we are learned in languages and play musical instruments. Therefore what will you win if you kill us? Better to take us for wives and you will have great wealth too;" and she showed them what was on the ship (for the ship belonged to the trader's son, with his great wealth). The pirates agreed to her words. The pirates also showed them their wealth, and brought them to all their places. And it was agreed between them that they should not marry them all at one time, but only one after the other; and a selection should be made to give each one such a noblewoman as befits him, according to his greatness.

Afterwards she told them that she would honor them with very good wine which she has on board the ship, which she does not use at all; only, the wine is kept in store by her until God brings her her match. She gave them the wine in twelve goblets and said that all of them should drink to each twelve. They drank, got drunk and collapsed. She called out to the other noblewomen, "Go and each of you kill your man." They went and killed off all of them. And they found enormous wealth there, such as cannot be found with any king. They decided that they should not take any copper or silver, only gold and precious stones, and they threw out from their ship things which are not so important, and loaded up the entire ship with precious things, with the gold and precious stones that they found there. And they came to a decision to no longer go dressed as women, and they sewed men's clothing for themselves — German style — and went with the ship.

[The Bald King Prince; the Emperor's Daughter is Crowned]

And the day came to pass, and there was a king. The king had an only son, and he had made him a wedding and had transferred the kingdom to him. Once, he said to his father he would go on a leisurely trip with his wife on the sea so that she become accustomed to the sea air, lest at some time they would have to flee on the sea. The king's son went with his wife and with the royal ministers and set out on a ship, and they were very merry there and played freely. Later they said they would all take off their clothes; they did so, and nothing remained on them except their shirts. And they urged everybody who could, to climb up to the mast. The prince climbed up on the mast. Meanwhile, the emperor's daughter approached with her ship and saw this ship (of the prince with the ministers). Initially, she was afraid of going there, then she came a bit closer; she saw that they were playing intensely, so she understood that they were not pirates. She began drawing closer.

The emperor's daughter announced to her retinue, "I can throw that bald-head guy down into the sea (that is, the prince, who was climbing up the mast)!" For the prince had a bald head. They said to her, "How is that possible? We are very far from them!" She answered them: she has a burning-lens, and with it she will cast him down. And she decided she would not knock him down until he reaches the very top of the mast, because as long as he was in the middle of the mast, were he to fall he would fall into the ship, whereas when he reaches the top then when he falls he will fall into the sea. She waited until he was up on the top of the mast. She took the burning lens and held it facing his brain until it burned his brain. He fell down into the sea. When he fell down there was a great commotion there (on the ship) and they did not know what to do. How could they return home? For the king would die of heartbreak. They decided to go to the ship that they saw (that is, to the ship of the emperor's daughter); perhaps there would be some doctor there on board who could give them a solution. They drew close to the ship and told them (namely, the people who were on the emperor's daughter's ship) that they should not have any fear whatsoever for they [the men of the king's ship] would not do any thing at all to them, and they asked, "Maybe you have here a doctor who can advise us?" And they told the whole story and how the prince had fallen into the sea.

The emperor's daughter instructed [them] to draw him out of the sea. They went and found him and took him out. The emperor's daughter took his pulse with her hand and said his brain had been burnt. They went and tore open his brain and saw it was as she had said, and they were awestruck (that is, it was a great novelty to them how the doctor, that is, the emperor's daughter, had been so correct). And they requested that she go together with them to their home; she would be doctor to the king and would be very esteemed by him. She did not want to, and she said that she was not a doctor at all, only she knows such things. Now, the people of the prince's ship did not want to return home; the two ships went together. It pleased the royal ministers very much that their queen (that is, the wife of the prince) should take the doctor (that is, the emperor's daughter who was going dressed as a male and they thought that it was a doctor): for they saw she was exceedingly wise, therefore they wanted their queen (who was the wife of the prince who died) to marry the doctor (that is, the emperor's daughter) and he would be their king. And their old king (that is, the father of the king) they would kill. Only, they were ashamed to tell the queen that she should marry a doctor. But the queen too was pleased to marry the doctor, only, she feared the country — perhaps they would not want him to be king. They came to the decision to make balls (that is, banquets) so that while drinking, at a time of merriment, they would be able to talk about it. They made a ball for each one of them on a separate day.

When the day came for the ball of the doctor (that is, the emperor's daughter) he gave them of his aforementioned wine that he had and they got drunk. When they were merry, the ministers said, "How beautiful it would be if the queen would marry the doctor!" The doctor (that is, the emperor's daughter) replied, "It would surely be very beautiful! If only they said this with a not drunken mouth!" The queen also replied, "It would be very beautiful for me to marry the doctor! If only the country would agree to it!" The "doctor" repeated, "It would surely be very beautiful! If only they proposed this with not drunken mouth!" Afterwards, when they sobered up from their drunkenness, the ministers remembered what they had said and were embarrassed before the queen for having said such things. But they decided: the queen herself had also said it! And the queen too was embarrassed before them, but she decided: they themselves had also said it! Meanwhile, they began to talk about it, and so it was agreed; they betrothed — the queen with the doctor (that is, with the emperor's daughter whom they thought was a doctor, as mentioned) — and they went home to their country. When the country saw them coming, they rejoiced greatly, since it had been a long time since the prince was away with the ship. And they did not know where he was, and the old king had meanwhile died before they arrived. Meanwhile they noticed that their prince — who was their king — was not there. They (that is, the country) asked, "Where is our king?" They told them the whole story, that the prince had long been dead now, and that they had already taken a new king, who was accompanying them (that is, the "doctor" who was emperor's daughter). The countrymen were very happy that they had received a new king.

[The Wedding and Conclusion]

The king (that is, the emperor's daughter) ordered to announce in all countries that whosoever was present anywhere — foreigner, guest, refugee or exiled — should all come to his wedding. Not a single one should be absent. They would receive great gifts. And the king (that is, the emperor's daughter) also commanded to make fountains all around the city, so that anyone who wanted to drink would not have to go away to get a drink, but would be able to find a fountain next to him. And the king (that is, the emperor's daughter) also ordered for his picture to be drawn next to every fountain, and to station guards to watch for anyone coming along and looking hard at the picture (that is, at the portrait of the king, who was the emperor's daughter, as mentioned) and making a bad face [as someone who looks at something and is shocked or saddened]; they should grab him and put him in prison. All this was done. And these three men came along — that is, the first prince, who was the true groom of the emperor's daughter (who had become king there), the merchant's son (who had been banished by his father on account of the emperor's daughter who had fled from him with the ship and all its merchandise), and the deposed king (also on account of her, who had fled from him with the eleven daughters of nobility, as mentioned). And each of the three recognized that this was her picture, and they gazed intensely and remembered and became very anguished. They were caught and placed in prison.

At the time of the wedding, the king (that is, the emperor's daughter) commanded to bring the captives before him. The three were brought and she recognized them, but they did not recognize her, since she was dressed like a man. The emperor's daughter spoke up and said, "You, king (that is, the exiled king, who was one of the prisoners) — you were deposed on account of the eleven daughters of nobility who were lost. Take back your daughters of nobility. Return home to your country and to your kingdom." (Because the eleven daughters of nobility were there with her here.) "You, merchant (that is, first she spoke to the deposed king; now she turned to speak to the merchant, that is, the merchant's son) — you were banished by your father on account of the ship with its merchandise that was lost from you. Take back your ship with all the merchandise. And for your money being out so long, you now have a much greater wealth on the ship, many, many fold more than there was before" (for the same ship with all the merchandise belonging to the merchant's son, with which she had fled, was still with her in its entirety, and in addition to this was all the wealth which she had taken from the pirates, which was extraordinary wealth, many, many fold more).

"And you, prince (that is, the first prince who was truly her groom) — come here and let's go home." They returned home. Amen and Amen.

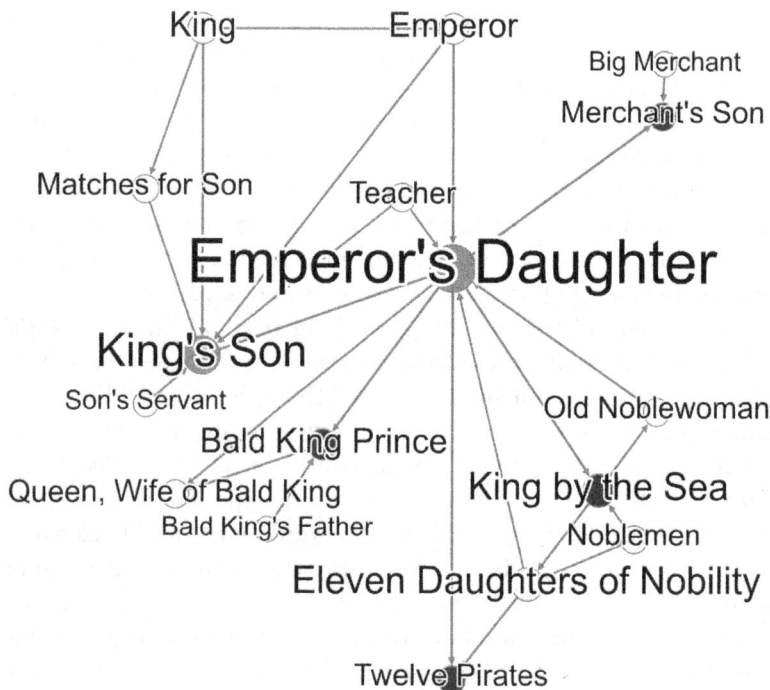

King———Emperor

Big Merchant

Merchant's Son

Matches for Son   Teacher

Emperor's Daughter

King's Son

Son's Servant   Old Noblewoman

Bald King Prince

Queen, Wife of Bald King   **King by the Sea**

Bald King's Father   Noblemen

Eleven Daughters of Nobility

Twelve Pirates

Tale 3: The Son Who Could Not Walk

[The Son's Trip to Leipzig, and Ambush by Robbers]

A tale. Once there was a sage. Before his death he called his sons and family and left them a will: that they should water fruit trees [*ilanoth*]. "You may engage in other needs as well, but this you must constantly do: water trees." Afterwards the sage passed away and he left children. And he had one son who could not walk; he could stand, but he could not walk. His brothers would give him his needs for livelihood, and they gave him so much that he had leftover. He would save up for himself bit by bit whatever remained beyond his needs, until he had amassed a certain amount. He then came to the decision, "Why should I get a stipend from them? Better that I begin some commerce." And though he could not walk, he came up with the solution to hire a carriage, an assistant (*ne'eman*, lit. faithful or trusted one) and a wagon-driver and to travel with them to Leipzig[34], and he would be able to conduct trade even though he could not walk. When the family heard this, it pleased them very much, and they also said, "Why should we give him subsistence? Better to let him make a livelihood." And they lent him more money so that he could conduct trade.

T hus he did; he hired a carriage, an assistant and a wagon-driver, and he set out, and they came to an inn. The assistant said that they should spend the night there, but he did not want to. They pleaded with him, but he was stubborn with them. They traveled away from there and got lost in a forest and thieves ambushed them. And the thieves had come about according to a story: There was once a famine. Someone came to the city and proclaimed: Whoever wants food should come to him. Numerous people came to him. When he saw that the men who came to him were not useful to him he would reject them. To one he would say, "You can be a craftsman," while to another he said, "You can be a miller." And he chose only intelligent youths, and went with them into the forest and proposed to them that they become thieves: "Being that from here there are roads to Leipzig, to Breslau [a city in Germany] and to other places, merchants travel through here. We will rob them. We will have money." (So did the thief who had earlier made the proclamation in the city tell them.) The thieves ambushed them (that is, the one who could not walk and his men, namely the assistant and the wagon driver). The assistant and the wagon driver were able to flee and they fled; and he was left on the wagon. The thieves came to him and took from him the chest of money and asked him, "Why are you sitting?" He replied he could not walk. And they stole the chest and the horses, and he remained on the carriage.

The assistant and the wagon-driver (who had fled away) came to the decision that inasmuch as they had taken out loans from feudal landlords [*poritzes*], why should they return home where they could be placed in chains? Better to remain there (where they had fled) and be an assistant and wagon-driver there. Now, the one who could not walk, who remained on the wagon, as long as he had the dry bread that he had brought from home, he ate it. Then when it ran out and he had nothing to eat, he thought about what to do. He threw himself out of the carriage to eat grass. He slept alone in the field and was frightened and his strength was so taken from him that he could not even stand, only crawl, and he would eat the grass that was around him. And as long as he could reach grass and eat, he would eat there, and when the grass around him ran out so that he could no longer reach, he crawled further away and ate again. Thus he ate grass for a time.

[The Son Finds a Diamond Having Four Charms]

Once, he came to an herb the likes of which he had never eaten before. This herb pleased him very much, because he had been eating grasses for a long time, so he knew them very well, and such an herb he had never seen before. He came to the decision to tear it out with its root. Under the root was a diamond. The diamond was quadrangular [Yid. *firekig*, Heb. *meruba`*] and each side had in it a different *segulah* [a charm or special ability]. On one side of the diamond it was written that whoever grasps that side, it would take him where day and night meet together, that is, where the sun and the moon gather in unison. When he tore out the herb with its root (which is where the diamond was) it happened that he grasped that side (that is, the side which the segulah of it was it would take him to the place where day and night come together). It took him there, where day and night come together. He looked around and now he was there!

He heard the sun and the moon talking, and the sun was complaining before the moon, "Inasmuch as there is a tree that has many branches, fruits, and leaves, and each of its branches, fruits, and leaves has a segulah — one is conducive [*mesugal*] to having children, another is conducive to livelihood, another is conducive to healing this sickness, another is conducive for another sickness; each tiny bit [*pitsel*] of the tree is conducive to something else — this tree should have been watered, and if it would be watered, it would be very specially potent [*mesugal*]. But not only do I not water it, I shine on it too and dry it out."

The moon answered and said, "You worry about others' worries. I'll tell you my worry. Inasmuch as I have a thousand mountains, and around the thousand mountains are another thousand mountains, and that [lit. there] is a place of demons, and the demons have chicken-like feet — they have no strength in their feet, so they take strength from my feet and because of this I have no strength in my feet. And I have a powder (that is, a dust) that is a cure for my feet, but a wind comes and carries it away."

The sun responded, "That is what you worry about?! I will tell you a cure. Inasmuch as there is a path, and many paths branch off from that path: One is the path of the *tzaddikim* [righteous]. Even someone who is a tzaddik here, the dust from that path is sprinkled underneath each his steps, so that with each step he is stepping on that dust. Another is the path of heretics. Even someone who is a heretic here, the dust of this path is sprinkled underneath each of his steps, as mentioned. And there is the path of the insane. Even someone who is insane here, the dust of this path is sprinkled underneath each of his steps, as mentioned. And so there are several paths. And there is a different path, being that there are tzaddikim who accept suffering upon themselves, the landlords march them in chains, and they have no strength in their feet: dust from this path is sprinkled underneath their feet so that they have strength in their feet. So go there, for there is plenty of dust there and you will have healing for your feet." (All this did the sun say to the moon.) And he heard all this. (That is, the one who had no strength in his feet heard all this.)

[The Son Is Healed, and the Robbers Repent]

Meanwhile, he looked at the diamond on another side and saw that it was written there that whoever grasps that side, it would bring him to the path from which many paths go out (namely, the path mentioned above, of which the sun informed the moon). He grasped that side and it carried him away to there (that is, to the path). He placed his feet on the path whose dust was healing for the feet and he was immediately healed. He went and took the dust from all the paths and bound each dust separately in a bundle. (Namely,) he bound the dust from the path of the righteous separately, and likewise the dust of the remaining paths he bound separately; so he made himself bundles from the powders and took them with him. And he came to a decision and went to the forest where he was robbed. When he arrived there, he chose a tall tree near the path from which the thieves go out to rob. And he took the dust of the righteous and the dust of the insane and mixed them together, and spread them on the path. And he went up the tree and sat there to see what would happen with them.

He saw the robbers going out, having been sent out by the elder robber (mentioned above) to rob. When the robbers came to that path, as soon as they took a step on the powder they became tzaddikim and began to cry out for their years and days for having robbed until then and having killed numerous souls. But since it was mixed there with the powder of the insane, they became insane tzaddikim and began to argue with each other. One said, "Because of you we killed," and another said, "Because of you!" So did they argue until they killed each other. The elder robber sent more robbers, and it was also as before and they also killed each other. And so it was each time until they were all killed off, until he (namely the one who previously had no strength in his feet, who was up in a tree) understood that there were none remaining of the robbers except for him alone (namely the elder robber who commanded them all) and one other. He went down from the tree and swept up the dust from the path, and sprinkled only dust from the path of the righteous, and went to sit in the tree again.

N ow, the elder robber was very puzzled that he had sent all the thieves and none of them had returned. He decided to go personally with the one that still remained with him. And as soon as he came onto the path (where the son mentioned above had sprinkled the dust of the righteous by itself), he became a tzaddik. He began to cry out to the other bandit over his soul [Heb. *nafsho*; Yid. *seine yar un tag*, his years and days], over how he had murdered so many souls and robbed so much. And he tore graves and was penitent and very remorseful. When he (the son who was sitting in the tree) saw he had remorse and was very penitent, he came down from the tree. As soon as the robber noticed a person he began to cry out, "Woe to me! I have done this and that! Woe! Give me penance!" He answered him, "Return to me the chest that you robbed from me." For, it was written by them on all the stolen goods, when it was stolen and from whom. He said to him, "I will immediately return it to you! I will even give you the troves of stolen goods that I have! Just give me penance!" He said to him, "Your penance is just to go into the town, call out and confess, 'I am the one who made the proclamation at that time [during the famine, that whoever wants food should come to me] and made many robbers, and I murdered and robbed many souls.' That is your penance." The robber gave him all his troves, and went with him into the city and did so. Judgment was passed in that town that since he had murdered so many souls, he should be hanged, so people would know: meaning, so that others would be edified.

[To the Two Thousand Mountains with the Demons]

A fter this he (that is, the one who previously had no strength in his feet) decided to go to the two thousand mountains (mentioned above) to see what takes place there. When he arrived there he stood far from the two thousand mountains, and he saw there were many, many millions and billions of demon families, for they are fruitful and they multiply and they have children as do humans, so they are very numerous. And he saw their kingship sitting on a throne, upon which no one born of a woman (meaning, no human) had ever sat on such a throne. And he saw how they make scoffery: one tells over that he had harmed someone's baby, another tells how he had harmed someone's hand, another tells how he had harmed someone's foot, and other such scoffery.

Meanwhile, he noticed a father and mother [demon] walking and weeping. They were asked, "Why are you weeping?" They answered: They have a son, whose routine was he would go his way and would return at the same time, but now it has been a long time and he still has not come. They were brought before the king. The king ordered to send messengers throughout the world to find him. As they were returning from the king, the parents met up with someone who used to go together with their son. He asked them, "Why are you weeping?" They told him. He answered them, "I will tell you. Being that we had a little island at sea, which was our territory — the king to whom this island pertained went and wanted to build palaces there and had already laid a foundation. Your son said to me that we should harm him. We went and took away the king's strength. He got involved with doctors but they could not help him so he started getting involved with sorcerers. There was one sorcerer there who knew his family. He did not know my family, therefore he could not do anything to me — but he knew his family, so he seized him and is torturing him severely." They brought him (that is, the demon who was telling all this) to the king and he told it over before the king too. The king said: "Let them return the strength to the king [to whom the island pertained]!" He replied, "There was someone by us who had no strength and we have given away the strength to him." The king said, "Let them take that strength away from him and return it to the king!" They answered him: He has become a cloud (that is, the demon to whom they have given away the king's strength has become a cloud). The king said that they should, "Summon the cloud and bring it here." They sent an emissary for him.

[How a Demon Becomes a Cloud]

He (namely, the one who previously had no strength in his feet, who has witnessed all this) decided, "I will go ahead and see how these people [i.e. these demons] become a cloud." He followed the emissary and came to the city where the cloud was. He asked the townspeople, "Why is it [such] a *cloud* here in town?" They answered him, "Here in town it is just the opposite; never a cloud here. Only for while has such a cloud enveloped the city." And the emissary came and summoned the cloud; it went away from there. He (that is, the one who previously had no strength in his feet) decided to follow them to hear what they were saying. He heard the messenger ask him, "How did it come to be, that you became a cloud here?" He answered him, "I'll tell you a story.

[The Sage-Elder Has No Fear of the Demons]

Once, there was a sage (Heb. an elder). And the emperor [*keisar*, Caesar] of the country was a big heretic, and he made the entire country into heretics. The sage went and summoned his whole family and said to them, 'Surely you see that the emperor is a big heretic and has made the entire country into heretics, and some of our family he has already made into heretics. Therefore let us set out for the wilderness so that we will be able to remain in our faith in God, blessed be He.' They agreed on this. The sage uttered a [Divine] Name; it brought them to a wilderness. This wilderness did not please him. He again uttered a Name; it took them to yet another wilderness. This wilderness too did not please him. He uttered another [*noch*] name; again it took him to another wilderness. This wilderness did please him. And the wilderness was close to the two thousand mountains (mentioned above). The sage went and made a circle around them so that no one would be able to come near them.

Now, there is a tree which if it would be watered, there would not remain any of us (that is, of the demons). Therefore, some of us stand digging day and night, allowing no water to reach the tree." The other one asked, "Why do they have to stand day and night digging? Once they have dug one time then the water will be unable to come; it should suffice." He answered him, "Since there are gossipers among us, and these gossipers go and instigate disputes between the one king and the other king, and this causes wars, and the wars cause earthquakes, and the earth around the ditches falls in, which allows water to reach the tree; therefore, they must constantly stand and dig. And when there is a new king among us, they make all the mockery before him and they rejoice. One jests in how he harmed a baby and how the mother mourns over it, another shows another mockery, and similarly many various mockeries. And when the king gets into festivity he goes and takes a walk with his ministers and tries to uproot the tree. Because if this tree would not exist at all, it would be very good for us. And the king fortifies his heart exceedingly in order to uproot the tree entirely. When he approaches the tree, the tree gives a great shout, so a great fear falls on him and he must turn around.

❝ Once, a new king was appointed among us (that is, among the demons, for all this did the cloud tell to the emissary, as mentioned). Great mockery was done before him, as mentioned, and he waxed quite joyous and made his heart very bold, and wanted to tear out the tree completely. So he went out walking with his ministers, brazened his heart exceedingly, and ran to tear out the tree completely. When he arrived at the tree it let out a great cry at him, and a great fear fell on him; he turned around and was very angry. And he was coming back and meanwhile took a look and noticed men sitting (this was the aforementioned sage with his men). The king sent from his people to do something (that is, to harm them, as was their custom). When the sage's family saw them, they were overcome with fear. The elder (that is, the sage) called out to them, 'Do not fear.' When the demons arrived there, they were unable to come close due to the circle that was around them. He sent other messengers but they too were unable to come close. The king came in great anger and went himself and he too was unable to come close to them.

❝ He asked the elder to let him in to them. The elder said to him, 'Since you request it of me, I will indeed let you in, however it is not customary for a king to go alone, so I will let you in with one other.' He opened a little door for them, they entered, and he closed the circle again. The king said to the elder, 'How do you come and settle on our place?' He said to him, 'Why is it your place? It is my place!' The king said to the elder, 'You have no fear of me?' He said, 'No.' He said again, 'You have no fear at all?' And he displayed himself becoming very big, up to the sky, and wanted to swallow him. The elder said, 'I still have no fear of you at all. But if I want, you will be afraid of me.' And he went and prayed a bit, and big thick clouds formed, and there was great thunder. And thunder kills them very effectively, so all his ministers that were with him were killed, and none remained except for the king and the one who was there with him in the circle. He begged him (that is, the king begged the elder) for the thunder to cease, and it ceased.

[The Demon King Gives the Elder a Book]

❝ The king replied and said to the elder, 'Since you are such a person, I will give you a book of all the demon families. For, there are miracle workers [ba`alei shemoth] who only know of one demon family, and even that family they do not know completely. But I will give you a book in which all the families are written. For, by the king they are all recorded, and even a newborn is also registered by the king. The king sent the one who was with him for the book. (Hence the sage did very rightly by letting him in with another, for otherwise whom would he send?) He brought him the book. He opened it and saw that inside were millions and billions of their families. The king promised the elder that they would never harm the elder's entire family, and he commanded to bring portraits of his whole family, and even if a baby was born, to immediately bring its portrait, so that they would not harm anyone from the elder's family.

❝ Afterwards, when the time came for the elder to leave the world, he called his sons and commanded them and said to them, 'I leave you this book. Surely you see that I have the power to use this book in holiness, and even still I don't use it; I just have faith in Hashem Yithbarakh. You too should not use it. Even if there will be one of you who will be able to use it in holiness, he still should not use it, but just have faith in Hashem Yithbarakh.' Then the sage died and the book was passed on as an inheritance and came to his grandson (his son's son). And he had the power to use it in holiness, but he just had faith in Hashem Yithbarakh and did not use it, as the elder wished.

❝ The gossipers that were among the demons tried to persuade the elder's grandson, 'Since you have grown daughters and are unable to support them and marry them off, therefore use this book.' And he did not know that they were trying to persuade him, and thought that his heart was advising him to do this. So he traveled to his grandfather, to his grave, and asked him, 'Being that you left a testament that we should not to use this book, but only have faith in Hashem Yithbarakh, now my heart is telling me to use it.' His grandfather (who was deceased) answered him, 'Even though you can use it in holiness, it is better that you should have faith in the Hashem Yithbarakh and not use it, and Hashem Yithbarakh will help you.' And that is what he did.

And the day came to pass, when the king of the country where this grandson of the elder lived became ill. He got involved with doctors, but they could not heal him. Due to the high heat there in that country, the treatments did not help. The king of the country decreed that the Jews should pray for him. Our king (that is, the king of the demons) said, 'Since this grandson has the power to use this book in holiness and he still does not use it, therefore we need to do him a favor.' He commanded me to become a cloud there so that the king (of that country) would be healed by the treatments that he had already taken and the treatments he would yet take. And the grandson knew nothing about this. And that is why I have become a cloud here." (All this is what the cloud told the emissary.)

And the one who previously had no strength in his feet was following them and heard everything. The one who was a cloud was brought before the (demon) king, and the king commanded to take the strength from him and return it to the other king (from whom they had taken away his strength because he had built upon their territory, as mentioned), and they returned the strength to him. The son of the demons (whose father and mother had wept for him, as mentioned) had returned, and he arrived very afflicted and without strength, because he had been severely tortured there. He was very enraged at the sorcerer who had tortured him so much there, so he ordered his children and his family to always stalk this sorcerer. But among the demons are talkers (that is, gossipers), and they went and told the sorcerer that they were waiting to ambush him, so that he could protect himself from them. The sorcerer performed some strategy, and called upon more sorcerers who knew more families, in order to protect himself from them. The (demon) son and his family were very enraged at the tattlers for having revealed his secret to the sorcerer.

[Nothing Remains of the Demons]

Once, it happened that some members of the (demon) son's family and some of the tattlers went together on the king's watch. The son's family went and made false accusations against the tattlers, and the king killed the tattlers. The remaining tattlers were enraged, and they went and made an upheaval (that is, a huge war) between all the kings. And there were hunger, infirmity, murder, and plagues among the demons. So wars were waged between all the kings, and this caused an earthquake, and all the earth [around the tree] fell in, and the tree was watered completely. None of them (that is, of the demons) survived whatsoever, and they became as if they had never existed. Amen.

[Notes Following the Story]

Rabbi Nachman's words:] *"Ashrei ha'ish asher lo-halakh... lo-`amad, uvmoshav leitzim... vehayah ke`etz shathul `al-palgei mayim"* — the entire story is alluded to in this chapter [Psalms 1]. Whoever has eyes, let him see, and whoever has a heart, let him understand, what on earth is happening.

Rabbi Nathan writes:] The secret of this story is alluded to in Chapter 1 in the Psalms:

- {v. 1} *"Ashrei ha'ish asher lo-halakh/* Fortunate is the man who has not walked..."* — the "path of the wicked" and the "path of the just." These are the aspect of the paths mentioned in the story that have the dust that they sprinkle, etc.
- {v. 3} *"Wehayah ke`etz shathul `al-palgei mayim, asher piryo yiten be`ito we`alehu/* And he will be like a tree planted by streams of water, which gives its fruit in its season, and its leaves...
- ...*Wekhol-asher ya`aseh yatzliach/* and all that he does will prosper"* — this refers to the tree in the story, that all of its fruit and leaves, everything in its entirety, are all very beneficial, as mentioned.

  Examine and you will find more allusions:

- "Fortunate is the man who has not walked" — for, initially he could not walk. *"Lo-`amad/* Has not stood" — for, later on, he could not stand either. *"Uvmoshav leitzim/* And in the company of scorners" refers to the settlement of the mockers who make mockery, etc., as mentioned.
- {v. 4} *"...Kamotz asher-tidfenu ruach/* Like chaff which the wind drives away" refers to the wind that carries away the dust.

A nd all this is just a few superficial allusions that he [Rabbi Nachman] enlightened our eyes with a little bit, in order to somewhat understand and comprehend the extent to which these things reach. But the things are still sealed in utter concealment, for all these stories that he [Rabbi Nachman] told are very, very high above human comprehension and hidden from the eye of all living creatures, etc.

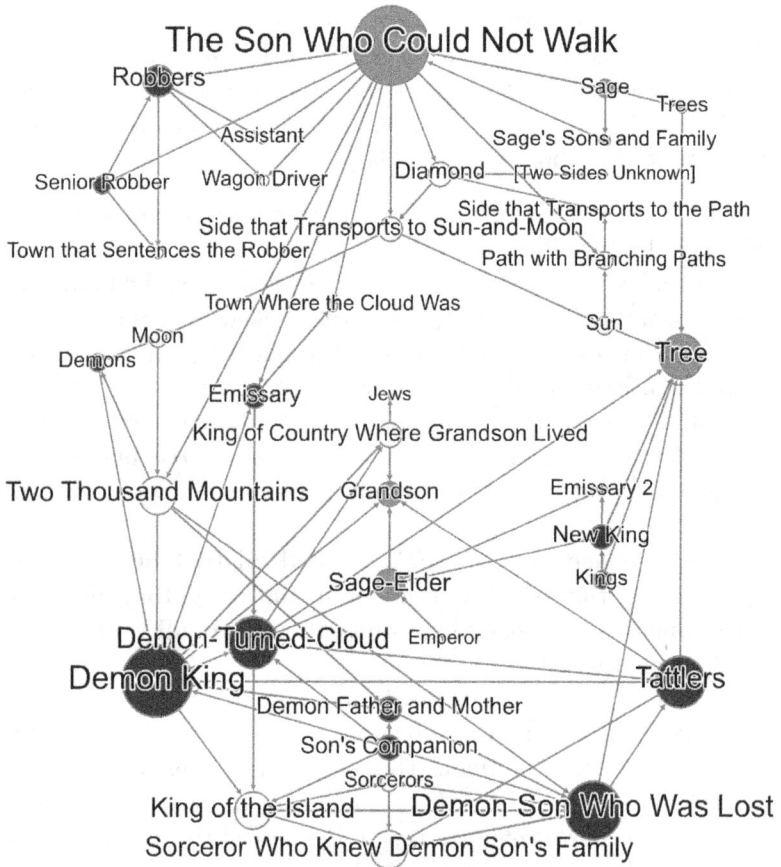

The Son Who Could Not Walk

Tale 4: The King Who Decreed Conversion

— A story of miracles —

[The King Decrees Forced Conversion upon the Jews]

Once, there was a king who decreed religious exile over the country: that is, whoever wanted to remain in the country had to convert, otherwise be expelled from the country. There were some who abandoned all their goods and wealth, and they left in poverty, in order to remain in the faith and be able to be Jews. But some had pity on their wealth and remained there; they became *anoosim* [lit. forced, compelled]: discreetly (that is, in concealment), they practiced the religion of the Jews, but publicly (that is, in front of people) they were not allowed to conduct themselves as Jews.

[The King's Son Allows the *Anoos* to Be a Jew in Public]

Later the king died and his son became king. And he began to rule the country very sharply (that is, forcefully; heavy-handedly) and conquered many countries; and he was very wise. And because he held the royal ministers with a tight grip (lit. very sharply in his hand), they banded together to attack him and kill him off with all his offspring.

And among the ministers was one of the anoosim. He decided, "Why did I become an *anoos*? Because I had pity on my possessions and my wealth. Now if the king will be killed and the country be left without a king, everyone will swallow his fellow alive, for a country cannot exist without a king." Therefore he decided to go and inform the king, without them knowing. And he went and told the king that they had conspired against him, as mentioned. The king went and probed whether it was true, and he saw it was true, and he stationed guards. On the night they fell upon him they were caught and judged, each one according to his sentence.

The king spoke up and said to the minister who was an *anoos* (forced convert), "What honor shall I give you for having saved me and my offspring? Shall I make you a minister (that is, a *herr*)? You are already a minister! Give you money? You have money! Say what honor you want; I will surely do it for you." The anoos answered, "But will you really do what I say?" The king said, "Yes, I will certainly do what you wish." The anoos said, "Swear to me by your crown and your kingdom." The king swore to him. The anoos replied, "My main honor is to be permitted to be a Jew in public — to put on *tallith* and *tefillin* in public." The king was extremely disturbed, because in his entire country there were not allowed to be any Jews. But he had no choice because of the oath he had sworn, that whatever he wished he would do for him. In the morning the anoos went and put on tallith and tefillin in public.

[The King's Son and Grandson Become King]

Later that king died and his son became king. The son began to rule gently, because he saw they had wanted to eliminate his father, as mentioned. And he conquered many countries and was extremely wise. The new king ordered a convening of all astrologers to tell him what sort of thing could cause his offspring to be cut off, so that he could guard against it. The astrologers told him that his offspring would not be cut off if he just guards himself from a bull and a ram (that is, from an ox and a lamb); this was written down in the record book. The king ordered his children to also rule the country as he did, gently. Later he died.

His son became king, and he began to rule the country stringently, like his grandfather, and conquered many countries. And he fell upon a wisdom, and ordered to announce that no ox or sheep should be found in his country, so that his offspring could not be cut off. So he thought he now had no fear of anything, and he ruled the country very stringently. And he became extremely clever.

[The King's Great-Grandson Makes an Effigy, Conquers the World]

The king fell upon a wisdom that he could conquer the entire world without battle, for there are seven parts in the world, for the world consists of seven parts, and there are seven planets (that is, seven luminaries that circle [that is, make a progression through] the seven days of the week) and each planet shines on one of the seven parts of the world, and there are seven kinds of metals (that is, seven different metals, namely gold, silver, copper, tin, etc.) and each of the seven planets shines on a specific metal. The king went and gathered all the seven different metals and ordered to bring him all the golden portraits of all kings, which hang in their palaces, and he made a man from this. Its head was of gold, its body of silver, and likewise the rest of the limbs, of other metals; in this man were all seven kinds of metal.

And he stationed the man on a high mountain, and all the seven planets shined in the man. And when a man needed any advice, or any commerce and did not know whether to do it or not, he would stand facing the limb of the type of metal pertaining to the part of the world where the man was from. And the man would contemplate whether to do the thing he needed or not. And if he needed to do it, that limb would light and shine and if not it would darken. (All this did the king do.) And thereby he conquered the entire world and amassed a huge amount of money.

[The King's Great-Grandson Resuppresses the *Anoos*]

However, this effigy that he had made from the seven various metals was not able to perform unless the king cast down the haughty and raised the lowly (that is, throw down big people from their greatness and pick up little people). He went and sent orders to all generals and other ministers who held positions of authority and orders (merit badges and special privileges). They all came and he demoted them, removing their positions. Even those who had positions which they served since his great-grandfather — he took them all away. And lowly people did he raise, appointing them to their places (of the great people).

Among the ministers whom the king was casting down was the anoos. The king asked him, "What is your position?" He answered him, "My position is just to be permitted to be a Jew in public, for the favor that I did for your grandfather." The king took this from him, and he was again an anoos.

[The King's Great-Grandson's Dream; the Sage's Tradition]

Once, the king lay down to sleep, and he saw in a dream the clear sky and he saw all twelve *mazaloth* [constellations] (that is, the stars in the sky are partitioned into twelve parts, corresponding to the twelve months; a section of stars resembles a ram, which is the *mazal* of *Nissan*, and the mazal of *Iyar* is called *shor*/bull, that is, an ox; and so each month has its mazal). And he saw the bull and the ram (that is, the ox and the lamb) that are among the mazaloth laughing at him. He awoke with great fury and was very frightened. He ordered to bring the chronicles (that is, the book wherein everything is written down), and he saw it written there that by bull and ram his offspring would be cut off, and a great terror fell over him. And he told the queen, and a great terror also fell on her and her children. And his heart pounded hard and he called for all the dream interpreters. And each one interpreted individually, but nothing would enter in his ears. And an extremely great terror fell on him.

A sage came and told him that inasmuch as he had tradition from his father that the sun has three hundred sixty-five courses (paths) and there is a place upon which all the three hundred sixty-five of the sun's paths shine and an iron rod grows there, whoever has a fear, when he comes to the rod, will be saved from the fear.

[The King's Great-Grandson's Excursion and Demise]

This pleased the king very much, and he went with his wife, children and all his descendants to that place, and the sage also went with them. But in the middle of the way stands an angel who is in charge over anger. For, by anger one creates a destructive angel (that is, an angel that destroys and ruins), and this angel is appointed over all the destroyers. And he is asked the way, for there is a good (Heb. straight) path for a man, and there is a path full of mud, and there is a path full of pits, as well as other paths. And there is a path where there is fire that incinerates from four "miles" [Heb. parsa'oth] away. (They asked the angel the way, and he told them the path where the fire is.)

And the sage kept looking around to see if the fire was there, for he had a tradition from his father that the fire was there. Meanwhile he saw the fire, and he saw kings and Jews dressed in tallith and tefillin going around in the fire. (Heb. only: This was because by those kings there lived Jews in their countries, therefore they were able to pass through the fire.) The sage said to the king, "Since I have a tradition that four 'miles' from the fire one is incinerated, I will go no further. You, if you wish, go." And the king thought that since he saw other kings walking around there in the fire, he would also be able to go there. The sage replied, "I have a tradition from my father, so I do not want to go. You, if you wish, go yourself." The king went with his entire offspring.

They caught the fire and he and his entire offspring were incinerated and all cut off.

[The Sage Comes Home and the Anoos Explains]

When the sage came home, it was a wonder to the ministers that the king and his offspring were cut off. Had he not guarded himself from a bull and a ram? How was it that his offspring and he were cut off? The anoos replied, "Through me has he been cut off. For, the astrologers saw (that by an ox and lamb his offspring would be cut off) but they did not know what they saw. For, an ox — from its hide they make tefillin; and a lamb — from its wool they make tzitzith for the tallith. And by them was the king and his offspring cut off.

For, the kings where Jews did live in their countries, wrapped in tallith and tefillin, were able to go in the fire completely unharmed. But this king, because no Jews dressed in tallith and tefillin were allowed to dwell in his country, was therefore cut off, with his offspring. And this was the bull and the ram of the mazaloth laughing at him. For, the astrologers saw that by bull and ram would his offspring be cut off; they did not, however, know what they saw, and the king was cut off with his offspring." Amen, so let all Your enemies be obliterated, Hashem!

[Notes Following the Story]

- *Lamah rageshu goyim/* Why are the nations in an uproar? ...*Tero'em beshevet barzel/* You will break them with a rod of iron" [Ps. 2] — the iron rod.
- "...*Pen-ye'enaf wetho'vedu darekh/* lest He be angry and you perish in the way," etc. And the words are extremely archaic and closed up... All this I [Rabbi Nathan] heard.

In addition I have found some more allusions from this story in this chapter:

- "...*Nenatekah eth-moserotheimo, wenashlikhah mimenu 'avotheimo/* Let us break their bands asunder, and cast away their cords from us" — bands are made of hide, the aspect of tefillin. "*Avotheimo*" — *avot* are cords, aspect of tzitzith, as our Rabbis obm expounded this verse in tractate *Avodah Zarah* [3b] regarding tzitzith and tefillin.
- "*Yoshev bashamayim yischak/* He Who dwells on High will laugh" — for, the bull and the ram laughed at him.

- *"Az yedaber eleimo ve'apo, uv'charono yevahaleimo/* Then He speaks to them in His wrath; and He panics them with His sore displeasure" — the anger, the panic and the fear mentioned above.
- *"Wa'ani nasakhti malki `al-tziyon har qodshi/* But I have poured/ anointed My king on Tzion, My holy mountain" — perhaps the allusion here is to the effigy that the king erected on the high mountain; *zeh le`umath zeh* (everything in holiness has its counterpart in evil), and this is counterpart to the king on the holy Mount Tzion, for, all the parts of the world are included there, and so forth, and this is the "mountain" there. *"Nasakh"* is a term as in *"nasakh wayitzok/* pouring and pouring-molding" [the statue] [Gen. 35:14].
- *"She'al mimeni/* Ask of me" — all the advices mentioned above. *"Goyim nachalathekha, wa'achuzathekha afsei-aretz/* Nations as your inheritance, and the ends of the earth for your possession" — to grasp together all ends of the earth, namely all seven parts of the world, and all the kings and nations as inheritance under him.
- *"'Ivdu/* Serve" — is tzitzith, *"be'yir'ah/* with awe" — is tefillin, and *"wegilu bir`adah/* and rejoice upon the trembling" — the trembling [of the wicked; Rashi there, citing Isa. 33:14].

The entire story is hinted in this chapter, so well-off is he who will know something of these stories, which are great secrets of the Torah throughout.

Tale 5:
The King's Son Who Was Made of Precious Stones

There was once a king who had no children. He went and got involved with doctors so that his kingdom should not be turned over to strangers, but they did not help him. So he decreed on the Jews to pray for him to have children. The Jews sought a tzaddik to pray and cause it happen that the king should have children.[35] They sought and found a hidden tzaddik, and they told him to pray for the king to have children.

He replied: he knows nothing at all [gar nisht]; they informed the king (inasmuch as there was a hidden tzaddik there, but he said he knew gar nisht). The king sent a royal order for him, and they brought him before the king. The king began talking kindly with him, "You know very well that the Jews are in my hands. I can do with them what I will. Therefore I ask you with goodness, pray that I have children."

The tzaddik ensured the king that same year he would have a child, and he went home. The queen bore a daughter, and this queen's daughter was extremely beautiful. When she was four years old, she knew all the wisdoms and languages, and could play musical instruments. Kings from all countries would travel to see her, and it was a great joy for the king.

Afterwards the king very much wanted to have a son so that his kingdom should not go away to a stranger, so he again decreed on the Jews that they should pray for him to have a son. They were searching for the first tzaddik, but they could not find him, for he had already passed away.

They continued searching and they found another hidden tzaddik. And they told him that he should give the king a son, and he said that he does not know anything. Again they informed the king, and the king said to the tzaddik also as before, "You know very well the Jews are in my hand, etc." The sage (that is, this tzaddik) said to him, "But will you be able to do what I order?" The king said, "Yes."

The sage said to him, "I need you to bring all the types of gemstones (lit. good stones), because each gemstone has in it a different segulah (ability, charm)." And by the kings there is a book wherein are written all the types of gemstones. The king said, "I will spend half my kingdom in order to have a son." And the king went and brought him all the types of gemstones.

The sage took them and ground them, and took a goblet of wine and poured them in the wine. And he gave a half cup of wine to the king to drink, and the other half to the queen. And he told them that they would have a son who would be thoroughly of gemstones, and he would have in him all the *seguloth* of all the gemstones, and he went home.

The queen gave birth to a son, and the king rejoiced very greatly, but the son that was born was not made of gemstones. When the son was four years old, he was extremely handsome, very wise in all the wisdoms, and knew all the languages. Kings traveled to see him. Now, the princess saw that she was no longer so important, and she was jealous of him. The only consolation for her was that the tzaddik had said that he would be completely of gemstones; good that at least he was not made of gemstones.

Once, the prince was carving wood and he nicked his finger. The princess ran to bandage his finger and she saw a gemstone there. She was extremely jealous of him, and she made herself sick. Many doctors came but were unable to heal her at all. Sorcerers were called. A sorcerer was there, to whom she disclosed the truth, that she had made herself sick because of her brother, as mentioned.

And she asked the sorcerer if it were possible to perform a spell on a man to become leprous. He said, "Yes." She said to the sorcerer, "What if he asks another sorcerer to annul the spell so that he will be healed?" The sorcerer said, "If the sorcery is thrown into the water, it can no longer be annulled." She did so and threw the sorcery into the water.

The prince became very leprous. He had leprosy on his nose, on his face and on the rest of his body. The king got involved with doctors and with sorcerers, but they were of no avail. The king decreed on the Jews to pray. The Jews sought the tzaddik (who had prayed for the king to have a son, as mentioned), and brought him before the king.

Now, this tzaddik would always pray before Hashem Yithbarakh, inasmuch as he had promised the king that his son would be completely made of gemstones, and it had not been fulfilled. And he complained to the *Eybishter* (the Most High; God), "Have I done this for honor's sake? I have done this only for Your honor, and now, it has not been fulfilled the way I said." And the tzaddik came to the king. The tzaddik had prayed (namely, for the leprosy of the prince to be healed), but to no avail. He was informed that it was sorcery.

N ow, this tzaddik was higher than all sorcery. The tzaddik came and informed the king that it was a sorcery, and that the sorcery had been thrown into the water, so the prince could not be healed except by throwing the sorcerer who performed the spell into the water. The king said, "I give you all the sorcerers to throw into the water so that my son be healed."

T he princess was afraid, so she ran to the water to pull the sorcery out of the water, for she knew where it was. She fell into the water. A great tumult erupted over the princess' falling into the water. The tzaddik came and said that the prince would be healed. And he was healed, the leprosy withered up and fell off, and his entire skin peeled off. And he was entirely of gemstones, as the tzaddik had said.

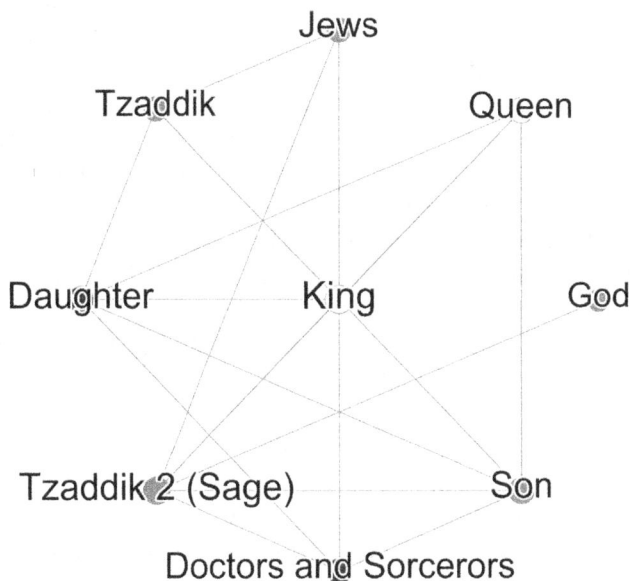

Jews

Tzaddik   Queen

Daughter   King   God

Tzaddik 2 (Sage)   Son

Doctors and Sorcerors

Tale 6: The Humble King

A tale. There was once a king who had a wise man. The king spoke up to the wise man, "Inasmuch as there is a king whose signature declares that he is a great man of might, and a man of truth, and humble (in other words, a truthful person who does not focus on himself [lit. "hold of himself"]): mighty — I know that he is a great man of might, for the sea flows around his country, and on the sea is stationed a navy on warships with cannons and they do not allow anyone to approach, and inwards from the sea there is a great swamp (a place where one drowns) surrounding the country, through which there is only one narrow path wide enough for only one person to pass; there too cannons are positioned, so that if someone comes to attack, the cannons are fired, so it is impossible to set foot there.

But his signing himself as being a man of truth and humble — this I do not know, and I want you to bring me this king's portrait." For the king had all the portraits of all the kings, but the portrait of that king (who signs himself in such fashion as mentioned) was not found by any king, for he is concealed from people, since he sits under a veil [Yid. *forhang*, Heb. *killah*], and he is far from his countrymen.

The wise man went to that country. He came to the realization that he must come to know the essence of the country (in other words, the "thing" of the country; how the country works). And how can he find out the country's essence? — by way of the country's jests [Yid. *katoves* < Slav. *katavasnik* prankster < Gr. *katavasis* descent]. Because when one needs to know [the essence of] something, one must know its jesting. For there are many types of jesting: there is one who really wants to smite the other with his words, and when the other takes notice [lit. "looks around"] he says to him, "I am joshing! (*Ikh treyb katoves*, lit. 'I drive a jest')" as in the verse, "Like one who wearies himself shooting firebrands... and says, 'Am I not joking?'" [Prov. 26:18-19], and so there is someone who really means a jest but still harms the other with his words. Thus there are several kinds of jesting.

N ow, among all the countries, there is a country that includes all countries (that is, the country is the principle and rule for all countries), and in that country there is a city that includes all cities of that whole country that includes all the countries. And in the city is a house that includes all the houses of the entire city that embodies all cities of the country that includes all countries. And there in the house is a person who includes the entire house which includes etc. And there, there is someone who makes all the wisecracks and jesting of the entire country.

S o the wise man took a large amount of money with him and went there. He saw them making all types of fun and joking. He understood from the jests that the country is full of falsehood through and through. For he saw them making fun of how people are cheated in business, and how he goes to the *manistrat* (lower court) and there it is utter lies and they take bribery there; and he goes to the *sand* [higher court, <? Ger. *Gesandte*, emissary]; and there as well it is utter lies. And they were all making fun and jest, enacting all these things.

T he wise man understood from this jesting that the country is full of lies and deceit, lacking any truth in the land whatsoever. So he went and did some commerce in the country and allowed himself to be cheated in the exchange, and went and brought suit before the *sands* [Yid. *sandes*, Heb. `arkhaoth* registrar, archivers' office < Gr. *arkhi, arkhion*], they being all full of falsehood and bribes. On this day he gave them bribery; the next day they didn't recognize him.

S o he went to a higher *sand* and there too it was full of falsehood. Until he came before the *senat* (highest court) and there too it is falsehood and bribery throughout. Until he came to the king himself.

W hen he came to the king he spoke up and said, "Over whom are you king? The entire country is full of falsehood throughout, from beginning to end, and there is no truth in it here whatsoever." And he began to tell over all the falsehood of the country.

W hen the king heard his words he bent his ear to the veil to listen to hear his words for it was a great wonder to the king that there should exist a man who would know all the falsehood of the country. And the royal ministers who heard the wise man's words grew very angry at him but he still continues reporting all the country's falsehood.

The wise man spoke up, "One could say that the king is also like them; that he likes falsehood as the country does. But on the contrary one sees what a man of truth you are, and because of this you keep your distance from them: on account that you cannot bear the falsehood of the country." And he began to praise the king very very much.

And the king, because he was very humble — and "in the place of his greatness, there is his humility," for that is the way of a humble man, that the more he is praised and extolled, the smaller to himself and the humbler he becomes — so on account of the wise man's great praise and exaltation of the king, the king entered into great humility and extreme tininess, until he became absolutely nothing; and he could no longer withhold himself and he threw aside the veil to see the wise man: who is it that knows and understands all this?

The king's face was revealed, and the wise man saw him, depicted his portrait and brought it back to the king.

[Notes Following the Story]

"*Darkei Tziyon aveloth* / The paths of Tziyon are mournful" [Lam. 1:4; since the Temple has been destroyed, one is obligated to remember and mourn it, and unbridled joking and laughter are forbidden; v. *S"A O"C* 560. Also, there are no festivals or times when God can be "seen:" Ex. 23:15 etc.].

Tziyon is the aspect of the *tziyunim* [markers; placemarks] of all the countries, for they all gather there, as it is written, "*wera'ah `etzem*[36] *adam uvanah etzlo tziyun* / and see the bone of[36] man, then shall he set up a sign by it." [Eze. 39:15].

This is [the meaning of], "*Chazeih Tziyon Qiryath Mo`adeinu* / Look upon Tziyon, the city of our assemblies" [Isa. 33:20], the acronym of which is *MeTzaCheiQ* (jesting), for that is where all the *tziyunim* [signs] gathered, and whoever needed to know whether to do something or some business transaction would know it there. May it be His will that it be rebuilt speedily in our days, Amen.

Look, discern and gaze, reader, how far these matters reach. Fortunate is he who attends to and will attain knowing and grasping a little of the secrets of these stories, the likes of which have not been heard since ancient times.

And know, that all these verses and allusions that are brought after some of the stories are only hints and a scant disclosure of the subject matter, so that they might know "*ki lo-davar reiq hu/* it is no empty thing," God forbid. As was heard from his holy mouth, saying that he is revealing a few mere hints from a few verses that hint to the secret of the stories, so as to know that he is not saying, God forbid, prattle. But the essential secret of the stories is far from our knowing; "*Amoq `amoq, mi yimtzaenu/* Deep-deep; who can find it out?" [Eccl. 7:24]

King

Other Kings   Sage

Country

Humble King

Country of All Countries

City of All Cities

House of All Houses

Person of Entire House

Wisecracker

Tale 7: The Fly and the Spider

He [Rebbe Nachman] announced,
"I'll tell you my entire trip that I had."[137]

A tale. There was once a king who had a number of hard wars up against him, and he conquered them and took many captives. (In the midst of his words as he began telling this story he interjected and said, "You might think [mistakenly] that I will tell you everything and that you will be able to understand.") The king made a big banquet (a ball) every year on the day when he vanquished the war. There at the ball would be all the royal ministers and all the gentlewomen, as the usual way of kings goes, and comedy shows would be made and they would make fun of all the nations: of the Turk (Heb. Ishmaelites) and of all the nations. And they would imitate every nation in the way that their manner and conduct is, and they probably made fun of Jews as well.

The king ordered to bring the book in which the mannerisms and customs of every nation are recorded. And whenever the king would open up the book, he would see [Heb. only: that written in it were the practices and mannerisms of the nation] exactly as they performed the parody of them, because probably the one who performed the comedy also saw the book. While the king was poring over the book, he saw a spider crawling on the edge of the book's pages, and on the pages stood a fly. Presumably, where does a spider go? — toward a fly. Meanwhile as the spider was crawling and going toward the fly, a wind came along and lifted that page from the book; the spider could no longer go to the fly. It turned around and crawled exactly as if it were turning around and no longer wants to go to the fly. Meanwhile, the page fell back in its place and again the spider wanted to go toward the fly. Again the page lifted and did not permit it; again the spider turned back. Thus it happened several times. Afterwards again the spider went towards the fly and was crawling along until it had already gotten itself up with one foot on the page. Again the page lifted up — and the spider was already somewhat on the page — then the page lay down completely, until the spider was left between one page and another; and it was crawling around there, but kept getting left deeper and deeper until nothing whatsoever was left of it. (And the fly — I will not tell you what happened to it.)

And the king had been watching all this and was very astonished; he understood that this is no empty thing but rather he is being shown something through it (and all the ministers saw that the king is gazing and wondering at it). And the king began thinking: what does this signify? And he dozed off over the book. The king dreamed that he was holding a diamond in his hand and looking at it. An exaggerated number of people were emerging from it and he threw the diamond down out of his hand. And the usual way by kings is that over them hangs their portrait and on top of the portrait hangs the crown. He saw in the dream how the people who had emerged from the diamond took the portrait and cut off its head, then they took the crown and threw it into the mud, and they ran towards him to kill him. A page from the book upon which he was lying lifted itself and shielded him and they were unable to do anything to him so they went away, then the page returned to its place. Then again they wanted to kill him and again the page lifted itself as before. Thus it happened several times. The king very much wanted to see what sort of page is shielding him (that is, protecting him); what mannerisms are written on it; from which nation it is. But he was afraid to look and he began to scream, "Woe! Woe!" All the ministers who were sitting there heard and they wanted to wake him up; however, this is no sort of protocol, to wake up a king. They rapped around him in order to wake him, but he did not hear.

Meanwhile, a tall mountain came to him and asked him, "Why are you screaming so? It is such a long time already that I sleep and nobody at all has woken me up — and you have woken me up!" He said to him, "How shall I not scream, when they are rising up over me and want to kill me, except that this page is shielding me?!" The mountain answered him, "If this page is shielding you then you need have no fear of anything whatsoever, for many enemies rise against me as well, but this same page shields me. Come, I will show you." It showed him how around the mountain stand thousands and myriads of enemies and they make feasts and rejoice, playing musical instruments and dancing. And the joyful occasion is that some group from them, one of them thinks and arrives at some wisdom how to go up on the mountain, hence they make a big celebration and a feast with music and dancing, and thus with each group (that is, faction) from among them — "except that this page of these mannerisms that shields you shields me."

A nd on the mountain's peak is a tablet, and on it were written the mannerisms of the page that shields him; from which nations it is. But since the mountain is high, one cannot read the writing. However at the bottom was a tablet; there it was written that whoever has all [his] teeth — he can go up on the mountain. Hashem Yithbarakh provided that there grows such a grass there where one needs to go up on the mountain, that whoever comes there, all his teeth fall out; whether he was going by foot, riding, or driving a carriage by animals, always his teeth would fall out. Lying there were piles white with teeth, like mountains.[38]

L ater the people from the diamond took the portrait and put it back together as previously, and they took the crown and washed it up, and they hung them back in their place. And the king woke up and immediately looked at the page that had shielded him — which mannerism of which nation is it? He saw that written on it is the mannerisms of Jews [Heb. Yisrael]. He began to look at the page honestly and he understood the right truth, and he came to a decision that he himself would definitely be a Jew [Heb. Yisrael]; however, what does one do to return the entire world back to the best state [*machzir lemutav*], to bring them all to the truth? He came to the decision that he would journey in search of a sage who would solve the dream according to its essence (that is, he should interpret the dream exactly as it is). And he took two men with him and traveled around the world, not as a king but as a simple person, and he traveled from one city to the next and he asked: where does one find such a sage who can solve his dream according to its essence? They informed him that there-and-there is found such a sage. He went there and came to the sage and told him the truth: that he is a king and he had vanquished wars, and the entire story that happened, as mentioned, and he asked him to solve his dream. The sage answered him, "I myself cannot interpret; however, there is a time on this day and in this month — then, I gather together all the spices of the Incense (that is, all the herbs from which they would make the Incense) and I make from them a compound (in other words, he mixes them all up together) and the person is smoked with the incense and this person thinks in himself what he wants to see and know, and then he knows everything."

The king resolved: since he has already in fact spent so much time on it he would wait longer until that day and that month (which the sage had told him). The day came and the sage did for him so, as described above, and smoked him with the incense. The king began to see even things that had happened to him before he was yet born, when the soul was still in the upper world (in other words, on the other world); how they led his soul through all the worlds and they announced, "Whoever has something to say for the prosecution (that is, to speak evil) against this soul, let him come." There was no one who found fault. Meanwhile someone did come and was running and shouting, "Master of the World! Hear my prayer! If this one should come upon the earth, what then have I to do any longer, and for what have You created me? And this was the *Samekh-Mem*[39] (in other words, the one who was shouting was the *S.M.* himself; he was yelling: if this soul should go down on the earth he will no longer have anything to do). He was answered, "This soul must go down on the earth, and you — give yourself advice." He went away (that is, the one who was yelling).

They led the soul further through worlds [`olamoth, pl. of `olam, a term for "world" whose root also denotes concealment; hence, the world as a clothing and concealment of the Blessed Unity] (in other words, worlds) in order to swear it in already, in order that it should go down on the earth. And he had not yet arrived (that is, the *S.M.*, who was yelling earlier, had not come yet), so they sent an emissary after him. He came and brought with him a little oldster, a hunched-over one, with whom he was long familiar (that is, the Accuser had been acquainted with this old one from long ago), and he laughed and said, "I have already given myself an advice; this soul can now go down on the earth." They released the soul and it went down on the earth. And he (that is, the king) saw everything that happened to him from beginning to end, how he became king, the wars he had, etc.

And he took captives, and among the captives was a beautiful woman who had every kind of charm in the world. However, this charm was not from herself; rather, she would hang a diamond upon herself and the diamond had all kinds of charm, and on account of that it seemed she had all kinds of charm. And upon that mountain can no others ascend except the wise, the rich, etc. (And more than this he did not tell.)

And there is a great deal more in this. (From "And he took captives" until the end — was not written properly as he told it.)

[Notes Following the Story]

- *Mizmor leDawidh bevorcho/* A psalm of Dawidh when he fled... *Hashem, mah-rabú tsarai, rabim kamim `alai/* Hashem, how many are mine adversaries become; many are they that rise up against me...

- *We'atah Hashem magen ba`adi, kevodi umerim roshi/* But you, Hashem, are a shield about me: my glory and the lifter up of my head...

- *Qoli el-Hashem eqra weya`aneni mehar qodsho selah/* With my voice I call out unto Hashem, and He answers me from His holy mountain, Selah — the mountain mentioned above.

- *Ani shakhavti wa'ishanah/* I lay down and I sleep — as mentioned above.

- *Haqitzothi/* I awake...

- *Lo-ira merivevoth `am/* I will not fear a multitude of people...

- *Ki-hikitha eth-kol-oyvai léchi; shinnei resha`im shibbarta/* for you have smitten all my enemies on the cheek; You have broken the teeth of the wicked — for their teeth would fall out when they wanted to go up on the mountain.

- *`Al-amekhá virkhathékha selah/* May Your blessing be on Your people, Selah. [Psalms 3]

Stand and contemplate these wonders! If you are a living being [*ba`al nefesh*], take your flesh up in your teeth and place your life [*nefesh*] in your palm; stand trembling and amazed. Let the hairs of your head stand on edge, and return again and wonder at these words which stand in the highest of heights.

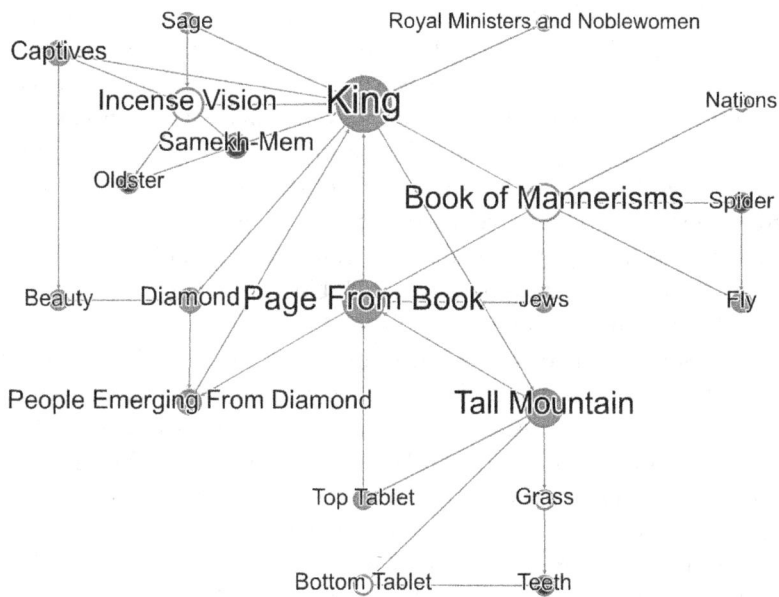

Tale 8: The Rabbi and His Only Son

A tale. There was once a rabbi who had no children. Later, he had an only son and he raised him and made him a wedding. The son would sit in an attic room and learn [i.e. study], as is the way with the wealthy. He would study and pray constantly, except that he felt in himself that he's lacking [due to] some deficiency, but he did not know what, and he had no taste in his learning and praying. He told this to two young people and they advised he should travel to a certain tzaddik. Now, this son had done a *mitzvah*[40] through which he had reached the aspect of the Smaller Luminary. The only son went and told his father inasmuch as he feels no taste in his service (in other words, in his serving God, that is, praying, learning and other mitzvot) and it's lacking for him but he doesn't know what — therefore he wants to travel to this Tzaddik about whom they had told him, as above. His father answered him, "How do *you* arrive at traveling to *him*? You are, after all, more of a scholar than he and more pedigreed than he. It doesn't suit you to travel to him. Desist from this way!" Until the father thus prevented him from traveling to the Tzaddik.

The son returned to his learning and again he felt the deficiency as mentioned above, and again he took counsel with those young people. Again they gave him the advice that he should travel to the Tzaddik. Again he went to his father and again his father diverted him and prevented him. Thus it happened several times. And the son kept feeling that he is lacking something and he greatly wanted to fill his lack (in other words, he should make corrections with something so that he should not be lacking) but he did not know what the lack is, as mentioned earlier. He went yet again to his father and implored him a great deal until his father had to travel with him, for the father did not want to let him travel alone, since he was an only son for him. So the father said to him, "Look, I will go with you. I'll show you that he's nothing at all (in other words, that the Tzaddik is nothing)." They harnessed the carriage and set out. The father said to his son, "With this I will make a test: if everything goes orderly, it is from Heaven, and if not, it is not from Heaven that we should travel and we will return." They set out, and they reached a small bridge, a horse fell, the carriage turned over and they nearly drowned. His father said to him, "You see that it's not going orderly and the journey is not from Heaven." They returned. Again the son returned to his studies and again he saw that something is lacking and he does not know what. Again he implored his father, as above, and his father had to once again travel with him. As they were traveling, his father again set up a test as before: if it goes orderly (then etc., as mentioned). As they were traveling, both axles broke. His father said to him, "See that [things are] not going so that we should travel. For is it a natural occurrence that both axles should break? How many times have we traveled with this carriage and such a thing has never happened?!" Again they returned. And the son returned to his learning and so forth as above, and again he felt the deficiency as mentioned earlier, and the young people advised him to make the journey. Again the only son went to his father and again pressed him; once again he had to travel with him. The only son said to the father: that we should no longer set up such a test, for this is a natural occurrence, that sometimes a horse falls or axles can break — unless it will be something very wild.

They traveled and came to an inn to spend the night. They met a merchant there, and they began talking with him as merchants are wont, not telling him that they are going there (to one "good Jew"), for the rabbi was embarrassed to say that he is traveling to the good Jew. So they were speaking worldly things until in the conversation they began talking about good Jews [Heb. tzaddikim]; where tzaddikim are found. He (the merchant) told them that there (in a certain place) there is a tzaddik, and there and there. They began speaking about the tzaddik to whom they are traveling. The merchant answered them, "*That* person (in an expression of amazement)? He is plainly a *qal* [lit. "light one"] (in other words, not at all an earnest Jew)! Just now I am traveling from him; I was there when he did a transgression!" The father spoke up (to the only son), "Do you see, my son, what this merchant is telling [us] innocently (in other words, he is not intending trash-talk, to speak evil of the Tzaddik; only by way of the conversation did he tell it)? Look, he's coming from there." They returned home (that is, the father and the only son).

The son died, and appeared in a dream to his father, and his father saw him standing in great anger. His father asked him, "Why are you so angry?" He answered him (that is, the son, who is dead, answered his father in the dream) that he should travel to that Tzaddik (to whom they had wanted to travel), "and he will tell you why I am angry." He awoke and thought to himself: it's a chance occurrence (in other words, just a dream; not any truth). Afterwards he dreamed the same again, and again he thought it's a false dream, and so it happened three times. He understood that this is no empty thing and he traveled there (that is, the rabbi traveled to the Tzaddik toward whom he had previously traveled with his son). On the way he again encountered the merchant whom he had previously encountered when he traveled with his son, and the rabbi recognized him. The rabbi said to the merchant, "Aren't you the one I saw at that inn?" He answers him, "Certainly you saw me!" and opens up his mouth and says to him, "If you want, I'll just swallow you down now!" He says to him (that is, the rabbi to the merchant), "What are you talking [about]?" He answered him, "Do you remember when you traveled with your son and first a horse fell down on the bridge and you returned, then the axles broke, then you met me and I told you he is a *qal*? Now that I have exterminated your son — now you may travel. For your son was an aspect of the Minor Luminary, and that Tzaddik to whom he wanted to travel is an aspect of the Major Luminary, and if they both would have assembled together, Mashiach [Messiah] would have come. And now that I have exterminated him, you are permitted to go." And in the midst of speaking, he disappeared (in other words, the merchant vanished suddenly while talking) and he didn't have whom to talk with. The rabbi traveled to the Tzaddik and cried, "Woe! Woe! What a loss in the perished and no longer present (woe for the one who is lost and can no more be found)!" (Heb. only: May Hashem Yithbarakh return our exiled ones soon, Amen.)

[Notes Following the Story]

And the merchant was the *Samekh-Mem*[41] himself, who disguised himself as a merchant and deceived them, and then when he met the rabbi the second time, he himself teased him for having followed him. For such is the way of the *yetzer hara`* [evil inclination]: initially he incites a person, and when the person follows him, Heaven forbid, he himself teases the person afterwards and personally takes vengeance upon him for having followed him. Hashem Yithbarakh save us from him and return us to the truth proper, Amen.

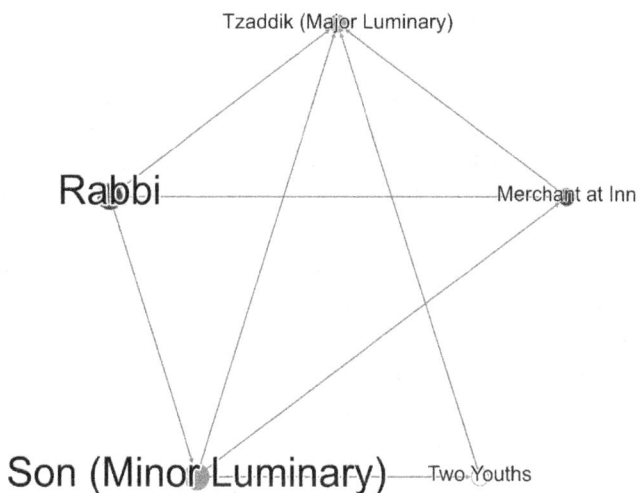

Tale 9: The Clever Man and the Simple Man

[Introduction]

Once there were two proprietors in a city, and they had great wealth and large houses. The two proprietors had two sons; that is, each one of them had a son; and the two children learned together in the same schoolhouse. And one of them was a *chakham* [clever, smart, sophisticated, wise] and the other was a *tam* [simple, innocent, artless, wholesome] (not that he was a fool; rather, his intellect was simple, without sophistication). And the two sons loved each other very much, even though one was clever and the other was a *tam* and his mind simple; they still loved each other very much. Around a certain time the two proprietors began to decline from their wealth and kept declining and declining until they became entirely possessionless and destitute and nothing more remained for them except their houses. And the sons began to grow up and the proprietors told the sons: We haven't [wherewithal] to pay for you; we cannot sustain you. Do for yourselves what you can.

[The Simple Man and the Clever Man Learn Trades]

The tam went and learned shoemaking. The chakham became a discerning person [*bar havanah*] (in other words, a smart and understanding person); he didn't want to apply himself to such a common trade so he decided he would travel the world and look and see what he should do. And he was going around in the marketplace and he saw a large wagon with four horses in harness speeding through. He called out to the merchants, "Where are you from?" They answered him, "From Warsaw." "Where are you going?" "To Warsaw." He asked him, "Maybe you need a helper?" The merchants saw that he is a smart youth and motivated, and they liked him and took him along. He traveled off with them and served them on the road quite finely.

When they arrived in Warsaw, since he was astute he decided, "Since I am already in Warsaw, why should I remain with these merchants? Maybe here there is a better place than them; let me go search." And he walked around in the marketplace and began to inquire and ask regarding the men who had brought him, and whether here there is a better place than them. They answered him that these people (who had brought him there) are honest people and it's good to be with them, but on account of this it's very difficult to be with them since their dealing and trading is in very distant places.

Meanwhile he went on and he noticed shop servants as they were going around the marketplace, and they were going around as they are accustomed to, with all their charm, with their caps and the pointy shoes and the rest of the charms which they have in their gait and how they go dressed. And he was a smart youth and this thing pleased him very much, since it's a nice thing and it's at home in one place. He went to the men who had brought him and gave them thanks and told them that it is not good for him to be with them, and as for them having brought him here, for that he had served them on the road.

And he went ahead and offered himself to a proprietor. And the way it goes with servants is first one has to be a lowly worker (earning less and doing hard work), then later one reaches the levels of higher workers. The proprietor did hard work with him and would send him off to nobility to carry merchandise in the manner of servants, who must carry cloth upon their elbows; this work was very hard for him. Sometimes he needed to go up with the merchandise to upper floors, and this work was very hard for him. He decided, since he was a philosopher, a discerning person: "Why do I need this work? The essential is only for the ultimate purpose: so that I can have a wedding and be able to support myself. I don't need to see to that yet; there will be time for that later. Meanwhile I would rather be out in the world seeing countries." He walked along in the marketplace and saw merchants riding on a large wagon, and he asked them, "Where are you going?" They answered, "To Lagorna[42]." He asked them, "Would you take me there?" They answered him, "Yes." They took him there. From there he traveled to Italy, and from Italy he traveled further on to Spain.

Meanwhile, many years passed and he became even more knowledgeable[43] on account of having been in many countries. He decided, "At this time a person needs to look at a purpose," and he began to think with his philosophy (that is, with his knowledge) what he should do. It seemed to him that he should

learn goldwork, which is a major occupation and a nice craft, re-
quiring great insight; and it's a profitable craft. And since he was
a discerning man and a philosopher, he didn't need to study the
trade many years; merely in a quarter year he received the skill,
and he became quite a great craftsman. And he knew the work
better than the one who had trained him.

Afterwards he concluded, "Even though I have such a trade in
hand, nonetheless I will not content myself with it, for today
this is distinguished; maybe at another time some other thing will
be considered important" — and went ahead and placed himself
with a gem cutter. And on account of his cleverness he acquired
this skill in a short time as well — in a quarter year.

Then he thought to himself with his philosophy, "Even though
I have two trades in hand, who knows if perhaps both will
not be important. Therefore it is good for me that I should learn
such a profession that will always be important." He probed out
with his insight and with his philosophy that he should learn
medicine, for this is something that is always needed and always
esteemed. And the routine is when one will study medicine one
must first learn Latin, the language and its writing, and one
must learn philosophy. And he on account of his insight (that is,
understanding) mastered this also in a short time, in a quarter
year; and he became a big doctor and a philosopher and an expert
in all fields of wisdom.

[The Clever Man Afflicted, the Simple Man Joyful]

Then the world began to be like nil to him (in other words the
entire world became like nothing to him); that is, he maintained that nobody has any sense at all; for on account of his
great wisdom, since he was such a great craftsman and such a
smart person and such a doctor, every person in the world was
like nil to him (equal to nothing). So he decided that he would
now accomplish a purpose and take a wife. He thought with this
opinion: "If I would have wedding here, who will know what has
become of me? Let me rather go back home, so that people will see
what has become of me. I left as a young boy and now I have come
to such greatness." And he picked up and traveled home, and he
had great afflictions on the way, for on account of his sophistication he didn't have anything to talk about with anyone and he

had no lodging like he desires. So he kept having great affliction continually.

Meanwhile let us set aside the story of the clever man; we will begin to tell the story of the simple man. The simple man learned shoemaking, and since he was a simple person he had to study the trade a great deal until he got it, and he did not know the art entirely. And he took a wife, and he sustained himself from his work. And since he was a simple person and did not know the work as one should, therefore his livelihood was with a great deal of pressure and very limited. And he didn't have time even to eat, because he always had to work, since he didn't know his work entirely; except that while he was working, when he had inserted the nail and pulled through the cobbler's thread, then he would take a bite on a piece of bread and he ate. And his usual way was that he was always happy and constantly only joyous.

And he had all foods, all drinks and all clothing. He would say to his wife, "My wife, give me to eat;" and she gave him a piece of bread and he ate. Then he said, "Give me the sauce with buckwheat groats," and she cut him off another piece of bread and he ate, and he gave much praise and said, "What a goodness and niceness this sauce is!" And similarly he ordered himself served meat, and again she gave him bread and he ate and also praised greatly and said, "What a niceness this meat is!" And so too other foods which he kept ordering himself given; and for each type of food which he ordered himself she kept giving him a piece of bread and he had a great pleasure from this and very much praised the dish. "What a goodness it is!" — just as if he actually ate it, for he would really and truly feel, in the bread that he ate, the taste of all the foods he wanted; on account of his great *temimuth* [the quality of being *tam*; simplicity; wholesomeness; naivete; innocence] and his joy, he sensed the bread's taste just as if he were eating all those foods.

And similarly he would say, "My wife, give me a drink of beer;" she gave him water and he would praise, "What a niceness this beer is!" Then he would summon, "Give me mead;" she gave him water and he also praised the same way, "What a good mead this is!" "Give me wine" or other drink; she continued giving him water and he had delight and praised the drink just as if he's drinking it.

A nd so too with clothing it was also thus. He and his wife to-gether had one *pelts* [Yid. pelt coat; unfinished skin-with-fur coat]. When he needed a *pelts*, namely, to go to the market, he would say, "My wife, give me the *pelts*," and she gave it to him. When he needed a *tulep* [fancy overcoat with fine fur on the inside and the fur rolled over onto the collar], to go amongst people, he would say, "My wife, give me the tulep," and she gave him the *pelts*. He would have great delight and would praise, "What a niceness this tulep is." When he needed a *kaftan* [long suit coat] to go to synagogue he would summon and say, "My wife, give me the kaftan," and she gave him the *pelts*. He would give praise and he said, "What a niceness and what a beauty this kaftan is!" And so too when he needed to don a *yupa* [a long silk robe worn for for-mal occasions] she would also give him the *pelts*, and he would also give praise and had delight: "What a niceness and what a beauty this yupa is!" And thus with all things; and he was full of joy, happiness and wellbeing constantly.

W hen he had finished a shoe — and probably the shoe had three corners, because he wasn't able to perform his craft totally well — he would take the shoe in his hand and praise it highly. And he had enormous delight from it and would say, "My wife, what a beauty and what a niceness this little shoe is! What a sweetness this little shoe is! What a honey, what a sugary little shoe this is!" She would ask him, "If that is so, why do other shoe-makers take three gulden for a pair of shoes, and you take only a half thaler (that is, one and a half gulden)?" He replied, "What's that to me? That's the other person's business and this is my busi-ness. And besides, why do we have to talk about other people? Let's just start calculating how much I win here in this little shoe when it changes hands. The leather costs me so much, tar and thread cost so much, the filling between the skins so much, and likewise other items so much; now I profit ten groschen when changing hands. Well, why should such a profit from changing hands bother me?"

S o he was only happy and cheerful at all times, but to the world he was a laughingstock; here they got what they de-sired, for here they had someone to mock however they pleased, for he seemed to them like a lunatic. People would come and in-tentionally start speaking with him, in order to have something to make fun of. And the simple man would say to them, "Just without mockery." And as soon as they answered him, "No kidding," he listened to them and started talking with them, for he did not want to further suspect witticisms — that perhaps this itself [their reply] is mockery — for he was a tam. But when he would eventually see that their intention is to ridicule, he would say, "So what if you are cleverer than me? You'll still be a fool, for what do I amount to? So if you'll be cleverer than me you'll still be a fool!" (That was all the usual way of the simple man. Now we will again talk about the clever man.)

[The Clever Man Arrives Back in Town]

I n the meantime, there was a commotion, that the clever man is traveling and is coming with great pomp and great sophistication. The simple man too came running to greet him with great joy, and said to his wife, "Give me quick the yupa! Let me go and greet my dear friend; let me see him." She gave him the *pelts* and he ran out towards him. Now the clever man was riding in a carriage pompously; the simple man came out to greet him and welcomed him joyously, with great love (and said to him), "My dear brother, how do you do? Praised is God for bringing you and giving me the privilege of seeing you." And the clever man looks at him; for him the entire world was also nothing (as it was stated above, that all the people of the world amounted to nothing in his regard, for he considered himself smarter than all the world) — all the more so such a person who looks like a crazy. But nonetheless, on account of their childhood love, that they loved each other very much, he drew him close and traveled with him into town. Now the two proprietors, the fathers of these two sons (that is, of the clever man and the simple man), had died during the time when the clever man was out in countries, and had left behind their houses. The simple man was in his place, so he moved into his father's house and inherited it.

T he clever man, however, was in foreign countries and had no one to take possession of the house. The clever man's house came to an end and was lost and nothing at all remained of it, so the clever man had no house to enter in when he arrived. He traveled to an inn and suffered anguish there because it wasn't the kind of inn that he wanted. And the simple man had now found himself a new thing to do and would always run to the clever man

with love and joy. And he noticed that the clever man had affliction from the inn, so the simple man said to the clever man,
"Brother, come over to me into my house. You'll stay with me and
I will gather my entire belongings into one bunch and you'll have
my entire house." This was agreeable to the clever man, so he
went into his house and stayed with him. And the clever man was
always full of suffering, for he had left a reputation that he is a
great wise man, a great craftsman, and very much of a great doctor. A nobleman came and ordered for him to make him a gold
ring. He made him quite a wonderful ring and etched out engrav-
ings with very wonderful paths, etching out in it a tree that was a
total marvel. The nobleman came and the ring did not please him
at all. He had enormous suffering, because he knew in himself
that if this ring with the tree would be in Spain it would be quite
esteemed; it would be a novelty there, but here it's not liked at
all. And similarly, one time a great nobleman came and brought
an expensive diamond that was brought from distant lands, and
he brought with him another diamond with an image and bid him
to etch out just as this image is; so should he etch out on the diamond that he brought him (which was from distant lands). He
etched out precisely like the image, except he lacked one thing
which nobody at all would discern except him alone. The nobleman came and took the diamond and he liked it very much. But
the clever man had great agony from the shortcoming that he
lacked; he thought to himself: "As smart as I am, now should *I*
make a mistake?"

And similarly in medicine he suffered as well: when he came
to an ill person and he gave him treatments of which he
knew clearly that if the patient should just survive he would certainly have to be healed from the treatments since they're very
excellent treatments — then however the patient died. The public
said that he died because of him, and he had great affliction from
this. And likewise sometimes he gave an ill person treatments
and the ill person became healthy, and the public said it's a
chance occurrence (in other words, he became so healthy not
through him). He also suffered very much from that. So he was
full of afflictions constantly.

And similarly, when he needed a garment he summoned the
tailor and took pains with him until he taught him to make

the garment in the fashion like he wants, in the way he knew. The tailor hit upon it and made the garment just as he wanted, except the tailor erred on one lapel and didn't hit it off well. He suffered great anguish from that because he knew in himself that although here no one discerns it, "If I were only in Spain with this lapel, they would laugh at me and I would look ridiculous." And so he was always full of suffering.

And the simple man used to always run, coming to the clever man with joy, with happiness; but he always found him in affliction and full of suffering, and he asked him, "Such a wise person and such a wealthy person as you — why do you always have anguish? Why am I constantly happy?" For the clever man this was a mockery, and he seemed crazy to him. The simple man said to him, "Even plain people, when they make fun of me, are fools as well, for if they're already smarter than me, they are first fools themselves [as mentioned above]! All the more so such a clever person as you are. So what if you are smarter than me?" The simple man proclaimed and said to the clever man, "The Supreme One grant that you should come up to my level (in other words, that you should also become a simple person)." The clever man replied, "It could happen that I should reach your level — if God would take away my intellect, God spare us; or if I, God forbid, should became sick it could happen that I should also become insane. For, what are you anyway but a madman? If only you could come up to my level; this is by no means possible, that you should be such a clever person as I." The simple man answered, "With Hashem Yithbarakh everything is possible. It can happen like the wink of an eye (like an eyeblink) that I should arrive at your smartness." The clever man ridiculed him a great deal.

[The King Sends for the Clever Man and Simple Man]

Now these two sons, the public would call them "Clever" and "Simple:" this one they called "Clever" and that one they called "Simple." Even though there are many clever ones and simple ones on the earth, still, here it was very apparent, because they were both from one town and had studied in one schoolroom, and this one became quite an extraordinarily clever person, while that one became quite an extremely simple person; consequently they gave them the nicknames "The Clever Man" and "The Simple Man." Now in the registry (the book listing the residents) everyone is written down with all their family names, so they wrote down after this one the nickname "Clever Man" and after that one, "Simple Man."

One time the king came by the registry and he found the two as they were recorded, this one with the nickname "Clever Man" and that one with the nickname "Simple Man." This was a wonder to the king, that the two should have such nicknames, "Clever Man" and "Simple Man." The king very much wanted to see them. The king decided, "If I suddenly send for them to come before me they will be very frightened, and the clever man won't know at all what to reply, and the simple man might go crazy from fear." The king decided to send a clever man to the clever man and a simple man to the simple man. But where does one get a simple man in a royal city? For in a royal city (that is, the town where the king lives) the majority are smart people. However, the one who is a warden over the treasuries — he is specifically a simple person, because one doesn't want to make a clever person any sort of warden over the treasuries, for perhaps through his cleverness and his intellect he will embezzle the treasuries; therefore one specifically puts a simple person in charge of the treasuries.

So the king summoned a clever man and the simple man (who is a warden over the treasuries) and sent them to the two (that is, to the clever man and to the simple man) and he gave each one a different letter. And he gave them an additional letter to the governor of the province whom the two, that is, the clever man and the simple man, were under. And the king commanded in the letter that the governor should send letters on his behalf to the clever man and the simple man so that they shouldn't be frightened, and he should write to them that the matter is not obligatory and the king is not specifically decreeing that they should come but rather the choice is theirs: if they want, they should come. But the king does want to see them.

The emissaries traveled off, the clever one and the simple one, and came to the governor's and delivered him the letter. The governor inquired after the two children and they told him that the clever man is an extraordinarily clever person and quite a wealthy man and the simple man is quite a very simple person and has every kind of garment from the *pelts* [sheepskin coat] as mentioned before. The governor decided that it is certainly not nice that they should bring him before the king dressed in a *pelts* so he made for him clothes as appropriate and placed them in the simple man's carriage. And he gave them the letters, as mentioned.

The messengers traveled off and came to them and delivered the letters to them; the clever one delivered to the clever man and the simple one to the simple man. And the simple man, as soon as he was delivered the letter, spoke up to emissary (who was also a simple man, as mentioned) who brought him the letter, "I don't know what is written in the letter. Read it to me." He answered him, "I'll tell you externally [Yid. *oysveynik* < Ger. *auswendig*; Heb. *be`al peh* by rote] what is written in it. The king wants you to come to him." Immediately he asked, "Just without mockery?" He answered him, "It's a definite truth; without mockery." He was immediately filled with joy and he ran and said to his wife, "My wife, the king has sent for me!" She asked him, "What is it? Why has he sent for you?!" He had absolutely no time to answer her at all. He immediately rushed himself joyfully and went ahead and sat himself in the carriage so that he could travel off with the messenger. Meanwhile he noticed the clothes there (which the governor had made on his behalf and placed in his carriage, as mentioned). He became even happier: now he has clothes as well! So he was extremely happy.

[The King Appoints the Simple Man as Governor, Minister]

In the meantime the king was delivered leaks regarding the governor, in that he is committing fraud, and the king removed (in other words, deposed) him. The king made up his mind: it's good if a simple person would be governor, that is, a *tam*, for a simple man would conduct the country with truth and justice, since he doesn't know any cleverness or contriving. So the king felt that he should make the simple man (that is, the simple man who is the friend of the clever man, whom the king had sent for) a governor. The king sent an order that the simple man, whom he had sent for, should become governor. Now, the simple man must travel through the provincial capitol, thus they should station themselves at the city gates so that as soon as the simple man arrives they should detain him and give him the appointment that he should be governor. They did so, and they stood at the gates and as soon as he drove through they stopped him and told him that he has become governor.

He asked, "Just without mockery?" They answered him, "Definitely! Without joking! We are not mocking you!" The simple man immediately became governor, with authority and power. And now that his mazal[44] had improved — and *mazal machkim*[45] (that is, the mazal makes [a person] smart) he now acquired a bit of discernment (that is, understanding). Nonetheless, he did not make use of his wisdom at all but just conducted himself with his *temimuth* as before, and he led the state with temimuth, with truth and with integrity. And he dealt absolutely no falseness or injustice to anyone. And for the management of a state one needs no great intellect nor special knowledge, just uprightness and temimuth. When two people came before him for judgment, he would say, "You are clear and you are liable," purely according to his temimuth and his truthfulness, without any deceit or falseness. And thus he led everything with truth.

The country loved him very much and he had loyal advisers who truly loved him. And on account of love, one of them gave him an advice: "Inasmuch as you will certainly have to appear before the king, since he has already sent for you, and moreover the procedure is that a governor has to come before the king, therefore, even though you are very sincere and the king will not find any falseness in you in your leadership of the country, still however it is the routine of the king when he converses that he enters the discussion through the side and starts discussing special knowledges [*chokhmoth*] and languages. So it is fitting and it is the etiquette that you should be able to respond to him; therefore it is right that I should teach you knowledge and languages." The simple man accepted this and received wisdoms and languages. It immediately came to his mind that his friend the clever man had said to him that it is impossible in any manner that he should reach his wisdom. "Here I have already arrived at his wisdom!" (And still even though he now knew wisdoms, he did not use the wisdoms at all but conducted himself with simplicity as before.)

Afterwards the king dispatched that the simple man, the governor, should come to him. He traveled to him. First the king discussed the leadership of the country with the simple man, and the king was very well pleased, for the king saw that he leads justly and with great honesty, without any wrongdoing and completely without falseness. Then the king began to talk about fields of knowledge and languages; the simple man replied to him as one should, and the king was even more pleased. The king said, "I see that he is such a smart person and yet conducts himself with such an innocence." He pleased the king very, very well, and the king made him a minister over all the ministers; and the king ordered to give him a special city where he should live, and commanded to wall him about with very beautiful walls as is befitting, and gave him a writ regarding the fact that he shall be minister. And so it was; they walled him about with very fine beautiful walls in the place where the king ordered, and he took on his greatness in full effect [*betokef*].

[The Clever Man Denies There is a King]

The clever man, when the letter from the king came to him, replied to the clever person who brought the letter, "Wait, and spend the night here. We'll talk it over and we'll come to a decision." At night he prepared for him a great feast. During the meal the clever man (the simple man's friend) started being clever and analyzing with his cleverness and his philosophy. He spoke up and said, "What can this mean, that such a king should send for such a lowly person as I? Who am I that the king should send for me? What's the sense? Such a king who has such authority and such prestige, and I, as little as I am versus such a great king — well, how is it conceivable that such a king should send for me? If I should say on account of my wisdom he has sent for me, what do I amount to next to the king? After all, doesn't the king have any wise men? And the king is certainly a great sage himself, so what is this, that the king should send for me?" So he was very, very astonished about this, and as he was wondering thus, he called out (to the other clever person, the messenger who had brought the letter), "Do you know what I'm going to tell you? Well, my opinion is that it clearly must be that there is no king whatsoever here in the world. And the entire world is mistaken in this; they think that there is a king here. Just the opposite. Understand — how can it be that the entire world should entrust itself into the hands of one man, that he should be the king? There is certainly no king on the earth at all." The clever person, the messenger, replies, "Haven't I brought you a letter from the king?" The clever man (the simple man's friend) asks him, "Did you personally receive the letter at the king's, from out of his hand?" He answers him, "No, but another person gave me the king's letter." He calls out, "Well, on the contrary, now see with your eyes that I am correct, that there is absolutely no king." Again he asks him, "Just tell me. You are from the royal city and you grew up there. Tell me, have you once seen the king?" He answers, "No." (For in fact it is so, that not everyone is privileged to see the king, for the king is not seen but on rare occasion.) He declares, "Now see that I am correct, that there is definitely no king whatsoever, for even you here have never seen the king." Once again the messenger answered the clever man, "If it is really so, who then rules the country?" He (that is, the clever man, the simple man's friend) answered him, "That — I'll make clear to you, for I am expert in this, so it is me you should ask, for I have been abroad in countries; I've been in Italy and the practice is thus: there are seventy senators and they rise up and lead the country for a while. With this system of authority the entire country participates one after the other (that is, first these are the senators, then these go down and others rise up and lead the country, and similarly other people each time)." His words started to get into the other clever person's ears (that is, the messenger), until they were both left with the conviction that there definitely isn't any king on earth. Again the clever man (the simple man's friend) spoke up, "Wait until morning and moreover I'll prove to you clearly that there is definitely no king."

The clever man got himself up in the morning and woke up the other clever man, the messenger, and said to him, "Come with me on the road. I will show you how the whole world is mistaken and there is no king whatsoever. They went in the marketplace and noticed a soldier. They took hold of him and asked him, "Whom do you serve?" He answered, "The king." "Have you in your life seen the king?" He answers, "No." He announced (that is, the first clever man, the simple man's friend; we always call him the "first" clever man) and said, "See! Is there such a foolishness?" (In other words, the soldier serves the king but doesn't know him — for the clever man still wanted to demonstrate with his foolish wisdom that there is no king at all, as mentioned.) After that they went on to an army officer and they entered in conversation with him until they asked him, "Whom do you serve?" He answered, "The king." "Have you seen the king?" "No." He proclaimed, "On the contrary — look and see with your eyes that they are all mistaken and there isn't any king here." (For the officer had also not seen the king.) It was settled among them that there is no king here. The first clever man declared, "Come, let's travel the world; I'll show you moreover that the entire world is very mistaken with great foolishness."

They went and traveled about in the world and wherever they arrived they always found the world in error. (In other words, the clever men through their "wisdom" fell into such foolishness, to the extent that they thought that the whole world is always mistaken.) And the matter of the king (that is, the fact that for them it was proven that there is no king) had already become a byword for them, and wherever they found the world in error they took the king as an analogy: "Just as it is 'true' that there is a king, so too is this ['true']." Thus they were out in the world and they traveled until they ran out of what they had. They began by selling one horse and then the other until they had sold everything, until they had to go on foot. And constantly they kept examining the world and kept finding that the world is in error. And they became foot-going beggars and they were already not at all distinguished, for by now people paid no attention at all to such beggars.

[The Clever Man Meets with the Simple Man]

So they were out in the world until it turned out that they came to the city where the minister lives (that is, the simple man, the clever man's friend). And there in that city was a genuine *baal shem* [lit. "Master of the (Divine) Name;" a holy man and miracle worker]. And the baal shem was held in high esteem because he had done truly wild things, and even among the nobility he was a renowned person and was highly regarded by them. And the clever men came into the city, walked about and came before the house of the baal shem. They saw many wagons stationed there with sick people, forty or fifty. The clever man thought that a doctor lives there. He wanted to go inside to him; since he too was a great doctor, he wanted to go in to make his acquaintance. He asked, "Who lives here?" They answered him, "A baal shem." He made a heavy laughter and said to the other (that is, to the messenger wise person), "This is another lie and a foolishness! This is even more nonsense than the mistake about the king! Brother, let me tell you about this falsehood, how much the world is mistaken and so deceived."

Meanwhile they became hungry and found that they still had three or four groschen. They went into the food kitchen [Yid. *gorkekh*, everyman's kitchen] and there one can get food for even three, four groschen and they ordered themselves served with food and they were served. While they were eating they talked and made fun of the "lie" and the "error" of the baal shem (how the world is in error). And the food kitchener [*gorkekher*] heard their talk and it upset him very much, because the baal shem was highly esteemed there. He said to them, "Eat up what you have and get out of here." Then a son of the baal shem arrived there, and they kept on ridiculing the baal shem before his son's eyes. The food kitchener screamed at them for making fun of the baal shem before his son's eyes, until the kitchener beat them altogether harshly and pushed them out of his home. It made them very furious and they wanted to obtain a judgment over his beating them. They decided that they will go to their proprietor where they had deposited their bundles so as to take counsel with him as to how to attain a judgment against the food kitchener who had beaten them. They went and told it to their proprietor that the food kitchener had severely beaten them. He answered them: Why? They told him: Because they had spoken against the baal shem. The proprietor answered them, "It definitely isn't upright that people should be beaten. But you however behaved entirely not right by talking against the baal shem, for the baal shem is highly regarded here." They saw that he too was in "error." They left him and went to the commissioner, and the commissioner was a gentile. They told him the story that they had been beaten. He asked: Why? They said: Because they had spoken against the baal shem. The commissioner also beat them deathfully and pushed them out.

They went away from him and went to a superior who had authority and still could not bring about any judgment. And thus they kept going from one to another, each time to a higher one (and still accomplished nothing but were well beaten every time) until they came before the minister (who was the simple man, as mentioned). And there before the minister were stationed sentries. They announced to the minister that a person needs him and he ordered that he should come in. The clever man came before the minister. As he was coming in the minister immediately realized that this is the clever man, his friend. But the clever man did not recognize him, since he's in such greatness now. Immediately the minister started talking to him and said to him, "See what my temimuth has brought me to — to such a greatness — and what your cleverness has brought you to." The clever man spoke up and said, "That you are my friend the simple man — we can speak about this later. Right now, give me a court hearing for them having hit me." He asks him, "Why did they hit you?" He answers him, "Why, because I spoke against the baal shem, that he is a liar and it's all a swindle." The simple man, prime minister spoke up to him, "You still adhere to your contrivances? Look, you said you can easily reach mine [i.e. my level], but I cannot reach yours. Now see that I have already long reached yours (for the simple man has already become a big wise man as well, as mentioned) but you still have not reached mine. And I see that it is more difficult that you should arrive at my temimuth." But notwithstanding, since the simple man, the minister, had known him from long ago when he was great, he ordered him to be given garments to be clothed with and he bid him to eat with him at meal time. While they were eating they began to converse, and the clever man tried to demonstrate his (foolish) opinion that there is no king whatsoever. The simple man, the minister, screamed at him, "What are you saying?! I myself have seen the king!" The clever man answers him with laughter, "You yourself know that it was the king? You know him? You have known his father, his grandfather to have been kings? From where do you know that it was the king? People have told you that this is the king. They have deceived you." It annoyed the simple man a very much regarding the fact that he denies the king.

Meanwhile someone came and said, "The Devil [Yid. *Toivl*, Heb. `*Azazel*] has sent for you [plural]." The simple man trembled severely and ran and told his wife with great fear that the Devil had sent for him. She gave him an advice, that he should send for the baal shem. He sent for him; the baal shem came and gave him *kame`as* [amulets containing holy names] and [other] protections and told him that now he need no longer fear at all. He had great faith in this.

L ater the clever man and the simple man sat together some more. The clever man asked him, "What were you so terri-fied about?" He answered him, "Because of the Devil, who had sent for us." The clever man ridiculed him and said to him, "You believe that there is a Devil?!" The simple man, the minister, asked him, "Who then sent for us?" The clever man answered him, "This here is definitely from my brother; he wanted to meet with me; he set this up and sent for me with that disguise." The simple man asked him, "If it is so, how did he get through past all the sentries?" He answered him, "He definitely bribed them, and they are telling a lie in colluding that they did not see him at all." Meanwhile again someone comes and says again thus: "The Devil has sent for you." And the simple man now already did not trem-ble at all and did not have any fear whatsoever, on account of the protections he had taken from the baal shem. He calls out (that is, the simple man) and says to the clever man, "Well now, what do you say?" He answers him, "I will tell you. I have a brother who is angry at me. He is the one who made this disguise in order to frighten me." And the clever man got up and asked the one who had come for them, "What kind of appearance has the one who sent for us? What color is his hair?" etc. and other such things. He answered him: Such and such. The clever man replies and says, "See! That there is my brother's looks!" The simple man says to him, "Will you go with them?" He answers him, "Yes, I will go with them; you should only give me a few soldiers for *azalaga* (es-corting guards) so that they shouldn't cause me any travail." He gave him azalaga and the two clever men went with the one who had come for them (that is, with the Devil, because they did not want to believe that this is the Devil, as mentioned).

T he soldiers of the azalaga returned and the simple man, the minister asked them, "Where are the clever men?" They replied: They know nothing of where they've gone [Heb. how they've disappeared]. And he (that is, the Devil's emissary) had snatched the clever men and carried them off into a mire with clay. There the Devil sat on a throne amidst the mire. And the mire was thick and sticky just like a glue, and the clever men were completely unable to move in the mud. And the clever men screamed, "Wicked ones! Why are you dealing out tortures on us? Is there indeed a Devil on the earth? You are wicked people for torturing us for no reason!" (For these clever men still did not want to believe that there is a Devil; instead they said that wicked people are causing them agony for nothing.) The two clever men lay in the thick mire and probed, "What is this? These are nothing else but the hooligans with whom we had once quarreled, and now they are dealing out such afflictions on us." The clever men remained there in the mire several years, and they dealt them out wild sufferings along with wild tortures.

[The Clever Man Admits There is a King on the Earth]

One time the simple man, the minister passed by in front of the baal shem's home and he recalled his friend the clever man and went in to the baal shem and bowed to him in the proper way [Heb. in the way of ministers] and asked whether it is possible for him to show him the clever man and whether he can extricate him. And the simple man, the minister, said to the baal shem, "Do you remember the clever man whom the Devil sent for and carried away? And from that time I have not seen him." The baal shem answered him, "Yes, I remember." The simple man, the minister, bid him that he should show him the place where the clever man is and that he should extricate him from there. The baal shem said to him, "I can certainly show you his place and take him out, however, no one else can go; only I and you." Both went off and the baal shem did what he knew and they arrived there. He saw how they lay there in the thick mire, in clay. When the clever man noticed the simple man, the minister, he screamed to him, "Brother, look! They are beating me! And these hooligans are smiting me so hard for nothing!" The minister gave him a yelling, "Still you hold to your contrivances and don't want to believe in anything at all?! And you say that this is people. Well, look now. This here is the baal shem whom you had denied. You will be shown that specifically only he can take you out (and he will show you the truth)." The simple man, the minister, bid the baal shem that he should take them out and show them that this is a Devil and not humans.

The baal shem did what he did, and they were left standing on the dry land and there was no mire there at all. And the harmful angels became plain dust (that is, they became earth altogether). Then for the first time the clever man beheld the truth and had to admit everything, that there is indeed a king and there is indeed a genuine baal shem, etc.

[Notes Following the Story]

Regarding this story was said the torah [*LM II* #12] that discusses *temimuth,* that the essence of Judaism is not any mental scheming but only *temimuth* and simplicity etc.

(After he concluded the story he announced:) And when the prayer is not as it needs to be, it's a "three-cornered shoe" [*a shikhele mit drei ecken*]. Understand well what is said, as one can live out the world with bread, water and a coat and would have a better life and a happier life than the most clever person and the wealthiest person, as we see that they are full of travails constantly. And ultimately it is certainly altogether good for the *tam* who sufficed with what he had and was constantly happy. And whoever will be a wise guy and over-thinks a great deal will have difficulty from beginning to end and is full of afflictions constantly and never has any life, and ultimately becomes lost, until the tam has to have pity on him and help him. Aside from this, here in the story are more very great secrets, for all the tales are great secrets of the Torah throughout.

[In Hebrew:]

Regarding this story was said the torah [*LM II* #12] which discusses *temimuth;* that the essence of wholeness is only temimuth and simplicity; and the concept of 'Amalek who was a wise guy and became apostate at the root etc.; see there regarding the verse, "*ShevA` yipoL tzaddiK wekaM/* Seven [times] the tzaddik falls, but rises" — end-letters `AMaLeK, for the root of the downfalls are through wisdoms etc.; see there. Also Agag, from the seed of `Amalek, even though he was seeing his fall when Shmuel came to Shaul to kill him, still did not believe, as written, "*Vayelekh Agag ma`adanoth/* Agag went to him in chains" [I Sam. 15:32] and [Targum] Yonathan translated: "[Agag went to him] *mepanka/* with a noble or indulgent manner," for he still did not believe in his fall, until he saw with his eyes the end of his fall; then, "W*ayomer akhen sar mar-hamaveth* / Surely the bitterness of death has turned [hither]," for until now he did not believe. (Put your eyes on this story and you will discern wonders of wonders). And if the prayer is not as it ought to be, it is a *min'al be'g` ketzavoth* / shoe with three corners; and understand. And see also at the end of the book the Rav's explanation, and you will see wonderful analogous commentaries.

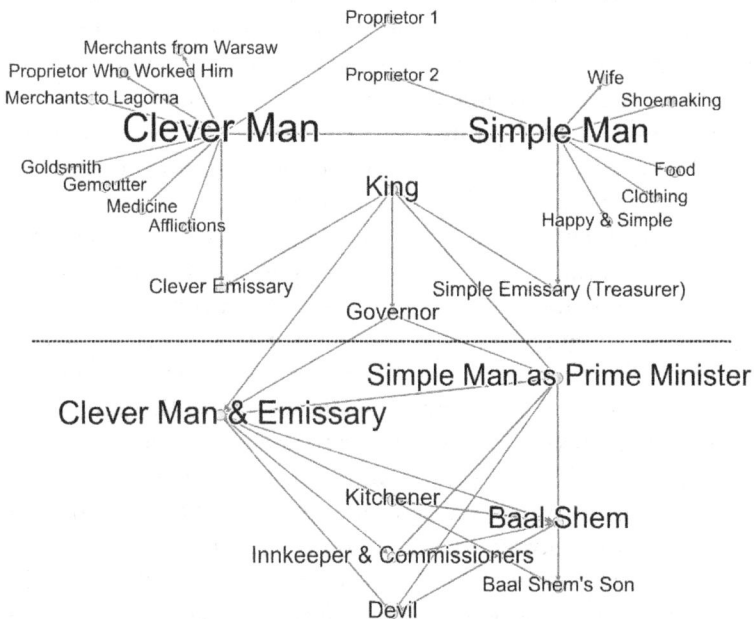

Tale 10: The Burgher and the Pauper

[Introduction; the Dream of the Burgher and the Pauper's Wife]

A tale. Once there was a burgher (that is, a [member of the] great merchant [class in Medieval Europe]) [*burgh* denotes a (fortified) city and is related to the word *berg*, mountain; see Rabbi Nathan's notes at the story's end] who was an extremely rich man and had a vast amount of merchandise. His promissory notes [*vekhseln*] and letters of credit [*briv*] circulated over the world and he had everything good. Below him lived a pauper who was an extremely poor man and had the complete opposite of the burgher (that is, the complete reverse: just as the burgher was a very rich man, so the pauper was conversely a very poor man). But both of them had no children: the burgher had no children and likewise the pauper also had no children.

Once, the burgher dreamed that people came to his house and were making packages and packages. He asked them, "What are you doing?" They replied: they will carry it all away to that very same pauper (that is, the pauper who lived under him, as mentioned). It annoyed him very much and he grew very angry that they wanted to carry away all his wealth to the pauper. To be wroth at them was impossible, for they were a good many people. So they continued making packages and packages of all his belongings, all his wares and all his goods and they carried absolutely everything away to the aforementioned pauper, leaving him nothing in the house but the bare walls; and it upset him very, very much. Meanwhile, he woke up and saw: it's a dream. And even though he saw it's only a dream and, thank God, all his belongings were with him — still all the same his heart pounded mightily and the dream could not be got out of his mind and the dream upset him severely. The pauper and his wife used to be cared for by the burgher and he would give to them often. But now after the dream he cared for them more than before. However, whenever the poor man or his wife would come into his house, his facial expression would change and he became frightened of them because he would recall the dream. And they, that is, the pauper and his wife, would often go to his house and were often with him.

One time the pauper's wife came to his house and he gave her what he gave her, and his expression changed and he became stricken with fear. She asked him and said, "I beg pardon of your honor. Tell me why it is that whenever we come to you your face becomes drastically changed." He told her the whole story: that he had had such a dream (as above) and since then his heart has been pounding him mightily (as above). She replied to him: did the dream take place on such and such a night (which she said)? He answers her, "Yes. What about it?" She replies to him, "On that night I also dreamed: that I'm a very wealthy person, and people had come to my house and were making packages upon packages. I asked them, 'Where are you bringing this?' They replied, 'To the pauper (that is, to the burgher, whom they already called a poor man now).' Therefore why do you pay attention to a dream? What for? — I also had a dream." Now the burgher has become all the more frightened and confused, since he has heard her dream as well, because it seems that his wealth and property are to be brought to the pauper and that the pauper's poverty are to be brought to him. He has become extremely panicked.

[The Wives' Trip and the Pauper's Wife's Capture; Rescue by the Burgher & the Pauper's Wife's Oath]

And the day came to pass — the burgher's wife took a trip by coach, taking other wives along with her, and she took the pauper's wife too. And while traveling along on their tour, meanwhile a general and his army passed through. They got off the road and the army passed through. The general saw that women were traveling and he gave orders that one of them should be taken out, and they went and took out the pauper's wife, snatched her into the general's coach and drove away with her. Getting her back was certainly impossible now, for he had driven off with her, and especially a general with his army... And with her he rode to his country. And she was a Heaven-fearing person (that is, she had fear of God) and she was not willing to listen to him at all and she wept very profusely. They implored her a great deal and coaxed her but she was, however, an exceedingly Heaven-fearing person. And she (the burgher's wife, and the other wives) returned from their tour but the pauper's wife was not there. The pauper wept very, very much, beating his head against the wall and constantly mourning for his wife bitterly.

One day the burgher passed by the pauper's house and heard the poor man crying so bitterly and beating his head against the wall. He went in and asked him, "Why are you crying so intensely?" He answered him, "Why shouldn't I weep? What do I have left? Some people are left with wealth or with children. I have nothing at all and my wife has also been taken from me. What do I have left?" The burgher's heart was very touched [*angekhapt*, lit. captured] and he had great pity on the pauper on account of seeing his bitterness, his acute sorrow, and he went and did a reckless thing; it was so truly an insanity — and he went and asked in which city the general lives, and he journeyed there. Then he did a reckless [Yid. *vild* wild, extraordinary; Heb. *mevohal me'od* very panicked] thing: going into the general's house. Now, before the general there are sentries posted, but he [the burgher], on account of his severe agitation, suddenly with extreme turmoil went and paid no attention to the guards whatsoever; and the guards became shocked and extremely confused due to suddenly seeing a man beside them in great agitation, so they became very shocked: "How did this guy get here?" And due to their panic all the guards permitted him and he passed through all the guards until he went in the general's house, in the place where she [the pauper's wife] was lying. And he came and woke her up, and said to her, "Come!" When she caught sight of him she took fright. He said to her, "Come with me right away!" She went with him, and now again they passed by all the guards until they emerged outside. Only then did he first come around and realize what he had done there, such a wild thing, and he realized that for certain there would right away be a big uproar at the general's, and that's just what happened: there was a big commotion at the general's.

The burgher went and hid himself with her in a pit where there was rainwater until the commotion died down, and he tarried there with her for two days. She saw the great self-sacrifice that he has for her sake and the troubles that he suffers for her, and she swore by God that all the *mazal*[46] that she has — possibly she has some kind of mazal, that she will have supreme grandeur and success [*gross gedulah un hatzlocheh*] — then all her success will not be withheld from him (that is, from the burgher), and that if he should want to take for himself all her success and greatness, so that she should remain just as she was before, it would not be withheld from him whatsoever. However, how does one get witnesses there? She took the pit as a witness.

After two days he went out of there with her and went further. And he went with her further and further. And he understood that there in that place, she [Heb. he] is also being sought. He went and hid himself with her in a *mikveh* [ritual bath]. There once again he recalled the great sacrifice and the suffering which he endures for her sake and she once again swore as before: that all her mazal etc. as mentioned, taking the ritual bath as her witness. They were there as well for approximately two days and they went out and went further. Again he understood that they are searching here too and again he hid himself along with her. And so it happened several times, hiding himself with her each time in another place, namely in seven different waters, that is, in a pit with water and in a mikveh as mentioned, and ponds (mucky waters), a spring, rivulets (creeks), rivers and seas. And in every place where they hid she kept remembering his self-sacrifice and the troubles which he endures for her sake, and she kept swearing: that her mazal etc. as mentioned, each time taking the place as witness, as mentioned. And they kept going in this manner, always hiding themselves in those places (mentioned above), until they came to the sea. When they came to the sea — and the burgher was a great merchant and knew the sea lanes — he negotiated [lit. cut himself] to get to his country, until he traveled the way and came home with the pauper's wife and brought her back to the pauper. There was great rejoicing.

[The Burgher's Son and the Pauper's Daughter; the Match; Rise of the Pauper]

The burgher, because he had done such a thing, and in addition had withstood trial (passed the test) with her (that is, he had the fear of God and did not touch her), therefore he was "remembered" (that is, "thought about" by Hashem Yithbarakh) [*nifkad*; see Gen. 21:1 etc.] and that year he had a son.

And she too, that is, the pauper's wife, because she withstood such a trial, both with the general and with the burgher, she therefore merited to have a daughter. And she was a supreme beauty, an extraordinarily great beauty which was unlike any human beauty whatsoever, for among mankind one never sees such beauty. Everyone [di velt, lit. the world] would say, "She should just grow to maturity!" (for it is hard for such an extraordinary novelty to reach maturity) because her beauty was absolutely extraordinary, the likes of which one doesn't see on earth. Everyone in the world would travel in and come to see her, and they would be very astonished at her beauty which was very, very extraordinary, and would give her gifts all the time out of affection, and they so kept presenting gifts until the pauper became rich.

As for the burgher, it entered his mind that he should arrange a match with the pauper due to her great beauty which was such a marvel, and he thought to himself: maybe this is what the dream will mean; that what's his is brought to the pauper and what's the pauper's to him; maybe the dream signifies this, that they will have a match; they will be mixed into one through the match.

One time, the pauper's wife came to the burgher and he told her that he has desire to have a match with her; and maybe through this the dreams will be realized, as above. She replied to him, "I've had this in mind as well, but I didn't have the boldness to talk of this, that I should be related to you through marriage. But if you want, I am certainly ready and will certainly not hold back from you, for I have already sworn that all my good and my success will not be withheld from you. And the son (of the burgher) and the daughter both learned in one schoolroom, languages and other things as was the order among them. And people would come to see the daughter on account of the exceptional novelty and kept presenting her with gifts until the pauper became rich.

And nobility would come see her and they liked her very much, and her beauty was an extreme marvel, for it was no human kind of beauty; and because of her extraordinary beauty the nobility got the idea of contracting a marriage with the pauper, and [any] minister who had a son wanted very much to contract a marriage with her. However, it would not befit the nobility to have a match with him (that is, with the pauper); they therefore needed to see to exerting themselves to make this man big (that is, the pauper), and they saw to it that he should perform a service for the emperor [Yid. *keisar* < Lat. *Caesar*].

And he was first an ensign [Rus. *práporshchik*, the lowest military officer rank < Slav. *prápor* flag] and afterwards continually higher and higher, for they saw to it to quickly promote him each time, until he rapidly became each time higher and higher, until he became a general. By now the nobility already wanted to have a match with him, however there were many nobility who wanted this, for many nobility had aimed at this [*deroyf gefalen* lit. fallen on it] and busied themselves with it, to continuously promote him. (Therefore he could not have a match with any of them.) And furthermore he could not have a match with any of them on account of the burgher, for it was already discussed that there would be a match with him.

And the pauper, who has now become a general — he became more and more successful. And the emperor would send him into battles and he was successful each time, and the emperor promoted him still higher each time and he was continuously very successful, until the emperor died. The entire country came to the decision to make him emperor, and all the nobility assembled together and all agreed that he should be emperor. He became emperor (that is, the aforementioned pauper has now become emperor) and he waged wars and was very successful, conquering countries, and waged more wars and was continuously successful, continually taking over countries until the other lands themselves submitted themselves under him with good will, for they saw his success is extremely great, for all the beauty of the world and all the mazal of the world was with him. So all the kings met together and agreed that he should be emperor over the entire world, and they gave him a document written with golden letters[47].

[The Ex-Pauper Emperor Reneges on the Match, but His Wife Adheres; The Emperor Schemes to Bring Down the Burgher and Eliminate His Son]

And the emperor (that is, the pauper who has become emperor over the entire world) no longer wanted to have a match with the burgher, for it is not fitting that an emperor should have a match with a burgher. But his wife the empress — she did not desert the burgher. (That is, she stood by the burgher because he had risked his life for her sake, as mentioned.) The emperor therefore saw that he cannot make any match on account of the burgher, particularly since his wife supports him very, very much. Therefore he began to think thoughts about the burgher; and in the beginning he saw to it to place him in poverty and he made schemes just as if it were not from him at all, and he continually saw to it to cause him damages; and an emperor can certainly do this. He was continually caused losses and continuously beaten out of money until he became impoverished and became an absolute pauper. But she, the empress, kept adhering to the burgher.

Then the emperor realized that as long as the son is alive, (that is, the burgher's son) he can make no other match. The emperor exerted himself to rid the young man [*bachur* in both Yid. & Heb.: chosen one; or young man, youth, unmarried] from the earth and he thought out plans to eliminate him. And he set up false charges on him and called the judges into session to try him. The judges understood that the emperor's will was that he be eliminated from the world, and they delivered the sentence that he be put in a sack (that is, the burgher's son) and thrown into the sea.

[The Empress Saves the Burgher's Son; Her Daughter Sends Him a Note in Captivity; He Escapes and Becomes Lodged Alone in a Wilderness]

As for the empress, her heart was very pained at this, however, even the empress too can do nothing up against the emperor. She went to the designees who were appointed to throw him into the sea, and she came to them and fell at their feet and pleaded with them direly that they should do for her sake and let him go, for: why does he deserve execution? So she begged them very much that they should take another captive who had to be executed and throw him into the sea, and the young man they should release. This she achieved with them; they swore that they would release him and so they did. And they took another man and threw him into the sea, but him they released (saying): "Go! Go!" And he went away. And the young man was already of mature mind [*bar da`at*, lit. "son of knowledge"], so he went his way.

And before this, that is, prior to the young man leaving, the empress went and summoned her daughter and said to her thus: "My daughter, you must know that this burgher's son is your groom;" and she told her daughter the entire story that happened to her, and "how the burgher sacrificed his well-being for my sake and was with me in the seven places (that is, in the seven types of water), and I swore to him every time by God that all my good would not be withheld from him, and I took those seven places as witnesses (that is, the pit, the *mikveh,* and all the rest of the seven types of water.)" Therefore now — you are all my good and all my mazal and my success; you are certainly his, and his son is your groom. And your father because of his haughtiness wants to kill him for no reason, but I have already made efforts to save him and have brought about that he be released. Therefore you should know that he is your groom (that is, the burgher's son), and you must not agree to any other groom in the world." The daughter accepted her mother's words, because she too was a God-fearing person, and she replied to her mother that she would certainly uphold her words.

The daughter went and sent a note to the burgher's son in prison, that she retains herself by him and he is her groom. And she sent something like a piece of a map, and she drew on it all the places where her mother had hidden with his father, which are the seven witnesses, that is, the pit, the mikveh and the rest as mentioned; that is, on it she drew something like a pit, a mikveh, and the rest of the seven types of waters. And she ordered him very, very strongly that he should guard this note very, very much, and she signed herself underneath; then things took place as mentioned: the deputies took another man, and him they released and he went on his way.

And he went and went until he reached the sea and he boarded a ship and set out upon the sea. A big storm wind came along and carried away the ship to a coast that was desert (that is, desolate) and on account of the great tempest, the ship was broken up; however, the passengers were saved and made out to dry land. And there it was a wilderness; the people from the ship went off in search of food. Each one looked for something to eat, for at that location it was not the norm that ships should arrive there, for it was desert. Therefore they did not think there, that some ship would come so that they could return home. They went along in the wilderness in search of food and became scattered here and there, each one separate. And the young man wanted to turn back but he no longer could, and the more he wanted to turn back, the farther he got, until he saw he can no longer return; so he went where he went in the wilderness. And he had in his hand a bow with which he protected himself against the vicious animals of the wilderness, and while walking he found himself something to eat there. And thus he walked and walked, until he emerged from the wilderness. And he arrived at a habitable spot that was a vacant place, and there was water there, and fruit trees around with fruit, and he ate of the fruit and drank of the water. And he resolved in his mind that he would settle down there for as long as he lives, for after all, anyhow it is already difficult for him to return to civilization, and who knows if he would again arrive at such a place if he would leave this place and go away? Therefore he wanted to dwell away there, and there live out this world. For it was good for him there, as he had fruit to eat and water to drink; and sometimes he would go out and shoot with his bow a rabbit or a deer and he had meat to eat. And he would catch fish there, for there were very good fish in the water there. It pleased him to live out his years there.

[The Emperor Proceeds to Make Other Matches with His Daughter and Makes Her a Court; She Is Courted but Refuses]

As for the emperor, after the sentence had been carried out on the burgher's son and he was now free of him (for the emperor thought that they had indeed truly executed the judgment on the young man and he is no longer on the earth), now then he can already make a match with his daughter [that is, for his own daughter].

They began proposing matches to her with this king and with that king, and he made her a court in the appropriate way, and she remained there. And she took young ladies, daughters of nobility, to be her companions and she lived there, and she would play on musical instruments in their usual fashion. And whatever they proposed match to her, she always replied that she did not want any talk (that is, talk about the match) but that he himself should come (that is, he who wants to marry her). And she had very expert knowledge of the wisdom [*chokhmah*] of song (that is, the *chokhmah* to speak very beautiful lyrics with great *chokhmah*); and with skillful artisanship she made a place for him to come to (that is, he who wants to marry her) and stand facing her and say a song, that is, a song of desire, just as a desirer speaks to his desired (that is, words of love). Kings would come to be matched with her and they arrived at that place and they each one spoke his song.

To some of them she sent a reply through her ladies, also with a song and with affection. And to some whom she liked more, she herself responded and she would raise her voice with a song and reply to him as well words of affection. And to some whom she liked even more she would personally show herself face to face; so she showed her face and replied to him with a song with affection. But to all of them she always concluded in the end, "The waters, however, did not pass over you [*Di vassern zenen aber iber dir nit ariber gigangen*]." And none of them understood what she meant. And when she showed her face people would fall down due to enormous beauty, and some were left weak and some became insane on account of lovesickness due to her great beauty which was very, very extraordinary. And nonetheless, even though they became insane and were left weak, despite this kings would still come to be matched with her; and she gave them all the same answer, as above.

[The Burgher's Son Muses with the Note; the Note is Lost and He Reaches Settlement; Three Kings Betray Him]

And the burgher's son remained in that same place and he made himself a place to dwell in and he lived there. And he too could play and knew the wisdom of song; he selected wood out of which musical instruments can be made and he made himself instruments, and from the veins of animals he made strings; thus he would musically accompany himself. And he would take the note that he had which she had sent him (at the time he was in captivity) and he would sing and play and remember what had befallen him, and how his father had been a burgher etc., and now he has been cast off to here. And he went and took the note and made a sign on a tree and made a place there in the tree and hid the note there, and he dwelled there for some time.

One time there was a great storm wind and it broke all the trees that were standing there. He could not recognize the tree where he had hidden the note, for when the trees were standing in their place he had a sign to recognize, but now that they had fallen the tree became mixed among the other trees which were very numerous there; he could no longer recognize the particular tree. And it was impossible to split open all the trees and look for the note, for there were very many trees. He cried exceedingly and was extremely sad and he realized that if he would stay there he would certainly become insane on account of great anguish that he had.

He came to the decision that he must go further away and whatever should happen to him, let happen — go away he must, for he is anyway in great danger due to severe anguish. So he got some meat and fruit into a sack and went wherever he would go. And he made signs in the place from which he left and he went along until he reached a settled area. He asked them, "What land is this?" They answered him. He asked if they had heard about the emperor here. They answered him, "Yes." He asked if they had heard about his daughter, the beauty. They answered him, "Yes, but no one can be matched with her (as mentioned, for she wants none of them, as mentioned)." He came to a decision, since he can't get there anyway — and he went to the king of the country and spoke his heart out entirely: And that he is her groom and because of him she wants no other match. And he cannot get there, therefore he gives over to the king all the signs that he has, that is, the seven waters mentioned above. And the king should himself go there and he will match himself with her; and he should give him money for this.

The king recognized that his words are true, for one cannot think up such things out of one's heart. The thing pleased the king. However, he decided: if he brings her here and the young man will be here, this is not good for him. Should he kill him? He did not want to do such a thing, for why should one after all kill him for the favor? Therefore the king decided he would exile him two hundred miles away. He was very upset at him exiling him for such a favor as he had done him. There as well he went to another king and told likewise too as before. (That is, the young man, the burgher's son, because it upset him that the first king exiled him, went to another king and told him as well the whole story with all the signs, so that the other should make haste to marry the beauty.) So he related to him all the signs and to this other king he added an additional sign. And he ordered him and rushed him to set out immediately; maybe he can overtake the other king, in order to get there first; and even if he does not arrive first, he still has one sign more than the first. And the second one decided as well like the first (that it is not good for him if the young man should be here); the other king also exiled him two hundred miles further. He was again very upset and he went again to a third one (that is, the young man, the burgher's son, again went to a king who was now the third, and also told him as before, the entire story); so he went another time, to a third king. He also told him the whole story, as with the others. And to the third one he gave even more signs, very good signs.

The first king got up and traveled there and arrived there at the location of the emperor's daughter, that is, the beauty. And the king composed a song and embedded in the song, with wisdom, all the places, that is, the seven aforementioned witnesses (that is, the seven types of water, which were the essential signs of her groom that she had, as mentioned). However, in accord with the science of song the seven places came out for him not in order (that is, for example he had to say the pit first and then the mikveh etc., but he said in reverse), for so it came out for him according to the wisdom of the song. And the king came up on the place (that is, on the place where the one who wanted to be matched with her had to come upon and say a song with wisdom as mentioned), and he said his song. When she heard the places (that is, the seven types of waters) it was extraordinary news for her. It felt to her that this was certainly her groom, but it was difficult for her why he said them not in order. However, notwithstanding, she thought perhaps due to the science of the song, this order came out for him. It was accepted in her heart that this is he himself. She wrote to him that she designates herself as matched with him. There was a grand celebration and a commotion inasmuch as the beauty has at last found her match, and they were already preparing for the wedding.

Meanwhile, the other one arrived (that is, the other king, to whom the young man had also divulged all the signs plus one more sign, as mentioned). And the other one also ran there and they told him that she has already made a match; but he paid no mind to this [lit. he didn't look at it] and he said: nonetheless, he still has something to tell her; that he will certainly have an effect. He came (that is, the other king) and said his song — and this other one has now arranged all the places in order, and moreover he gave one more sign in addition. She asked him, "From where does the first one know?" If he were to tell the truth it would not be good for him (that is, the other thought he cannot tell her the truth, that the young man told the first one, for it's not good for him if she should know that). So he said he doesn't know (from where the first one knew the signs). It was a big wonder to her and she was left standing bewildered, for the first one also told out all the places; and from where should a man know these signs? But notwithstanding, it felt to her that this other [second] one is her groom, for she saw that he told in sequence, and in addition one more sign; and the first one, maybe it came out to him through the science of song that he mentioned the places. Albeit, now she remained standing (in other words she could no longer give herself counsel; she stayed put and now was not willing to be matched with anyone).

And the young man, that is, the burgher's son, when the second king exiled him, was again very upset, and he went to a third king and told him the whole entire story as above, and he told him even more signs, very good signs. And in front of this third one he told out his entire heart: Inasmuch as he had a note on which all these places were drawn (that is, the seven types of water); therefore he [the king] should draw on a piece of paper all those places and bring [it] to her. And the third king also exiled the young man two hundred miles further yet, and the third one also ran there. And he got there; he was told that the other two (that is, the two kings) are there already. He replied, "Nevertheless," for he has such a thing that he will definitely have an effect. And the world [i.e. people] did not know whatsoever why she wants these kings more than others. And the third one came and said his song with very excellent signs, better than the first ones, and he showed the note (where he himself had re-drawn the places) with all the places drawn. She became very panicked (in other words, scared and disturbed), however, she did not at all know a thing to do, since regarding the first one she also thought that this is he; and then regarding the second. Therefore, she said that she would believe no longer until her very own writing itself is brought.

[The Young Man Goes Himself, but She Pays No Mind and He Returns to His Place in the Wilderness]

Then the young man decided (that is, the burgher's son): how will he always be sent further away? So he made up his mind he himself would set out for there (that is, to the emperor's daughter); perhaps he will have effect. And he went and went until he got there. And he said he has something that will definitely have effect. And he approached and said his song. And he said even more signs, very good signs, and he reminded her that he had learned with her in one schoolroom, and other signs too. And he told her everything: that he had sent the aforementioned kings, and hidden the writing in a tree, and everything that had befallen him.

But she did not regard this at all (and the first three kings certainly also had to say some reasons for not having the note). And to recognize him is certainly impossible, for a long time had already passed. So she already no longer wanted to regard any signs at all until the writing of her own hand is brought, for regarding the first one she also thought that this is he for certain, and likewise regarding the second, etc.; therefore she no longer wanted any signs etc. as mentioned. And the young man (that is, the burgher's son) decided he can make no delay whatsoever here (in other words, he cannot tarry here, for it may become known that he is here; the emperor will kill him, as mentioned).

He made up his mind he would again return back to his spot in the wilderness where he was before, and there he would live out his life. And he went and traveled to get to that wilderness and he arrived there at the wilderness. Meanwhile as the above was all happening, very many years went by. And it remained in the young man's mind that he should sit away there in the wilderness and live out his years there. According to how he had evaluated the entire mortal life on earth, it was clear in his mind that it is good for him to live out his years here in the wilderness; and he lived there and ate from the fruits, etc. as mentioned.

[A Murderer Kidnaps Her; She Arrives at the Young Man's Place]

Now, on the sea was a murderer, and the murderer heard that there exists such a beauty on the earth. He wanted to abduct her even though he did not need her since he was a eunuch; he only wanted to grab her in order to sell her to some king; he'll get a great deal of money for her. So the murderer began to busy himself with the thing. And a murderer is a reckless person, so he abandoned himself: if he accomplishes, he accomplishes, and if not, what will he forfeit here? For he is after all a reckless person, as the way of a murderer is. So the murderer went and bought a vast amount of wares — extraordinarily much. And he made golden birds, and they were made with craftsmanship so that one would think they live; they were just like living birds in nature. Moreover he made golden grain stalks, and the birds stood on the grain stalks and this alone was a novelty, that the birds stand on the stalks without the stalks breaking, for they were large birds. And furthermore he made devices so that a person thought that the birds make music; one clicked its tongue, one chirped, and one sang. And this was all done with cunning, for men stood there in a room that was on the ship and the men stood under the birds and the men did it all, and it was thought that the birds themselves make music, for they were cunningly made with wires; it was thought the birds themselves do all this.

And the murderer went off with all this to the land where the aforementioned emperor's daughter was. And he came to the city where she was and he brought himself to a standstill with the ship in the sea and anchored the ship and made himself out to be big merchant. People would go to him to buy expensive wares, and he stayed there a while, a quarter year and longer, and people always carried off beautiful wares that they bought from him.

The emperor's daughter also desired to buy wares from him; she dispatched to him that he should bring her merchandise. He dispatched to her: he has no need to bring merchandise to a buyer's house, even if she is an emperor's daughter; whoever needs merchandise should come to him. And no one can force a merchant into that, so the emperor's daughter decided to go to him. And her custom was: whenever she would go in the marketplace she would veil her face in order that one should not gaze at her, for people would be liable to fall down and be left in weakness etc. due to her beauty. The emperor's daughter went, covering her face, and she took her ladies with her and a watch [Yid. *vakh* guard, lit. wake, vigil; a squad of guards] followed her. And she came to the merchant (that is, to the murderer, who disguised himself as a merchant) and she bought some wares from him and went her way. He told her (that is, the murderer, the merchant), "If you come once more, I will show you even more beautiful articles than this, very wonderful things." And she returned home. After that she came once again and bought merchandise from him and again went home. And the murderer stayed there for a while. Meanwhile the emperor's daughter already became accustomed to visiting him; she would go to him often.

One day she came to him. He went and opened for her the room where the golden birds and so forth were located. She saw it being a very extraordinary novelty; and the other people who were with her (that is, the watch, etc.) also wanted to go in the room. He said, "No, no! I don't show this to anyone except you because you are the emperor's daughter; but for others I don't want to show this at all." She alone entered in there, and he too went in the room, and he locked the door and did a crude thing and took a sack and forcefully put her in the sack. And he took off all her clothes from her and dressed a sailor with the clothing, veiled his face, pushed him out, and said to him, "Go!" And the sailor, not knowing whatsoever what's happening to him, as soon as he emerged with his face covered, the soldiers (that is, the watch) being unaware immediately began walking with him; they thought that this is the emperor's daughter. And the sailor went along with the troop wherever they led him; and not knowing whatsoever where in the world he is, he came there into the room where the emperor's daughter lived. His face was uncovered and they noticed that this is a plainly a sailor. There was a tremendous uproar there. (And the sailor was slapped quite thoroughly in the face and was shoved out, since he is after all not responsible, for he didn't know at all.)

And the murderer took the emperor's daughter, and he knew that he would certainly be chased after. He left the ship and hid himself together with her in a pit containing rainwater until the uproar would subside. And the ship's sailors he ordered to immediately cut anchors and flee right away, for they would certainly be pursued; and the ship would certainly not be shot at on account of the emperor's daughter, for they will think that she is there on the ship. "However, they will pursue you; therefore you should flee immediately. If they catch you, so what?" — as the way of murderers is; they do not look at themselves at all (in other words, they disregard themselves). And such is what happened; there was a big outcry and they were immediately chased; however, she was not found there. And the murderer hid himself together with her in a pit of rainwater, and they lay there. And he scared her so that she wouldn't scream, in order that people should not hear. And he said to her thus: "I have risked my life for your sake in order to capture you, and if I should lose you again, my life is not worth anything at all to me: for since you are already in my hand, if I should lose you again and you be taken away from me, then my life is already worth nothing to me. Therefore as soon as you just give a yell I will strangle you right away, and let whatever happens to me happen, for I consider myself worthless in that case." She was terrified of him (in other words, the emperor's daughter who was lying in the pit with the murderer, was afraid to scream since the murderer had scared her).

Then he departed from there with her and he brought her to a city and they traveled on and traveled on, and they came to a place and the murderer understood that there too they are searching. He hid himself together with her in a mikveh. And then he went out from there too and came to another place, and there also he hid himself with her in another water, and thus he hid himself with her each time in another water, until he had hidden himself with her in all the seven kinds of waters that the burgher had hidden himself in with her mother, as mentioned, which constitute the seven witnesses, as mentioned, until he came with her to the sea. The murderer searched there for even a small boat from which they catch fish, in order to cross with her. He found a ship; he took the emperor's daughter, and he did not need her, for he was a eunuch as mentioned, but just wanted to sell her to some king. And he had fear lest she be snatched away from him, so he went ahead and dressed her in sailor's clothes; she looked like a male. And the murderer traveled with her on the sea (that is, with the emperor's daughter, whom we refer to in male terms, as the murderer disguised her thus, as mentioned).

A storm wind came and carried away the ship to a shore, and the boat was broken and they came to the shore where the wilderness was, where the young man was living. When they came there, and the pirate was expert in routes as usual, he knew that here it is desert; that no ships come here. Therefore, he no longer had any fear of any man and he let her loose. And they walked (that is, the murderer and the emperor's daughter), he this way and she that way, to find themselves some bit of food. She distanced herself from the robber and the robber went his own way, and he noticed that she isn't here beside him. He began to shout out to her, and she made up her mind and did not respond to him at all, for she thought to herself, "My end is that he will sell me. Why should I answer him? If he reaches me again, I will reply to him I did not hear, especially as he does not want to kill me, for he wants to sell me." She did not respond to him and she went further on. And the robber sought her here and there and could not find her. And he went further and still could not find her; so probably vicious animals ate her up.

A nd she went further and further and was able to find some food, and walked on thus until she came to the place where the young man was living (that is, the aforementioned burgher's son). And by this time she was now overgrown with hair, and in additional she was dressed as a male in sailor's clothes as mentioned. They did not recognize one another. And immediately when she came he turned very happy that another person had come here. He asked her, "Where have you come here from?" [S]he answered, "I was with a merchant on the sea" etc. She asked him, "Where did you come here from?" He also answered her, "Through a merchant." The two of them remained there.

[The Empress and Emperor's Strife, Her Banishment, and His Decline; Reversal of the Banishment; the Empress Restores the Burgher and His Wife]

A fter the emperor's daughter was snatched away from the emperor, as mentioned, the empress lamented a great deal and struck her head on the wall over the loss of her daughter, and she ate away at the emperor with words a great deal and said to him, "Because of your pride you've wasted the young man, and now our daughter has become lost!" And she said to him, "She was our entire fortune and our entire success. Now we've lost her. What is left for me?" So she ate away at him severely. And for himself as well this was certainly also very bitter that his daughter had become lost; in addition the empress ate away at and infuriated him very much. So there were severe quarrels and bickering between them; and she would say nasty things to him until she angered him very much, until he ordered her banished. And he had judges sit trial on her; they ruled that she be banished, and she was banished. Afterwards the emperor sent out into war and was not successful; he blamed this on some general: "Because you did so, therefore you lost the war." He banished the general. After that he sent off again into war and again was not successful. He banished more generals, and so he banished a number of generals. The country saw that he was doing bizarre things: first he banished the empress, then the generals. They decided (that is, the citizens): maybe the other way around — the empress should be sent for, he should be banished and she should lead the country. They did so and banished the emperor; and the empress they took back and she led the country. And the empress immediately sent for the burgher and his wife the burgheress to be brought back (as the emperor had brought them low and made them into paupers as mentioned, etc.). And she brought them into her palace.

[The Emperor's Release and Arrival at the Same wilderness as the Young Man and His Daughter]

And the emperor, while he was being sent into exile, went ahead and begged those who were leading him that they should release him, "for, after all, I have been your emperor and must certainly have done good things for you. Now do this for me and let me go, for I will certainly not turn back to the country any longer. You need have no fear. Release me. Let me go my way. Let me at least be free, the little bit of life that I have yet to live." They released him, and he went on and went on. Meanwhile several years passed by and the emperor went on and went on until he reached the sea. The wind carried away his boat too and he too reached the aforementioned wilderness, until he came to the place where the other two were living (that is, where the young man, the burgher's son, and his daughter the beauty who was now going dressed as a male, were). They did not recognize one another, for the emperor had already become overgrown with hair and already several years had passed; and they too had become overgrown with hair as mentioned. They asked him, "Where have you come here from?" He answered them, "Through a merchant." And they answered him thus as well. The three of them stayed there together, eating and drinking there, as mentioned. And they played on musical instruments there, for they all were able to play, for this one is an emperor and likewise they too were able to play.

And he, that is, the young man, was the highly capable person [Yid. *beryeh*] among them, for he had been there since long ago already. And he would bring them meat, and they ate, and they would burn wood there, which was more precious than gold in settled places. The young man used to prove to them that here it is good for them to live out their years. According to the benefits that people have on earth in settled places, it is better that they should stay here, living out their worldly existence here. They asked him, "What sort of good did you have, that you say it is better for you here?" He answered them and told them what had happened to him: how he had been a burgher's son etc. until he came here, and what his being a burgher's son resulted in for him. Here too he has all the good. (Thus did the young man keep saying to them.) And he kept proving to them that here it is good to live out their worldly lives.

The emperor asked him, "Have you heard of the emperor?" He answered him: he had heard. He asked him about the beauty: whether he had heard of her. He answered him also: Yes. The young man began to talk angrily and said, "That murderer!" (As one who gnashes his teeth at the other person, so did the young man talk angrily about the emperor of whom they were speaking, for he did not know that the emperor himself is talking with him.) He asked him, "Why is he a murderer?" He answered him, "Because of his cruelty and because of his arrogance I've arrived here. He asked him, "How did that happen?"

The young man made up his mind that here he has no need to fear anyone, so he spoke to him and recounted the entire story that happened to him. He asked him, "If the emperor should come into your hand would you take revenge on him now?" He answered him, "No," (for he was a good person and merciful) "on the contrary, I would provide sustenance for him just as I sustain you." Again the emperor began to sigh and groan, saying, "What an evil and bitter old age this emperor has!" For he had heard that his daughter the beauty had become lost, and he himself has been banished. Again the young man spoke up, "Because of his cruelty (in other words, mercilessness) and because of his pride he squandered himself and his daughter and I have been cast off to here — all because of him." Again he asked him (the emperor to the young man), "If he should come into your hand would you take revenge on him?" He answers him, "No. I would sustain him precisely as I sustain you." The emperor made himself known to him and informed him that he himself is the emperor, and what has befallen him. The young man fell on him, kissed him and hugged him. And she, that is, the beauty, who was also present, only in disguise, etc. was listening to everything as the two were talking to one another.

[Searching for the Note]

And the young man, it was his routine that he would go every day and make a sign for himself on three trees and look for the writing there (that is, in these three of the trees). For there were millions of trees, so he would make himself a sign on those which he searched, in order that he should no longer need to search in these three trees tomorrow. Thus he kept doing every day; perhaps he would still find the writing (that is, the note she had sent him which he had lost among the trees, as mentioned). And when he would return from there he would come with wept-out eyes, for he would cry when he searched and could not find. They asked him (that is, the emperor and the beauty) asked him, "What do you look for among the trees and then come back with wept-out eyes?" He told them the entire story: insofar as the emperor's daughter (that is, the beauty) had sent him a writing; he had hidden it in one of the trees; a storm wind came, etc. as mentioned. Now he searches; maybe he'll find it. They said to him, "Tomorrow when you go look we will also go with you. Maybe we will find the note." And so it was; they went with him too. The emperor's daughter found the note in a tree, and she opened it up and saw this is her own writing from her hand. She reckoned if she immediately discloses to him that this is she herself, that if she will again remove these clothes and return again to her beauty and again be a good-looker as before, he may collapse and pass away. And she wants that it should be done in a kosher way, according to traditional practice (in other words, she cannot marry him here in the wilderness, for she needs to have a wedding with him, as it ought to be). She went and returned the writing to him and told him that she had found the writing. (In other words, she did not tell him that this is she herself; rather, she simply told him that she had found the writing.) He immediately dropped down and was left faint. They restored him to health and there was great rejoicing among them.

Later the young man said, "What use is the writing for me? How will I ever be able to find her? For surely she is now with some king (for he thought that she had been sold by the murderer, just as the emperor had told him). What use is it for me? I will live out my years here." And he went and gave her back the writing and said to her, "Here! Take the note for yourself and you go and marry her" (for she was disguised as a male). She allowed herself to go but asked him to go with her as well. "For I will certainly take her; things will be good for me; I'll give you a share of my good." (In other words, the emperor's daughter who was disguised as a male said thus to the young man.) And the young man saw that "he" is a wise man and will certainly take her; he was willing to go with him (that is, with the emperor's daughter who he thought is a male). But the emperor was left alone, for he was afraid to go back to his country. She asked him to go too: for he will surely take the beauty. "You no longer have anything to fear. (In other words she said to him, 'I will certainly seek out the beauty, so you no longer have anything to fear, for the mazal will turn back when she is found.') And you will also be ordered to return."

[The Three Set Out to the Empress, the Daughter Reveals Herself, and the Wedding Takes Place]

The three set out together and they hired a ship and came to the country where the empress lives, and they came to the city where she is located and they put the ship down. The emperor's daughter figured: if she immediately informs her mother that she has come back, she may pass away. She went and dispatched to her mother inasmuch as there is a man who has knowledge of her daughter. Then she herself went to the empress and told her what had happened to her daughter, telling her the entire story. And at the end she said to him (in these terms), "And she (that is, the daughter) is also here." She told her the truth: "I myself am she!" And she informed her that her groom, that is, the burgher's son, is here too; however, she said to her mother that she wants it no other way except that her father the emperor be restored to his place. However, her mother did not want this at all, for she was very upset at him, because all this was due to him; but nonetheless she had to do it for the sake of her daughter. They wanted to bring him back (the emperor); they searched for the emperor — and he's not there at all. Her daughter told out to her that the emperor is also here with her. The wedding took place; the joy was entire. And the kingdom and the empire they took over, that is, the burgher's son with the beauty who got married; and they reigned over the face of the earth [*zey zinen molekh bekipah given*], that is, they reigned over the entire world, Amen and Amen.

[Notes Following the Story]

A fterwards as well the old emperor had no greatness, for it [the trouble] was all because of him. The burgher had enormous greatness — he is the emperor's father, who is the essential one [*ikar*, the root]. The sailor was smacked and smacked in the face and expelled.

R egarding Lot it says, *"Ha'hárah himmalét/* to the mountain flee for salvation" (Gen. 19:17) — this is a burgher [a play on words: Yid. *barg* mountain, pl. *berg* < Ger. *Berg* mountain; ME *burgh* city < OE *burg* fortified town; O. High Ger. *Burg* fortified castle, all from Indo-European root *bhergh*], and from him comes [Heb. is born] Mashiach. [Note: Rabbi Nachman's surname was Horodenker, as his grandfather, also named Nachman, was from the Ukrainian city Horodenka, the name of which stems from Ukrainian *gorod*, city. Thus "Burgher" might be interpreted as an allusion to this name.]

J ews had, in Mitzrayim, signs who would be the Redeemer etc. [Heb. only: *paqódh paqádh'ti* (Ex. 3:16: "I have remember-remembered you;" alternately, "a chief I have appointed"?) — he who says to them these terms is the Redeemer. And it is an astounding thing, since all Yisrael knew of this — so then what is this sign? Possibly it was not transmitted except to the elders.] And upon the [Heb. final] Redeemer [Yid. to come] there are certainly signs [Yid. *do*, here] as well.

Mashiach will say to every Jew everything that has happened to him every single day [Heb only: to every member of Yisrael individually]. Tamar also lost the signs, as it says in the Midrash. Also when she was going to be burned the *Samekh-Mem* came and removed the signs from her, and the angel Gabriel came and returned them, as it says in Midrash; out from her comes Mashiach, speedily in our days, Amen.

All this the Rebbe discussed after the story so that one can make some kind of surmise how far the story reaches. So, good for one who is privileged to know the stories' secret even in the other world!

Regarding that which is explained in the story, that every one comes with his song of desire and some are replied to via an emissary etc. as mentioned — so there are a number of great people who each do what they do [Heb. only: And each says songs and so forth] and each busies himself and wants to reach {Yid.: the truth; Heb.: the desired purpose. But there is none who attains the essential true purpose completely} — except the one who is worthy/ fit/ eligible [*re'ui*] for it. And some are answered via an emissary, or from under [Heb. behind] the wall, or they show them the face etc. as in the story. However, in the end, when they leave this world, they answer them that they've still done nothing at all, like it is written in the story, how the beauty ultimately answers them, "*Di vassern haben aber iber dir noch nit ariber gigangen*," until the right leader comes — speedily in our days, Amen! This too the Rebbe z"l discussed.

Pauper — Burgher

Dream of Exchange

Pauper's Wife — General   Burgher's Wife

Nobility and Ministers — Emperor

Seven Waters

Daughter — Son

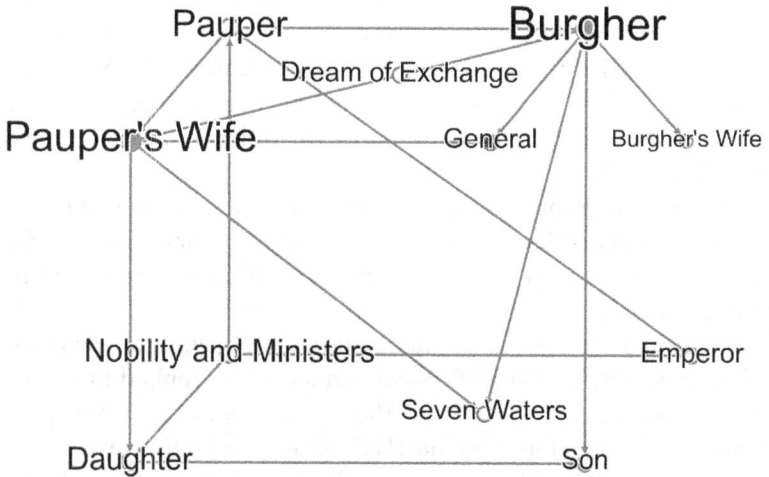

Pauper as Emperor

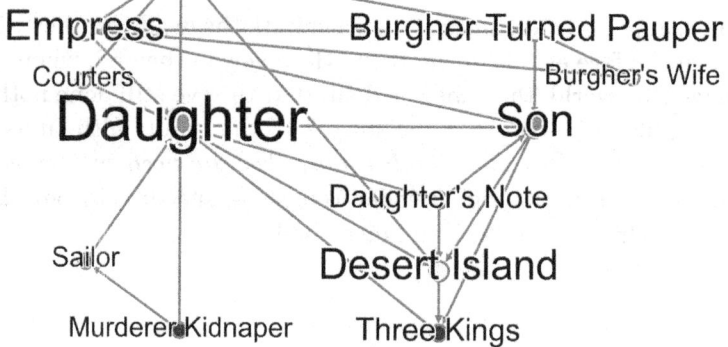

Empress — Burgher Turned Pauper

Courters   Burgher's Wife

Daughter — Son

Daughter's Note

Sailor   Desert Island

Murderer Kidnaper   Three Kings

Tale 11:

The King's Son and Maid's Son Who Were Exchanged

[The Switch]

A Tale. There once was a king. In his home there was a bond-maid [Yid./Heb. *shifchah*] who served the queen. (Generally no cook may enter in the king's presence, but this bondmaid had some other service, a minor service.) The time came when the queen was supposed to have a child, and the bondmaid had to give birth at that time as well. The granny [Yid. *bubbe*, Heb. *meyaledeth*, midwife] went and switched the babies to see what will happen; what will arise from this. So she took the king's child and put him down next to the bondmaid, and the bondmaid's son she put by the queen.

A fterwards the children began to grow up, and the king's son (that is, the child who grew up at the king's whom they thought was the king's son) they promoted (that is, made great) and kept raising higher and higher until he became extremely great and was a very important person[48]. And the bondmaid's son (that is, he who was reared by the bondmaid, who in truth was the king's son) also grew up at the maid's, and both children studied together in one schoolroom. And the king's true son (who shall be called "the bondmaid's son"), his nature was drawn to the manners of royalty, except that he was brought up in the home of the servant[49]. Conversely, the bondmaid's son (who shall be called "the king's son"), his nature was drawn to a different deportment not like the bearing of a king is, except that he was brought up in the king's home so he had to act according to the manners of a royal person, because those were the manners they brought him up with.

N ow the granny, because women are *da`athan kaloth* [lit. light minded], in other words, they cannot hold themselves back, went and spoke out the secret to some person, inasmuch as she had exchanged the children. Now, every person has a friend, and that friend has another friend, thus one person told the other until the secret was revealed, as the way of the world is, until the world was talking quietly about it, that the king's son was switched. But it was not permitted to speak about it outright, so that the king should not become aware of it, for what will the king be able to do in such a case, since he cannot correct it? For he cannot believe it, as perhaps it is a lie, so how can one reverse the exchange? Therefore one certainly may not say it out in front of the king; however, amongst themselves the public talked about it quietly.

The day arrived when someone came along and told out the secret before the king's son, inasmuch as they say about him that he was exchanged. "However, you cannot investigate this, for it does not befit you. And how can one probe such a thing? Just, I am telling it to you in order that you should know. For perhaps there will once be a conspiracy against the monarchy; the conspiracy will be able to prevail through this, for they will say that they are taking to themselves the king's son as a king, that is, the one who they say of him that he is the king's true son, as mentioned before. Therefore you need to outwit the fellow." (All this said that person to the king's son who in actual truth is the bondmaid's son, as mentioned.)

The king's son (that is, the one who is called the king's son. And the rule is that wherever simply "the king's son" is mentioned, it refers to the exchanged one. That is, he is actually the bondmaid's son, except that he is called the king's son because he was raised at the king's. And similarly with the "bondmaid's son" where a bondmaid's son is mentioned: only where "the king's true son" or "the bondmaid's true son" is mentioned, then the meaning is the actual truth.) went and began to do mischief to the other one's father (who was really his own father), and arranged everything to constantly do him evil. And he kept dealing him mischiefs one after another in order that he should have to be uprooted[50] along with his son. Now the whole time the king himself still lived, he did not yet have so much authority; nonetheless he kept dealing him woes.

Afterwards the king grew old and died, so he assumed the reign (that is, the bondmaids's son who is now called the king's son, as mentioned above); then he dealt even more evil to the other son's father (that is, to the father of the bondmaid's son who in truth was the king's son; and this father was really his own father, of the one who had taken up the reign, for they were exchanged, as above). And he dealt him evil disguised so that people would not know that it's from him, for it's unseemly in front of people, and kept dealing him mischiefs one after another.

This one [the son's father] understood that he is dealing him woes on account of the matter (that is, because the public discusses that the children were exchanged). He (that is, the bondservant, the bondmaid's husband who was constantly dealt woes in order that he should drive out his son because they say that the children were exchanged, as mentioned) spoke up and said to his son and told him the whole affair and said to him, "I have great pity on you, for any way you approach it [*mimah nafshakh*[511], lit. "from wherever your soul (is drawn)," possibly a double meaning here]: if indeed you are my child, of course I certainly have great pity on you; if indeed you are not my child but are in truth the king's son, there is even greater pity on you, because that one (that is, he who took over the reign) wants to expel you entirely, perish the thought. Therefore, you must pull up (that is, run away) from here."

It irritated him very much and he felt very bad about the thing. However, the king (that is, the one who became king in place of his father, because it seemed he is the king's son due to the interchange) meanwhile kept constantly dealing out woes one after another, so the son (that is, the king's true son who was exchanged) decided he must run away. His father gave him a great deal of money and he left. It upset him very much that he was driven out of his country for nothing, for he looked around him: "Why do I deserve it that I should be driven out? If indeed I am the king's son, I certainly don't deserve this, that I should be driven out. And even if I am not the king's son, I also don't deserve this, that I should be a fugitive (that is, one who has run away) for nothing. For, what is my sin? What am I guilty of here?" It upset him very much, and on account of this he took to the drink and went to brothels (that is, to houses where there are whores). And with that he wanted to spend his years, getting drunk and following after what his heart desires, because he was driven away for nothing.

And the king (that is, the false prince, the exchanged one who became king) took over the kingship strongly, and when he heard anything about people murmuring and discussing anything about it (that is, that they were switched, as mentioned) he penalized them (in other words, punished and tortured) and took his revenge on them. So he ruled with force and strength.

And the day came to pass when the king went with his noblemen on a catch (*"na ulavi"* [<Rus.]: that is, catching animals) and they came to a pleasant place. And a river of water was ahead of that spot, so they stopped there to rest themselves and they wanted to walk around. The king lay down for a little bit, and the deed that he had done, that he had driven away that certain person for nothing, came to his mind. For, any way you look at it[51]: if he's indeed the king's son, is it not enough that he was exchanged? Why should he in addition be driven out for nothing? And if he is not the king's son, he also does not deserve to be driven away, for what had he done wrong? The king thought himself away in this matter, and had remorse over the transgression and the great injustice that he had done. And the king could give himself no advice what he should do here. And to talk about it — one cannot do such a thing with any person at all, to take counsel with him (for one is obviously ashamed to discuss such things with people). So the king became very laden with great worry. He ordered the nobles to turn back, because since worry has befallen him there is no need to tour any more. They returned home. When the king returned home, he of course had numerous affairs and concerns, and he busied himself with his concerns and the thing left his mind (that is, the worry and the remorse that he had over the fact that he had driven away the other for no reason).

And the one who was driven away (that is, the king's true son) — well, he did what he did and squandered his money. One time, he went out alone for a walk; and he lay down and it came to his mind what had happened to him and he thought: "What has God done to me? If I am indeed the king's son I certainly don't deserve this, and if I am not the king's son I also don't deserve this selfsame thing, that I should be a fugitive and an exile." Then he reached settledness in his mind, "Just the reverse. If it is so, that Hashem Yithbarakh can indeed do such a thing, that they should exchange a king's son and such things should befall him — do I turn myself to behave this way? Is it right, what I have done? Does it befit me that I should behave thus, the way I have done?" And he began to have great anguish and very much regret the bad deeds he had done. Then he turned back home, there where he was staying, and further took to the drink. However, because he had already begun to have remorse, the thoughts of remorse and repentance which came to his mind all the time would confuse him.

[The Dream, the Job and the Forest]

One time he laid himself down to sleep and the dream came to him to the effect: In such and such a place there is a fair on such and such a day; therefore he should go there, and whatever he strikes first — any gainful service — he should immediately do it, even if it won't be according to his dignity (thus went his dream). And he woke up with a start and the dream was very much in his thought. For sometimes it happens that the matter immediately goes out from the thought. But rather, this dream very much entered in his thought. Albeit, nonetheless, it seemed very hard for him to do this, and he went more to the drink. And the dream appeared to him again several times, and the dream confused him a great deal.

One time they said to him in the dream, "If you want to have pity on yourself, do thus" (that is, he should go to the fair etc. as mentioned), so now he had to carry out the dream. And he went ahead and left the remaining money he still had, leaving it at the inn where he was staying; and the good clothes which he had, he also left at the inn; and he took for himself a simple garment like merchants, that is, a coverall, and he set out for the fair and arrived there. And he got up very early and went to the fair.

A certain merchant encountered him and said to him, "Would you like to earn something?" He answered him, "Yes." He said to him, "I need to drive herds [behemoth, dumb beasts][52] here. Will you hire yourself out to me?" And he didn't have time to settle his mind, due to the dream (for the dream had been that he must take on the first gainful work etc. as mentioned), and he immediately answered, "Yes." And the merchant immediately hired him and immediately began to lord over him like a master over his servants. And he began to look around himself, what he had done, for he certainly doesn't deserve such a servitude, for he is a delicate man and now he'll have to drive herds and go by foot next to the beasts. However, one already can't have any regret, and the merchant is lording over him like a master. He asked the merchant, "How shall I go alone with the herds?" He answered, "I have more herdsmen driving my herds. You'll go together with them," and he gave over to his hands certain herds to drive. He led the herds out of the town, and there, gathered together, were the rest of the herdsmen driving beasts.

They went together; he was driving the herds, and the merchant was riding on a horse and going along with them. And the merchant was driving cruelly (that is, with anger and without compassion), and against him he was extra cruel, and he grew more and more terrified of the merchant, since he saw in him that he has extremely great cruelty and anger against him. And he feared in case he deals him a blow with his stick then he'll die instantly (for the king's [true] son was quite a frail person and on account of his sensitivity he was very terrified, thus he thought that way). So he was walking with the herds, and the merchant with them. And they came to a certain spot; they took the sack wherein lies the herdsmen's bread, and he (the merchant) gave them to eat; him too they gave from the bread and he ate.

Afterwards, they were walking by a very thick forest; two beasts from his herds (of this son who had become a herder for the merchant) walked off into the forest. The merchant yelled at him and he went after the beasts to capture them. And the beasts ran away further and he pursued them more; and since the forest was very thick, it was as soon as he entered the forest that they already could not see each other, so he immediately disappeared (that is, became hidden) from their eyes (that is, from the rest who were going with him). And he (that is, the king's [true] son) from whom the two beasts walked off, kept going and still chasing after the beasts and they kept running away. And he chased after them a great deal, until he arrived in the thick of the forest.

He made up his mind: "Either way [lit. be what will be], I'm already going to die, because if I return without the beasts I'll die through the merchant" (for on account of the great fear that he had of the merchant, it seemed to him that the merchant would kill him if he returns without the beasts). And if I'll be here I will also die by the animals of the forest." He decided, "Why should I return to the merchant? How can I come to him without the beasts?" For he had great fear of him. He went and chased further after the beasts and they kept running away. Meanwhile it became night, and such a thing he has never had, that he should have to sleep alone at night in such a thick forest. And he heard the roaring of the beasts which roared in their usual way. He made up his mind and went up on a tree and spent the night there, and he heard the sound of the beasts yelling in their usual way.

In the morning he took a look: he saw that the beasts are standing close by him. He got down the tree and went to catch them; they got away further. He went after them more and they got away more. And the beasts found themselves some grasses to eat there and they stopped to graze. He went further to catch them; they got away further. And thus he kept going after them and they run away, he goes after them more and they run away — until he has arrived in very thick forest where there were already animals[53] that have no fear whatsoever of any people, because they are far from settled places. And again it has become night and he heard the sound of the animals roaring and he was very terrified.

Meanwhile he noticed that a very large tree is standing there, and he got up on the tree. As soon as he was up on the tree he noticed: a man is lying there. He took fright but still he was relieved for the reason that he has found a human here. They asked one another, "Who are you?" "A man." "Who are you?" "A man." "From where have you come here?" He did not want to tell what had happened to him, so he answered him, "By way of the dumb beasts which I tended. Two beasts walked off here, and thereby I've arrived here." In return he asked the other man whom he found there on the tree, "From where did you get here?" He answered him, "I got here by the horse. For I was riding on a horse; I stopped to take a rest and the horse went off into the forest. I chased after it to catch it and the horse ran away further, until I arrived here."

They made up between them that they should remain together, and they agreed that even when they will come into civilization they should also remain together. And the two of them slept the night there and they heard the sound of the beasts roaring and screaming very much. Towards day he heard a very great laughter ("*kha kha kha*") over the entire forest (in other words, the sound of the laughter went over all the forest), for it was a very great laughter, to the extent that the tree trembled from the sound of the laughter, and he became very terrified and had great fear from it. The other person said to him (that is, the man whom he had found there on the tree), "I already have no fear of it whatsoever, for I've slept here already several nights. All nights are like this; as it gets close to day, one hears the laughter, to the extent that all the trees tremble and quake."

He was very frightened and said to the other, "It seems that here is the place of 'those people' (that is, of the demons), for in settled areas one does not hear such a laughter at all, for who has heard a laughter over the entire world?" Then immediately it became day. They took a look; they saw: the beasts of his are standing, and the horse of the other is also standing. They went down and started chasing after — this one after the beasts and that one after the horse. And the beasts ran away further, and he chases more, etc. as before. And likewise the other keeps chasing after the horse and the horse keeps running away, until they [the two men] have gone off, one from the other, and one already did not know of the other['s whereabouts].

Meanwhile he (that is, the king's son who was still chasing after the beasts) found a sack with bread. Now this is certainly very important in a wilderness, so he took the sack on his shoulders and went after the beasts.

[The Man of the Forest]

Meanwhile he encountered a man. Initially he was afraid; however, still he had a little relief because has he found a person here. The man asked him, "How did you get here?" He asked the other man in return, "How did you get here?" The other man answered him, "*I* (with an expression of amazement) — my parents and my parents' parents were raised here. But you, how have you come here? For, no man whatsoever comes here from the settled areas." He was very frightened, for he understood that this is no human being at all, for he says his ancestors were raised here and no man from civilization comes at all here, so he understood that this is no human at all. But still he did not do anything to him whatsoever and was welcoming (that is, this man of the forest did not do any harm to the king's [true] son who was going after the beasts).

And the man of the forest said to him, "What are you doing here?" He answered: he is chasing after the dumb beasts. The man (of the forest) said to him, "Stop chasing after your sins already, for it is not beasts at all but rather your sins are leading you around like this. Enough already! You have already received yours (that is, your punishment you've already received). Now stop chasing them any more. Come with me; you will arrive at the thing that is fitting for you." He went with him, and he was afraid to speak with him and to ask him anything, for a man like this may open up his mouth and swallow him down. He followed him.

Meanwhile, he encountered his friend who was chasing after the horse. As soon as he saw him he immediately winked at him (to signal) that "this is no human being at all; don't have any dealings with him whatsoever, because this is not at all a human." And he immediately went and whispered it to him in his ear, that this is not a human being at all, etc. Meanwhile his friend (that is, the horseman) took a look and he saw: he has a sack with bread on his shoulder! He began to appeal to him, "My brother! It is already days that I have not eaten. Give me bread!" He answered him, "Here in the wilderness nothing helps, for my life takes priority; I need the bread for my sake." He began to beg him and beseech him greatly, "I'll give what I'll give you!" (Except, in the wilderness certainly no gift helps at all for bread)." He answered him, "What can you give me for bread in the wilderness?" He said to him (that is, the horseman who begged for the bread said to the herdsman, who is the king's true son), "I give away myself entirely; I will sell myself to you as a servant for the bread." He (that is, the herdsman) decided: "To purchase a man it's worth it to give him bread," and he bought him as a permanent slave. And he swore him in with oaths that he shall be a slave to him forever, even when they arrive in civilization, and he will give him bread, that is, they shall both eat from the sack of bread until it runs out.

And the both of them went together and followed the man of the forest, and the slave walked behind him (that is, the horseman who sold himself as a slave followed after the herdsman, for he was already his slave, and the two of them walked after the man of the forest). And meanwhile now it became a little bit easier for him (since he has a servant already). When he needed to lift up some object or do something else he ordered his slave to lift it or do something. So they followed together behind the man of the forest and they came to a place where there were snakes and scorpions; he grew very terrified, and on account of fear he asked the man of the forest, "How will we get past here?" He answered him, "*Ella ma'i* (but what then? isn't this too a wonder?)[541] — how will you enter my house?" — and showed him his house standing in the air. They went with him and he brought them over in peace, and he brought them into his house, gave them [things] to eat and to drink, and went away.

And he (that is, the king's true son who had driven the beasts) ordered his slave around for whatever he needed. It upset the slave very much that he had sold himself as a slave for the sake of a single hour when he needed bread to eat, because now he already has what to eat and just for the sake of a single hour he will be an eternal slave. And he made a big sigh and groaned, "What have I come to, that I should be a slave?" He asked him (that is, the king's true son, who was his master, asked him), "What kind of greatness did you have, that you sigh that you have come to this?"

He answered him and recounted to him to the effect: He had been a king; they said about him that he had been exchanged etc., as above (for this horseman was really the king himself, who was actually the bondmaid's son); he drove his friend away (that is, the king's true son). One time it came upon his mind that he has done not right and he regretted etc. Regrets kept coming to him constantly over the evil deed and over the great injustice that he has done against his friend. Once, the dream appeared to him that his correction is that he should throw away the kingship and go wherever his eyes will bring him, and by this he will rectify his error. He didn't want to do it, but those same dreams kept perplexing him constantly, that he should do so, until it remained in his mind that he should do so. So he threw away the kingship and went where he went until he came here. And now he'll be a slave.

Now the other one hears all this and keeps silent (that is, the king's true son who had driven beasts heard out all this that he told him), and he thought to himself, "I will know well enough how to deal with you."

At night, the man of the forest came and gave them to eat and to drink, and they spent the night there. Towards day they heard the great laughter (mentioned earlier), until all the trees trembled; it broke all the trees (the sound of the laughter). He urged him (that is, the slave urged the king's true son, who is his master) to ask the man of the forest what it is. He asked him, "What is this such great laughter, close to day?" He answered him, "This is the day laughing at the night, for the night asks the day, 'Why when you come do I have no name?' The day lets out a big laugh and then it becomes day. And this is the laughter that is heard close to day." This was a big wonder to him, for this is something extraordinary, that the day laughs at the night. (He could already ask no more, when the other answers with such language.)

In the morning again the man of the forest went away and they ate and drank there; at night he came back and they ate and drank and spent the night there. At night they heard the sound of the animals as they all screamed and roared with wild [i.e. extraordinary] sounds. The lion screamed, the leopard roared with another sound, and similarly the rest of the beasts, each beast roaring with a different sound, and the birds whistled and clicked, and so all gave voice with wild sounds. And at the beginning they became very scared; they did not listen correctly to the sound on account of fear. Later, they bowed their ears and listened; they heard it's a sound of a melody; they sing quite a nice tune which is an extraordinary novelty. They listened even more; they heard it's an extraordinarily fine melody that is quite a wild marvel which was an extremely great pleasure to hear, [such] that all the pleasures of the world are completely nothing and amount to absolutely nothing in compare to the wildly great pleasure that one has when one hears this wondrous tune. They discussed between themselves that they want already to remain here, since for eating and drinking they have, and they have such a delight that is such a marvel that all kinds of delights of the world were entirely nullified against this pleasure. The slave urged his master (that is, the king's true son) to ask him (that is, the man of the forest) what it is; he asked him.

He answered him: Inasmuch as the sun has made a garment for the moon, all the animals of the forest have spoken up to the effect that the moon does them great favors, for the animals' dominion is mainly at night only. For sometimes they need to go into a settled area, and by day they cannot, so of course the main time of their dominion is only at night. And the moon does them such a favor by shining for them at night; therefore they agreed that they should make a new melody in honor of the moon, and this is the tune that you hear. When they heard it's a melody they listened even more; they heard it's quite a lovely, sweet melody that is an extremely wild novelty.

He replied to them (that is, the man of the forest) "What — is this such a novelty for you? *Ella ma'i* [But what then?][54] — I have an instrument[55] which I've received from my forebears, who inherited it from their forebears' forebears, which this instrument was made with such things, with such leaves and with such colors, that when one takes the instrument and puts it on whatever beast or on whatever bird then it immediately begins to play this melody (that is, the melody that the animals played)." Then the laughter happened again and it became day; the man of the forest again went away and he (that is, the king's true son) went searching for the instrument. And he searched out the entire room and did not find, and he was fearful to go any further. And they (that is, the king's true son with his slave who is the bondmaid's son who before was king) were afraid to say to the man of the forest that he should lead them into settlement.

Later the man of the forest came and said to them that he would lead them into settlement. He led them into settlement, and he took the instrument and gave it to the king's true son and said to him, "The instrument I give to you. And with him (that is, with his slave who before was king etc.) — you will know how to deal with him." They asked him, "Where shall we go?" He said to them that they should inquire after the land that is called by this name: "The Foolish Land with the Wise King (*Das Nayrishe Land un der Kluger Malchus*)." They asked him, "To which side [Yid. *tsayt*[56]; compare with *zayt* further below; Heb. *tzad*] should we start to ask after this land?" He showed them with his hand: right here (as someone points with a finger). The man of the forest said to the king's true son, "Go there, to the land, and there you will come to your greatness."

[The Foolish Land with the Wise King]

They went where they went, and they very much wished to find any animal or beast to test the instrument, whether it would be able to play (as before). However they still did not see any sort of animal. Then they arrived further into settlement. They found some beast and laid the instrument down on it and it began to play the tune (as before). So they went and went until they came to the land. And the land was walled about and one could not enter in the land except by one gateway. One must go around several miles until one comes to the gateway. They went around until they came to the gateway. When they had now arrived at the gateway, they did not want to let them enter, inasmuch as the king of the land had died; the king's son remained and the king had left a will: "Inasmuch as the land has hereto been called *Das Nayrishe Land un der Kluger Malchus* ("The Foolish Land with the Wise King"), now it will already be called the reverse: *Das Kluger Land un der Nayrisher Malchus* ("The Wise Land with the Foolish King"). And whoever will undertake that he should return the land to the first name, that is, that they will once again call the land by its first name, *Das Nayrishe Land un der Kluger Malchus* — the same shall become king" — therefore they do not let any man into the land except he who will undertake the same, that he should return the land to the first name. They said to him, "Can you undertake this, that you should return the country to its first name?" He certainly could not undertake this, so they could not enter. His slave urged him that they should return home. However he did not want to return because the man of the forest had said to him that he should go to this land and there he will arrive at his greatness.

[Another Horseman; Understanding One Thing From Another]

Meanwhile another man arrived who was riding on a horse, and he wanted to go in but they also did not let him in on account of this (as mentioned). Meanwhile he noticed that this other man's horse is standing so he went ahead and took the instrument and laid it down on the horse and it began to play the very fine melody (as above). The horseman pleaded him very much that he should sell it to him, and he replied, "What can you give me for such a wondrous instrument?"

The horseman said to him, "Well, what can you do with this instrument except perform theatrics and take in a *gulden?* I however know a thing that is better than your instrument. I know a thing I've received from my parents' parents: to be an extrapolater [*mevin davar mitokh davar*]. That is, I know such a thing that I've received from the forebears of my forebears, that through this thing one can make inference. When somebody says just any utterance, one knows, through that which I have received, one should discern something from one thing (that is, one thing from the other). And I have not yet spoken out the thing before any man in the world. Therefore, I will teach out to you this certain thing, and you will give me this here instrument for that."

He decided (that is, the king's true son, who had the instrument) it is truly a great wonder to be an extrapolater. So he gave away the instrument to him and he (that is, the horseman) went ahead and instructed him so that he should be an extrapolater. Now the king's true son, since he has now gotten the ability to extrapolate, was walking around there by the gate of the country, and he understood that it is indeed possible for him to undertake it to return the land to its first name. For he had now after all become an extrapolater; thus he understood it is possible, even though he did not yet know just how and by what way he will be able to do this, to restore the first name to the country. But nevertheless because he had become able to extrapolate, he understood it is possible.

He made up his mind he would order himself let in and he would undertake it that he would return its first name to the country. What would he lose here? He said (to those people who did not want to let him in) that they should let him in and he will take under himself that very thing, that he would return the first name to the country. They let him in, and they informed the noblemen that there is found a man who wants to undertake it to return the land to the first name. They brought him to the noblemen of the land.

The noblemen said to him, "You should know that we too are no fools, God forbid, except the king that had been[57] — he was a very extraordinarily great sage, such that against him we were all fools. Therefore the land used to be called 'The Foolish Land with the Wise Government (*malkhuth*).' Then the king died; the king's son remained, and the king's son is also a wise man, except against us he is not at all smart. Therefore the land is now called conversely: 'The Smart Land with the Foolish Government.'

"" The king left a will: when there will be found such a wise person that he should return the land to the first name, he shall be king. And he commanded his son that when such a man will be found, he shall step down from the reign for him: that is, when there will be found such a wise man that he will be such an extraordinarily great sage that against him everyone will be fools, he will become king, for this man will surely bring back the land once more to its first name, 'The Foolish Land with the Smart King,' for they are after all fools against him. Therefore you should know what you are taking under yourself here." (All such did the noblemen say to him.)

[The Test: The Garden and the Man]

In addition they (that is, the noblemen again; this is all a continuation of their words) said to him, "The test will be whether you are this wise: Inasmuch as there is a garden that is left over from a king who had been, who was a very great sage, and the garden is quite an extraordinary novelty — metal instruments grow in it (that is, tools of ironwork), silver instruments and gold instruments — so it is an extremely wild novelty: However, one cannot go in the garden, for when a person goes in the garden then immediately they begin chasing him. So they chase and he screams and he doesn't at all know and doesn't at all see who is chasing him, and so they chase him continuously until they make him run away from the garden. Therefore, we shall see whether you are wise; if you'll be able to go into the garden."

He asked whether they beat the person who enters. They said to him: the main thing is they chase him and he doesn't at all know who they are that chase him and he has to run away in very great panic. For thus people who had gone in there told them. (All thus did the noblemen say to the king's true son.)

He got up and went to the garden. He saw there is a wall around it, and the gate is open and there aren't any guards there, for one certainly doesn't need any guards for this garden (for no one is able to go in it, as mentioned)! He (that is, the king's true son) was walking by the garden and he took a look: he noticed that standing there by the garden is a man. That is, a man was portrayed there.[58] He looked some more and he saw that above the man there is a sign, and there it is written that the man — this was a king several hundred years ago, and in the king's times there was peace, for until this king there were wars and likewise after him there were wars but in the days of this king there was peace.

He understood, because he had already gotten the ability to extrapolate, that it all depends on this man. When one enters the garden and they start to chase him, he needs not run away at all but just put himself next to the man; thereby he will be saved. Moreover even if one takes this man and inserts him inside in the interior[59] of the garden then every man will be able to enter in peace into this garden. (All this the king's true son understood because he had become able to infer.)

He got up and went inside the garden, and as soon as they started chasing him he went and put himself next to the man standing by the garden from the outside, and thereby he emerged in peace and it did not harm him at all. For, others when they entered in the garden and they started chasing them would run away in very great panic and were consequently battered, but he emerged in peace and tranquility by placing himself next to the man.

And the noblemen saw this and were astonished that he got out safely. Then he ordered (that is, the king's true son called) that they should take the man and insert him inside within the midst of the garden. They did so and then all the noblemen entered inside the garden and they passed through and got out safely.

[Another Test: The Throne and the Things Around It]

The noblemen spoke up to him, "Still, even though we have seen from you such a thing, nevertheless for the sake of one thing you do not yet deserve to be given the kingship. We will try you further with one thing. Inasmuch as there is a throne here from the king who was, and the throne is very high and by the throne stand all sorts of animals and birds carved out of wood: And in front of the throne stands a little bed, and by the bed stands a table, and on the table stands a lamp. And from the throne emerge paved roads[60] and the roads are walled and the roads go out from the throne to all sides [*zaytin*[61]; see above[56] where it is spelled with a *tzaddi*], and no man knows whatsoever what it is, the matter of the throne with these roads. And these roads, when they go out and extend for some piece [i.e. distance] — a golden lion is standing there. And if some man should go to it, it will open its mouth and swallow him down. And beyond this lion the road extends even further, and likewise with the rest of the roads that go out from the throne. That is, with another road that goes out from the throne to another side it is also like that: when the road extends away a piece, a different animal is standing there, namely a leopard [Yid. *lempert*, Heb. *lavi'* lion] of ironwork. And there too one cannot go to it (as before, because it will swallow him down). And beyond the leopard the road extends further, and so it is with the rest of the roads. And these selfsame roads extend and go throughout the entire land, and no man whatsoever knows what is the thing of the throne with all these things and the roads. Therefore you shall be tested with this, whether you will be able to know the matter of the throne with all these things."

They showed him the throne and he saw that it was very high, etc. He went to the throne, took a look and understood that the throne was made of the little box's wood (that is, the instrument that the man of the forest had given him). He looked some more and he saw the throne is lacking some little rose at the top [*rayzile*, Heb. *shoshanah*], and if the throne would have this rose the throne would have the power of the little box (that is, the aforementioned instrument which had the power that when one would lay the instrument on some beast or animal it began to play, as mentioned). He looked some more and he saw that this rose which is missing at the top of the throne, this rose is lying at the bottom in the throne. One needs to take the little rose out from below and seat it above and thus the throne will have the power of the little box. For the king who had been[57] had done everything with wisdom and had disguised everything in order that no one should understand the matter — what it means — until there would come such an extraordinarily great sage who would surmise and would be able to hit upon interchanging everything and arranging all the things as needed.

And so too the little bed: he understood that one needs to move it a bit away and back from the place where it's standing. And also the table: one also needs [to move it] a bit away and back from [its] place; and one also needs the lamp a bit away and back from its place. And so too the birds and animals: one also needs to relocate them all; one should take this bird from this place and put it on that place. And thus with everything; one must reposition everything. For the king had purposely disguised everything cleverly in order that no one should know what is meant, until there would come the wise man who would be able to understand he should arrange everything properly.

And so too the lion that stands there, where that road goes out: one needs to put it yonder. And likewise all of them; one needs to relocate all of them. He ordered that they should arrange everything as needed: they should take out the little rose from below and seat it above, and likewise all the things — they should reposition all things and arrange them differently (as needed; in the way he called for).

As soon as they did so, they all began playing the exquisite melody that is quite a wild novelty, and they all did what they needed to do. So they gave him the kingship (that is, the true king's son who demonstrated all the clever things, as above). He spoke up and said to the [actual] bondmaid's son: "Now I understand that I am indeed the real son of the king and you are really the bondmaid's son."

[Notes Following the Story]

Translator's note: "Y" indicates notes that appear after the Yiddish text, "H" indicates notes that appear after the Hebrew text, and "YH" indicates notes found in both.

H: (These too are the words of Rabbeinu n"y [nero ya'ir, "let his light shine"]; after he told this story he spoke up and said these words:)

Y: In former generations when they would discuss kabbalah it would be talked about in such language (as this story is). H: For until Rashbi they would not discuss kabbalah openly; only Rashbi disclosed kabbalah openly; and before, when the friends would speak kabbalah they would speak in such language: "When they placed the ark upon the oxen they began singing."[62] Now understand this.

H: For there are new states of the moon, when the moon receives innovations from the sun, and this is the aspect of when they bring the Ark to Beith Shemesh [lit. "House of the Sun," I Sam. 6], and then all the creatures bearing the Throne make a new melody, the aspect of *"Mizmor shiru laShem shir chadash/* A Song: Sing to Hashem a new song," which is the song that the cows of Bashan sang. And this is the aspect of: bed, table, chair and lamp; they are the restoration of the Shekhinah. And the aspect of the garden: for Adam haRishon was driven out of the Garden, and Shabbath guarded over him, as is brought [in the books of kabbalah]. And Shabbath is the aspect of "the king unto whom peace belongs," the aspect of the aforementioned man, who is the king during whose days there was peace; and therefore he stationed himself by Shabbath. And the rest he did not explain.

H: (He spoke up and said after telling this story, in these words:) YH: This story is a big wonder, and it's entirely one: the herds etc., the throne etc. and the garden; it's all one. At times it (the aspect hinted to in the story) is called by this name, at times by this name; H: all according to the *inyan/* interest and the aspect.

H: And the things are very, very deep, wondrous and awesome. (These too are the words of Rabbeinu *n"y*.) And there is more, but there is no need to reveal everything. There is also that the king that was in that land did something corresponding to the sun and something corresponding to the moon (that is, that these things alluded to the sun and the moon), and the moon was holding a lamp in its hand, and when the day arrives then the lamp does not shine, for *"shraga betihara/* a lamp at midday"[63] etc. [is superfluous]. And this is that the night said to the day, "Why is it that when you arrive I have no name?" (as expressed above), for in the day a lamp does not avail whatsoever.

YH: The explanation of the story is like the throne which the king made, as mentioned, as the main wisdom is that one needs to know how to order the things; therefore whoever is adept in the books and his heart is whole can understand the explanation; however, the things have to be ordered well, for sometimes it is called this and sometimes it is called that, and likewise with the rest of the things, that is, with the explanation of the story, sometimes the man of the above story is called by this name, and sometimes by a different name, and similarly with the rest of the things. Fortunate is he who will be privileged to understand these things to their truth. Y: All this he himself *a"h* said after the story. H: *Barukh Hashem le`olam, amen ve'amen/* Blessed be Hashem forever, Amen and Amen. (These are entirely Rabbeinu haKadosh's words, *a"h* ztz"l.)

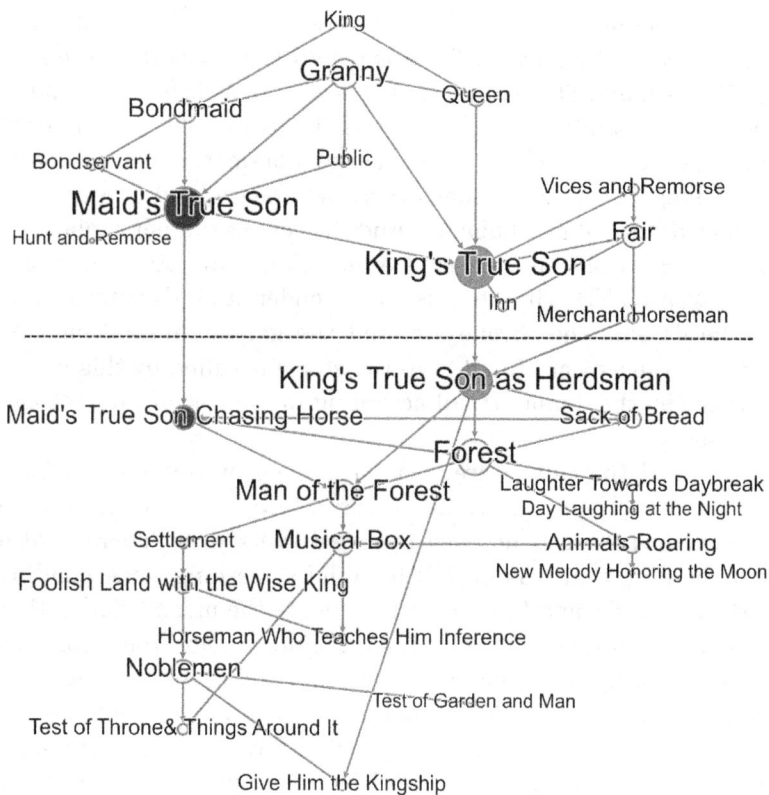

King

Granny

Bondmaid   Queen

Bondservant   Public

Maid's True Son   Vices and Remorse

Hunt and Remorse   Fair

King's True Son

Inn   Merchant Horseman

King's True Son as Herdsman

Maid's True Son Chasing Horse   Sack of Bread

Forest

Man of the Forest   Laughter Towards Daybreak
Day Laughing at the Night

Settlement   Musical Box   Animals Roaring

Foolish Land with the Wise King   New Melody Honoring the Moon

Horseman Who Teaches Him Inference

Noblemen

Test of Garden and Man

Test of Throne&Things Around It

Give Him the Kingship

Tale 12: The Prayer Leader

[The Prayer Leader]

A tale. Once, there was a Prayer Leader [ba`al tefilah: master of prayer; prayer man; the leader of a prayer service] who was always involved just with prayers, songs and praises to Hashem Yithbarakh (the Blessed Creator), and he dwelled outside of settled areas [yeshuv]. And his program was: he would regularly go into settled areas and enter in [conversation] with some person — typically going in [conversation] with lowly people, such as poor people and so forth — and he would start talking with the person regarding the purpose of the whole world, that truthfully there is no purpose whatsoever in the world except for serving God all one's life, spending the years just with prayer to Hashem Yithbarakh, with songs and praises to Hashem Yithbarakh, etc. And he would speak a lot of such talk with the person to wake him up, until his words entered his heart, until the person would be willing to join him, and as soon as the person agreed with him he would immediately take him and bring him to his place which he had outside of settled areas (that is, outside of settled places; not where people dwell). For the Prayer Leader had chosen for himself a place outside of settled areas, and there was a river there in front of him, as well as trees and fruits there too, and they would eat of the fruits and they would not look at clothes whatsoever — how you go, you go (Heb. he was not strict about clothes at all).

A nd so was the constant schedule of the Prayer Leader, going into settled areas and persuading people to go his way, to only serve Hashem Yithbarakh and only be involved with prayers etc.; and whoever listened to him, he would take and bring to his place outside of settled areas, as mentioned, and they would be involved there just with prayers, songs and praises to Hashem Yithbarakh, and confessions, fasts, privations (that is, torturing one's body), repentance and so forth; and the Prayer Leader would give them his compositions (that is, books) that he had of prayers, songs, praises and confessions, and they would be involved with them constantly, to the extent that there would be found among his people that he brought there, those who could

now also bring people to Hashem Yithbarakh. He would sometimes give permission to one of his people to now also go into settled areas and awaken people to the Almighty, that they should
just serve Hashem Yithbarakh.

The Prayer Leader kept doing so, time after time attracting
his people and taking them out of settled areas, as mentioned, until an impression was made on the world and the thing
began to be known, because suddenly people would disappear
from the country and no one knew where they went: this one had
a missing son, that one had a missing son-in-law, and no one
knew where they were, until it became known that there exists a
Prayer Leader who goes and talks people into (serving) Hashem
Yithbarakh. Except, catch him they could not, because the Prayer
Leader would conduct himself very craftily and would present
himself differently for each person. For this one he presented
himself as a poor man, for that one as a trader, and for another he
disguised himself still differently. Furthermore, when he would
come to talk to a person, when he understood that he could not
accomplish with the person what he wanted, he would so spin the
person around with talk that it was not at all possible to detect
that he meant that — that is, to draw him closer to Hashem Yithbarakh. And it was impossible to realize that he meant that, even
though in truth his whole intention was only that. For in the
things he chatted and talked about with people, he meant nothing
other than this, that is, to draw them close to Hashem Yithbarakh. Only when he understood that he was not influencing
him, he would so deceive and misguide him with talk until he
thought that he did not want that at all. (Therefore they could not
catch the Prayer Leader.) The Prayer Leader remained occupied
with this matter, until there was an impression and publicity
over the world; and they wanted to catch him but it was impossible, as mentioned.

So the Prayer Leader, with his people, dwelled outside of settled areas, and were involved only with prayer, songs and
praises to Hashem Yithbarakh, and confessions, fasts, afflictions
and repentances. It was also the Prayer Leader's business that he
could provide for each person what he needed. If he understood of
one of his people that in relation to his brain he needed for his
serving Hashem, to go dressed in *gilden geshtik* (gold-embroi-

dered clothes), he supplied it for him, and vice versa, when sometimes some rich person would draw close to him and he took him out from settled areas and understood that this rich person needed to go in tatters, he would make him go [dressed] that way. Whatever way he knew a person needed to go, he supplied it for him. And for the people whom he drew close to Hashem Yithbarakh, a fast or the biggest privation (that is, torturing oneself) was dearer than all the world's delights, for they had more delight from the big privation or fast than from all the world's delights.

[The Land of Riches]

And the day came to pass — there was a country where there were enormous riches; they were all rich. Only, their behavior was quite disturbing, because by them everything went according to wealth. Everyone's status and honor was only according to his wealth. It was determined by them that whoever had its particular amount — thousands or ten-thousands of money — deserved one class, and whoever had such and such an amount of money deserved another class. And similarly all the classes by them were all according to the money each person had. And he who had so many, so many thousands and ten-thousands, as was determined there by them — is already a king. And similarly they had flags, that whoever had so much money is in this flag, and deserves status and honor in that flag; and whoever had so much money is in another flag and deserves the status in that flag, all according to his money. So it was determined for everyone how much money he should have in order to have the status in this flag, and how much money he should have in order to be already in another flag and have some kind of status and honor there. And so every man's honor and all his status was all only according to how much money he had, as had been determined by them for every status and honor, how much money he needed to have. And similarly it was determined by them if he has only so much money he is a plain human, whereas if he has even less he is already no man at all, just a beast or bird (that is, it's just a beast that looks like a human). So they had beasts and birds, that is, if he has this little money, it's just a lion — it's a human lion; but if he has that little money, he is a mere bird. And similarly they had other beasts and birds, as someone who has less money is no man at all by them, just a beast or a bird. Because the main object for them was money, and the status and honor of everyone was only according to his money.

People heard in the world that there is such a country. The Prayer Leader would make a very big sigh over this and would say, "Who knows how far they can stray through this?" Some men from his people were present, and did not ask his opinion at all and they picked up and went there to that country to get them out of it. Because they (that is, the Prayer Leader's people) had great pity on that country which was so led astray in the craving of money; and especially since the Prayer Leader had said that they could go further astray, therefore these people of the Prayer Leader went to that country. Perhaps they could bring them out of their nonsense.

They entered the country and approached one of them who was apparently a low-status person whom they call a beast. And they began to talk with him, that truthfully money is not a purpose at all, and the main purpose is only serving Hashem, and so forth. But he did not listen to them at all, because it was already rooted in their thinking that the main thing is only money. And so did they chat with another, and he too did not listen. And they wanted to talk with him more, but he replied, "I have no more time to talk with you."

They asked him, "Why?" He replied, "Because we all must leave the country and go to another country, for we have seen that the main goal is only money, therefore it has become ingrained in us that we must go to such a country where they make money (that is, there, there is a kind of earth from which they make gold and silver). Therefore we all must now go to that country."

It also got into them that they wanted to have stars and constellations too, that is, whoever has so much and so much money, according to the amount they had determined for it, he should be a star, because since he has so much money he must have the power of the star, because the star generates the gold, because the fact that there is earth from which they make gold is, after all, due to the star that generates such earth there from which they make gold. Since the man has so much gold, he must have the power of the stars, therefore he himself is a star. And likewise they said they wanted to have constellations too. That is, when someone would have so much and so much money, however much they had determined for it, he should be a constellation. And likewise they made for themselves angels, all according to money. Until they agreed that they should have gods too, that whoever would have very much money, so many and so many thousands and myriads, however much they had determined for this, he would be a god, because since God gives him so much money, he himself is a god.

They said furthermore that they ought not dwell in the air of this world, and they must not at all be together with other people, so that they should not contaminate them, because the other people of the world are completely impure compared to them; therefore they decided that they should find for themselves very high mountains that are higher than all the world, and they should dwell there, so that they can be higher than the air of the world. They sent people to seek high mountains, and they found very high mountains. The whole country went and settled there on the high mountains; that is, on each mountain a gathering of people from the country (in other words, a city) settled, and around the mountain they made a big fortification and great trenches around the mountain, until it was impossible for any man to reach them, because there was no longer even a hidden path to the mountain, so that no other person would at all be able to reach them; and likewise on the next mountain, and so on all the mountains they always made a fortification etc. as mentioned. And they appointed guards far from the mountain, so no one would be able to reach them.

So they dwelled there on the mountains and conducted themselves as mentioned earlier, and they had many gods, that is, according to money, as mentioned. However, since wealth was the main thing for them — so much so that via great wealth a person could become a god — they had a fear of murder and theft, because anyone would be a murderer or thief in order to become a god via the money he would steal. But they said since the wealthy one is a god he will protect himself from theft and murder. And they established devotions and offerings to offer and pray to the gods, to get money through them, and they would sacrifice people and their very selves to the gods in order to be included in them and later be reincarnated as a rich [person]. Because their main creed [emunah] was in money. And they had devotions, sacrifices and incenses with which they served their gods (that is, those who had much money). But despite this the country was definitely full of murder and theft, because whoever did not believe in the devotions became a murderer and thief in order to get money, because the main thing for them was wealth, since through money one can buy anything — food and clothing — so the root of a man's life is through money; therefore money was their main creed (such was their foolish and confused thinking). And they all endeavored to not lose any money, because money was for them the fundamental creed and the god; on the contrary, they needed to try to bring money into the country from other places. Traders would go out from them to trade in other countries, in order to win money, in order to bring even more money into the country. And charity was certainly a great prohibition for them, because how can someone be permitted to give away the money that God has given him — which was for them the main thing, to have money — how can someone be permitted to give that away? So for them it was definitely forbidden to give charity.

And they had officers who were appointed to observe of everyone whether he has as much money as he says, because everyone had to show off his wealth at every moment in order to remain in the status and honor that he had according to his money (in other words all the rich people who for them were gods, stars, angels etc. due to their money would always be inspected whether he has so much money; whether he is not in vain a god and so forth, and people were appointed to constantly watch this). And sometimes among them an animal would become a person, or a person an animal. Namely when a rich person lost his money he already became a non-human — a man became an animal, because he already had no money for himself; and conversely when someone won money, so an animal became a human; and so on with the other classes, which by them was all according to money (it was that way too, as sometimes one became a non-god because he has already lost the money). And they would have the figures and portraits of the gods (that is, those who had much money), and everyone had the portraits, and they would hug and kiss them, because money was their entire devotion and religion.

A nd the Prayer Leader's people (who were previously there in that country) returned to their place and they told the Prayer Leader of the nonsense of the country, how they were so fooled and lost in the craving of money, and that they wanted to already leave their country for another country (where they make money as mentioned) and wanted to make stars and constellations already. The Prayer Leader spoke up and said that he feared lest they stray more and more. Then people heard that they had already made themselves gods (as mentioned).

T he Prayer Leader spoke up and said, "That is what I meant; that is why I feared" (that is, by his always saying he feared lest they get further lost, he meant this). The Prayer Leader had great pity on them and came to the decision to personally go there; perhaps he would return them from their error. The Prayer Leader went there and came to the guards who stand around each mountain (as mentioned). And the guards, it would reason, were people of low status who were able to stand in the air of this world, because the people who had status from their money were not at all able to be together with the people of the world and could not stand in the world's air, so that they should not contaminate them, and they were not at all able to speak with people of the world, so that they should not contaminate them with their breath (in other words the foolish country considered the world entirely impure compared to them, as mentioned). Therefore the guards who stood outside the city were surely of low status, except the guards also had the portraits (of their gods) and would hug and kiss them all the time, because with them too was money the main object of faith.

T he Prayer Leader came to one of the guards and began talking with him about the ultimate purpose, inasmuch as the only ultimate purpose is Godly devotions — Torah, prayer, good deeds etc. — and money is utter foolishness and not the ultimate purpose at all, etc. But the guard did not listen to him at all, for it was already ingrained in them for a long time that the main thing is only money, as mentioned. And likewise the Prayer Leader went to all the guards and talked with them likewise as mentioned and they did not listen to him whatsoever. The Prayer Leader came to a decision and went into the city which was on the mountain (as mentioned). When he arrived inside the city it was a great novelty to them and they asked, "How did you get in here?" since no one was able to reach them. He answered them, "Why do you ask? I am already inside the city, all the same."

The Prayer Leader began talking with one of them about the purpose of the world, that money is no purpose at all, etc. (as was his custom) but the man did not listen to him at all, and likewise another, and likewise all of them, because they were already so lost in their mistake that they already could not listen to anybody, as mentioned. And it was a wonder to the people of the city that such a man exists and should come to them and say to them such things, the complete opposite of their faith. It struck them that this man must be the Prayer Leader, because they had already heard that there is such a Prayer Leader in the world, since the matter of the Prayer Leader had already become publicized in the world (as mentioned), and people in the world would call him *"Der Frummer Baal Tefilah"* (the devout Prayer Leader). But catch him they could not, because he would make himself appear different to each person: to one he appeared as a merchant, to another as a pauper, etc., immediately afterwards disappearing from there (in other words, he was quickly gone away).

[The Warrior (The Strong Man)]

And the day came to pass: now there was a Mighty Warrior [*gibbor*, lit. mighty; strong; overpowerer], unto whom other warriors [*gibborim*] had gathered. Now, the Warrior and his warriors were going around taking over countries, the Warrior wanting nothing else but submission (in other words, that they should be subject under him). And when the people of the country submitted to him he would release them; and if not — he would ruin them. So he went around subjugating countries, without any desire for money whatsoever — only submission; that they should be under him. And the way of the Warrior was: he would send his warriors to a country when he was still very far from it — fifty miles — for them to surrender to him; and so he was continually taking over countries.

And the merchants of the aforementioned wealthy country, who used to conduct trade in foreign countries, returned to their country and told about the Warrior, and a great terror fell on them. And even though they were willing to submit themselves under him, the thing that prevented them was they heard that he loathes money and does not want any money at all, and this was contrary to their faith, therefore they could not submit themselves under him, because for them it would be like apostasy, since he did not at all believe in their creed, that is, in money. And they were very afraid of him, and they began to perform their devotions and bring their sacrifices to their gods (that is, to those who had much money); and they would take a beastie (that is, someone with little money, who was considered by them a beast) and bring him for a sacrifice to their gods (as mentioned), and similarly they performed their other devotions (that is, the things with which they would serve their gods). And the Warrior was continually coming closer to them, and had started to send his warriors ahead [to ask]: What do they want? — after his usual custom, as mentioned. A great terror came over them and they did not know what to do.

Their own merchants gave them a suggestion: Inasmuch as they had been in a country where the entire populace were gods and traveled about with angels — that is, that country is where everyone, from the smallest to greatest, are all extraordinarily great [*vild-groiss*, lit. "wild-great"] wealthy people in the extreme, such that even the smallest among them is also a god according to their foolish delusion (because the smallest person in the country is exceptionally wealthy and has as much money as was reckoned by them that with that much money one becomes a god, as mentioned). And they "travel with angels" since their horses are covered with such great wealth, with gold and so forth, that the covering of one horse was worth the amount that an angel had. Thus, the riders "travel with angels," tying three pairs of "angels" to a carriage and riding with them. "Therefore you need to send to this country and they will surely help you, for they are all gods." (All this was still the advice of their merchants.) Their advice pleased them very much, for they believed that they would surely be saved by the other country, since they are all gods there, as mentioned.

And the Prayer Leader came to the decision he would go once again to that country; perhaps he would still lead them out of their folly. And he went there, came up to the guards, and began speaking with one guard in his usual way. The guard told him about the Warrior, that they are in great terror of him. The Prayer Leader asked him, "What do you have in mind to do?" The guard told him the matter mentioned above, that they want to send to the country where they are all gods etc.

The Prayer Leader made much laughter of him and said to him, "That is quite a great folly! Because they are humans like we are. And all of you, with all your gods, are all merely humans and not one of them is any god at all. There is no more than only one God in the world: He who created everything, and He alone should be served and only to Him one should pray; and this alone is the main purpose in the world." And such other words did the Prayer Leader speak with the guard. And the Prayer Leader kept speaking more of the same kinds of words with the guard, while the guard continued to not listen, because their mistaken belief had already been set within them from a long time ago, as mentioned.

However, the Prayer Leader debated with him extensively, until finally the guard answered him, "What else can I do? I am only one individual, after all (and compared to me are the numerous residents of the country)." Now this already had the semblance of some *teshuvah* [repentance, response], as the words which the Prayer Leader had spoken before with the guard, and the words which he spoke now, joined together until they stirred him somewhat. (Because the *teshuvah* that the guard had answered, "What can I do?" etc., made it known that the words of the Prayer Leader were starting to already enter his heart a little bit.)

And so the Prayer Leader went to another guard and also spoke with him in his usual way, as above; and he too did not listen to him, but in the end also replied as above, "I am one person" and so forth, as above. And so all the guards answered him this teshuvah in the end.

Afterwards the Prayer Leader entered the city and began talking with them in his usual way: inasmuch as they are all very much in complete error, and money is no goal at all; rather, the essential purpose is solely to delve in Torah and prayer and so forth. They did not listen to him, for they were all very much rooted in money from a long time ago. And they told him about the Warrior, and that they want to send to the country where they are all gods, etc. He laughed at them too and told them that was a folly and they all are only humans, etc. "And they will be unable to help you at all, because you are human and they are human, and they are no god whatsoever. There is only one God, the All-Blessed One, etc." As for the Warrior he replied to them (with a wondering expression), "Isn't this that Warrior?" (the one he knows?) They did not understand what he meant. And so he went from one to the other, and continued talking thus with them, as above. And as for the Warrior he said to everyone, "Isn't this that Warrior?" etc., as above. They did not understand his words; what he meant.

Meanwhile, a commotion broke out in the city, inasmuch as there was found someone who says such things, making laughter of their faith, and saying that there is only a single Unity, that is, Hashem Yithbarakh, the All-Blessed One, etc.; and as for the Warrior, always saying, "Isn't this that Warrior?" etc. as above. They understood that this must certainly be the Prayer Leader, because he was already notorious among them, as mentioned. They ordered for him to be sought and caught. Even though he appeared different each time (that is, at times presenting himself as a merchant, at times as a poor person, and so forth, wherefore they were not able to catch him, as mentioned), nonetheless they knew of this too, that the Prayer Leader constantly presents himself differently. They ordered an investigation into him, for him to be captured. He was sought out until they caught him, and they brought him to their elders.

When they began talking with him he told them also as above, "You are all mistaken and in great folly, and this is no purpose whatsoever (that is, money is no goal at all). Instead there exists a singular all-blessed One, namely the Creator, blessed be His name, Who has created everything. He alone should be served, and money is an utter nonsense, etc. And the country where you say they are all gods — they will be unable to help you whatsoever, for they are only human, etc."

They considered him insane, because the entire country was already so immersed in money and they were already so crazed that whoever said something contrary to their foolishness was for them a madman.

[The King and the Hand]

They asked him, "What is this that you say about the Warrior, 'Isn't this that Warrior?'" as above. He answered them, "Inasmuch as I used to be with a King, and to the King a Warrior was lost; then if this is that Warrior, I am acquainted with him. And furthermore, your relying on the country where you say they are all gods — this is nonsense, because they will be unable to help you whatsoever. Just the reverse — this will be your very downfall, if you rely on them." They asked him, "Where do you know this from?"

He answered them: Insofar as the King whom he was with, had with him a **Hand** [*yad*, יד]. That is, the King had something resembling a hand with five fingers and with all the grooves (that is, all the creases and ruts) that are on a hand. And the Hand was the map of all the worlds, and all that has been since the creation of heaven and earth until the end and what will be afterwards was all depicted on the Hand. For depicted in the scratches and folds of the Hand was the diagram of all the worlds, how every world stands, with all of every world's things in detail, every thing standing out on the and as depicted on a land map (as is known to those who are used to land maps, that is, depicted on a paper is each town, every country and every bridge; and similarly other things: streams, woods etc.; and by every thing it is all written down, that this is this town and this is that country and so forth).

Thus all the worlds were depicted on the Hand by the ruts and folds of the Hand, and in the Hand's ruts were as if letters, just as letters are inscribed on a map next to each thing so that they may know what it is, that is, that they should know that here is this town and here is this stream and likewise other things. In exactly the same way by the ruts of the Hand were depicted the likeness of letters next to every thing depicted on the Hand so as to know what is every thing depicted there. The same for every separate city, every town and all the rivers, bridges, mountains and other objects (whatever is found in the world and in all the worlds): everything was depicted on the Hand by the ruts and folds on the Hand, and there were always letters standing next to every thing, that this is this thing and that is that thing, etc. Similarly all the people who go around in every country, and all their experiences (that is, everything that passes over a man during his lifetime), were all depicted on the Hand.

❝ And even all the paths from one country to another, and from one place to another, were written on it, and on account of that I knew the way to come in here to this town which no man can enter (because the wealthy country had dug around their cities and nobody could come to them, as above). And so if you want to send me into the other town I know that way too, all through the Hand. And also imprinted on the Hand was the way from one world to another world. For there is a path and a course on which one can ascend from earth to heaven (for, one cannot go up from earth to heaven, due to not knowing the way; but depicted there was the way to go up to heaven). So depicted there were all the paths that exist from one world to another world. For, Eliyahu ascended to heaven with this path, and that path was written there; Moshe Rabbeinu [Moses] went up to heaven with a different path, and that other path was also written there; and likewise Chanokh [Enoch] ascended to heaven with yet another path, and that path was also written there. Thus from one world to the other (farther, higher) world was all depicted by the ruts and folds of the Hand.

❝ Also represented on the Hand was every thing as it was at the time the world was created, as it is now, and as it will be afterwards. For instance, Sedom [Sodom] was depicted there as that city had been (while inhabited) before it was overturned; in addition depicted there was Sedom being upheaved, as a city turning over; and again depicted there was Sedom as it appears today after the upheaval. For on the Hand was depicted what was, what is, and what will be. And there on the Hand I have seen that the country of which you say they are all gods, together with all the people who come to them for help (that is, that the city should help them) will both all be obliterated." (All this the Prayer Leader told them.)

This was an extraordinary novelty to them, for it was recognized that this is true talk, because it is known that on a map all things are depicted, so they understood that his words are true since such things cannot be thought up, because one can see for himself that he can put together two ruts of the hand and a letter will become of them. For this reason they understood this is no contrived thing; hence it was an extraordinary novelty to them. They asked him, "Whereabout is the King? Perhaps he will show us a way how to find money."

He answered them (with an expression of someone awestruck and angered), "You still want money?! Don't talk about money at all!" They asked him, "Nonetheless, tell us where the King is." He answered them, "I too don't know of the King; where he is. And this is how the story happened:

[The Prayer Leader Tells the City About the King Etc.]

" Once, there was a King and a Queen, and they had an only daughter. And it came near the time to marry her off, so they seated advisors to give counsel as to whom she ought be married off to. And I too (that is, the Prayer Leader, who is still relating this in front of them) was there among the advisors, because the King liked me, and my advice was that they should give her the Warrior, because the Warrior had wrought us many benefits, for he had conquered many countries; therefore he ought to be given the Queen's Daughter for a wife. My advice was very liked and they all agreed upon it, and there was a big celebration there for having found a groom for the Queen's Daughter. And they wed the Queen's Daughter with the Warrior, and the Queen's Daughter had a Child. And the Baby was quite an extraordinary beauty, being no sort of human beauty whatsoever: his hair was golden and had all the colors, his face was like the sun and his eyes were other luminaries. And the Child was born with mature wisdom, because they saw in him immediately when he was born that he is already a great sage, for when people were talking, in the place where one needs to laugh he would laugh; and so with other such things they likewise recognized him being a great sage — except not yet having the motions of an adult, namely he had not yet the faculty of speech and other such things — but this they saw right away: that he is already a big genius.

" And with the King was an Orator, that is, a speaker who is a master of language and rhetoric, who was able to talk very fine talk: very beautiful speeches, songs and praises for the King. And the Orator was on his own account a fine Orator too, but the King showed him the hidden path and the way for him to go up and get the power of the science of rhetoric, and thereby he became a very superb orator. The King also had a Sage, and the

Sage was also a sage on his own account, but the King showed him the way for him to go up and get wisdom, and thereby he became an extraordinary, superb sage.

And similarly, the Warrior was mighty on his own, but the King showed him the way for him to go and get strength, and thereby he became an extraordinary, superb warrior. For, there is a Sword that hangs in the air, and the Sword has three powers. When the Sword is lifted then all the officers of the [opposing] army flee, so as a matter of course they fall, because when the officers flee, there is no one to lead the battle, so they certainly fall. But despite this, the survivors may still be able to wage war — however, the Sword has two sharp edges, and they have two powers: through one edge they all fall down, and through the other edge they get the sickness called "*dör*" (wasting; consumption), namely they (the enemies whom they are fighting) become meager of flesh and lifeless, as is known of this sickness; the Merciful One spare us. So by merely making a move with the Sword in its place, the enemies are stricken with the aforementioned things, that is, by using one edge the enemies have defeat, and by using the other edge the enemies are stricken with *dör*, as mentioned. And the King showed the Warrior the path that there is to the Sword and from there he attained his great strength.

And to me the King also showed the way to get my thing; I got from there what I need. (In other words the Prayer Leader, who is telling all this, said that the King showed him the way from which he should get his thing, namely, prayer.)

And likewise the King had a Faithful Friend [*Ohev Ne'eman*, lit. faithful one who loves] (in other words, *a gutn freund, a getreuen*: a good, trusty friend) who was in love with the King [*vas er hat sich lieb gehat mit dem melekh; she-hayah ohev eth `atzmo `im hamelekh, lit.* who loved himself with the King] with a very extraordinary love. They loved each other so much that it was utterly impossible for them to be one without seeing the other for some amount of time. But nonetheless there must be times when they need to be apart, so they had portraits in which both their images were depicted. They would delight themselves (in other words, take pleasure and satisfaction with) the portraits when they could not see each other. And the images depicted how the King and his Faithful Friend love each other and hug and kiss each other with great love. And the portraits had the special ability that whoever looked at the images attained great love (in other words, one received the trait of love when looking at the images). And the Faithful Friend also received the love (that is, the amorousness) from the place which the King showed him.

There came the time when they all went, each one to his place, to receive there his power for his thing — that is, the Orator, the Warrior, and all the King's people, each went up to his place to renew his power. And the day came to pass: there was a very great Storm Wind upon the world. And the Storm Wind mixed up the entire world, and overturned sea to dry land and dry land to sea, and wilderness to settled area and settled area to wilderness; so it overturned the entire world. And the Storm Wind went into the King's chamber and did nothing at all there (in other words, there at the King's it wrought absolutely no damage), except that the Storm Wind went in and snatched away the aforementioned Child of the Queen's Daughter. And amidst the commotion, as soon as the Storm Wind snatched away the dear Child, the Queen's Daughter followed [him] immediately (in other words, the Princess immediately started running after the Child in order to snatch him back; she too went off someplace no one knows where). So too the Queen, and so too the King: they all went after the Child, until they all became dispersed and no one knows where they are. But all of us were nowhere nearby during this, for we were gone away then, each to his place to renew his power, as mentioned; and when we came back we could no longer find them all, as mentioned. The **Hand** too became missing then.

So from that time on we have all become scattered and can no longer each go to his place to renew his power, for since the entire world has been overturned we now need different paths today; therefore we have no longer gone up each to his place to renew his power. However, the impression that remains by each of us (meaning the token, that is, the little bit that has remained by each one from long ago) is also very great — and if this mighty one (which the country feared) is the King's Warrior, he is certainly a very mighty warrior." (All this the Prayer Leader told the people.)

And they heard out his words and were very amazed, and now they held the Prayer Leader fast by him and would no longer let him go from them (because perhaps the warrior upon them is the King's Warrior mentioned above, with whom the Prayer Leader is acquainted).

[The Warrior's Guard Speaks]

And the aforementioned Warrior kept coming closer to the country, always sending his emissaries to them, until he reached the country. And he stationed himself below the city and sent his emissaries inside to them (for them to tell him what they want: to submit themselves or not, as above). They were very terrified of him and they begged the Prayer Leader that he should give them a suggestion. The Prayer leader told them it was necessary to inspect the conduct of this warrior in order for him to recognize thereby if this is the aforementioned Warrior of the King. The Prayer Leader left and went out towards the Warrior, and he reached the Warrior's army and began talking with one from among the Warrior's accompanying warriors (that is, with one of his sentries) (in order to examine if he is the Warrior with whom he is familiar). The Prayer Leader asked him, "What are your doings? And how have you gotten together with the Warrior?"

He answered him (that is, that same warrior replied to the Prayer Leader), "What took place was like this: It is written in their chronicles how there had been a great Storm Wind upon the world, changing sea to dry land and dry land to sea, and wilderness to settled area and settled area to wilderness, mixing up the entire world. And after the noise and upheaval, the entire world having become so mixed up, the world's people decided to make a king for themselves. They started to investigate who ought to be made king over them and they reasoned, 'Inasmuch as the essential thing is only the ultimate purpose [takhlith] therefore whoever most occupies himself with and exerts himself in the purpose of the world — he deserves to be king.' They began probing what is the purpose, and there arose several opinions among them.

One faction said that the main object is honor, for, 'We see that the world considers honor the main thing. Because when a person is not given his respect — that is, when some word is uttered against his honor — he experiences bloodshed, because the main thing is honor, for the entire world. And even after death people are careful to give to the dead his honor, burying him with respect and so forth (and telling him, 'What is being done for you is all being done on account of your honor'). Even though after death one no longer wants any money and the dead person certainly has no desire for anything, nevertheless they are particular about the dead's honor and they guard his honor. Therefore it is honor that is the main object. They continued saying more such conjectures and deductions of that sort, that honor is the main object of the world, until it became settled among them that the main purpose is honor. Therefore they needed to search for an honorable person (that is to say, a person who attains honor) and moreover the person should also pursue honor, for since he receives honor and pursues it, and assists [human] nature which desires honor, therefore this person exerts himself and pursues after the main goal and has reached it, because the goal is, after all, honor, as mentioned; therefore such a person deserves to be king." (All this was the foolish opinion of one sect of them; and so they found foolish conjectures and deductions until they became led astray therein and said that honor is the purpose.)

Likewise all the other factions that will appear below all had foolish reasonings for their foolish notions. (Heb. only: Some of them are explained below, but Rabbeinu z"l did not want to explain all the perplexed reasonings for these beliefs, because there are some rationales in this that are so convoluted that it is possible to indeed be led astray by these false rationales; the Merciful One spare us.)

They went searching for such a person and they went and saw an old Gypsy beggar being carried while following him were perhaps five hundred Gypsies. And the beggar was blind, hunchback and mute, and all these people followed him because they all were his relatives, for he had sisters, brothers, and seed of his loins, until there came to be so many of them, all of whom followed him and carried him. And the old beggar was very particular about his honor, for he was a very angry person and always heaped his great indignation upon them, always ordering that others should carry him and always scolding them. Hence this elderly beggar is a very 'honorable' man, because he has such an honor, and also pursues honor, because he is so strict over his honor. Therefore this beggar pleased them and they accepted him as a king. And because land also has an effect, for there is a land that engenders and is conducive to honor, and similarly there is a land that is specially suited for another trait, therefore this faction (which regarded honor as the main purpose) sought a country that engenders and is conducive to honor; and they found such a country that is conducive to it and they settled there.

One faction said that the main object is not honor, and they conceived that the main object is murder, for, 'We see that all the things that are found on the earth — grasses and all plants and people, and all that is in the entire world — must all ultimately cease to exist. Hence the very goal of all things is to be finished off (that is, destroyed). Therefore a murderer who kills and destroys people is really bringing the world to its purpose.' Therefore they came to the conclusion that the goal is murder. They looked for a person who would be a murderer; an angry person and an extremely vengeful person, for such a person is closest to the purpose (according to their deluded mindset) and he deserves to be king. They went looking for such a person and they heard a shriek. They asked, 'What is this, such a screech?!'

They replied to them this shriek is: someone has slaughtered his father and mother. They spoke up, 'Where else can one find such a stronghearted and angry murderer, that he should murder his own father and mother? This here man has reached the purpose (that is, the one who has slaughtered father and mother)!' And they were extremely pleased by him and they accepted him as a king over them. And they sought for themselves a country that causes (that is, brings about) murder and they chose a place among mountains where killers abide and they went there and settled there with their king.

A faction said that he deserves to be king who has a great abundance of food and does not eat the fare of other people but only fine foods (such as milk, so that his mind should not become coarse); such a person ought to be king. However, they could not immediately find such a person who would not eat the foods of other people. In the meantime they chose for themselves a rich man who had plenty of food (and whose food was a bit finer) until they would find such a person as they want, who would not eat etc. as above. And meanwhile they made the rich man into a king until they would find such a person as they want, as above; then the rich man would descend from the reign and the other one would be taken up as a king. And they chose for themselves a country suited for this and they went and settled there.

A faction said that a beautiful woman is fit to be king, for the main object is, after all, that the world should be inhabited with people, since for that reason the world was created. And since a beautiful woman brings about that desire, through which the habitation of the world grows greater (since more people come about), it follows she brings the world to the goal. Therefore a beautiful woman deserves to be king. They chose for themselves a beautiful woman and she became king over them. And they sought for themselves a land conducive to this, and they went there and settled there.

A faction said that the main object is speech, because the distinction between a man and a beast is only speech, and since that is the essential in which a man is greater than a beast, therefore it is the main purpose (that is, speech). They sought for themselves a speaker (that is, a talker) who would be eloquent and who would know many languages and would always talk a great deal all the time, for such a person is at the goal. They went and found a French lunatic who was going around and talking to himself. They asked him if he knows languages, and he knew several languages. Now such a man has certainly already reached the goal (according to their foolish deluded ideas), since he is a master of language, knows many languages and talks a great deal — for he talks even to himself, after all! Therefore they were very pleased by him and they accepted him as a king. And they chose for themselves a land conducive to this and they went and settled there with their king. And he surely led them on the straight path!

A faction said that the main purpose is happiness. For, when a boy is born, people are happy; when there is a wedding, people are happy; when conquering a country, people are happy. It follows that the main purpose of everything is only happiness. Therefore they sought a man who would always be happy, for he is, after all, at the goal, and he should be king over them. They went searching and they saw a gentile going along with a disgusting shirt and carrying a bottle of brandy while following him were several other gentiles. And this gentile was very happy because he was very drunk. They saw that this gentile is very happy and has no concern whatsoever, and they liked him very much, this gentile, because he has reached the goal, since the goal is only happiness. They accepted him as a king over them, and surely he led them on the right path! And they chose for themselves a land conducive to this, that is, where there are vineyards so that they should make wine, and from the seeds of the grapes they would make brandywine; and nothing whatsoever of the grape bunches should go to waste, because this for them was the main purpose: to drink and go drunk and always be happy, even though one doesn't know at all about what, for they had nothing at all to be happy about. Nevertheless it was the main purpose for them to be always happy. And they chose for themselves a land conducive to this, as above, and they went and settled there.

❝ A faction said that the main thing is wisdom. They sought for themselves a great sage and made him a king over them, and they sought for themselves a land conducive to wisdom and they went and settled there.

❝ A faction said that the main goal is to attend to oneself with food and drink, which is called *pilevin* [Yid. < Ger. *pflegen*], in order to enlarge his limbs [*evarim*]. And they sought a *ba`al evarim* [lit. master of limbs], that is, someone who has large limbs and nurses himself to grow his limbs (that is, the members of the body), for since he has big limbs he has, after all, a larger portion in the world because he takes up more space in the world. So this man is closer to the purpose because the purpose is, after all, to grow the limbs; therefore such a person ought to be a king. They went and found a tall man (which is called a *veynger* [Yid.]); they were pleased by him, because he has, after all, large limbs and is at the goal. They accepted him as a king and they sought a land conducive to this and they went and settled there.

❝ And there was a different group that said that all these things are no goal at all; instead the right purpose is to only be involved in prayer to Hashem Yithbarakh and to be a humble person and a lowly person etc. (in other words, one should not deem anything of oneself), etc. And they sought for themselves a prayer leader, and they made him a king over them."

(One will understand by himself already that all the previous factions were all gravely mistaken and deluded in great folly, each faction in their folly through their foolish hypotheses and foolish deductions. Only this last faction hit the truth proper — so, fortunate are they!)

All this was related by one of the strongmen before the Prayer Leader. And he went on to tell him that they (namely the strongmen who joined themselves to the Warrior as mentioned) — they are from the faction of the limb-masters mentioned above (that is, the faction that said that the main object is only to nurse oneself to grow his limbs) who had taken up as a king over themselves a master of limbs (that is, a large person, as mentioned).

"And the day came to pass, and a company [*machneh*, camp] of them were going along (in other words, a great deal of the ample-limbed people were going along) with wagons in train (which are called *ibez* [< Ukr. *oboz*, train]) bringing along food, drink and other such things. Now, of these large-limbed ones the world was certainly very afraid, for they were large and mighty men, and whoever encountered them was sure to step off the road. Meanwhile, as the camp of the ample-limbed was going along like that, up against them from the opposite direction came a big Warrior [lit. mighty one] (and this was the Warrior who now goes with them). And this Warrior did not step off the road for them and he went into the camp and dispersed them here and there, and the people of the camp were terrified of him. And he (that is, the Warrior) went inside among the aforementioned wagons which trailed behind them and ate up everything that was there. This was an extraordinary novelty to them (that he is such a mighty man that he is not afraid of them whatsoever and entered among them and ate up all that was on the wagons) so they immediately fell down before him, saying immediately, 'Hail [lit. live] the king (meaning they immediately made him a king)!' because he certainly deserves the reign, according to their notion that the main accomplishment is someone who is ample-limbed, as mentioned. And (their) king will certainly forgo the kingship for him because since he is so strong and so well-limbed that he certainly deserves the reign. And so it was: they took him up as king (that is, the Warrior who came against them, as mentioned). And this is the Warrior with whom we now go about conquering the world. But he says (that is, the Warrior who has now become king over them) that he means something else in his going about conquering the world, for he does not at all intend that the world should be under him; instead he means something else." (All this, one of the strongmen told the Prayer Leader who had asked him how they had joined the Warrior; he answered him all this.)

[The Prayer Leader and Warrior Reunite; the Prayer Faction]

Asked the Prayer Leader, "Wherein is the strength of the Warrior who is now your king?" He answered him, "Inasmuch as there was a country that did not want to submit themselves under him, the Warrior took his Sword which he has, and his Sword has three powers: when it is lifted, all the army officers flee" etc. (and he recounted the three powers explained above, from which the King's Warrior got his strength, as mentioned).

When the Prayer Leader heard this, he realized that this is definitely the King's Warrior mentioned above. The Prayer Leader asked if it were possible to be seen by the Warrior who is their king. They answered him it must be announced for approval before him. They went and announced, and he summoned that he should come in, and the Prayer Leader entered to the Warrior. When the Prayer Leader entered to the Warrior, they recognized each other and there was very great rejoicing between them over their being privileged to reunite together. And between them was rejoicing and crying (happiness and weeping), for they recalled the King and his men — they cried over that — therefore between them was rejoicing and crying. The Prayer Leader began to discuss with the Warrior by what experiences they had arrived here.

The Warrior told the Prayer Leader that from the time that there was the Storm Wind — when they all became dispersed — when he returned from where he went to renew his power and did not find the King with all his people, as mentioned, he then let himself go wherever he would go. And he passed by them all: that is, he understood he was at the place where the King is and where all his people are. That is, he was at a certain place and he understood that there is certainly where the King is found, however he was unable to seek and find him. And similarly he passed by another place, understanding that the Queen is certainly there, however he was unable to seek and find her; and thus he passed by all the King's people.

Only you have I not passed by!" (That is, the Warrior who is telling this said to the Prayer Leader that he passed by all the places of all the people; only the place of the Prayer Leader did he not pass by.)

The Prayer Leader replied to him saying, "I passed by all their places, and by your place as well. For, I was passing by a certain place and I saw the King's crown standing there and I understood that the King is certainly here, however I was unable to seek and find him. And so I went further and passed by a sea of blood and I understood that this sea is certainly made from the tears of the Queen who weeps over all this and the Queen is certainly here, however I could not seek and find her. And so I passed by a sea of milk and I understood that the sea is certainly made from the milk of the Queen's Daughter whose son was lost, and the milk pressured her and from this the sea of milk came to be; and the Queen's Daughter is certainly here, however I was unable to seek and find her. And so I went further and saw the golden hairs of the Child laid out, and I did not take from them whatsoever, and I knew that the Child is certainly here, however it was not possible to seek and find him. And so I went further and was passing by a sea of wine and I knew that this sea is certainly made from the speech of the Orator, who stands and speaks consolations before the King and the Queen, and then turns his face and speaks consolations to the Queen's Daughter, and from his speech the sea of wine comes to be (as written, '*Vechikekh keyayin hatov*/ And the roof of your mouth is like best wine' [Song 7:10]), however I could not find him. And so I went further, and I saw a stone standing there upon which was etched out just like the **Hand** with its ruts (that is, just like the Hand with all the furrows etc. which had been at the King's, as mentioned), and I understood that the Sage (of the King) is certainly here and the Sage has engraved for himself the shape of the **Hand** on the stone, but it was not possible to find him. And so I went further and I saw arranged on a mountain the golden tables, the credenzas [display cupboards] and the rest of the King's treasures, and I understood that the King's Treasurer [lit. Warden

Over the Treasures] is certainly here, however it was impossible to find him." (All this the Prayer Leader told over to the Warrior.)

Replied the Warrior, "I too passed by all these places, and I did take from the golden hair of the child, for I took seven hairs that had all sorts of colors, and they are very dear to me. And I settled down and sustained myself with whatever possible, with grass and so forth, until I had nothing whatsoever to sustain myself. I let myself go where I would go, and when I went away from my place, I forgot my bow there." The Prayer Leader replied, "I saw your bow! And I knew that it was certainly your bow, but I could not find you."

The Warrior went on telling the Prayer Leader that, "When I went away from the place, I went until I encountered the troops mentioned above (that is, the troop of the ample-limbed mighty men mentioned above), and I entered in their midst, because I was very hungry and wanted to eat; and as soon as I entered among them they immediately took me up as a king, as mentioned. And now I go conquering the world, and my intention is: perhaps I will be able to find the King and his people mentioned above."

The Prayer Leader began discussing with the Warrior: "What to do with these people!?" That is, with the country that is so fallen into craving money until they have gone out to such extraordinary folly that those who have much money are gods for them; and so forth the other follies the country has.

The Warrior answered the Prayer Leader that he had heard from the King that one can take out from any craving someone who has fallen into it except someone who has fallen in the lust for money; it is impossible to extract him from it by any means. "Therefore you will have no effect on them whatsoever, for it is impossible to extract them from this at all. Albeit through the way that there is to the Sword mentioned above" — from where he gets his power as mentioned — "only through this way can one extract from the lust of money someone who has sunk into it." (So he had heard from the King.)

The Warrior remained together with the Prayer Leader for a while, and as for the country which had beseeched the Prayer Leader that he should go out to the Warrior on their behalf, as mentioned, they extended the time. That is, the Prayer

Leader convinced the Warrior that he should give them a span (that is, until which he should do nothing at all to them). He alloted them time, then they made signs between themselves, that is, the Prayer Leader and the Warrior exchanged signs so that one would be able to get information from the other, then the Prayer Leader went off on his way.

As the Prayer Leader went on he saw people going along and entreating God, Blessed is He, praying and carrying prayer books. He was afraid of them and they were frightened of him too. He stood to pray, and they also stood to pray. Then he asked them, "Who are you?" They answered him, "Inasmuch as when there was the Storm Wind, the world separated into many factions, these choosing this thing, and those choosing that thing (just as all the different factions are explained above). At that time we chose for ourselves that the main purpose is only to be constantly involved in prayer to Hashem Yithbarakh. We sought and found a master of prayer and made him a king."

When the Prayer Leader heard this it pleased him exceptionally, for this is what he himself wants. He began to talk with them and showed them the order of his prayers and his books and his ideas he had regarding prayers. When they heard his talk their eyes opened and they saw the greatness of the Prayer Leader. They immediately made him a king over them, for their king deferred the kingship to him since they saw that he is quite a great man [Heb. that he is set apart on a very, very high level]. The Prayer Leader taught them and opened their eyes and showed them how pray to Hashem Yithbarakh, and he made them into very great complete tzaddikim, for they had been tzaddikim before as well since they had involved themselves only in prayer, albeit the Prayer Leader opened their eyes until they became extremely great tzaddikim. The Prayer Leader sent a letter to the Warrior and informed him how he was privileged and had found such people as he wants and had become king over them.

[The Treasurer (The Warden Over the Treasures)]

Now the aforementioned country (that is, the wealthy land for whom money was the main object etc. as mentioned) continued occupying themselves with their devotions (that is, they kept doing wild things and offering sacrifices to their gods, that is, to those who had much money, as mentioned), and the time that the Warrior had granted them was already about to run out. They were very frightened and they did their devotions and offered sacrifices and incense and involved themselves in their prayers which they prayed to their gods. They caught a "little critter" [a *chayeleh*], that is, such a person who has little money, and offered him for a sacrifice to their gods. And it remained their opinion that they must perform their first plan which they had been given, that they should send to the country where they are all gods there, because they have very extraordinary riches there (which according to their opinion entails that they are all gods) and that country would certainly save them, since they are all gods after all, as mentioned. They did so, and they sent emissaries there to that country.

Meanwhile on the way as the emissaries were going they went astray and they noticed a man walking with a stick, whose stick came to more than all their gods. That is, his stick was set with very expensive diamonds so that the stick was worth more than the riches of all their gods. Should one put together all the riches of their gods and even of the gods of that country they're going to, the stick would be worth more than all their riches. Furthermore the man was walking with a hat in which there were diamonds so that the hat was also worth extraordinarily much. As soon as the emissaries noticed this man they immediately fell down before him in kneeling and prostration (that is, they bowed profusely before him), because according to their foolish opinion this man is a god over all gods, for he has such extraordinarily great riches. (And this man whom they encountered was the King's Treasurer mentioned above.)

The man said to them, "This here is a novelty for you!? Come with me — *I'll* show you riches!" He led them atop the mountain where the King's treasury was laid out in order and he showed them the treasure. As soon as they saw the treasure they immediately fell down with bowing and prostration, because he is, after all, a god over all gods (according to their foolish and deluded opinion, as for them the essence of creed was money, as mentioned). Albeit they brought no sacrifices, for in accordance with their belief that he is such a god etc. they certainly would have offered themselves to him, however (when these emissaries went out) the emissaries were warned that on the way they should offer no sacrifices, for they were afraid that should they want to offer sacrifices along the way, none of them would remain, for maybe one of them will find a treasure on the road. Maybe one of them will enter an outhouse and find a treasure there (Heb. only: which would be a god for him); he will want to sacrifice himself to it, and none of them will remain; therefore the country warned the emissaries that on the way they should offer no sacrifices whatsoever. [Heb. only: Therefore these emissaries did not offer sacrifices to this aforementioned Warden. But this was clear for them: that he was a god over all gods, since he possessed such astounding and vast wealth.]

The emissaries came to the decision: Why should they any longer go to those other gods, that is, to the country they were sent to, where they are greatly wealthy people whom they considered to be gods? Isn't it better that this man will surely be able to better help them, for he is, after all, a god above all of them (according to their crazed notion), since he has such extraordinary, great riches more than them all (many, many times over)? Therefore they beseeched this man that he should go with them into their country. He was amenable with them and went with them and entered their country. There was a great celebration in the country, that they had acquired such a god, for they were already sure now that through him they would have a deliverance, for he is such a god, since he has, after all, such great fortune. The man (who was the King's Treasurer, as mentioned, who was accepted by the countrymen as God) ordered that until there would be a proper order in the country, no one in the meantime should offer any sacrifices. (For this Warden was in fact a great tzaddik, for he was of the King's people, who were all very great tzaddikim. The Warden certainly loathed the foolish practices of the country but he was still incapable of leading them out of their evil way; however, for the time being he ordered them that in any case no sacrifices should be brought.) The countrymen started beseeching him regarding the aforementioned Warrior of whom they were very terrified, and the Warden also replied to them, "Could this be the Warrior (whom he knows)?"

The Warden got up and went out to the Warrior and asked the Warrior's people if it were possible to be seen by him, and

they said they would announce it. They announced it. He ordered
[for] him [to be] let in, and the Warden entered before the Warrior. They recognized each other, and there was celebration and
crying between them, as above (that is, they were very happy that
they were privileged to find each other but they still wept very
much: how can the rest of the aforementioned people be brought
as well?). The Warrior spoke up to the Warden, "Our kosher
Prayer Leader is also here, and I have already seen him, and he
has already become a king!" (Heb. only: And they told each other
how it had evolved that they arrived here.) The Warden told the
Warrior that he had passed by everyone, that is, by the King's
place and all the aforementioned people; only by the two of them
did he not pass, that is, by the place of the Prayer Leader and the
Warrior he did not pass. The Warden talked with the Warrior
about the country that has become so errant and so deluded in
money that they have fallen into such nonsense.

The Warrior answered the Warden that which he had told the
Prayer Leader, that he had heard from the King that whoever has fallen into the craving of money cannot be taken out of it
by any means except by that way as mentioned. Again they extended time: that is, the Warden convinced the Warrior that he
should give the country yet another date. The Warrior gave them
another date. Then they made signals between themselves — the
Warden and the Warrior — and the Warden went away from the
Warrior and returned to that country. (Now, the Warden certainly kept rebuking them severely over their evil way in which
they had become so abased in (craving) money, but he could not
lead them out of it, since they were already very deep-rooted in it.
But nonetheless since the Prayer Leader and the Warden had
talked with them very much, they had already become a little
confused and kept saying, "Aderaba (Just the reverse)! Take us
out of it!" Even though they still held themselves fast in their foolish notion and did not want [to get] out of their nonsense at all,
nevertheless they kept saying when they were rebuked, "Aderaba
— if it is indeed so that we are mistaken, please (na) take us out
of our error!")

The Warden replied to them, "I will give you a suggestion
(against the Warrior). I know the Warrior's power and from
where he gets his strength." And he told them the matter of the

Sword, mentioned above, from where the Warrior gets his strength. "Therefore I will go with you to the place of the Sword, and by this you will be able to stand up against the Warrior (for you will also get strength from there)." And the Warden's intention was: when they arrive at the Sword's place they will already be out from their money craving (for by means of that way to the Sword, thereby a person gets out of the money craving, as mentioned). The country accepted his advice and sent their magnates who to them were gods and they went together with the Warden to the Sword. (And the gods, that is, their magnates who went with the Warden, certainly went dressed in gold and silver jewelry since this was the main thing for them). So they went together, the Warden and the country's magnates whom they called gods.

[To the Place of the Sword, and the Conclusion]

The Warden made the thing known to the Warrior, inasmuch as he is going with them to seek the place of the Sword and his intention is maybe he will be privileged on the way to find the King and his people. The Warrior replied, "I too will go with you." The Warrior disguised himself (so that the people going with the Warden should not know that he himself is the Warrior) and also went with the Warden. They decided (the Warden and the Warrior) they would inform the Prayer Leader of this as well. They informed him, and The Prayer Leader replied he will also go with them. The Prayer Leader went to them and the Prayer Leader ordered his people before he went away that they should pray about this, that Hashem Yithbarakh should make their venture successful; that they should be privileged to find the King and his people. For the Prayer Leader had always kept praying about this, that the King and his people should be found, and always kept ordering his people that they should also pray about this, and he had composed prayers for them which they should pray for this; and now that he wanted to go the Warden and the Warrior so that they should go together to search for the King and his people, he urged them even more to pray for it constantly that they should be privileged to find them. The Prayer Leader came to the Warden and the Warrior and there was certainly great rejoicing among them — celebration and weeping, as before. They, all three, went together, that is, the Warden, the Warrior and the

Prayer Leader, with the "gods," that is, the country's magnates (who were called "gods" in their country) going with them.

They went and went, and they came to a certain country, and there were guards there standing around the country. They asked the sentries, "What sort of country is this, and who is your king?" The guards replied: Inasmuch as when there was the Storm Wind, at which time the world became separated into numerous factions (that is, into many opinions, as each sect had a different opinion, as mentioned), then the people of the country chose for themselves that the main thing is wisdom, and they took up for themselves a great sage as a king. Not long ago they found quite an exceptionally great wise man, who is strangely an extraordinarily great sage. The king relinquished the kingship to him and they took him up as king, since for them the main thing was wisdom. The three of them said (that is, the Warden, the Warrior and the Prayer Leader) that it appears that this must be our Sage (that is, the King's Sage). They asked if it were possible to be seen by him, and they answered them, "It must be announced." They went and announced, and he ordered them to come in. They (that is, the three of them) entered in to the Sage, who had become king in the country. They recognized each other, for this sage was indeed the King's Sage mentioned earlier. There was certainly great celebration there — rejoicing and weeping, for they wept, "How to be privileged to find the King and the others as well?!"

They asked the Sage if he knows anything about the King's Hand. He answered them that the Hand is with him, but since the time that they had become dispersed by the Storm Wind — from that time onward he does not want to gaze at the Hand at all, because the Hand belongs exclusively to the King. Albeit, he had carved out the Hand's form on a stone in order to use it a little for his thing (i.e. wisdom); but upon the Hand itself he doesn't look at all.

They discussed with the Sage how he had come here, and he told them that since the time the Storm Wind happened, he went where he would go (and as he went he passed by everyone [Heb. only: of the King's people]; only by the three of them, that is, by the place of the Prayer Leader, the Warrior, and the Warden he did not pass by), until this country found him and took him up as a king; and now in the meantime he must guide them according to their way, according to their sophistries, until later he will lead them out to the truth proper.

They talked with the Sage regarding that country that had become so deluded about money, etc., and they said, "If we had been thrown around and dispersed for nothing more than on account of that country, in order that we should correct them and turn them to the truth, it would also be worth it, for they have become so deluded." Because in truth, all the aforementioned factions, each one having chosen its nonsense, this one wanting honor, and this one murder, etc. — they have all become deluded and need to be led out to the proper goal. For even the sect that had chosen for itself that the main thing is wisdom, they too have not reached the true purpose and also need to be led out from that, for they have clung to alien and heretical wisdoms. Still, one can more easily lead [people] out of all [the other] follies, except these ones are so deluded in the idolism of money and are so fallen into it that it is impossible to extract them from it. And the Sage also replied to them that he too had heard from the King that it is possible to extract someone who has fallen into any craving, but from the craving of money it is impossible to extract, other than by the way that there is to the Sword, as mentioned. The Sage said he too would go with them, and they all four went along, and the "gods" (that is, the wealthy ones of the country) went with them too.

They came to a certain country and they also asked the watchmen, "What sort of country is this and who is your king?" They answered them: Inasmuch as when the Storm Wind occurred, then the people of this country chose for themselves that the main purpose is speech. They took up an eloquent talker as a king. Later they found quite a superb, eloquent bard and orator; they accepted him as a king, because the king relinquished the kingdom to him because he is so eloquent. They realized, "This must surely be our King's Orator." They also asked if it were possible to be seen by the king. They answered them, "We must announce it." They announced it, and he ordered that they should come in. They entered to the king, and that was the King's Orator. They recognized each other, and there was also great rejoicing and weeping between them. The Orator also went with them as well and they went further in search; maybe they would find the rest of them, for they saw that Hashem Yithbarakh is helping them; that they successively find their friends. And they attributed all this to the merit of their kosher Prayer Leader who is always praying for this, and through his prayers they were privileged to always find their friends. They went onward; maybe they will find the rest in addition [noch].

They went along and they came to a certain country, and they also asked, "What sort of country is this and who is your king?" They answered them that they are of the faction that had chosen for itself that the main goal is to go drunk and be happy. They had taken up for themselves some drunkard as a king because he is always happy, but later they found a man sitting in a sea of wine and he pleased them very much more, because this is certainly a very big drunkard, for he's seated in a sea of wine. They took him up as a king. They also asked to interview with him and they [the guards] went and announced it. They entered to the king, and this was the King's Faithful Friend who had been sitting in the sea of wine that had come about from the talk of the Orator who consoles them, as mentioned. (And the countrymen reasoned that he is a great drunk since he sits in a sea of wine, so they took him up as a king.) When they entered to him, they recognized each other, and between them was a great rejoicing and weeping, as before. And the Faithful Friend went with them as well.

They went onward and came to a certain country. They asked the watchmen, "Who is your king?" They answered that their king is a beautiful woman, insofar as she leads to the goal, because the goal is habitation of the world (that is, that the world should be inhabited with people, as mentioned). And initially they had a beautiful woman as a queen; then they found a beauty who is a very exceptional beauty and they accepted her as a queen. They realized: this must surely be the Queen's Daughter. They also asked to interview with her, and they went and announced, and they entered to the queen and recognized that this is the Queen's Daughter herself. And the rejoicing that was there is certainly unimaginable. They asked, "How have you come here?"

She told them that after the Storm Wind happened and had snatched away the dear boy-Child out of the crib as men-

tioned, immediately in that frantic moment she ran after the
Child but did not find him. The milk pressured her and from this
the sea of milk came about. Then the country found her and accepted her as king over them. And there was a great celebration
there. But they also wept severely over the dear boy-Child who's
not there, and over her father and mother whom she [the Queen's
Daughter] doesn't know about. But now already the country has a
king too, because already here is the husband of the Queen's
Daughter who has become queen here — for the Warrior himself
is her man — so now the country has a king!

The Queen's Daughter asked the Prayer Leader for the time
being to go in her country and meanwhile cleanse of their re-
pulsive vice, because since for them the main purpose was a beautiful woman, they were certainly very defiled and deep in this
lust, therefore she asked the Prayer Leader to meanwhile go
cleanse them of it a little in the meantime (that is, he should tell
them *mussar*/exhortation, so that they should not be so deep in
this craving of promiscuity), so that they should not be so crude in
this vice, because beyond it being a craving, it was additionally
for them just like a creed that this is the goal (because all the factions that had each chosen its bad thing as the purpose, as mentioned — for each of them the thing was just as a creed that this
is the purpose), therefore she asked the Prayer Leader to go and
cleanse them a little in the meantime.

Then they all went searching for the rest. They went along
and they came to a certain country, and they also inquired,
"Who is your king?" They answered them that their king is a one
year old, for they are from the faction that had chosen for themselves that whoever has an abundance of food and is not nourished from what other people eat — he deserves to be a king.
They temporarily accepted a wealthy man as king. Then they
found a man who was sitting in a sea of milk, and they were very
pleased by him, because this man was nourished his whole life
from milk and was not nourished from what other people eat,
therefore they took him up as a king. And for that reason he is
called a *"ben shanah*/ one-year-old," since he lives on milk like a
one year old. They realized that this is surely their Child. They
requested to interview with him; and they went and announced.
They entered to him and they recognized each other, for he also

recognized them, even though he was only a little child when he was snatched away — nevertheless because he was a mature sage since his birth, since he was born with a complete wisdom, as mentioned, therefore he recognized them; and they of course recognized him. There was certainly a very great celebration there, albeit they still wept that they did not know of the King and the Queen. And they asked him, "How did you get here?"

He told them that when the Storm Wind had snatched him away, it carried him away where it carried him and he was there in that place and sustained himself with what he found there, until he came to the sea of milk. He understood that this sea was certainly made from his mother's milk, for the milk certainly pressured her, and that is how the sea came about. He settled there on the sea of milk and was nourished by the milk until these countrymen came and took him up as a king.

Then they went onward and came to a country. And they asked, "Who is your king?" And they replied that they had chosen for themselves that murder is the goal. They accepted a certain murderer as king, then they found a woman sitting in a sea of blood, so they took her up as a king, because they saw that she is surely a very great murderer since she is seated in an ocean of blood. They also asked to interview with her, and they went and announced. They entered to her, and this was the aforementioned Queen who keeps crying constantly and her tears come to be the sea of blood as mentioned. They recognized each other, and there was certainly a very great celebration there, albeit they still wept that they still did not know about the King.

They went onward and came to a certain country. They asked, "Who is your king?" They replied that they had chosen for themselves as a king a certain honorable person (that is, a person who has honor, as mentioned), because for them the main purpose is honor. Then they found sitting in a field an old man wearing a crown on his head. They were extremely pleased by him, for he is a dignitary, for he sits in a field adorned with a crown, and they accepted him as king. They realized that this is certainly their King himself, and they also asked if it were possible to be seen by him. They went and announced, and they entered to him and recognized that he is the King himself. And the rejoicing that was there is certainly inconceivable in the brain. And the foolish "gods" (that is, the very wealthy ones from the land of riches who went with them) are traveling with them, and they do not know whatsoever for their lives what is happening here, why there is such happiness here.

And now the entire holy group was restored and gathered together united: that is, the King and the holy people. They sent the Prayer Leader to all the countries (that is, the countries of all the factions that had each chosen for itself a bad thing as a goal, as mentioned) to correct them and cleanse them; to lead them out of their error, each country out of its vice and its nonsense, for they had all become deluded, as mentioned, and now the Prayer Leader definitely had the power to go to them and turn them around to the right way, for he had received power and permission from the kings of all the lands, since here were all their kings, as mentioned (because the King and his people who had come together — they all were the kings of all the lands of the factions mentioned above). The Prayer Leader went, with their authority, to cleanse them and bring them back in *teshuvah* (repentance), while the Warrior spoke with the King regarding the country that is so fallen in the idolism of money. The Warrior said to the King, "I heard from you that through the way that I have to the Sword — through it, it is possible to extract someone who has fallen in the idolism of money."

The King answered him, "Yes, it is so." The King told the Warrior (the thing, just how through that way one can take them out of the craving of money): Inasmuch as on the way where he goes to the Sword there is a way on the side; by this way one comes to a Fiery Mountain, and on this Mountain crouches a Lion. And the Lion, when he needs to eat, goes and falls on the flocks and takes for himself sheep and cattle and eats them up. And the shepherds know of this and guard the sheep intensely from him, yet the Lion does not look at this whatsoever — just whenever he wants to eat he falls on the flocks, and the shepherds bang and strike and storm at him, however the Lion does not hear this at all; he just takes sheep and cattle for himself and roars and eats them. And the Mountain of Fire is entirely invisible (in other words, there, there is a Mountain of Fire, only, one doesn't see it).

And moreover, from the side there is yet another way; with this way one comes to a place called *"Kech"* (Kitchen). And there in that Kitchen there are all sorts of food, and in the Kitchen there is no fire whatsoever; rather, the foods are cooked by way of the Fiery Mountain mentioned above. And the Fiery Mountain is very far from there, but channels and pipes go from the Fiery Mountain to the Kitchen, and thereby all the foods are cooked. And the Kitchen too is not seen at all, but there is a sign: standing there are Birds upon the Kitchen, and by them one knows that the Kitchen is there. And the Birds hover with their wings, and thereby they kindle the fire and put out the fire, that is, by the Birds' flapping they blow on and inflame the fire, and also by their very flapping they put out the fire so that the fire should not flame too strongly, more than necessary. And they blow on the fire according to what is necessary for the foods, that is, for one food is needed such a fire, and for another food is needed a different fire — all according to the food, so do the Birds blow on the fire. (All this the King tells the Warrior.)

“ Therefore lead them (that is, these people from the Land of Riches who are "gods" there) first against the wind, so that the smell of the foods should get to them. Then when you give them from the foods they will definitely just cast away the craving of money."

The Warrior did so, and took these people, that is, the magnates from the Land of Riches who are gods in their country, who came here with the Warden, as mentioned. Now, when they left their country with the Treasurer, the countrymen gave them power that whatever they do shall be done and the whole country must abide by whatever they do. The Warrior took the people and led them on the way (which the King told him, as mentioned) and he brought them up until the Kitchen where the foods are. And first he led them against the wind and the smell of the foods went to them and they began begging him intensely to give them from these good foods. Then he led them [away] from the wind and they began to scream, "There is a tremendous stench!" He again brought them against the wind and again the good smell of the foods reached them and again they begged intensely that he should give them from the foods, then he again led them [away] from the wind and they again began to scream, "It stinks unbelievably (lit. very wildly)!"

The Warrior responded to them, "Don't you see that there is nothing whatsoever here that should have a bad smell? It must certainly be that you yourselves make the stench, for here there is nothing that should have a bad smell." Then he gave them from the foods. As soon as they ate of these foods they immediately began to cast away from themselves their money, and each one dug for himself a grave and buried himself in the pit due to the great disgrace, as they were intensely ashamed, for they felt that money stinks intensely (Heb. only: which smells like actual feces) because they had tasted of the foods. And they scratched their faces and buried themselves and could not lift their faces at all, and each one was ashamed in front of the other (because such is the special power [*segulah*] of the foods, that whoever eats of the foods is very repulsed by money) because there in that place money is the greatest disgrace of all disgraces, and when someone wants to say something derogatory about another (lit. throw something out at another) he throws out at him, "You have money," for money there is a huge disgrace, and the more money someone has, the more he is ashamed, therefore they buried themselves out of great disgrace, and each of them was unable to lift his face even in front of the other; even more so in front of the Warrior. And whoever still found with himself some *gilden* or *grush* would rid himself of it immediately and throw it away from himself. Then the Warrior came to them and took them out of their pits that they had dug for themselves there out of disgrace, and he said to them, "Come with me, because now you need no longer have any fear of the Warrior, for I myself am the Warrior!" They begged the Warrior to give them from the foods, to bring to their country, because they themselves would surely just hate money, however, they wanted the whole country to go out from this money craving.

The Warrior gave them from these foods and they brought the foods into their country, and as soon as they gave them from these foods they all immediately began to cast away their money and buried themselves in the earth out of disgrace; and the very wealthy and the gods were most ashamed, but even the lesser people who were called "animals" and "birds" by them were also ashamed for having been so little until now in their own eyes because they had no money, because now they knew that on the contrary it's just the reverse: money is the main disgrace. For these foods have such an effect, that whoever eats from the foods is very repulsed by money, for he senses the bad smell of money, just like feces exactly. They all cast away their money and their gold and silver. Then they sent them the Prayer Leader and he gave them *teshuvoth* [ways to make amends and return to God] and *tikkunim* [repairs; remedies], and he cleansed them. And the King became king over the entire world, and the entire world returned to God, Blessed be He, and they all were involved only in Torah, prayer, *teshuvah* and good deeds. Amen, so be His will. Blessed is Hashem for eternity, Amen and Amen.

[Notes Following the Story]

T he verse states that Hashem Yithbarakh has an oven in one place and fire in a different place, distant from the oven, as written [Isa. 31:9], *"Ne'um-Hashem asher-ur lo beTziyon wethanur lo Birushalaim/* Says Hashem, Whose fire is in Tziyon and His furnace in Yerushalaim;"* see there the entire chapter, which speaks of this whole story. *"Hoi hayordim Mitzrayim le`ezrah, `al-susim yisha`enu/* Woe to those who descend to Egypt for assistance and rely on horses... *uMitzrayim adam welo-El, wesuseihem basar welo-ruach/* The Egyptians are men and not God, and their horses flesh and not spirit"* — alluding to the country that the Land of Riches relied on to save them, for according to their mistaken beliefs they considered them all gods and their horses angels, as explained above in the story; see there. This is why the verse concludes, *"uMitzrayim adam welo-El, wesuseihem basar welo-ruach"* etc. Understand this.

" *...Washem yateh yado, wekashal `ozer wenafal `azur, yachdaw kulam yikhlayun/* So when Hashem shall stretch out his hand, both he that helped shall stumble and he that was helped shall fall; they shall all perish together"* — alluding to the Hand, for on the Hand they saw that both together would perish, the helper and the helped, as mentioned.

" *...Ka'asher yehgeh ha'aryeh wehakfir `al-tarpo, asher yikare `alaw melo ro`im/* Like as the lion, or the young lion, growling over his prey, though a band of shepherds be called

forth against him" etc. and "*Ketziporim `afoth* / Like flying birds"
— alluding to the Lion and the Birds mentioned. Take a good look
above inside the story and understand. "*Ki bayom hahu yim'asun
ish elilei khaspo we'elilei zehavo* / For on that day each man will
detest his silver idols and gold idols" etc.

    *Wenafal Ashur becherev lo-ish... wenas lo mipnei-cherev...
wesal`o mimagor ya`avor* / And Assyria shall fall by the
sword not of man... and shall flee from the sword... and his rock
shall disappear from fear" — alluding to the three powers of the
Sword in the story. *Wenafal* and *wenas* allude to two of the powers. And *wesal`o mimagor ya`avor* alludes to the illness of *dör*,
where one's strength and power wither and disappear, for *sal`o*
refers to their strength; this alludes to the third power of the
Sword. Take a good look and understand. Then the verse con-
cludes, *Ne'um-Hashem asher-ur lo beTziyon wethanur lo Birusha-
laim* — these are the furnace and fire in the story. Look and see
and understand how this chapter explains the entire story. (All
the above were the Rebbe's words.) And thus said the Rebbe explicitly, that the entire story from beginning to end is alluded to
in entirety in this chapter [i.e. Isa. 31] and he said that all the
words of the story can be found in Scriptures and so forth. But the
essence of the story is all stated in the above chapter, for there it
is all explained and alluded to entirely. However, we do not know
how, beyond what the Rebbe revealed to us explicitly (that is,
what is explained above). Still, the rest of the matters of the story
we were not privileged to perceive how they are hinted in that
chapter, but he stated explicitly that the entire story is alluded to
there.

    For instance, "*Wetime'them eth-tzipui pesilei khaskpekha
we'eth-apudath masekhath zehavekha; tizrem kemo davah, tze
tomar lo* / You shall defile your graven images overlaid with silver,
and the adornment of your golden molten image; you shall put
them far away as an unclean thing; 'Go away,' you shall say to it"
[ibid. 30:22]. And as written [ibid. 2:20-21], "*Bayom hahu yash-
likh ha'adam eth elilei kaspo we'eth elilei zehavo... lachpor
peroth... lavo beniqroth hatzurim* / On that day, a man will cast
away his gods of silver and his gods of gold... digging ditches... to
go into the clefts of rocks," that is, they will cast away the craving
of money, which is actual idolatry, and bury themselves in

ditches, etc., as explained in the story. Because money stinks like actual feces, as written, *"tizrem kemo davah/* you will put them far away as an unclean thing; *'TzE'/* Go away' [akin to *TzO'AH,* feces], *tomar lo/* you shall say to it." And so forth one can find all the words of the story in the Scriptures, etc.)

The order of the King and his men is as follows: The Prayer Leader and the Warrior; the Warden and the Sage; the Orator and the Faithful Friend; the Queen's Daughter and her Child; the King and the Queen. That is their order, and they correspond to `Olam haTikkun/* the World of Repair. And they are ten things, but they are not reckoned in order, that is, these ten are not reckoned according to the order explained in books of kabbalah. But there are hidden things behind this. It is also explained in the books that when the influx of one attribute passes through another attribute, when the influx tarries there then it is named after that attribute. That is, the attribute in which is tarrying the influx of another attribute that is passing through it, that attribute is named after the attribute from which that influx is coming. And because of this the order here is changed. There are also other matters in this, which will be very clear to those who are adept in the books. The Rebbe z"l said all this explicitly.

I also understood from his words that *Mitath haMelakhim* ["Death of the Kings;" shattering of the pre-Creation sefirot] and their repair is alluded to in this story, although neither the aspect of their destruction nor the aspect of their rebuilding are mentioned as the order of the ten aforementioned aspects, for the same reasons above. But still the things are hidden and sealed, because the utmost secret of the story he did not reveal at all; he only enlightened our eyes with the verses and ideas above so that we should know that there are very great and awesome hidden secrets in the story. But we do not know the extent. Fortunate is one who is privileged to understand a bit of the secrets of these stories explained in this book, because they are all extremely wondrous and awesome novelties; *"Amok `amok, mi yimtza'enu/* Deep, deep; who can find it out?" [Eccl. 7:24] *"Mah nomar... mah nedaber/* What shall we say... what shall we speak?" [Gen. 44:16] *"Mi-shama` kazoth, mi ra'ah ka'eleh/* Who has heard such a thing? Who has seen such things?" [Isa. 66:8]

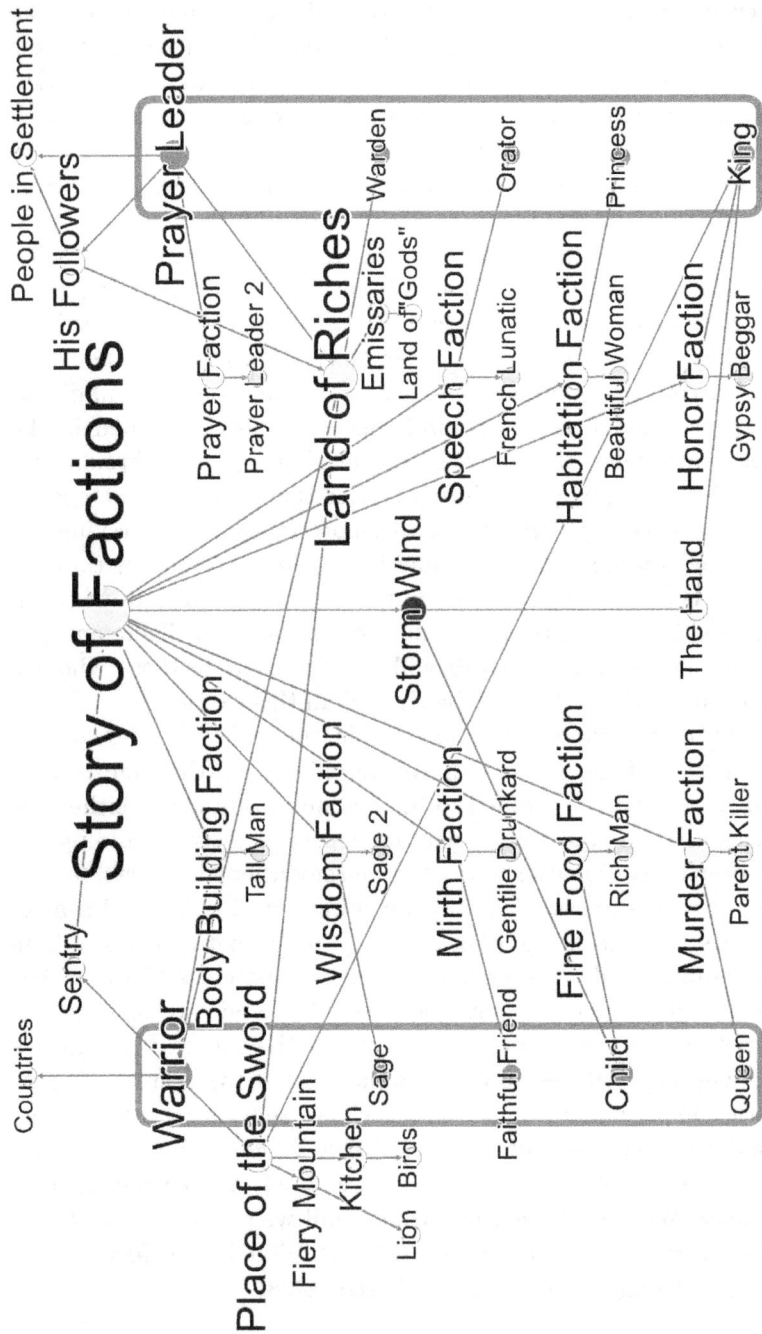

Story of Factions

Countries

Sentry

Place of the Sword

Warrior

Body Building Faction

Tall Man

Wisdom Faction

Sage 2

Sage

Fiery Mountain

Kitchen

Lion Birds

Mirth Faction

Storm Wind

Gentile Drunkard

Faithful Friend

Fine Food Faction

Rich Man

Child

Murder Faction

Parent Killer

Queen

People in Settlement

Prayer Leader

His Followers

Prayer Faction

Prayer Leader 2

Land of Riches

Emissaries

Warden

Land of "Gods"

Speech Faction

Orator

French Lunatic

Habitation Faction

Princess

Beautiful Woman

Honor Faction

King

Gypsy Beggar

The Hand

Tale 13: The Seven Beggars

[Introduction]

I'll tell you about being happy!

[THE KING WHO TRANSFERRED HIS KINGDOM TO HIS SON DURING HIS LIFETIME]

A tale. Once there was a King who had an only son. The King wanted to transfer the kingdom to his son during his lifetime, so he threw a grand party (which they call a "ball"). Now, when the King throws a ball there is certainly great merriment, so especially now that he was transferring the kingdom to his son during his lifetime, there was certainly a very great celebration. And there at the ball were all the royal officers and all the dukes and gentry, and people were very merry at the ball. And the country too was enjoying this — the king's transferring his kingdom to his son in his lifetime — for it is a great honorific event for the King. So a very great celebration took place there, and there were all types of festivities there: song groups, drama groups and so forth, as well as everything useful just for merriment — it was all there at the ball.

And when they had waxed very merry, the King got up and said to his son, "Being that I am a stargazer, I see that you will at some time fall from the kingship. Therefore see to it that you have no sadness (that is, no grief) when you fall from reign; just be happy. And if you will be happy, I will also be happy. Even if you will have sadness I will still be happy that you are not king, since you are not fit to be king if you cannot keep yourself happy. (In other words, if you are the kind of man that you cannot keep yourself happy even when you fall from reign then you aren't fit to be any sort of king). But when you will be happy then I will be extraordinarily happy."

The King's son took over the reign very sharply, appointing his own royal officers, and he had dukes, gentry and soldiers. Now, this son of the King was a clever person and loved wisdom very much, and very great intellectuals accompanied him. And whoever came to him with some sort of wisdom was very esteemed by him, and he would grant them honor and riches for their wisdom. Whatever each one wanted, he gave him: one wanted money — he gave him money; another wanted honor — he gave him honor; anything for wisdom. And because studying was so important to him, they all took to wisdom and the entire country was occupied with philosophies [*chokhmoth*], because this one desired money — in order to get money for it [being his motive] — and that one desired status and honor. And because all of them were busy only with philosophies, therefore they all forgot there in that country the strategies of war (in other words, how to wage a war), for they were all busy exclusively with philosophies, to such a degree that the smallest person in that country was the greatest sage in another country, while their own wise men were utterly wild scholars. And on account of their philosophies those wise men of the country fell into heresy and drew the son of the King too into their heresy. Albeit the simple folk were not harmed and did not become disbelievers, for there was great depth and subtlety in the sages' wisdom, so the common folk were not able to enter into their wisdoms, therefore it did not harm them. Only the wise men and the King's son became heretics.

And the King's son, because there was good in him, for he was born with goodness and had good character traits, would frequently remind himself, "Where am I in the world? What am I doing?" etc. and would make a very big groan and sigh deeply over it. He would ponder, "What is this? I should be carried away with such things?! What's going on with me? Where am I in this world?" as he kept sighing intensely. Albeit as soon as he began to use his intellect the heretical philosophy became strong again in him. This happened numerous times, that he would still contemplate where he is in the world, what he is doing, etc. as above, with groaning and sighing — but as soon as he began using his intellect the heretical belief became strong in him again, as above.

[THE EXODUS, AND THE BOY AND GIRL GET LOST; THE BEGGARS COME AND FEED THEM]

And the day came to pass — there was a flight in a certain country — everyone fled, and as they were fleeing they went through a forest, losing two children there, a male and a female; someone lost a male and someone lost a female. And they were still little children of four or five years and did not have anything to eat, and they screamed and cried because they had nothing to eat. Meanwhile there came up to them a beggar going along with his sacks (which are called *torbes*), carrying bread in them, and these children started to nudge him and huddle after him. He gave them bread and they ate. He asked them, "Where have you come here from?" They answered him, "We don't know," for they were little children. And he started going away from them and they asked him to take them with him. He said to them, "This I do not want, that you should go with me." Meanwhile they took a look — the beggar is blind! It was a marvel for them: since he is blind, how does he know how to go? (But in truth this itself is a novelty, that such a question should occur to them, for they were still young children. However, they were clever children; therefore it was a wonder to them.) He blessed them (this blind beggar), "You should be as I am; you should be as old as I," and he left them more bread and went away, and the children understood that Hashem Yithbarakh was watching over them and had sent them here a blind beggar to give them food.

Afterwards their bread ran out, and again they started screaming for food. After that it became night and they passed the night there. In the morning they still had nothing to eat so they screamed and cried. Meanwhile again a beggar comes up who is deaf; they started talking to him and he shows them with his hands and says to them, "I don't hear anything whatsoever." And this beggar also gave them bread to eat and started going away from them. They also wanted him to take them with him but he did not want. And he too blessed them, "That you should be as I am!" and also left them bread and went his way.

Later on their bread also ran out and again they screamed as above. Again there came to them a beggar who was tongue-tied (that is, he stammered with his mouth). They began to speak with him and he was mumbling his speech so they didn't know what he was saying — but he did know what they were saying — only they did not know what he was saying, because he was stammering. This beggar also gave them bread to eat, and also started to go away as before and also blessed them that they should be as he, and he went away, all as before.

Then there came again a beggar who had a crooked neck and it transpired as before. Then there came again a beggar who was hunchbacked (which is called *hoikir*). Then there came again a beggar without hands. Then there came a beggar without feet. And each one of them gave them bread and blessed them that they should be like him, just as the other beggars.

Afterwards the bread ran out by them yet again and they started walking toward a settlement until they came to a way. They went with that way until they came to a village. They (these children) went into a house, and they had pity on them and gave them bread. They continued into another house and there too they gave them bread, so they kept going around into houses and they saw [things are] good for them and they are being given bread. The children decided between them that they should always be together, and they made themselves large sacks (which are called *torbes*) and went around to the houses, and went to all happy occasions, to *brissim* [rite of circumcision] and to weddings. And they continued further along, going into cities, to the houses; and went to market fairs, and would sit among the beggars in the same way they sit there on the *prizbes* [banks of earth] with a *teller* [a plate for collecting alms], until these children became famous already among all the beggars, for all of them recognized them and knew of them; that they were the children who had been lost in the forest as mentioned.

[THE BEGGARS MATCH THE BOY AND THE GIRL]

One time there was a big fair in a big city, and all the beggars went there, as well as the children too. It came to the mind of the beggars that they should match the children; that they should marry each other. And as soon they started discussing it, it pleased all of them and they were matched. But how to make them a wedding? They came to the decision, inasmuch as on such and such a day the King would have his birthday feast (which is called a *myenines*) [<Slavic *myena* name, i.e. "name day"], all the beggars would go there, and from what they would request for themselves there, meat and bread, they would make a wedding. And so it was; all the beggars went to the myenines and requested out for themselves bread and meat and also collected what was left over from the banquet, meat and bread, which is called *kolitch* [big loaves special for celebrations]. And they went ahead and dug out a big trench which could contain a hundred

people and covered it with sticks, earth and trash, and they all went inside and married the children there, setting up a chuppah for them, and they were very, very happy there; and the groom and bride also were extremely happy. Now the groom and bride started recalling the kindnesses Hashem Yithbarakh had done for them when they were in the forest, and started crying and greatly yearning, "How can the first beggar, the blind one, be brought here, who brought us bread in the forest?"

[First Day]

And just as they were longing very much for the blind beggar he immediately calls out and says: I am here. I have come to you for the wedding, and I'm presenting you with a *derashah geshenk* [commonly meaning gifts given to the groom in reward for his pre-chuppah *derashah,* lecture; but possibly meaning a gift that is free for the seeking, *derashah*, as per Ps. 24, Deut. 4:29 etc.], that you should be old as I. For previously I had blessed you with this, that you should be as old as I; now I present it to you as a completely free gift, *derashah geshenk*, that you should live as long as I. You think that I am blind. I am not blind at all, except all the time of the whole world does not come across me as much as an eye blink (thus he appears blind, for he doesn't peek into the world whatsoever, for all the entire world's time doesn't come across him whatsoever, even as an eyeblink, therefore no sight or any glimpse of the world at all is relevant to him), because I am very old and I am yet entirely young [Heb. *yanik,* suckling, i.e. infantile] and have not yet begun living at all — but I am still very old. And it is not I alone that say this; on the contrary I have an approval upon it from the Great Eagle. I will tell you a story. (All this the blind beggar is saying.)

[THE GREAT EAGLE AND THE CONVERSATION REGARDING FIRST MEMORIES]

One time there were people traveling on many ships on the sea. A storm wind came and broke the ships, and the people were saved. The people came to a tower; they went up on it and found there all kinds of food, drink, clothing, and whatever one needs. And all good was there, and all the delights in the world. They spoke up and said that each one should tell an old story —

what he remembers from his first memory, that is, what he remembers since his memory began. There were old and young there and they honored the biggest *zaken* [elder, old; akin to *zakan,* beard] among them to tell first.

He answered and said, "What shall I tell you? I remember back when they cut the apple off the branch." No one at all knew what he was saying, however there were wise men there and they said, "*Oowah!* — that is a totally old story." Then they honored the second zaken, who was younger than the first, that he should tell. The second one replied, "That there is an old story?!" (expressing wonder) "I remember that story, but I remember back even when the candle was burning." Those who were there replied, "That story there is older yet than the first," and it was a marvel to them that the second one is younger than the first, yet remembers an older story than the first. Then they honored the third zaken, that he should tell. The third one, who was younger yet, spoke up saying, "I remember back even when the construction of the fruit was just beginning; when the fruit was just starting to become a fruit. They answered there, "This is an even older story." Then the fourth spoke up, who was even yet younger, "I remember back even when they were bringing the seed so as to plant the fruit."

The fifth answered, who was even yet younger, "I recall even the sages who thought up and brought out the seed." The sixth, who was even yet younger, called out, "I remember even the taste of the fruit before the taste entered into the fruit." The seventh called out, "I recall even the smell of the fruit before the smell entered the fruit. The eighth answered and said, "I remember even the appearance of the fruit before it went upon the fruit."

And I at the time was just an infant (that is, the blind beggar who is telling all this), and I too was there and I announced, "I remember all these stories — plus I remember *absolutely nothing* (*un ich gidenk gor nisht*). They replied, "That is a story completely older than all of them," and it was a great marvel to them that the child remembers more than them all. In the midst of this came a Great Eagle and knocked on the tower and said to them, "Cease being poor! Return to your treasures and use your treasures," and he said to them that they should go out from the tower age by age; whoever is oldest should go out first. He took them all out from the tower, removing the babe first, for truthfully he is, after all, older than all of them, and likewise whoever was younger he brought out first, and the hoariest elder he brought out at the very end, for the one who was younger was in fact older (because the younger he was, the older a story he kept telling), and the most aged elder was younger than all of them.

The Great Eagle replied to them, "I will explain to you all the stories that everyone told. The one who told that he remembers back when they cut the apple off the branch means: he remembers back even when they cropped his navel (that is, even what happened to him immediately as soon as he was born — when they cut his navel cord — even this he remembers); and the second who said that he remembers back even when the candle was burning means: he remembers back even when he was in utero, when a candle burns over one's head (for it says in the Gemara that when a child is in the mother's womb a candle burns over his head etc.); and he who said that he remembers back even when the fruit began to form, it is that he remembers back even when his body began to take form, when the fetus was only beginning to take form; and the one who remembers back when they were bringing the seed to plant the fruit, it means he remembers back even when the droplet was being drawn down [during relations]. And he who remembers the sages bringing out the seed means he remembers back even when the droplet was still in the brain (for the brains emit the droplet); and the one who remembers the taste — it is the *nefesh* [vital lifeforce]; and the smell — it is the *ruach* [spirit]; and the appearance — it is the *neshamah* [uppermost soul]. And the babe said that he remembers "absolutely nothing" because he is greater than all of them and remembers even what he was prior to nefesh, ruach and neshamah; thus he said he recalls absolute nothingness. (In other words he recalls not existing at all; he remembers even what was happening there, which is highest of all.)" And the Great Eagle said to them, "Return to your ships, which are your bodies which have been broken and will be rebuilt; now return to them," and he blessed them. And to me (that is, the blind beggar [who was a babe then] who is telling all this) said the Great Eagle, "You come with me, for you are like me, for you are 'very old and completely young' and haven't at all started to live and are yet nonetheless very old. And

I am like that too, for I am very old and still entirely young, etc."
It follows I have a testimonial from the Great Eagle that I am
very old and completely youthful, etc.

N ow I present it to you as a completely free gift, *derashah*
geshenk, that you should be as old as I. There was a great
celebration there with great jubilation and they were extremely
happy.

[Second Day]

O n the following day of the seven days of *mishteh* [lit. drinking (celebration)] the *chathan-kallah* [lit. groom-bride
(unit)] thought back again about the other beggar, who was deaf,
who had enlivened them and given them bread. And they were
crying and longing, "How can the deaf beggar, who enlivened us,
be brought here?" Meanwhile as they were longing after him he
comes in and says, "I am here!" And he fell upon them, kissed
them and said to them, "Today I present you in a gift that you
should be as I am, that you should live as good a life as I do. Because previously I had blessed you with this; today I give you my
good life in a full gift, *derashah geshenk*. You think that I am
deaf. I am not deaf at all, except that the whole world does not
matter to me whatever so that I should hear their lacking. For,
each and every voice in the world is only about needs, since everybody screams about his deficit, that is, what he hasn't got; and
even all the world's celebrations are all exclusively about deficits,
as someone rejoices over what he didn't have whereas now he has
what he didn't have. But the entire world doesn't come across me
at all, that I should hear their deficit, for I live such a good life
that it hasn't any lack at all; and I have an attestation about this,
that I live a good life, from the Land of Wealth." And his good life
was: he ate bread and drank water. (He told them:)

[THE LAND OF RICHES AND THE CONVERSATION RE-GARDING GOOD LIFE]

I nasmuch as there is a land where there is great wealth — they
have enormous fortunes — one time the wealthy people gathered together and each one began boasting of his good life, how he
lives such a good life, and each one described the routine of his
good life.

I spoke up and said to them (that is, the deaf beggar who is telling all this): I live a better "good life" than you, and this is the proof: for if you live the good life, help out that country — for there is a country where they had a garden, and in the garden were fruits having all kinds of tastes in the world and all kinds of smells in the world; there too in the garden were all kinds of shapes of every color and all the *kvetin* [flowers] in the world; everything was there in the garden. And over the garden was an *agradnik* [gardener] [that is, someone who sees to the garden], and the people of the country would live a good life through the garden. The gardener there got lost, so naturally whatever there is in the garden must surely cease to exist since the gardener is no longer there to see to the garden and go about with what needs to be done around the garden. But despite this, they would have been able to live from the garden's aftergrowth (that is, from the regrowth, that is, what grows in a garden by itself from that which falls down).

A cruel (in other words, merciless) king came over the country and could do nothing against them, so he went and spoiled the country's good life that they had from the garden. It was not that he spoiled the garden, rather he left behind in the country three crews of henchmen and commanded them to do what he ordered them. And by doing there what the king ordered them they ruined the taste, for through what they did there they made it that whoever wanted to feel any taste, it would have the taste of rotten carcass. And similarly they ruined the smell so that all the smells would have the smell of galbanum, and similarly they destroyed the appearance, for they made it be dark in the eyes just like when it's cloudy. (All this did the three crews of workers accomplish in the country by doing there what the king ordered them, as mentioned.) Now if you live the good life let me see if you can help out that country. (So is the deaf beggar still saying to the Land of Wealth which had bragged that they live the good life, as mentioned.) And I say to you: if you won't help them out, it will harm you too (that is, the fact that in that country the appearance, taste and smell were ruined, will reach you too).

[THE RICH ONES AND THE DEAF ONE GO TO THE LAND]

The rich men mentioned above got up to go to that country, and I went with them too, and on the way they lived their good life, each his own, for they had fortunes as mentioned. When they came nigh to the country, there began to spoil also by them the taste and the other things, and they felt in themselves that it had become spoiled with them. I spoke up to them, "Just consider — if now when you have not yet entered the country, the taste, appearance and smell have already become spoiled for you, how will it be when you go in? And all the more so, how can you still help them?" I took my bread and my water and gave it to them. They felt in my bread and water all the tastes (and all the smells etc.) and everything became corrected that had been ruined for them (that is, the taste, appearance and smell).

[THE PEOPLE OF THE LAND SEND MESSENGERS, MEETING UP WITH THEM]

And the other country, that is, the country where the garden was (where the taste etc. had been ruined, as mentioned), started to look around to repair the country's ruined taste and so forth. They came to a decision: inasmuch as there is a Land of Wealth (that is, that very land mentioned above with whom the beggar had spoken, as mentioned), it felt to them (that is, it felt to the country where the garden was) that their gardener who had become lost (through whom they had lived the good life) is from the same root as [the people of] the Land of Riches who also live the good life; therefore they liked the idea that they should send off to the Land of Wealth — they will surely help them! They did so and sent messengers to the Land of Wealth. The messengers went, and they encountered each other (that is, the emissaries came up against the people of that very Land of Riches on the way, for the Land of Wealth themselves wanted to go to them, as mentioned). They asked the messengers, "Where are you going?" They answered, "We are going to the Land of Wealth so that they will help us." They spoke up, "We ourselves are that rich country and we are going to you."

I spoke up (that is, the deaf beggar who is telling all this) to them, "Don't you need me? For you cannot go there and help them," as mentioned above (because when they only so much as came near the country, they themselves were already affected; all the more so when etc. as mentioned). "Therefore you stay here and I will go with the emissaries to help them."

[THE DEAF ONE GOES WITH THE MESSENGERS TO HELP THEM]

I went with the emissaries, arrived at the country and entered a city. I saw people approaching and one of them saying a *vartel* [a word of mockery], and then more people came up, until a small crowd was formed and they said *vartlach* [wisecracks] and they laughed. I listened up to what they were shmoozing about and heard them speaking lewd speech [*nivul peh*]. This one says a quip of lewd speech, that one says a bit finer, this one laughs, that one enjoys, and so forth, as their way is.

L ater I went further to another city (of that country) and saw two people fighting with each other on account of some trade transaction. They went to the courthouse to bring suit and the court decided for them: this one is entitled and that one is obligated — and they went out from the court. Afterward they again bickered with each other, and said that they no longer want this courthouse — they just want another courthouse — and they chose for themselves another courthouse and brought their case before the other courthouse. Afterward one of them again got into an argument with someone else, and again they selected a different courthouse, and so they fought on and on there, this one with that one and that one with this one, always choosing a different court, until the entire city was filled with courthouses. I took a look and saw that this was due to there being no truth there; now this one tilts the verdict and favors this one (in other words he curries favor with him and decides in his favor), and later the other one favors him (in other words later the other decides in his favor in return), for they take bribery and they have no truth there.

A fterwards I saw that they are full of adultery, and there are so many illicit relations there that it has already become like an altogether permissible thing for them. And I said to them that on account of this, the taste, the smell and the vision were ruined for them, for the aforementioned cruel king had left them the three aforementioned squads of agents so that they should go and ruin the country. For they went around and spoke lewd speech among them, bringing lewd speech into the country, and through lewd speech the result was that the taste was ruined, so that all the tastes had the same taste as *nevelah* [carcass of an animal that died on its own; same root as *nivul* < *nbl* decayed]. And likewise they brought bribery into the country, and thereby their vision was ruined and it got dark in their eyes, for so it states, *"Ki hashochad ye`aver `einei chakhamim,"* in other words bribery blinds the eyes of the wise [Deut. 16:19]. And similarly the henchmen brought lechery into the country, and through this the smell was ruined, for lechery results in ruined smell (and look in another place in our words [*Likutei Moharan* II 1:12] that lechery blemishes one's smell). Therefore you should see that you repair the country from these three sins and seek after these people (that is, the agents who brought the three sins into the country, as mentioned) and drive them out. And when you do so and you purge the country from the three sins, I say to you that not only will the taste, vision and smell be repaired, but that moreover even the gardener who was lost from you will also be recoverable.

They did so, and they began cleansing the country of the three sins. And they sought out the people (that is, the henchmen mentioned above) and they would grab someone and ask him, "From where did you come here?" — until they caught the cruel king's agents and drove them out, and they cleaned out the country from the sins. Meanwhile a noise was made: Maybe the insane one is the gardener after all? For there is an insane man going about who keeps saying that he is the gardener, and everyone holds him to be insane, and stones are thrown at him and he is driven away — but maybe he in fact is the true gardener?! They went out and brought him (that is, before these ones who sat and repaired the country; and also he, namely the deaf beggar who is telling all this, was there). And I said, "Of course he is the gardener!" (That is, the one whom they had previously called insane.) Hence, I have a testament from there that I live the good life, for I myself repaired the Land. Now I present you with my good life as a gift.

A big celebration and great blissfulness started up there, and they were extremely happy. The first one had given them *chayim arukhim*, that is, long life, and the other had given them *chayim tovim*, that is, good life. And so all the beggars came afterwards to the wedding and gave them for a wedding-discourse present the same thing that they had previously blessed them, to be like themselves; they now gave this to them in total gift, *derashah geshenk* [for a] (wedding-discourse present).

[Third Day]

On the third day the groom and bride again thought back, crying and longing, "How can the third beggar be brought here, who was a *kaved-peh* [tongue-tied]?" (That is, who stammered with his mouth.)

Meanwhile in he comes and says, "I am here!" And he fell on them, kissed them, and he too said to them as before: Previously I had blessed you to be like me. Now I give you, *derashah geshenk*, that you be like me. You think I am speech-impaired. I am not speech-impaired at all, rather: the utterances of the world which are not praises to the Supernal One have no integrity (in other words thus he appears like a tongue-tied person who cannot talk, for he has absolutely no wish to speak any worldly speech which is not praise to Hashem Yithbarakh; since talk that is not praise to Hashem Yithbarakh has no integrity, thus he stammers in his speech). But in truth I am not speech-impaired at all. On the contrary I am an orator and a speaker, that is, one wild novelty of a good talker. And I can say such wildly innovative riddles, poems and songs that when I begin to speak my riddles, poems and songs, there can be no creature in the world that will not want to hear me (in other words there is not a creature in the world that will not want to hear his poems etc.). And contained in them (that is, in the riddles and poems that he says) are all the wisdoms. And I have testimony to this from that great man who is called "The Truly Gracious Man" (*Der Grosser Man; Der Emetir Ish Chesed* — with these terms did Rabbeinu of blessed memory tell it). And there is a whole story to this.

[THE CONVERSATION REGARDING WISDOMS]

For, once upon a time all the wise men sat, and each one boasted of his wisdom. {1} This one boasted that with his wisdom he had invented the production of iron (that is, the ability to make iron from earth is what he brought out to the world), {2} that one boasted that he had invented another type of metal (that is, another type of metallurgy: zinc or lead etc.), {3} another boasted that with his wisdom he had invented the production of silver — this is already more momentous (that is, the ability to make silver is what he had brought out); {4} another boasted that he had invented the ability to make gold, {5} and another boasted that he had invented weapons of war (that is, the instruments with which war is conducted, namely guns, cannons and so forth — the technology of making these instruments is what he brought out); {6} yet another boasted he can produce metal wares without those things that they produce these metals from, {7} and another boasted of other wisdoms, for there are numerous things in the world that have been invented through wisdoms, namely salt-peter, gunpowder and the like. So each one boasted of his wisdom.

Someone there called out, "I am cleverer than you all, for I am wise as the day." No one there understood what he was saying, that he is "wise as the day." He replied to them, "Because all your wisdoms can be put together and they will constitute no more than one hour, even though each wisdom is obtained from a different day, according to the creation that came into being on that day. For all of those wisdoms are composites (that is, several things are mixed together and from them the thing is produced; therefore each wisdom is taken from the day in which God created the things from which the materials are taken and combined with wisdom to make the thing they want to make: silver, copper and so forth); in spite of this, all of these wisdoms of yours can be put together by wisdom, constituting no more than one hour. But I am wise like an entire day." (So did that final wise man boast.) I (that is, the tongue-tied who is telling all this) called out to him, "Like which day?" (In other words, "Like which day are you wise?") He (the wise one mentioned) responded, "This one here (that is, the tongue-tied) is wiser than me for he's asking like which day. But like whatever day you wish, that's how wise I am." However, why, after all, is he smarter for having asked like which day, if the wise man himself is also as smart as any day he wishes? But there is a whole story:

[THE HEART AND THE SPRING]

For, the Truly Gracious Man is in truth a very great man. And I (that is, the speech-impaired who is telling all this) go about, gathering up all true generosities, and bring them to the Truly Gracious Man. And the root of time's genesis (that is, that [such a thing as] time should exist, for time itself, that is, the very existence of years and days in the world, is itself also created by Hashem Yithbarakh) is solely through true kindnesses. And I go about and gather up all true kindnesses and bring them to the Truly Gracious Man, resulting in time coming into being.

And there is a Mountain, and on the Mountain stands a Stone, and from the Stone emerges a Spring. Now, every thing has a heart, and the entire world also has a heart, and the Heart of the World is a complete structure, with face, hands, feet etc. But the nail of the foot of the World's Heart is heartier [Yid. *hertziker*] than the heart of anything else. And the Mountain with the Stone and the Spring stands at one end of the world, while this Heart of the World stands at another end of the world, and the Heart stands facing the Spring, desiring and hoping continuously, exceedingly, that it should come to the Spring, and the longing and desire of the Heart to come to the Spring is just extraordinary. It screams nonstop, the Heart, to come to the Source, and the Source longs for the Heart too.

Now, the Heart has two things that make it weak. One, because the sun pursues it exceedingly and scorches it (because it always yearns and desires to come to the Source), and the second thing that tires the Heart is due to yearning and desiring, that the Heart constantly yearns and wishes; it keeps pouring out its soul for the Source and screaming and so forth, as above, so as to come to the Source, for the Heart is always standing facing the Source, and screams *"Na! Gevald!"* [Yid. Please! Woe!], and keeps on yearning most exceedingly for the Source, as mentioned.

However, when the Heart needs to rest a bit, so as to draw a little breath [Yid. *oyf zoyfn*] then comes a Big Bird and spreads its wings above it, shielding it from the sun; then the Heart gets a little rest. But even then while resting it also looks facing the Spring and still longs for it. But since it longs so much for the Source, why does it not go to the Source? Only, as soon as the Heart wants to go close to the Mountain upon which is the

Source then it no longer sees the peak; it cannot look at the
Spring — and as soon as it would not look at the Spring it would
expire, for the Heart's entire vitality is only from the Source, so
when it stands facing the Mountain then it sees the Mountain
peak where the Spring is, but immediately as soon as it wants to
go to the Mountain, the peak no longer appears (for such indeed is
the way with a tall mountain; standing from afar the peak is visible, but upon going nearer the peak is no longer visible). Then it
can no longer look at the Source and could — Mercy save us! —
expire, and if this Heart — Mercy save us! — would expire the
whole world would be destroyed, for the Heart is the very vitality
of every thing, and how can the world endure without the Heart?
Therefore the Heart cannot go to the Spring; it only stands facing
the Spring, longing and screaming without cease to be able to
come to it, as mentioned.

And the Spring is completely timeless, for the Spring is not
within time at all (in other words the Spring has no time at
all, that is, because it is completely above worldly time). So how
can the Spring exist in the world? (For in the world nothing can
exist without a time.) But all the Spring's time is simply the
Heart giving the Spring a day as a gift. And when it comes time
for the day to be let out and terminated — and should the day go
away the Source would no longer have any time and would depart
from the world — then when the Source is no longer, the Heart
itself would also expire, Mercy save us, then the whole world
would become nil, Mercy save us, as mentioned. Thus, when it
gets very close to the end of the day then they begin to take leave
of each other (which is called *gizeginin*) [wishes and blessings
upon departing] — the Heart and the Source — and begin saying
wonderful riddles, poems and songs to one another — very fine
riddles and songs — with great love and tremendous yearning
(one for the other, the Heart for the Source and the Source for the
Heart).

Now, the Truly Gracious Man supervises and keeps watch
over this, and when the day reaches its very end and needs
only to give out (at which very instant when the day lets out and
the Source shall no longer have any day, as mentioned, it will
pass away and thus, Mercy save us, the Heart will expire too; the
whole world will be destroyed) — at that moment the Truly Gra-

cious Man arrives and gives the Heart a day and the Heart gives the day to the Source; thus the Spring once again has time (that is, that day the Source can again maintain its existence and consequently the Heart too can maintain its existence, etc.). And when this day comes from the place whence it comes, it comes along with riddles too and with fine poetry which contains all wisdoms. And there are distinctions between the days, for there is a Sunday, a Monday, etc., and similarly there is a first of the month and holidays (in other words, according to what sort of day comes along, with such poetry does it arrive).

A nd all the time that the Truly Gracious Man has, is entirely through me (that is, through the tongue-tied one who is telling all this). For I go along and gather up all true generosities, from which all the time comes to exist, as mentioned. (And therefore the tongue-tied one is even smarter than the sage who boasted he is wise like any day one wishes, for time itself and its days altogether come to exist entirely through him, the days coming along with poetry and riddles containing all wisdoms, etc., as mentioned). Hence I have a testimony from the Truly Gracious Man that I can say riddles and poetry containing all the sciences (because all the days, with the riddles and their poetry, come to exist entirely through him, as mentioned). Today I present you in a full gift, *derashah geshenk*, that you should be like me. There was a grand celebration and superb gladness there, and they had a ball (*Zei haben a Hilva gitan*)!

[Fourth Day]

W hen they had completed that day's celebration and passed the night afterwards, in the morning they again thought back and yearned, and so forth, for the beggar who had a crooked neck. Meanwhile in he comes and says: I am here! (and so forth...) Previously I had blessed you to be like me. Today I present it to you, *derashah geshenk*, that you should be like me. You think I have a crooked neck. I have no crooked neck whatsoever. On the contrary, I have a very even neck, a very beautiful neck, except there are vapors [*havalim*] of the world (that is, worldly nonsense), and I wish to release no breath or spirit [Yid. *duch*] whatsoever into the world's vanities (and therefore it appears his neck is crooked, since he twists his neck from the world's vanities world and wants to release no breath or spirit whatsoever into the world's vanities). But in truth I have a very beautiful neck, an extremely fine neck. For I have a superb voice, and all kinds of sounds [*qolot*] in the world, which are only sound without speech — I can mimic all of them with my voice, for I have a very superb neck and voice. And I have testament to this from that country —

[THE COUNTRY OF MUSICAL EXPERTS AND THE CONVERSATION REGARDING MUSICAL PROWESS]

For there is a country where they are all expert in the science of music making, and they are all involved there in this wisdom, even little children. There is not a child there who cannot play on some musical instrument. And the most minor person that is in that country is the greatest expert in another country in musical knowledge. And the sages and king of that country, and the cappellas [song groups], are extraordinarily great masters of that wisdom.

One time the country's sages were sitting together and each one boasted of his musical prowess [*chokhmah*]. {1} This one boasted he could play on this musical instrument, {2} that one boasted he could play that musical instrument, {3} and another boasted: on another musical instrument. {4} Someone else boasted he could play several musical instruments, {5} and another boasted he could play on all kinds of musical instruments. {6} This one boasted he could perform with his voice like a certain musical instrument, {7} that one boasted he could perform with his voice like a certain musical instrument, {8} and another boasted he could perform with his voice like several musical instruments. {9} Still another boasted he could perform with his voice exactly like a drum (which is called *poyk*) when it is struck, {10} and another boasted he could perform with his voice like shooting from cannons (which are called *urmatis*) [?<Ukr. *garmata*, cannon]. And I too was there (that is, the one with the crooked neck who is telling all this). I spoke up and said to them: My voice is better that your voices, and this is the proof: because if you are indeed such experts in musical sound, help the two lands —

[THE TWO LANDS, ONE THOUSAND MILES APART]

For there are two lands, a thousand miles apart from each other. And there in these two countries when night arrives no one can sleep, for when it becomes night they all begin crying out with wailing voices — men, women and children. If a stone were to rest there it would melt down, for at night they hear an exceedingly wailing sound, and because of it, all of them there must start wailing — men, women and little children, etc. (And this happens in both countries), for in one country they hear the wailing sound and must all lament as mentioned, and likewise in the other land it too is so, and the two countries are a thousand miles apart. So if you are such expert musicians (that is, you can play and sing), let me see if you can help the two countries, or at least reproduce the sounds (that is, mimic the wailing sound that is heard there). They said to him, "Will you take us there?" He said, "Yes, I take you there [present tense]," and they arose to all go there.

They went and arrived there (that is, at one of the two afore-mentioned countries). When night came, it was as always — they all began wailing, and the experts too wailed as well. (So they saw for sure they could not help the countries.) He said to them (that is, the one whose neck was crooked said to the afore-mentioned sages), "Anyway, tell me where this comes from, that they hear this wailing sound. Where is the sound from?" They said to him, "And do you know?" He replied, "I know indeed."

[THE TWO BIRDS]

"For, there are two birds, one male and one female, and they are just one pair in the world. The female got lost. He seeks her and she seeks him. They had sought each other very long, until they lost their ways and saw they can no longer find each other, so they stood still and made themselves nests. He made him a nest nearby one of the two countries — and not actually near it, except that in consideration of the bird's voice it is called near, since from the place where he stopped and made him a nest they can already hear his voice in that country. And likewise she also made her a nest near the second country (that is, likewise, not right nearby, except from there her voice could be heard over there). And when night comes then this pair of birds begin both wailing, for he bemoans her and she bemoans him, wailing with a very big yell. And this is the wailing sound heard in these two countries, because of which they must all begin wailing intensely there and they cannot sleep." (So did the crooked-neck continue telling.) But they would not believe this, and said to him, "Will you lead us there (that is, to the birds)?"

He said, "Yes, I can lead you there. Except how can you come there? For if even here you cannot bear the sound and must all wail — when you will come there you will surely be unable to stand it at all! And by day one cannot stand the joy there, for by day the birds gather together by each of them separately, that is, to him and to her, and console them and make them happy with extremely great joys, and they tell them words of consolation: "You will still find each other," making them very happy, so much so that by day it is impossible to bear the joy there. And the sound of the birds making them happy is not heard from afar, but only when one arrives there. But the sound of the pair wailing at night — it is heard far away; you cannot, therefore, come there." They said to him, "Can you correct this?"

He replied, "Yes, I can correct it. For I can mimic all the world's sounds (that is, all kinds of sounds in the world, he can emit them with his voice, making it exactly like any sound at all); furthermore I can throw voices, that is, I can throw a sound which here, in the place where I let it out, will not be heard at all — only somewhere far away will it be heard — and therefore I can throw her voice to him, that is, the sound which I will let out will arrive close to the place where he is, and likewise I can throw his voice so that it arrives close to her; thereby will I draw them together" (until he brings them together). But who would believe this?

[SOUNDS IN THE FOREST]

He went and led them into a forest. They heard as if someone opens a door, shuts it again and slams the bolt shut (which is called a *klaymke*); and firing from gun (which is called a *biks*), sending the dog to fetch (the thing that he was shooting), and the dog thrashing in the snow [Yid. *gigraznit in shney*]. The sages heard all this, and they looked around — they saw nothing at all, and also from him they heard nothing at all. (It could only be that he, the crooked neck, was throwing those sounds. So they saw for sure that he can replicate all kinds of sounds exactly, and also throw sounds.) (And he did not tell more about this, but went up afterwards.) Hence I have testament from that country that I have a wonderfully fine voice and I can replicate all the world's sounds. Today I present this to you completely in a gift, *derashah geshenk*, to be like me. There was a grand celebration there, and extremely high spirits.

[Fifth Day]

On the fifth day they were also happy. They remembered the beggar who was a hunchback [Yid. *hoikir*], and they yearned very much, "How can that hunchback beggar be taken here? For if he were here, the joy would be immense." In the midst of this he arrives and says, "I am here! I have come to you for the wedding." And he fell on them, hugged them and kissed them, and said to them:

Previously I had blessed you that you be like me; today I present you, *derashah geshenk*, that you should be like me. And I am not hunchback [*hoikir*] whatsoever. On the contrary, I have the sort of shoulders [Yid. *pleytses*] that are the little that holds the much. And I have a testament to this.

[THE CONVERSATION REGARDING THE LITTLE THAT HOLDS THE MUCH; THEY SCOFF AT ONE]

For, there was once a conversation in which people boasted about this matter, each one boasting that he has this feature of the little holding the much (in other words, a small space containing very much). They laughed and scoffed at one of them; and the rest who boasted about this feature of the little holding the much were accepted. But my little that holds the much is greater than all of them.

For, one of them boasted that his brain is a "little that holds the much," for he carries in his brain thousands and myriads of people with all their needs, all their customs, and all their discussions and movements. He carries all this entirely in his brain, so he is a little that holds the much, since a bit of his brain bears on it so many people with their needs and so forth. (Therefore he is called a little that holds the much, that is, a bit of space containing and bearing so much, namely the bit of brain bearing so many people with all their affairs etc.) They laughed him off and those present there replied, "You are nothing and your people are nothing."

One of them spoke up and said, "I have seen such a 'little that holds the much.' For, once I was passing by before a mountain and I saw a huge amount of garbage and filth on it. It was a novelty for me — from where does so much garbage and filth come on the mountain? There was a man there by that mountain. The man said, 'It's all mine.' For he was dwelling there beside the mountain, and kept throwing on the mountain his garbage and secretions from his eating and drinking, and defecated there, until there was so much garbage and feces from him on the mountain. So this man is a 'little that holds the much,' insofar as so much garbage comes about from one man. That's what this is too." (That is, so is the little-that-holds-the-much of the one who boasted that his brain bears so many people etc.)

[THE BIT OF COUNTRYSIDE, AND THE ORCHARD]

One of them boasted he has the feature of the little that holds the much, inasmuch as: He has a bit of countryside that produces a great quantity of fruits. Afterwards they reckon the fruit that the country has produced and they see that the country does not in any way hold as much space as the fruits need to take up; there is not at all in the country so much space as the fruits need to occupy. So this is what a little that holds the much is (namely, a little space that holds so much). His words pleased them, for in truth this is certainly a little that holds the much.

One of them said inasmuch as he has an orchard [Heb. *pardes*] (namely, a garden) — a very fine one — where there are fruits and so forth: A great many people and noblemen travel there, for it is quite a nice orchard. And when summer comes, very many people and noblemen travel there to take walks there, and in truth there is in no way to be found in the orchard so much space as to contain that many people. This, then, is a little that holds the much. His words also pleased them.

[THE SECRETARY, AND THE RETICENT ONE]

One of them said that his speech is a little that holds the much, for he is a private secretary for a great king, and to the king very many people come. One comes with praises to the king (that is, each one says a praise to the king), another comes with petitions for the king, and so forth; and the king certainly cannot hear out all of this. "I gather up all their words into just a few words, and tell the king just these few words. Contained in them are all their praises and petitions, with all their words entering into my few words which I tell the king. Therefore my speech is a little holding the much."

One of them said that his keeping silent is a little that holds the much, for he has against him very many accusers and slanderers who gossip very much about him, for they argue with him and talk about him very much. And to whatever they slander him, bicker with him, and accuse him with much gossip, he performs some silence, and that is the solution to all the questions and all the utterances spoken against him. Hence his silence is a little holding the much.

[THE SMALL PERSON LEADING THE BLIND GIANT, AND THE TREE THAT IS BEYOND SPACE]

One of them said that he is a little that holds the much, for there is a poor person who is "well-visioned" [that is, blind] and very large, whereas he (that is, the one who was boasting and telling this) is very small and leads about the large poor one who is blind. Hence he is a little holding the much, for the blind one could slip and fall, but he holds him up with his guidance, and due to this he is a little that holds the much, since he is a small person and holds the big blind one.

And I (that is, the hunchback who was telling all this) was also there. I declared: It is true that you have the feature of the little that holds the much. And I know what all of you meant (that is, all those who boasted one by one of their little that holds the much — he knows what each of them meant); even the final one who boasted that he leads around the big blind one. He is greater than all of you. But I am still greater and higher than all of you. For, he who boasted that he walks the big blind one, his meaning is that he conducts the lunar cycle (that is, the heavenly orb where the moon is), for the moon is called "blind," for she does not shine in-and-of herself, and she has nothing of her own what-soever [*veleith lah migarmah klum*], and he (that is, he who boasted in this) conducts the moon, even though he is small and the moon is very great; and this gives the entire world sustenance (in other words, by means of this the entire world has existence), for the world needs the moon. Hence he is definitely a little that holds the much, for sure. However, all the same, my little that holds the much is completely higher than all of them. And here is the proof:

For, once there was a group that investigated: Inasmuch as every beast has its shade (that is, its shadow) in which it specifically wants to rest, and conversely there is a special shadow for each animal, because each and every beast chooses for itself some shadow, and only in that shadow specifically does it want to rest; similarly, each bird has its branch on which it specifically wants to rest, and not on any other branch, while another bird has its own branch and only there can it rest and not on any other; and so each and every bird has its own special branch — therefore the group investigated if there could be found such a tree in whose shadow all the beasts could rest, in that all the beasts would want to dwell in the shadow of that tree, and upon whose branches all the birds of the sky [*tziperei shemaya*, Dan. 4] would rest. And they discovered that there is such a tree. They wanted to go there to that tree, for the delight that there is there by that tree is absolutely limitless, since all the birds and all the beasts are found there, and there there is no harm whatso-ever from any animal (that is to say, no beast injures anyone there), and all the animals there are freely mixed. They all en-gage in play there and it is certainly a very wonderful pleasure to be there at that tree. They began to examine rationally which side [Heb. *tzad*] they needed to go to come to that tree, and there fell a dispute between them regarding this, without there being anyone among them to decide, for one said that they needed to go to this side to the east, and another said to the west side they needed to go; one said here, another said there, and so on, until they could not discern the right side to go to in order to come to that tree.

A sage came along and said to them, "Why are you investigat-ing by which side to go to the tree? Find out first *who* are the people who can come to the tree! Because to that tree not every man can come, since no one can come to the tree except one who has the tree's attributes (Heb. *midoth*). For, this tree has three roots: One root is faith (that one should believe in God, blessed be He), the other is awe, and the third is humility (that is, to not have special regard for oneself), and truth is the tree's body, that is, the tree itself is truth, and from there go out branches. Therefore no one can come to the tree but one who has these traits of the tree." (That is, faith — he should believe in God; fear — he should have fear of God, and humility — he should not have any special regard for himself; and truth. So did the sage say to the group.)

The group, however, did not all have these attributes; only some of them had in them these traits. But they had between them very great unity (that is, the group all loved each other and held themselves tightly together). They did not want to separate from each other in order that some of them should go to the tree (that is, those who already had these traits of the tree) and the rest should stay behind — they did not want this, for they held themselves very much together. Instead they had to wait until the rest of the men would exert themselves in attaining these attributes so that they could all come to the tree.

And so they did, toiling until they all came to those traits mentioned above. (That is, they all waited for each other until each had toiled and they all came to those virtues mentioned above, that is, by now they all have faith, fear and so on, as mentioned.) No sooner did they all come to the attributes, when they all came to one mindset and all agreed on one way by which to go to the tree. They all went. They went along for a while until they could see the tree from afar. Meanwhile, they take a look and the tree is standing on no place at all, for the tree has no space whatsoever. And since it has no place whatsoever, how can anyone come to it?

And I (that is, the hunchback) was also there with them. I announced to them, "I can bring you to the tree. For the tree has no place whatsoever, for the tree is completely above space (in other words, it is higher than worldly space; it has no place whatsoever), and the aspect of the little that holds the much still takes place in space, for although it is a little that holds the much, that is, a little space holding much more than can be put in the space, in any case it still takes place in space, because after all it still occupies some sort of space in any case. But I (that is, the hunchback) have such a little that holds the much that it is the absolute edge of the place beyond which there is no space whatsoever. Therefore I can carry you all to the tree, which is above space completely. (For, this hunchback is something like an intermediary, that is, a midpoint, between space and above space, for he is the ultimate degree of the little holding the much, which is the actual end of space, above which there is no unit of space whatsoever, since from there and above is the aspect of completely beyond space. Therefore he can take them out of space and bring them above space. Understand this.) I took them and carried them to the tree. Hence I have a testament that I have such an ultimate degree of the little holding the much. (And that is why he appeared as a hunchbacked person, for he carries a great deal on him, for he is a little holding the much.) Today I give you this very thing in a gift, that you should be like me. A great joy took place there, and a superb gladness.

[Sixth Day]

On the sixth day they also rejoiced, but they also yearned, "How can the one without hands be brought here?" Meanwhile in he comes and says, "I am here! I have come to you for the wedding." And he too spoke to them as the others, falling on them, kissing them and saying to them: You think I am crippled in the hands. I am not at all crippled in the hands. I do have power in the hands, only I do not use the power in my hands in this world, for I need the power for something else — and regarding this I have a testament from the Watery Castle *(fun das vasirikn shloss)*.

[THE CONVERSATION REGARDING POWER IN THE HANDS]

For, once several of us were sitting together. Each one was boasting of his power he has in his hands. This one boasted he has such a strength in his hands, that one boasted he has such a strength in his hands, and so each one boasted of his strength he has in his hands.

[RETRIEVING ARROWS]

N amely, one was boasting that he has such a power and a
strength in his hands, that when he shoots an arrow he can
pull it back to him again, for he has such a power in his hands,
that although he has already shot the arrow, he can yet turn it
around and tow it back to him again.

I asked him, "What kind of arrow can you pull back?" For there
are ten kinds of arrows, since there are ten kinds of poison.
For, when one wants to shoot an arrow, one smears it with a poison. There are ten kinds of poison, and when they soak it in one
poison, it injures like so, and when they soak it in another poison
it does more damage. And so there are ten kinds of poison, each
one worse than the other, that is, more harmful. (And this in itself is ten kinds of arrows, for the arrows are one sort; it is only
because of the variety of the poisons that they smear the arrows
in, which are ten kinds as mentioned above, that they are called
ten kinds of arrows.)

S o he asked him, "What kind of arrow can you pull back?" In
addition he asked him whether [only] before the arrow has
struck someone he can pull it back, or whether even after the arrow has already struck someone he could also pull it back. Upon
this the other answered: "Even after the arrow has already struck
someone, I can still pull it back." "But still, which sort of arrow
can you pull back?" He answered: Why, this-and-this kind I can
pull back.

I (that is, the one [without hands] who is telling all this) called
out to him, "You cannot heal the Queen's Daughter. If you can
pull back no more than one kind of arrow, you cannot heal the
Queen's Daughter."

[GIVING BY RECEIVING]

O ne was boasting that he has such a power in his hands that
whoever he receives from, he gives to (that is, by his very
getting something from someone, he gives to that person), and
hence he is a master of charity. I asked him, "What kind of charity do you give?" (For there are ten kinds of charity.) He replied:
he gives tithe. I called out to him, "If so, you cannot heal the
Queen's Daughter, for you cannot at all come to her place (because you only give tithe), for you can enter in no more than one

wall (in the place where she is dwelling), therefore you cannot come to her place."

[CONFERRING WISDOM, AND KNOWING PULSES]

One boasted that he has the following power in his hands: "Inasmuch as there are officials in the world (that is, senior men who are encharged with giving orders over a city, a country, etc.), each one needing wisdom: I have such a power in my hands, that with my hands I can give him wisdom, by laying my hands on him." I asked him, "What kind of wisdom can you give with your hands?" For there are ten measures *(kabin)* of wisdom (that is, ten varieties of knowledge). He replied: Such-and-such a wisdom I can give. I called out to him, "If so, you cannot heal the Queen's Daughter, for you cannot even know her pulse, because there are ten varieties of pulses, and you cannot know but one pulse, since you can only give one wisdom with your hands."

[RESTRAINING WIND, AND PLAYING MELODIES]

One boasted that he has such a power in his hands: when there is a *ruach se'arah* [lit. tempest spirit] (that is, a storm wind) he can detain the storm wind with his hands. He can seize the storm wind with his hands, restraining it, and can moreover with his hands make the wind with a mass, that it should be the sort of wind that is needed; with the [proper] weight.

I asked him, "What kind of wind can you grasp with your hands?" There are ten varieties of winds. He replied: Such-and-such a wind. I called out, "You cannot heal the Queen's Daughter, for you cannot at all play the melody for her. For there are ten varieties of melody, and the Queen's Daughter's healing is through melody, and you can play for her no more than one melody."

[THE WATERY CASTLE]

They called out, "What can you do?" He replied, "I can do what you all cannot do, namely, all the nine parts of each thing that each one boasted of, which you cannot do, I can do. For, there is a story:

For, one time a king desired (lit. cooked himself up about) a Queen's Daughter, involving himself with executing schemes to capture her, until the thing was attained and he caught her; then she was with him. One time the king dreamed that the Queen's Daughter stood over him and killed him. He awoke sharply (lit. caught himself up), and the dream entered deep in his heart. He called all the dream interpreters and they interpreted it for him according to its simple meaning, that the dream would be fulfilled according to its simple meaning, that she would kill him. The king could not give himself any counsel, what to do with her. To kill her — would pain him; to send her away from him — this vexed him severely, for another man would take her, and this vexed him very much, for he had made so much effort for her, and now she would come to another man's hand, and moreover if he let her go and she came to another man's hand, then certainly the dream could be fulfilled that she would kill him, since she was by another. To hold her fast by him — he feared because of the dream, lest she kill him. So the king did not know what to do to her. Meanwhile his love for her perished little by little because of the dream (that is, he no longer loved her so much as before) and at each moment the love perished more and more, and likewise by her the love perished more each moment, until it became by her a hatred of him. She fled from him.

The king sent after her to seek her, and they came and told him that she was circling around the Watery Castle. For there is a Watery Castle, and there are ten walls there, one inside the other, and all ten walls are completely of water, and also the ground in the Castle that they walk on is also of water. And likewise the garden, with its trees and their fruits, are entirely of water. As for the beauty of the Castle and the novelty of this Castle, there is no need to talk, for it is certainly a very wonderful novelty, for the whole Castle is of water. Entering the Castle is certainly impossible, for one would drown, for the whole Castle is entirely of water. Now the Queen's Daughter, upon fleeing, reached the Castle and was circling there around the Castle. They told the king that she was circling there around the Castle.

The king and his soldiers went to catch her. When the Queen's Daughter saw this she decided she would run into the Castle, for she wanted more to drown in water than that the king should catch her and she be with him; and perhaps she would be saved after all and she could slip into the Watery Castle.

When the king saw this, that she was running into the water, he said, "If that is the case, well then..." He ordered to shoot her; if she dies, she dies. They shot her and all the ten types of arrows that are smeared with the ten types of poisons struck her. And she, the Queen's Daughter, ran into the Watery Castle and entered into its interior, passing through all the doors of the watery walls. For there are doors there in the watery walls, so she passed through all the doors of all the ten walls of the Watery Castle, until she entered into the Castle's interior, fell down and remained faint.

" And I (that is, the handless one who is telling all this) heal her. For whoever does not have in his hands all the ten varieties of charities cannot enter past all the ten walls of the Watery Castle, for he would be drowned in water. So the king and his soldiers pursued after the Queen's Daughter and were all drowned in water. But I can enter past all the ten walls of the Watery Castle.

" Now, the walls of water are sea waves standing like a wall. The winds are what erect the waves of the sea and hold the waves up. And these waves, which are what the ten walls are, stand there constantly, but it is the winds that hold the waves and erect the waves. And I can enter past all the ten walls of the Watery Castle, and I can pull out from her (that is, from the Queen's Daughter) all the ten varieties of arrows.

" And I know all the ten varieties of pulsebeats through the ten fingers, for through each finger of the ten fingers one can know a particular pulsebeat from the ten varieties of pulsebeats, and I can heal the Queen's Daughter through all the ten varieties of melodies (for her healing is through melodies, as mentioned). Therefore I do, in fact, heal the Queen's Daughter. Hence I have such a power in the hands. Today I give you this very thing as a gift." There was a grand celebration there, and they were superbly happy.

[Notes Following the Story]

[Rabbi Nachman said:] This story is very hard for me to tell, but because I've already begun telling it, now I have to finish it. [But he did not actually finish telling it.] In this story there is not one word that will be void of meaning, and whoever is adept and versed in *sefarim* [mystical Judaic texts] can at least understand some of the hints. And the arrows — of which that [character] boasted he could pull back arrows — this is found in the verse, "[*Im shanothi beraq charbi*/ If I have twofold [unleashed] My sword [like] lightning {i.e. as lightning flashes from one end of the sky across to the other end, against My people in retribution}, *wethochez bemishpat yadi*/ My hand will yet have hold on [strict] justice..." [Deut. 32:41], and as Rashi explains, "Flesh and blood shoots an arrow and cannot retrieve it, but the Holy One, Blessed be He, shoots an arrow and does have the ability to retrieve it [as if He were holding them in His hand]." And the charity which safeguards against the walls of water — this is also found in a verse: "[*Lu hikshavta lemitzvothai; wayhi kanahar shelomekha*/ If you would listen to My commandments then your peace would be as a river] *wetzidkathekha kegalei hayam*/ and your charity (righteousness) as the waves of the sea." [Isa., 48:18]. And the wind — his grasping it in is hands — this is found in, "*Mi asafruach bechofnaw*/ Who has grasped the wind in his fists?" [Prov. 30:4] (Which is an aspect of producing melody, as explained elsewhere [*Likutei Moharan* #54].) And the ten types of pulses and ten kinds of melody — this is already explained in the Zohar [and see *LM II* pg. 32a (#24)]. [Rabbi Nathan adds:] All this we heard explicitly. But who, when and what? (Beyond this he said nothing more, that is to say, who they all are, what this is, and when this all took place — this is unknowable.)

The conclusion of the story — that is, what happened on the Seventh Day with the footless beggar, and the conclusion of the King's son with whom the story began — he did not tell; and he said he would not tell any more, and it will not be heard until Mashiach comes — speedily in our days, Amen!

He also said, "If I did not know any other thing besides this story, I would still be wild news." He said so explicitly. For this story is very wild news. Contained here in it are very many moral lessons and much Torah, for it contains many teachings and speaks of many ancient tzaddikim; of King Dawidh, peace be upon him, for King Dawidh stood at the world's edge and cried out to the Spring that flows from the Rock that is on the Mountain, as mentioned above, as written in Tehilim [Ps. 61:3], "*Miqtzeh ha'aretz eleikha eqra, be`atof libi; betzur-yarum mimeni* *tancheni/* From the end of the earth I will cry unto You, when my heart is faint. Lead me to the rock that is higher than I."

(All this we heard from his mouth explicitly. And what is understood from his words is that King Dawidh, peace be upon him, is the aspect of the Heart, as has been transmitted [*Zohar Shemoth* 108], and he is hinted to in the story regarding the Heart of the world, which stands at the end of the earth, facing the Spring, crying and longing for it constantly etc. But still the words are closed up; fortunate is whoever will merit attaining secrets of this story.)

The matter of King Dawidh and the aforementioned scripture, "From the ends of the earth," that is hinted to in the story, pertains to the Third Day, because there it speaks about the Heart and the Spring; look there and you will see wonders, how in each matter wonderful things are hinted. [In Yiddish: In this story are found very, very great secrets of the Torah, from beginning to end. All the stories of this book are thoroughly great secrets of the Torah; each word and each thing means something completely different — but this story is above them all.] And of the greatness of the awesomeness of this story it is not possible at all to tell, for it is above all of them. Exceedingly fortunate [*ashrei ashrei*] is whoever will merit even in the Coming World to know of it just a little bit. And whoever has [a] brain in his skull, let the hairs of his flesh stand on end; let him understand a little of the greatness of the Creator, Blessed be He, and the greatness of the true Tzaddikim, when he looks well into this awesome story, the likes of which will not be heard.

The matter of the verse, "From the ends of the earth," mentioned above, pertaining to the story of the Third Day — this I heard explicitly from his holy and awesome mouth, of blessed memory. Furthermore, look at this which I found afterwards — that the majority of the words of the chapter of *Tehilim* where this verse is written, which is Ch. 61 — virtually all of it is explained there [in] hints of the lofty secrets of the story of the Third Day mentioned above: "You will add days onto the days of the King" etc. — for he always needs that they should add days to his days etc. as mentioned. *"Chesed we'emeth, man yintzeruhu/* Summon mercy and truth, that he may preserve it" — this is the True Man of Kindness etc., *"Der Groyser Man; Der Emesir Ish*

Chesed" — because all the time and the days are made via the Great Man, who is the True Man of Kindness as mentioned there in the story, and he gives and adds at each moment, days to the days of the king, who is the Heart, which is the concept of King Dawidh, peace be upon him, as mentioned. And this is, "that he may preserve it" — because he guards and protects, for as soon as the day comes very close to ending — and then the Spring and the Heart and the entire world would end, God forbid — then the True Man of Kindness protects and guards this, and comes and gives a day to the Heart etc. as mentioned. And this is, "So will I sing praise unto Your name forever, that I may perform my vows day by day [*yom yom*]" — because each and every day which He gives him, he comes with songs and poems etc. as mentioned. "I will trust in the covert of Your wings, Selah" — for when the Heart needs to rest, a Great Bird comes and spreads Its wings over it etc., and this is, "I will trust in the covert of Your wings" etc.

P ertaining to the First Day: The matter of the elders, that each one boasted of what he could remember, where one boasted that he remembers even when they cut his umbilical cord etc. and he was the youngest elder of them all, etc. — our Rebbe of blessed memory said that in the Gemara (Yerushalmi) something similar is recorded: that Shmuel boasted that he remembers the pain of his circumcision etc.; see there.

W ho can glorify or tell? Who can evaluate? Who can estimate even one minuscule of the millions or billions of *hitnotzetzoth* [branchings/ revelations/ illuminations], a bit of the clues of wonders of wonders from the very, very awesome and high secrets of this awesome story, which is full of secrets of secrets from beginning to end? One who is enlightened in the matter will find goodness, and *hitnotzetzuth* of certain clues according to his capacity.

Flight from a Country
Someone 2   Someone 1
Lost Girl   Lost Boy
Seven Beggars
Settlement, Way, Village etc.
Other Beggars
Big Fair in a City
Match Boy & Girl
Wedding in Pit

Day 2: Deaf Beggar

GOOD LIFE

Land of Riches & Conversation of Good Life
Country with Garden
Purge of Spoilers & Repair
Gardener
Spoiled Senses

Cruel King and Agents

Day 4: Crooked-Neck Beggar

FINE VOICE & MIMICS SOUNDS
Sounds in the Forest

Country of Music Experts
2 Birds Near 2 Countries

Day 6: Handless Beggar

POWER IN HIS HANDS
Watery Castle

Conversation of Power in Hands

King
Ball
Menument
Son
Officers, Dukes & Gentry
Wisdoms & Heresy
Son's Officers etc.
Remorse

Day 1: Blind Beggar

Come with Me
Great Eagle **LONG LIFE**
Story of Storm, Tower, Memories
Return to Bodies
"Nothing At All"

Day 3: Tongue-Tied Beggar

SPEAKS RIDDLES & POETRY
CONTAINING ALL WISDOMS
True Generosities
Discussion of Wisdoms
Truly Gracious Man
Wise as Whatever Day
Heart & Spring

Day 5: Hunchback Beggar

Ultimate Little-Holding-the-Much

Conversation of Little-Holding-the-Much

Day 7: Footless Beggar

Notes Following the Stories

These parables and anecdotes appear only in the Hebrew.

[The Chandelier Maker]

A tale. One man left his father and was in other countries for a long time with foreigners. In time, he came to his father and boasted that he had learned there a great craft: how to make a chandelier, which is called a *hang laykhter/* hanging light. He told his father to assemble all the craftsmen of this art and he would show them his wisdom in this art. So did his father do, gathering all the craftsmen of this art to see his son's greatness; what he had accomplished all this time he was in the hand of others.

And the son took out one chandelier that he had made, but it was very ugly to all their eyes, and his father went to them and asked them to disclose the truth to him, so they were obligated to inform him of the truth, that it was very ugly. But the son boasted, "Have I not revealed the wisdom of my craft?" And his father informed him that it did not appear beautiful in all their eyes. But the son replied, "Well, with this I have shown my greatness, for I have shown to all of them their lackings, for in this chandelier are found the lackings of each one of the artisans found here. Do you not see that for this person this part is ugly and another part is very beautiful to him, but for another person it is the opposite: on the contrary, that piece that was ugly for his colleague is beautiful and wonderful in his eyes but only this piece is ugly; and likewise with all of them: whatever is bad in this one's eyes is beautiful in the eyes of his colleague, and vice-versa. And I have made this chandelier solely from lackings, to show to all of them that they do not have completeness and all have a lacking, for what is beautiful in one person's eyes is a lacking in the eyes of his colleague. But in truth I can make a perfect chandelier."

If [people] would know all the lackings that hinder a thing, they would know the essence of the thing, even if they had never seen it.

Great are the works of Hashem" [Ps. 111:2]. No two human beings are alike; all the [human] forms are included in the first man, Adam. That is, the very word "*ADaM*/man" contains all these forms. The same is true of other things: all luminaries are contained in the word "*OhR*/light;" the same for every thing, that is, all works of creation. And even two leaves of a tree are not alike, and so forth. And the Rebbe spoke at very great length about this, and he stated at that time, that there are wisdoms in this world through which a person could survive on these wisdoms alone, without eating or drinking. And he spoke at length then on this wonderful and awesome talk.

[The Pump]

Regarding the discussion which [some of Rebbe Nachman's chassidim] were having about someone who was then in one of the large non-Jewish cities and tarried there a long time because each time he imagined that now he would succeed: and so it was each time, until he was delayed there a long time. And he [the Rebbe] said that that is the way it goes when one comes to such places, that each time it seems to him, "Now I will accomplish, now I will accomplish," etc., etc. And he told this story:

There was one man who did not believe what the world says, that there are *leitzim*/tricksters from the *Sitra Achra*/ Other Side that come sometimes to mislead people, as has happened several times; he did not believe this. One night, a *leitz* came to him and called him to go outside. He went out and the *leitz* showed him that he had a beautiful horse to sell. He looked and indeed it was a very beautiful horse, so he asked him, "How much do you want?" Answered the *leitz*, "Four *adumim*/rubles." He saw that it was easily worth eight rubles, for it was a choice, fine horse. So he bought the horse from him for four rubles and he considered it a great find. The next day, he took the horse out to sell, and people stepped up to purchase and wanted to give him some amount. He said, "Probably, if they are willing to give me so much, it must be worth double!" So he was not satisfied and he took the horse onward, and they wanted to give him twice his desire. He said, "It is probably worth more than double this amount." So he brought the horse onward, until the price of the horse reached into the thousands. However, he was not satisfied with any of them to sell it, for whatever they wanted to give him, he said, "It is probably worth twice as much." Eventually, there was no one who could buy it except the king.

S o he brought it to the king, and the king wanted to give him an astounding amount, for the horse was exceedingly pleasing to everyone. However, he was not willing with the king either, for he said, "It is probably worth more." Thus, even the king was unable to buy the horse. So he went from the king with the horse to water it. There was a *plomf*/pump there from which people take water. The horse jumped into the pump, disappeared and was no more. (That is, it appeared to him as such, for the entire incident of the horse was made up by the *leitz*). He yelled out loud over this, and people gathered around in response to his screaming and asked him, "Why are you screaming?" He replied that his horse had jumped into the pump. And they beat him [with] injurious blows, for he appeared insane since the opening of the pump is very narrow, and how can a horse jump into it? He saw that they were beating him and that he appeared insane, and he wanted to go from there. As he wanted to leave, the horse began to stick its head out of the pump. So he began to scream again, "*Aha, aha* (look, look)!" since it appeared to him that his horse was there. The people gathered around and beat him again, since he was insane, as mentioned. Again he decided to leave; and as soon as he wanted to go, the horse again stuck its head out of the pump. He began shouting again as before and the people gathered upon him again and beat him.

T hus the *Sitra Achra* deceives a man each time with nothingness; complete lies having no substance. And he is incited by it, pursues it, and each time it appears to him that he will profit more and that he will fill his craving more. So he runs after it many times, and suddenly all his desires vanish, get away and go away from him — as has happened many times, that the cravings go away a little, and when the man wants to detach from them, then they come back and stick out their heads and he goes back to chasing them. And so it continues, that as soon as they stick out their heads, he goes back to chasing them. (And he explained the matter no further. Understand this well.)

[Flesh and Bones]

A story about a tzaddik, who was an extremely great tzaddik, who had totally, totally disengaged from that known desire, in the proper entirety, and he ascended to the upper worlds, and saw pieces of flesh and bones sitting in a cauldron. He asked,

"What is this?" They answered him that this was a very, very beautiful woman, and on account that she used to heat up her body for transgression, therefore they're cooking her here. And he wanted to see her. And they gave him divine names, that she should be reassembled as before, and he saw that she was an extremely beautiful woman. And from this it is proper to see the negativity of this desire. If they would cut her into little pieces, would his desire still apply?!

[The Tzaddik Who Fell into Sadness]

It is known that sadness is a very despicable trait, and one needs to keep very far away from it. And it is proper to enliven and raise oneself, just knowing that every single movement and change that one makes upon starting to serve Hashem is very, very precious in Hashem's eyes, even if he moves himself only a hairsbreadth, because since a person exists in a body in the physical world, any movement or change is very hard for him; therefore it is very precious in Hashem's eyes.

And there was a story about a *Tzaddik*/righteous man upon whom a great sadness and heaviness had fallen. And when sadness and heaviness grow worse on a Tzaddik it is very, very hard for him, for it attacks him more and more, until so much sadness and heaviness fell on him that he was really unable to move from his place at all due to the vastness of the heaviness and sadness that had become very strong upon him. And he wanted to make himself happy and pick himself up but he was unable to cheer himself up and lift himself with any thing, for with whatever thing he wanted to cheer himself with, the Accuser found sadness in it for him, until he was unable to make himself happy with any thing, because in any joy that he wanted to cheer and raise himself with, sadness found him in it. And he began to cheer himself with the joy of "*shelo `asani goy/* ...that He has not made me a heathen."

And this is certainly a very great joy that has no bound, for one cannot estimate the separation and difference, the millions of thousands of separations that are between the holiness of the lowest of lowest Yisraelites and the filth of the impurity of the idolaters. And when a person recalls the kindness Hashem had upon him in not making him a heathen, it is certainly proper for his joy to grow very great, and it is a joy that has no sadness upon it. For when a person makes himself happy with a thing that he himself did, which is a perfect thing to do, in this it is possible to find sadness in any joy, for lackings will find him in any thing, not letting him raise and cheer himself. But in this, "that He has not made me a heathen," which is only from Hashem Yithbarakh, since Hashem Yithbarakh did so and had mercy on him and did not make him a heathen, how is it possible to find a lacking in this joy, which is the sole work of Hashem Yithbarakh? For, certainly, however it may be, in any case it is a huge difference between him and the idolaters which has no bound or limit.

And the Tzaddik mentioned above began to cheer himself with this and began to rejoice and raise himself little by little. And each time, he raised and cheered himself exceedingly, until he came to such a great joy that he reached the joy that Moshe Rabbeinu, of blessed memory, had when he went up to receive the Tablets. And while he was raising and cheering himself, he flew up in the worlds many many thousand parsahs, and during this he took a look at himself and behold, he was very far from the place where he was at first. And he was very afflicted, for he thought he would fall down to some other place, and there would be an astonishment over him that he had disappeared suddenly, and the Tzaddik had always desired to be going along discreetly. And the joy began to end, for joy has limits, for it begins and it ends. And when the joy began to end, it ceased a little bit. And when he returned, fell, and was cast down from the place where he flew up to during the joy, he did not return to his first place where he flew up from in the same manner that he flew up, but rather he went down immediately to that place where he flew up from. And therefore it was a great wonder that he found himself afterwards going down in the original place. (Understand this well). Eventually he returned to the place where he was at first, and he took a look at himself and saw that he was actually where he was first, and did not depart from his place at all, except for possibly a hairbreadth which was impossible for a man to measure, only Hashem Yithbarakh. And it was a great amazement in the eyes of the Tzaddik, that he had flown up so much in the worlds while here below he did not move at all. So they showed him that a small motion and movement that a man moves himself with in this world is so precious in the eyes of Hashem Yithbarakh — even one that is less than a hairsbreadth — that many, many thousands of worlds and parsahs are incomparable to it.

And to understand this, it is known that this material world is only the central point of the [heavenly] orbs, as is understood by the astronomers; and all the more so, against the higher worlds the entire Earth is not considered more than a point. And it is known that all the lines which you draw from a central point are evidently near each other near the point, and the more they extend from the point, they become more distant from each other. And so when the lines extend exceedingly far from the point, the lines also become extremely far from each other, even though down below by the point they are adjacent, like this:

Hence if a person measures in his mind, lines drawn from the core of the Earth, even only out to the celestial orbs, thus even if he moves only a hair's thickness, nonetheless in the space of the orbs he is distanced from the place that was the projection of his head previously, being now distanced many, many thousands of parsahs, in accord with the immensity of the outermost orb in compare to the lower Earth, as is known, for innumerable stars are fixed there, and each star is as huge as this world and more. And all the more and all the more so, when he measures in his mind the lines drawn out to the upper worlds, compared to which the celestial orbs are totally insignificant. Hence there is no bound to the distance he spans there in the upper worlds by means of any traversal whatever, even less than a hairsbreadth that he spans and goes from the place he was at initially — even though here on the lower Earth he did not span and go even so much as less than a hairbreadth, that in his eyes he did not span any distance at all — for this is but undetectable except by Hashem Yithbarakh. Despite all this, there, in the upper worlds, he spans many, many thousands of worlds and parsahs — and all the more, all the more, when the Man goes a parsah or many parsahs in service of Hashem; "Eye has not seen..." [Isa. 64:3]

[The Two Palaces]

Know that there are two kinds of palaces, and the two palaces are identical. In one lives the king, and in the second lives a servant. And certainly in truth there is a vast difference between the palace of the king and the palace of the servant, but nevertheless it is possible to mistake one for the other, for there is a connection formed by many souls that bind to each other so that they become a house and palace, for one binds to another, and one to another, until they become a foundation, and then a covering, until they constitute a house and an abode. And this abode is an abode for truth, and when we need to request truth we find [it] there at that abode, that is, amidst the connection of the souls that constitute the abode for truth. And therefore the Torah has commanded, *"Acharei rabim lehatoth /* Turn [judgment] to the majority [opinion]"* [Ex. 23:2], for since many have bound together as one, surely the truth is there, as mentioned.

And this is the aspect of, *"Kol hanefesh haba'ah leveith Ya`akov/* All the souls that come to/ came to/ became the house of Ya`akov"* [Gen. 46:26-27 and Rashi there]. That is, the souls are what constitute the "house of Jacob," that is, an abode for truth, which is the aspect of Ya`akov, as is written, *"Titen emeth leYa`akov/* Grant truth to Ya`akov"* [Mic. 7:20]. However, be aware that diametrically opposed to this is the bond of the wicked, that many souls of the wicked bind together and become a house and abode for falsehood. And this is what the prophet warned us of, *"Lo-thomrun kesher, lekhol asher-yomar ha`am hazeh kesher/* You shall not call as a band everything that this people call a band"* [Isa. 8:12], for a band of the wicked is not considered, and for this it is written, *"Lo thihyeh acharei rabim lera`oth /* Do not follow a multitude to do evil"* [Ex. 23:2]. But behold, it is possible to mistake one of these abodes for the other, that is, between the one of truth and the one of falsehood. For falsehood imitates truth, for there too there is the binding of many souls, and a man can be mistaken and not know where the truth is nor where to drawn himself to. And know, that by means of the mitzvah of redeeming captives, one can discern between the two houses, between truth and falsehood, between the king and the servant, for falsehood is the aspect of the servant, aspect of the cursed, as in, *"Arur kena`an, `eved `avadim/* Cursed be Canaan — a servant of servants"* [Genesis 9:25].

[The Two Intellects]

And there are two types of intellects, and they are the aspect of, *"achor vakedem/* behind and before"* [Ps. 119:5]. That is, there is an intellect that comes to a man with time, and the more time passes in days, the more he knows, as in, "*Yamim yedaberu/* Days will speak" [Job 32:7]. This type of intellect is in the category of "achor," since it comes with the passing of time, for time is what this intellect needs. But there is an intellect that comes to a man in great abundance, very swiftly, in less than an instant, for it is above time; and no time at all is needed for this intellect, and this intellect is the category of "*panim/*face," which is the aspect of Ya`akov, who represents truth, as in, "...*mevakshei paneikha, Ya`akov. Selah/* those that seek Your face, Ya`akov. Selah" [Ps. 24:6].

[A Remedy for Pox]

After Shabbath *Parashath Vaychi* he said, "At this *Shalosh Se`udot* I became aware of a *segulah* for pox. Take chalk and take soap [*borith*] three times the weight of the chalk, and from the two make a bath to bathe the baby. And it is necessary to do this as soon as the baby starts to have fever from this, and it will be effective if the decree is not severe, but if the decree is severe it will not help."

And he said: The disease of pox resulted from the Sin of the Calf. So, in this regard the question arises: does this disease not exist also among the nations of the world? But it is brought in the Midrash that the nations of the world ought not have any diseases (since their portion is given them in this world), but only in order that they not oppress and overpower Yisrael, all the illnesses that Yisrael have were given to them, as Rashi has explained regarding the verse, '*Cherpath naval al-tesimeni/* Do not make me the reproach of an ignoble man' [Ps. 39:9]: Bring plagues and pains upon him as well so that he will not be able to say to me, 'You are stricken but we are not stricken;' and this prayer caused the afflictions of sicknesses to be brought upon the nations. But there is another apparent question: This illness certainly existed before the Sin of the Calf. However, beforehand, the illness was not severe, and the pox was only a result of blood that the baby had drawn in its mother's womb, as the healing sages know, but it was not a grave illness with deathly danger as it is now; and this is on account of the Sin.

[The segulah] is also alluded to in Yiremiyahu, where everything is mentioned in one verse: "Even if you wash yourself with *nether/* chalk and use a lot of *borith/*soap on yourself, the stain of your sin is before Me" [Jer. 2:22]. Rashi explains that this refers to the Sin of the Calf. (Thus, the secret of the segulah for this illness caused by the Sin of the Calf is alluded to here, that is, to wash with nether, which is chalk, and to use much borith, which is soap.) Understand the wonders.

[Sarah Esther]

[A story] from days of his youth. One time people came to him with a *pidyon*-redemption, to pray for a girl, *Sarah Esther bath Yehudith*. And he said that she would die, and that is what happened. And he said that he knew this from the holy Torah, since he had just seen the verse, "*Vehadagah asher ba'yeor meithah wayyiv'ash/* And the fish which were in the river died and stank" [Ex. 7:21]. And in the words, "*meithah wa'yiv'ash*" this was revealed to him — "*MeiThaH Way'YiV'ASh*" is an acronym of "*Sarah Aesther Vath Yehudith Wai [Vai!] MeiThaH* [Woe! Sarah Esther daughter of Yehudith shall die]*!*" Hashem keep us.

[The Ten Tehillim]

[The Rebbe] urged his men, when an unclean *mikreh*/accident happens to them (i.e. nocturnal emission) to go immediately and right away to a mikveh [ritual bath] to immerse, because a mikreh can cause, God forbid, what it causes. Therefore it is very good that before some [bad] thing starts to be done as a result of it, God forbid, the man should preempt, and immerse and purify himself.

And he urged us very much that a man should not fear this at all, for fear, worry and melancholy in this matter are very, very harmful, especially since he has revealed to us the ten chapters of *Tehillim*/Psalms to remedy this error, namely: 16, 32, 41, 42, 59, 77, 90, 105, 137, 150, as explained in the books which have already been printed [*Tikkun Haklali*; *Likutei Moharan*]. At that time he said, "Whoever manages to fulfill this, to say these the ten chapters of Tehillim on the same day he has a mikreh, God forbid, will surely have his error corrected, and should not [think] back and worry about it at all." He also made mockery of those chassidim and God-fearing people who, whenever some thought arises in their minds, have fear of having a mikreh, and due to this they are accustomed [to do the prohibited, God forbid] as if it were permitted — and he, of blessed memory, would make mockery of this. And his main intention was: that a man needs to not be scared or fear such things at all, without thinking any thoughts at all regarding this, but only be a valiant soldier standing against his craving and detach his mind from this completely and not be scared at all, and Hashem shall only let what is good in His eyes happen with him, whatever the Blessed One desires.

And he hinted with his words that this is the aspect of the blemish of King Dawidh, obm, with Batsheva, etc., but he did not explain the thing thoroughly. But a person very, very much needs to make himself strong in joy continuously, and not be cast down in his mind at all due to any thing in the world, no matter what happens to him. And if he is strong in his mind and does not get frightened at all, and does not contrive thoughts at all (which they call *iber trachten*/ over-thinking), but goes wholesomely in joy, he will merit to ultimately pass through everything in peace. And these things are impossible to explain in writing, "but a prudent one will discern the straight way he should go" [Prov. 14:15].

[A King's Hand]

In addition is what he told on Shabbath Chanukkah, of a king's son who was distanced from his father, etc., and he yearned very, very much, etc. And a letter from his father arrived to him, and he was very, very delighted by it, but still he yearned that he would extend him his hand, and if he would extend him his hand, he would hug it and kiss it. And afterwards he decided, "Is this letter not the writing of the king himself's hand? So therefore it *is* the king's hand," etc. etc. (All this has not been properly written, for it has been forgotten, since it was not written down at the time.)

Tam venishlam, shevach la'El, Borei ʿOlam
Done and complete, praise to God, Creator of the World!

Barukh hanoten layaʿef koach, ule'ein onim ʿatzmah yarbeh Blessed is He Who strengthens the weary and increases the might of the weak.

APPenoices

The Book of
Rimzei haMa`asiyoth
(Hints of the Stories)

on

Sipurei Ma`asiyoth

by

R' Nachman Goldstein of Tcherin, the "Tcheriner Rav" (d. 1894) z"l
ben R' Tzvi Aryeh ben R' Aharon the Rav of Breslev z"l
The Tcheriner was a student of R' Nathan of Breslev z"l

first published in the 1902 Lemberg printing of Sipurei Ma`asiyoth

♦ ♦

Zeh hasha`ar laShem tzaddikim yavo'u vo
This is the gate to Hashem, tzaddikim enter in it (Ps. 118:20)

In this book we have added hints about each story; what the things allude to, and their foundations in the holy mountains: in the holy Zohar, the *Tikkunim* and the writings of the Ari z"l. And also to explain the smart guidance that comes out of these stories according to the basic meanings of the things, as written, "*Lehavin mashal umlitzah/* To understand an allegory and a figure" [Prov. 1:6], and also to alert the reader's heart to the greatness of the matters that are told in them, from the rav, the genius, the pious; sharp and expert in the revealed and in the esoteric, and walking humbly, Rabbi Nachman [Goldstein] z"tzl, who was *Av Beit Din* in the city Tcherin, author of the book *Parpar'oth Lechokhmah*, the book *Yiqra deShabbata* and the book *Zimrath haAretz*, and compiler of the book *Lashon Chasidim*, the book *Derekh Chasidim*, the book *Likutei `Etzoth Chadash*, the book *Likutei `Etzoth 2/e (Mahadura Bathra)*, and several other books and collections, "*vehemah bakthuvim/* and they are [of those who] recorded" [Num. 11:26]. We have also interwoven into this the wonderful advices for the service of Hashem that flow out these holy stories that are explained in the holy book *Likutei `Etzoth 2/e* by the aforementioned holy rav, in order that whoever reads the stories can afterwards look at the advices, the inspirations and the wonderful guidance that comes from the story, and thereby merit to make himself strong in serving Hashem and to wake up from his sleep, which is the only reason the Admor z"l revealed to our fathers and to us these wonders.

STORY #1 (THE LOST PRINCESS)

E xplained in the holy Zohar, in several places, is regarding the six sons and one daughter that the King has. What is inferred is that it hints to the aspect of the six directions and the aspect of *malkhuth*/kingship; and this daughter is most precious to him. And he would play with her a great deal, as known: "One time... and he said that the Not-Good should take [her]" etc. And this is the secret of *"Lekhi um`ati eth `atzmekh, shetered utihyeh rosh leshu`alim/* 'Go and reduce yourself,' that she should go down and be a head of foxes" etc. [*Zohar Chadash Shir H'Sh Ma'amar Mi`ut HaLevanah*], until it comes about from this as written, *"`Eth asher shalet ha'adam be'adam lera` lo/* What time one man has power over another to his hurt" [Eccl. 8:9], *bikhdei levarer mimenu birurim/* in order to extract refinements from him etc. [*Sefer haGilgulim*]. And up until this time, when during the surge of the concealment she is hidden and concealed in this aspect of *"Yerushalaim... samtiyah/* I have put Yerushalayim" [among the gentiles, Eze. 5:5], and her father has, as it were, pain from this, in the aspect of *"Heviyu `alai kapara/* Bring atonement for Me" etc. [*Chullin* 60b] and the souls of Yisrael stir up, especially the souls of the tzaddikim, who are the aspect of the second to the kingship/the viceroy (for, *"Hemah hayotzerim vehayoshevei neta`im... `im-hamelekh bimlakhto/* They are the yotzerim {potters, craftsmen}, and the dwellers in plantations... with the king in his work" [I Chron. 4:23], and tzaddikim resemble their Yotzer {Creator, Potter} [*LM II* #52; Ps. 145:17; *Z"Ch* 119a, 122a]), and they ask that they be given an attendant, horse and money (which are the aspect of soul, body and broad wealth), and they will go and seek her; and the very seeking is also a great thing. And at present time they reveal that she still has some aspect of existence in the world; she just needs to be sought after. For, in accord with the surge of the Sitra Achra, they want to hide her so much, God forbid, until it seems as though she no longer has any existence, God forbid. Only, the tzaddikim delve in this, revealing her holiness even though she is where she is, in the aspect of *"Af gam zoth behiyotham/* Even this too, whilst they are" etc. [Lev. 26:44], until they merit to find her and bring her back to the place where her tent was at first. And behold, some little bit of the topic

of this story is somewhat explained in the second preface; see
there.

And behold, the first time, when he ate the apple and slept a
vast time, nevertheless afterwards when he awoke he went
there and found her in her first place; except he could not take
her out of there, and she showed a great deal of pain in front of
him, etc. But the second time, when he drank of the wine and
slept all the way through seventy years, which is the aspect of
falling from all the seventy faces of the Torah, as understood in
the lesson *Patach Rabbi Shim`on* [*LM #60*], then as it were, even
regarding the princess herself did the concealment overcome so
much that she too moved from her first place to another, very distant hidden place, until there it is exceedingly hard to seek after
her and find her. But nevertheless, *"We'atah marom le`olam
Hashem/* But You are on high for ever, Hashem" [Ps. 92:9], for
when a man is strong in his mind, to not give up his place, to
never despair himself of the asking and the searching after the
holiness, then he can be privileged that the descent be the utmost
ascent, which is the aspect that these who fell from all the seventy faces of the Torah — until it is no longer possible to awaken
them by any means to the Torah, as they are in the aspect of the
seventy "sleeps"— nevertheless when these ones also wake up a
little then the True Tzaddik involves himself in awakening them
and enlivening them by means of telling stories of *Shanim Qad-
moniyoth/* Ancient Character, which are, as it were, above the aspect of the seventy faces of the Torah, for they are in the aspect of
"*verav chesed/* and plenteous in mercy," the aspect of `Atik/the An-
cient One. And see *Parpar'oth leChokhmah* on the lesson
"*Pathach Rabbi Shim`on:*" a little is hinted in clues, and it may be
that this is the aspect of her informing him that now he needs to
seek a gold mountain and a pearl castle where he will find her,
that is, as mentioned. And also the first time, before the viceroy
came to her first place, it is explained that he set down and left
his horse and went to the castle; and now it is explained that he
also left the attendant and went alone to seek her. And all this is
hints in serving Hashem, for each person according to what he es-
timates in his heart.

And behold, the three aspects of man that are explained
there, one appointed over the animals, one over the birds,

and one over the winds, etc.: it is known and explained in the holy Zohar and the Tikkunim: *Ki it adam ve'it adam, adam de'atziluth ude'bri'ah/* there is an *Adam* (man; image-of-God) and there is an Adam — an Adam of Atziluth and [an Adam] of Beriyah etc. And similarly in the aspect of the sefiroth themselves, as it were, there are several aspects of *Adam*. And similarly there are several aspects of trees, as explained in the holy Zohar: "*Ilana `ila'ah binah, ilana tata'ah malkhut/* an upper tree, Discernment; a lower tree, Reign," as explained by the mekubbalim a great deal regarding these matters. And similarly the animals, birds and winds hint to what they hint, as known. And therefore even the man appointed over the animals was a very giant man and carried an extremely large tree. And nevertheless he pushed away the viceroy, etc., but afterwards he sent him to his brother appointed over the birds, and he told him his brother had sent him to him. And he too pushed him away, but nevertheless sent him to his brother appointed over the winds, and he too pushed him away. And all this is because the concealment had waxed so great that he was unable to receive his complete deliverance from all the aforementioned great aspects. Only initially did it seem to him as if all of them were distancing and pushing him off from his interest, God forbid, which itself is the aspect of falling from all the seventy faces of the Torah to the point that it is impossible to enliven him with any facet from them. For, the seventy faces of the Torah are made up of all the three aforementioned aspects, which are the aspect of animals, birds and winds, which allude to what they allude to in their upper root, and similarly they are made up of the three aspects of Adam appointed over them, and of the aspect of the giant trees that they carried (and see *LM* #15, what Rabba bar Bar Chanah said, *Saliq yativ be'ilana/* [Benayahu] went up and sat in a tree" [*Gittin* 68a], which is the aspect of what is written in *Zohar Mishpatim* 99b: "*Kol nishmatin me'ilana ravreva nafkin/* All the souls come from one vast tree;" and it is also the aspect of the hidden things of the Torah, etc.; see there. And it is known that also the seventy faces of the Torah are included in them). But insofar as the viceroy did not give up his place but was very strong in his mind and cried a great deal that he should attain his request perfectly, he merited afterwards that his deliverance was made complete and his desire fulfilled in whole, specifically by means of these aforementioned ones who seemed at first to be pushing away and distancing. For, this one sent him to that one, and that one to the other, until he came to the princess's place and merited to take her out and bring her to her father's house perfectly. And because all these things rise up to the top of heaven's heights etc. and we have no grasp of them at all, therefore we do not elaborate.

(*Likutei `Etzoth 2/e Ratzon* #3: The essence of Yisrael's job is to raise the Shekhinah from the dust and take out the Shekhinah, as it were, from the exile, as is known. But it is impossible to take it out except by a man choosing for himself a special place where he should remain every day; and any time he has free he should just yearn, ask and be watchful to take it out. And certainly it would be very good if he would regularly fast, but because fasting is a difficult thing, especially in these generations that are of meager strength, therefore the main thing is to choose for oneself a special place to remain, yearn, long, hope and look out every day and each moment to take out the Shekhinah, which is the root of the holiness of Yisraelite souls, from its exile. And he should minimize his cravings of eating as much as possible, and especially of drinking wine, in order to not fall into sleep: that is, because through the craving of eating and drinking, thereby he loses his face, which is the aspect of the intellect and life of holiness, and falls into constricted consciousness, which is the aspect of sleep. (And see the second preface and the lesson *"Pathach Rabbi Shim`on."*))

STORY #2 (THE KING AND THE EMPEROR)

The secret meaning of this story still has no explanation, therefore what can we say? how can we speak? Especially since we have no knowledge of the esoteric. But nevertheless from afar it can be discerned by whoever looks into it that it speaks of the secret of the upper holiness's union and how, as it were, (this union) arose in [the Blessed Creator's] thought first, and how immediately the concealment overcame it from both sides until the interest of the tie was completely forgotten. But nevertheless its mazal oversaw and they happened to be together at one teacher and there was such great love between them that they of themselves also made a bond between them and he put a ring on her hand etc. (and the esoteric meaning of this is known and clear).

Also understood from there is the great exaltedness of its eminence at its root, such that it is the aspect of *"esheth chayil `atereth ba`alah/* a woman of virtue is a crown to her husband" [Prov. 12:4], for she is the emperor's daughter, in the secret of *"Abba yasad barta"* (Wisdom founded Kingship), the aspect of *"Hashem bechokhmah yasad aretz"* [Prov. 3:19 and *Sha`ar haPesukim*] etc.

And understood, there, is the great abundance of the obstacles and obstructions that then occurred to separate the bond between them; and how by the loss of the ring, which was in real actuality the beginning of the bond, afterwards was made the surge of the concealment and separation between them so much that they strayed from each other and became so far from each other. But *"ve'atah marom le`olam Hashem/* But You are on high forever more, Hashem" [Ps. 92:9], and He "made the cure before the wound," and from the wound itself He fashioned a bandage. So specifically by coming to the merchant's son, which certainly was a great pain then, as inferred, still nevertheless by means of this specifically was the rise of the horn of salvation, through the good wine that was on the ship (the secret of which is somewhat understood), wherewith she made the sailors drunk and fled with the entire ship from the merchant. And even though for a while it was a great pain and he was expelled thereby from this father's house, nevertheless since he did the thing innocently, afterward he received his reward complete, as explained at the end of the story. Also with this wine she fled afterward from the king's home, and since he took her by circumstance, therefore he also had great suffering through her fleeing, but by the end returned to his place with the daughters of nobility, as a reward for carrying out his oath and not touching her. Also with this wine she was saved from the murderers and pirates, and they were completely destroyed; and similarly with this wine she was "married" with the queen etc., until thereby the salvation was made entirely complete. And the details of the interests of the wonderful secrets that are in each and every word and especially in each and every matter of this story, and also of the rest of the stories, they are all extremely "`amok amok, mi yimtza'enu/ deep-deep, who can find it out?" [Eccl. 7:24]

STORY #3 (THE CRIPPLE)

It is clear and understood by every one that the words of this story are exceedingly high, lofty and deep and there is no one to reveal them. But nevertheless it is understood and clear that discussed in it is the secret of *Olam haTikkun*/ the World of Repair, and the loftiness of the horn of holiness and the annulment of all the *qelipoth*/husks. And behold, the *chakham*/sage who drew his sons' and family's attention to water fruit trees, it is automatically understood that his meaning was to water the holy trees, which hint to what they hint to and as is explained a great deal in the holy Zohar and the Tikkunim and like Eliyahu's statement [*Patach Eliyahu*], *de'ihu shakiu de'ilana*/ that [Hashem's name] waters the tree [of the sefiroth] etc.; and as understood in this story itself regarding that the sun was talking with the moon regarding the holy tree, that it needed to be watered, and similarly at the end of the story a great deal is explained regarding the holy tree, that if it were watered then all the husks would be entirely nullified.

However, the whole concept of the story, the details of the interests in it, and their connection, are exceedingly awesome and wonderful: how it begins telling about the son who wanted to conduct trade etc., and about the thieves that fell upon them etc., and how he was forced to eat grasses etc. — which all this seems apparently at first glance to be a simple story. Immediately from there it leads into the matter of the grass that was good in his eyes, and he pulled it up with its root and under its root was a diamond and the diamond was quadrangular, and each side had a different *segulah*/special power. And on one side it was written that whoever grasps that side, it would take him to the place where day and night gather together etc., and it tells how this son arrived there and heard the conversation between the sun and moon, which is an exceedingly awesome and wonderful tale. And similarly how he gazed upon the diamond on another side and saw it written there that whoever grasps that side, it would take him to the path from which many paths go out. And he grasped that side and it took him there, and he put his feet on that road where the dust was healing for the legs and he was immediately healed, which this whole matter is awesome and wonderful. (And who knows the awesome and wonderful seguloth that were on the other two sides of the diamond, about which Rabbeinu z"l did not reveal any hint at all?) And it tells afterwards how the son picked up dust from all the paths and made packets for himself, and how he conducted himself wisely with this. And also within this matter he hints, incidentally, very necessary things: how even someone who is a tzaddik needs to be very wary of nonsense and craziness, for big mistakes can happen thereby, as explained there. And it also tells how the big chief thief among them repented, and returned his chest to him with the money, and also gave him all his stolen treasures that he had, and how they sentenced him to be hung, for it is understood that the thing also touches upon the secret of `Olam haTikkun, and how they will return to the holiness all the stolen things that they have stolen from us, in the secret of *"chil bala` vayki'enu/* he has swallowed down riches, and he shall vomit them up again" etc. [Job. 20:15]. And nevertheless this story also seems like a simple story, something that can happen according to its simple meaning, but immediately afterwards it tells that the son comes to the decision to go to the two thousand mountains, and it includes several wonderful and awesome stories within it, and amongst them are also some concepts that seem to be apparently as their simple meaning, until the matter ends with the tree being watered and none of them remain at all and they became as if they had never existed. So all these matters are exceedingly awesome and wondrous. *"Mi shama` kazoth; mi ra'ah ka'eleh/* Who has heard such a thing? who has seen such things!?"* [Isa. 66:8]

And similarly the clues that he hints afterwards, that the secret of this story is hinted in chapter one in the Tehillim, are very awesome and wondrous. And what is understood from them, slightly from afar, appears that the main watering of the holy trees in this matter is by means of the holy Torah, and this was the discussion between day and night, that the sun was complaining in front of the moon regarding the holy tree, that it is very *mesugal*, and it ought to have been watered etc., and if this tree is the very tree explained afterwards, which if it were completely watered then none of them at all would remain, then by the way it is understood that also the moon's complaint, which was concerning the demons that nurse from her feet, was also concerning this matter. And in truth if this tree was watered, none of them at all would remain, so anyways it would be healing for the moon too for its affliction (and look in the book *Zimrath ha'Aretz* regarding this story). And this can be found hinted to in the aforementioned chapter one, "*Ashrei ha'ish asher lo-halakh be`atzath resha`im/* Fortunate is the man that has not walked in the counsel of the wicked" etc. For, all the bad counsels and evil ways, everything is drawn from them, as mentioned there; also at the end of the story regarding the slanderers, that they coaxed the grandson of the elder who was a wonderful tzaddik to make use of the book that the elder commanded to not use, and the grandchild thought his heart was suggesting this to him. And if they tried to cause such a holy tzaddik to stumble by means of their evil counsels, all the more so how do they make most of the world stumble? And all the deteriorations explained there: whether it be the counsel of the thief who coaxed many people to be thieves, which is also the advice of the wicked; or also the king who made the people of his land apostates, which is the aspect of "*derekh chata'im/* the way of those who err," as explained there, that there exists a path of the apostates, for apostasy is the root and entirety of all mistakes entirely, as told; and this is the aspect of "*uv'derekh chata'im lo-`amad/* and has not stood in the way of those who err," such as the elder sage who gathered all the people of his family and emigrated with them from that country; and this is "*uv'moshav leitzim lo-yashav/* and has not sat in the seat of the mockers," for even though he settled with them close to the two thousand mountains, which is where the main residence of the mockers is, as explained there, nevertheless he was very far from them, for he made a circle so that the mockers would not be able to draw near them — and behold, all the aforementioned degradations of the wicked and those who err, everything is drawn only by means of the aspect of these mockers, which is the aspect of what our sages z"l said: whoever comes to defile himself, they open the door for him (*Yoma* 38b), as it says, "*im-laletzim hu yalitz/* regarding the scorners, He scorns them" (Prov. 3:34). And all of what keeps these in existence is only by the fact that the tree is not completely watered, for the sake of which there are those of them who stand day and night digging and not letting water get to the tree. And therefore the holy tzaddik who did not walk in the way of the wicked etc. — he is the real opposite of them and is involved day and night in Torah, by means of which is the main watering of the holy tree, as mentioned above. And this is *"Ki im beThorath Hashem cheftzo uv'thoratho yehgeh yomam valaylah/* But his delight is in none other than the instruction of Hashem, and in His instruction does he meditate day and night" specifically, as mentioned above; the opposite of them standing day and night digging and not letting water reach the tree, as mentioned. There is also reason to say that it also hints to the talk between the day and night, sun and moon; everything was regarding the Torah study of that tzaddik. For by means of his Torah the holy tree was watered, and the aforementioned mockers were finished and destroyed and became as if they had never been, and everything was repaired, including the sun's complaint and including the moon's complaint, who are day and night. Therefore the reward of this tzaddik was *"ke'etz shathul `al-palgei mayim/* like a tree planted by streams of water" etc., the aspect of that tree, as explained there.

(*Likutei `Etzoth* 2/e *Leitzanuth* #2: A man must guard himself against scoffery, for the place of the external forces, which are the *qelipoth/*husks, the Merciful One save us, is called *"moshav leitzim/* dwelling-place of the scorners," for they constantly practice mockery.

I bid., *Tzaddik* #84: The True Tzaddik, even though he has the power to use holy names, oaths, and so forth in great holiness, nevertheless he should not use this at all, but just have steadfastness in Hashem Yithbarakh at its basic level, and Hashem Yithbarakh shall help him. And sometimes it seems to the Tzaddik that he needs to use this, and that it is a big mitzvah, etc.; nevertheless he must think about it a great deal, for even though it seems to him that his heart counsels him thus, perhaps it is only from things that are coaxing him toward this.)

STORY #4 (A STORY OF MIRACLES)

H e begins telling of the king who decreed expulsion etc., and it seems like a simple story on the surface, for such a story can actually happen in its basic sense. And by the way, he tells how great is the love that Yisraelites love the mitzvoth, for even the anoos who was not able to withstand his test completely, nevertheless when a fit hour presented itself to him and the king swore to him to do his will and perform his request, even if he requests what he requests — the anoos did not ask of him anything except that he permit him to put on tallith and tefillin in public. And this itself was a great trial, for it upset the king a great deal; nevertheless he had to fulfill his request on account of his oath. Then it tells regarding the king who called all the stargazers etc., and they told him that his seed would not be cut off, but only he should be on guard against a bull and ram, etc., and how afterwards his son became king etc. and fell upon a wisdom to conquer the whole world, and regarding the man that he made from the seven kinds of metal etc., and this man did not have its special power unless the king would cast down the haughty and raise the lowly etc. This story is understood by everyone, that it is an awesome concept, especially what it tells afterwards, that there is a place where all the 365 processions of the sun shine upon, and an iron rod grows there. And incidentally it hints there of the gravity of the prohibition of anger, and the rest of the matter there until the end of the story, and how the matter of "*Lama rageshu*/ Why do [the nations] rage" (Ps. 2) is hinted to. All this is exceedingly awesome and wonderful.

And see *Likutei Halakoth* Vol. 5 *Hekhsher Kelim* #2.

Likutei `Etzoth 2/e *Tzitzith* #1: The great preciousness of the mitzvoth of tzitzith and tefillin are exceedingly great and dear, as our Rabbis z"l extolled them, and they are the main sign of the Yisraelite man's accepting the yoke of Heaven. And behold, when the anoos actually saved the king from death and the king swore to him that he would give him any honor he wants, the anoos spoke up and answered that this is his main honor, that he be permitted to lay tallith and tefillin in public, and this was his main authority and appointment. And afterwards when the one king from his grandchildren came along and nullified him from these commandments, he saw afterwards that the bull and ram constellations were laughing at him (for tefillin and tzitzith are the aspect of bull and ram; see there). And even though this king was great and conquered the whole world with his wisdom, nevertheless he and his seed were cut off, and the great fire had power

over them and they were all incinerated and cut off. But the rest
of the kings who had Jews living in their lands who were dressed
in tallith and tefillin, these kings were walking through this great
fire and it did not harm them at all, in the merit of the mitzvoth
of tzitzith and tefillin which the Jews in their lands were dressed
in. See and discern how great is the power of these mitzvoth's
sanctity, how they guard and deliver from all this; and all the
more so for Jews themselves who merit to be wrapped and
dressed in them.

Ibid., Anger #3: There is an angel appointed over anger, for by
anger one creates a destroying angel, and this angel is appointed over all the destroyers; and it is this angel whom they ask
the way, how to come to the iron rod where one is saved from fear
when he reaches there.)

STORY #5 (THE KING'S SON WHO WAS ENTIRELY OF PRECIOUS STONES)

Also apparent to whoever looks into it, is that this is an awesome and wonderful story, and incidentally it hints to
"Hashem li lo ira mah-ya`aseh li adam/ Hashem is for me; I will
not fear. What can man do to me" [Ps. 118:6] and *"Raboth
machshavoth belev-ish ve`atzath Hashem hi takum/* There are
many devices in the heart of man, but the counsel of Hashem, it
shall stand" [Prov. 19:21]. For specifically by the king's daughter
performing witchcraft on him and him becoming leprous, thereby
when he was healed then afterwards he became entirely gemstone etc. And it is also a wonderful encouragement regarding
what is explained elsewhere, that sometimes the descent is the
ultimate ascent; aside from many hidden things that are in this
story. And see *Sichoth haRan* #147, that there is reason to think
that this story contains the entire 42-letter Name. And I heard
something else, that there are those who say that this story also
touches upon that certain person's falling in water and almost
drowning, etc.

STORY #6 (THE KING WHO WAS MIGHTY AND A MAN OF TRUTH AND HUMBLE)

This is also a wonderful story, as discerned by anyone who
takes a look, and also the hints following it are wonderful

words, and incidentally hinted in it are wonderful interests regarding the kinds of jest that are in the world, through which one can know and understand the substance of every thing; and that contained in this are also many kinds. And the concept that the truth cannot tolerate falsehood; the concept of how the land was so full of lies and its king was such a wonderfully truthful man that they never saw his face; and the sage who discerned it all and praised the king and extolled him exceedingly, whereby he brought the king to such a state of humility and minuteness that he revealed the light of his holy face to him and he was privileged to see him, as explained there.

And see Isa. 33, "*Holekh tzedakoth vedover meisharim/* He that walks righteously, and speaks uprightly... *veno`er kapav mitemokh bashochadh/* and shakes his hand from holding of bribes" etc. (all this is the opposite of the conduct of the land in this story, where they were all full of lies and bribes). "...*Hu meromim yishkon, metzadoth sela`im misgabo/* He shall dwell on high; rocky fortresses shall be his defense" etc., the aspect of the king, who was exceedingly mighty, for he dwelled in great reinforcements, as explained there. And it ends, "*Melekh beyofyo techezeinah `eineikha, tir'einah eretz merchakim/* Your eyes shall see the king in his beauty; they shall behold a land stretching afar" etc., as this verse is brought there in the hints at the end of the story [but this verse is not printed there].

There in the hints at the end of the story, "*Darkei Tziyon aveloth/* the ways of Tziyon are mournful" etc., this is to say, in accord with the explanation that our rabbis z"l expounded on the verse, "*Mitziyon mikhlal yofi/* Out of Zion, the perfection of beauty" [Ps. 50:2], as from there went out sinews to all the lands, and King Shelomoh was expert in them etc. And here Rabbeinu z"l hints to us similarly, in matters that are much more spiritual and fine, for instance that the traits and mindsets of people are each different from each other, especially the general differences in these matters from one land to another, as known. But since each thing has some aspect of root also in holiness, as explained in the holy books, therefore everything was included in the holiness of Tziyon and Yerushalayim, especially the holiness of the Sanctuary and the holy Temple.

And see *Likutei Moharan*, in the lesson "*Chadi Rabbi Shim`on*" #61, that the *Even Shethiyah/* Foundation Stone includes in it all the constrictions in the universe; and all the aspects of the intellects through which the constrictions are sweetened shined in it, especially through the *Sekhel Hakolel/* General Intellect, which was the aspect of the *Kodesh Kodashim/* Holy of Holies; see there. And this is the aspect of "*Rabati vagoyim/* She that was great among the nations" [Lam. 1:1], where our sages z"l explained, "*rabati vade`oth/* great in wisdom" [*L. Rab.* 1:4]; "*sarati bamdinoth/* governess over the provinces" — for she was constituted of all of them. And perhaps this is the aspect of what is explained in this story, that there is a country that includes all the countries; this is the aspect of the general holiness of Eretz Yisrael's territory. And in that country there is a city that includes all the cities in that country; this is the aspect of Tziyon and Yerushalayim. And in that city there is a house that includes all the houses in this city; this is the aspect of the Sanctuary and the Temple. And in it is a man etc. — you can understand this by yourself. These matters cannot be expressed too explicitly.

And hinted somewhat in the words of Rabbeinu z"l is that when the Men of the Great Assembly prayed that the *Yetzer haRa`/* Evil Inclination be delivered into their hands, "A fire in the form of a lion-cub went out from the chamber of the Holy of Holies" [*Yoma* 69], and as explained in *Likutei Moharan* #72 regarding the supernal *Yetzer haRa`*: it has some aspect of supernal sanctity, as also explained in *Parpar'oth Lechokhmah* on this statement of Chazal. And there, it is only in the aspect of joking and pranks. And there are many kinds of jest. And another thing is what Rabbeinu z"l said regarding "*Yehu ya`avdenu harbeh/* Yehu will serve [Ba`al] a great deal" [2 Kings 10:18]: even though he said it jokingly and sarcastically, nevertheless he was ultimately made to fall by this [*Sichoth haRan* #237]. And similarly, there is an aspect of jesting that is lower than this, the aspect of "*Kemithlahleh hayoreh zikim/* Like a madman casting firebrands" etc. [Prov. 26:18] that is mentioned there. And so forth, from level to level going down from this. And similarly there are, as it were, these aspects higher and higher etc. For, the entire free will of man is only in regards to this jesting, for in truth the Yetzer haRa` which incites the man, it is only by way of prank, and the inside of its will is that he should not listen to it, as in the example of the harlot that is explained in the holy Zohar. And so on higher and higher etc. And are not all the strictures actually lovingkindness, and so forth? And it is impossible to be too explicit about this. And this is the aspect of *"Hoy moshekhei ha`avon bechavlei hashav/* Woe to them that draw iniquity with cords of vanity"* [Isa. 5:18], which is the aspect of the aforementioned jesting. And this is, *"Shuvah Yisrael... ki kashalta ba`avonekh/* Return, O Yisrael... for you have stumbled in your iniquity"* [Hos. 14:2]: for if you had known that the intention of the instigator was only a prank, you would definitely not have listened to it. Therefore *"shuvah/return"* from now anyhow. And thus it downchains from level to level down and down from this, until there is made the Yetzer haRa` that is coarse and thick, that makes the whole world err in its nonsense and vanities, each and every land according to its aspect, and likewise each and every city, each and every man. And thereby the world is made exceedingly far from Hashem Yithbarakh and does not merit to see the face of the King, the Ruler of the Universe. And it could be that included in this is the aspect of *"Shalosh pa`amim bashanah yera'eh kol zekhurkha/* Three times in a year shall all your males see [the face of Hashem your God]"* [Deut. 16:16], as also explained in *LM* #30, the lesson *"Meishra deSakina/* Bed of knives,"* and other places. And it is impossible to fully explain this, but this is what Rabbeinu z"l hinted to us here in *"Darkei Tziyon aveloth/* The ways of Tziyon are mournful (Lam. 1:4)... Tziyon is the aspect of the markers of all the countries, as they all meet up there"* etc.: the simple meaning is that those who make the pilgrimage have ceased; so it all goes up in one branch, as mentioned above.

And similarly what he wrote afterwards, *"**Chazeh Tziyon Qiryath Mo`adhenu/** Look upon Tziyon, the city of our assemblies"* [Isa. 33:20], the acronym of which is **MeTzaCheiQ** (jesting), for that is where all the tziyunim [signs] gathered, and whoever needed to know whether to do something or some business transaction would know it there;"* see there; this matter is also close to its simple meaning. For, since they were going up to there from all places together, thereby each person knew how to conduct himself in his business. And this is practiced in our land as well, as there is a council chamber for this. And in the spiritual sense, it means to say that a judgment can only be sweetened at is root; and all the doubts and division of counsel that exist in all worldly matters are all drawn only from the aspect of constrictions and judgments that have not yet been sweetened. But at the aspect of Tziyon that is mentioned there, it is all sweetened even at its uppermost root, where it is only in the aspect of jest and prank, as mentioned; it is only that all the Yetzer haRa's, corrupt ideologies, and evil traits are down-chained from this, and subsequently Hashem Yithbarakh who is the King of the Universe hides His face, as it were, as mentioned, and the judgments and constrictions dominate exceedingly, and so the nations of the world overtake Yisrael, until thereby Tziyon and Yerushalayim were ruined and the pilgrimage-goers were made to cease, in the aspect of *"Darkei Tziyon aveloth, mibli ba'ei mo`edh/* The ways of Tziyon are mournful, because none come to the solemn assembly." And the main damage is touching the aspect of the *Malkhuth diKdushah/* Holy Kingship, in the aspect of *"Zoth Yerushalayim, betokh hagoyim samtiyah/* This is Yerushalayim! I have set her in the midst of nations" etc. [Eze. 5:5], as known; and it may be that this is the aspect of all the portraits of all the kings — who are the aspect of all the holy traits, as known — being found with the king, for all the supernal traits-dimensions shine in it, as known. And it is known that he is mighty because all the construction of the aspect of Malkhuth is from rigors, as known. Only the portrait of the truthful king, who is the aspect of *Tif'ereth/*Splendor, and the humble one, who is the aspect of *Binah/*Discernment, *Ima Ila'ah/*the Supernal "Mother," which is the aspect of humility, as known, hid his face and distanced himself, as it were, from the world, on account of the great force of falsehood in the world, the aspect of *"Lo charvah Yerushalayim `ad shepasku mimenah ba`alei amanah/* Yerushalayim was not destroyed until there ceased from it honest men" [*Chagigah* 14a]. But the *Tzaddikei Emeth/* True Righteous Ones, *Chakhamei haDoroth/* Sages of the Eras, delve into repairing this, as understood in the words of Rabbeinu z"l in many places, until in the final end all will be repaired.

And this is the prophet's (Isa. 33) foretelling the fall of the idolater and the rise of the holy kingship, and that all the afflictions and fears will be done away from Yisrael by means of

Yisrael meriting to repair the character traits, which is the aspect of "*holekh tzedakoth vedover meysharim... no`er kapav mitmokh bashochadh*/ He that walks righteously, and speaks uprightly... that shakes his hands from holding of bribes..." [Isa. 33:15]: and thereby they will be privileged to the aspect of "*...melekh beyofyo techezeinah `eineikha, tir'enah eretz marchaqim*/ Your eyes shall see the king in his beauty; they shall behold a land stretching afar" [ibid. :17]. That is, the lands that have been made very distant from seeing the king's face, they too shall be repaired; so it ends, "*Chazeh Tziyon qiryath mo`adhenu*/ Look upon Tziyon, the city of our solemn assemblies" etc. [ibid :20], for all the judgments and constrictions shall be repaired at their upper root, as mentioned, and Yisrael will assemble together to go up on the pilgrimage-festivals to Tziyon and Yerushalayim, and the Holy King will shine His face upon us, and the holy kingship shall be in completion, which is the aspect of "*Hashem Shoftenu... Hashem Malkenu, hu yoshi`enu*/ Hashem is our Judge... Hashem is our King; He will save us" [ibid. :22]; look there some more and you will understand more. But we do not get involved in the esoteric.

And this is the scripture, "*Ki tavo'u lir'oth panai, mi-bikesh zoth miyedkhem*/ When you come to see My face, who has required this at your hand...?" [Isa. 1:12]: for has the King not hidden His face, as it were, from the world, since they are far from the truth? For, the truth is the aspect of the "*Ohr haPanim*/ Light of the Face," as brought in his words z"l in several places, and this is the aspect of, "*Dover sheqarim lo-yikkon leneged `einai*/ He that speaks falsehood shall not be established before My eyes" [Ps. 101:7], and Yerushalayim and Tziyon is called `*Ir Ha'emeth*/ the City of Truth [Zach. 8], and that is where the light of the King's face shines, especially during the Festivals, which are in the aspect of *Binah*/Discernment, the aspect of `*Anavah*/Humility, as explained in the lesson "*Ki eqach mo`edh*/ When I take the appointed time" [*LM* #135 on Ps. 75:3]. And therefore we ascend there for the Pilgrimage to receive the Light of the Face. But since you are so far from the truth, why do you come to see My face? And this is our rabbis' statement, "*Yir'eh yira'eh: kederekh sheba lir'oth kakh ba lira'oth*/ [Only] one who is able to see is required to be seen [on the festival]: in the way that he comes to see, thus he comes to be seen" [*Chagiga* 2a], that is, as mentioned. All this I have written only to somewhat appease the reader's mind; but in truth, Rabbeinu z"l's thoughts were utterly deep, and who can comprehend the inner aspects of his words? — even in his "worldly" conversations, as explained elsewhere [*CM* #243], and as written in stories about him.

(*Likutei `Etzoth 2/e Emeth ve'Emunah*/Truth and Steadfastness #27: Sometimes on account of the land being full of falsehood and the king being a man of truth, therefore he hides his face and he is exceedingly hidden, covered and concealed from them, until there is no man who is privileged to see the light of his pleasant face. For, "*Dover sheqarim lo-yikkon leneged `einai/* He that speaks falsehood shall not be established before My eyes" [Ps. 101:7]. But when there comes along a great sage who thoroughly discerns all the lies and recklessness, he comes before the king and goes on to tell all the lies of the country, and begins to exceedingly praise the king, how from this itself one sees that he is a man of truth, as for this reason he is so far from them, since he cannot endure their falsehood. And the king, because he is extremely humble — and the way of a humble one is that the more they praise and extol him, the more he enters into humility and tininess, in the aspect of "*bimkom gedulato sham anu motziyin `anvatnuto/* Where we find His greatness, there we find His humility" [*Megillah* 31a] — so on account of the enormity of the praise that the sage praises the king, thereby the king enters into such humility and tininess that he cannot hold back, and he moves away the veil from his face to see that sage: who is this that knows and discerns all this? And so the sage gets privileged to see the light of the king's face. And this parable is aside from the great secrets hinted in it, as understood there [in the notes following it]. But even according to its actual simple meaning it is also understood by everybody, each one as he estimates in his heart.

Ibid. *Leitzanuth*/Scoffery #1: From the kinds of mockery and jesting which are called "*katoyves*/pranks" in a country, one can discern what is the essence of the country's behavior.)

STORY #7 (THE KING WHO VANQUISHED MANY WARS)

Whoever looks into it will rightly judge that it is a wonderful and awesome matter, even though there is missing from it a great deal that he did not tell, as it states there. And in it is hinted the secret of his holy journey to Navritch, which also was a very awesome and wonderful matter, as somewhat explained elsewhere [*CM* #151 ff.]. The interest of this story also touches upon the matter of the big controversy that was unduly upon him, as known. And how wonderful is this matter explained in this story, of the mountain that none can ascend except one who has all his teeth, and Hashem Yithbarakh provided that there grew there a grass that whoever came there, all his teeth would fall out! Isn't this matter also wonderful and closed up? And "neither is there anyone among us" [Ps. 74:9] to understand his holy intention in this. However, we saw wonders in this, for we heard from our grandfathers that some many years before he told this story, it was still the start of the time when the controversy sprung up on him; one time he z"l spoke about this and said that he has no fear of that person, for he himself had already shown him that he has no teeth in his mouth (that is, they met together then one time, and the other apologized in his presence z"l that his intention is not to increase the controversy over him, for how could such a thing happen by such an old man who already has no teeth in his mouth? And he forcefully took the finger of Rabbeinu z"l into his mouth and showed him that he already has no teeth in his mouth. And there is a whole story in this, and perhaps it will be explained elsewhere [*CM* #123]). So now see and discern the depth of his thoughts z"l in each and every utterance from beginning to end. For, at that time it did not at all occur to his mind that he z"l would have deep meaning and wonderful hints in these words, for it seems to them that he's saying it as an expression like people use — until many years later when he told this matter of the mountain, it was understood anyhow retrospectively, for at that time too he had a deep secret in this utterance; and even now, is the secret of this matter not still entirely hidden, with no explanation at all?

So the rule is that each and every word of his z"l has supernal hints, and especially each and every utterance in these stories; and as heard from his holy mouth himself z"l regarding this and as explained elsewhere; and isn't there "no one among us that knows how far" [Ps. 74:9] to discern a little of the great, hidden wonders in them? Nevertheless it is understood and clear to everyone that they are exceedingly great wonders, and each and every matter is a wonderful thing and a hidden secret on its own, as also understood of this story, from the order of the narrative in it, as he starts in the beginning to tell of the matter of the king etc. — and immediately he reveals his mind that he will not tell everything and that we will not understand — and then he tells about the feast that the king made and the jokes and plays that were there, and then enters into the story of the spider and the fly (which is a wonderful and awesome story, as we have seen, as the king himself was astounded at this and discerned that it is not an empty thing, as explained there). And he abbreviated this story as well and did not want to tell what happened to the fly. And this alone is also a wonderful matter. And then he tells how the king dozed off over the book and what he dreamed then, and the matter of the mountain that came to him, and what the mountain told him etc. All of these are wonderful and awesome things. And then he tells about how the king gazed upon the page that protected him, and that he saw written on it were the habits of Yisrael etc., and he came to the decision that he would definitely become an Yisraelite. But what does one do to bring everyone back to the right state, etc.? And how he traveled in search of a sage to explain his dream to him etc., and how the king saw everything that had happened to him from beginning to end etc. So he abbreviated very, very much in this story as well, as explained there. And these are all wonderful and awesome things. And similarly the hints that he hinted afterwards, how this matter is hinted in [Psalms] chapter three, *Mizmor leDawidh bevorcho mipnei* etc., it is all very wondrous and awesome. If we would just be privileged, through all this, to wake up and be strong in serving Hashem as we should, in accord with His Blessed will, and in accord with the will of Rabbeinu haKadosh z"l, who just for this reason told and revealed to our fathers and to us all these wonders and by such wondrous and awesome ways!

And see *Chayey Moharan* [#90]: "On Purim I came to know" etc.; and see the holy *Zohar Tazri`a* p. 49 which expounds regarding Korach, his blemish and his repair, the matter of the scripture "*KeReaCh hu tahor hu/* he is bald, yet he is clean" (Lev. 13:40), and see the explanation of Rashi in Parashath *Tazri`a* on the verse "*pacheteth hi beKoRChato o begabachto/* it is a pene-

trating lesion, on the worn or on the new [garment] [ibid. :55]:
KoRaChath means old and *gabachath* means new, and possibly
this is the concept explained here when he brought an oldster
along with him etc. with whom he was already acquainted [at the
end of Story #7].

And see *Tikkunei haZohar*, at the end of *Tikkun* #70 [137b]:
"Like a king who had a faithful emissary... he said to his
forces '...if there is anyone who knows otherwise, speak.' When
there was found no one to accuse him, he said 'Let us make man'
['he who resembles,' Gen. 1:26]" etc.; see there. And see the book
Toledoth Ya`akov Yosef: Parashath Shoftim, what he heard from
his holy teacher the Ba`al Shem Tov z"tzukl about the verse [Ps.
89:49], "'*Al mah shav' barata/* For what futility have You created"
etc.; see there.*

* ולהבין הענין נראה לי כי שמעתי ממורי בפ' על מה שוא טענת (תהלים פ"ט) שהוא טענת היצר הרע והיה
התשובה כל בני אדם כי בעת רדת הנשמה קדושה מלמעלה [הס"ם אמר] מעתה לא יוכל לפעול פעולתו
להסטין ולפתות מאחר שזה יחזיר העולם למוטב ואם כן למה נברא לריק, עד שנותנים לו נגד זה איש בלע
ת"ח שידין יהודאין שנברא גם כן אשר יתלוצץ מזה איש השלם ומי שירצה ידבק בזה או בזה והבחירה
חפשית: תולדות יעקב יוסף פרשת שופטים דף תרס"ו

(*Likutei `Etzoth 2/e Tzaddik* #85: Before the soul of the True
Tzaddik, who is the true conductor of the world, descends, they
announce in all the upper worlds that whoever has something to
say against this soul should approach. And presumably there is
not even one who would bring accusation, God forbid, against
such a holy soul. Meanwhile the Accuser, who is the *S"M* himself,
comes, and screams, "If this Tzaddik comes to the world, what
have I any longer to do? and for what futility have You created
me?" For he will definitely bring the world back to its right state,
and the whole world will be repaired by him in entirety. Then
they reply to him, the *S"M*, "This soul needs to go down into the
world, for sure; and you — think for yourself a counsel." Then the
Accuser gives himself an advice, that this Tzaddik will be permitted to go down into the world, but nevertheless the light of his
truthfulness and the holiness of his righteousness will be very
hidden, concealed and covered from the world. And presumably,
the advice is by means that he will put up against him a popular
person in that period who will argue against this Tzaddik and
hide his light with great concealment. And this disputer, presumably the *S"M* already knows him, for there have already been
many, many stories like this throughout the ages, and in almost

each and every generation. And if not for the Accuser exerting such strength in each and every generation to close the light of the True Tzaddik, definitely the world's repair would already be complete. But nevertheless, "`Utzu `etzah vetofar/ Take counsel, and it will be brought to nought" [Isa. 8:10], and "Raboth machashavoth belev-ish [beLeibish] ve`atzath Hashem hi takum/ Many are the contrivances in a man's heart [Leibish], but it is Hashem's counsel that shall stand" [Prov. 19:21; also a pun on the name Leib; v. CM #123]. So this soul goes down into the world, and even though in truth what happens to it happens, "Lulei Hashem shehayah lanu/ If it had not been Hashem who was for us" etc. [Ps. 124:2]: nevertheless this Tzaddik, he vanquishes many many wars and in the very end the world will be perfectly repaired through him).

STORY #8 (THE RABBI AND HIS ONLY SON)

A wonderful and awesome story and a smart life lesson, how the Accuser surges up and attempts schemes to prevent people from drawing close to the True Tzaddik, and primarily away from the Tzaddik upon whom the whole hope of Yisrael depends. And the greater a person is and the higher a level and aspect he has, the more he exerts strength on him to hold him back, for if he would become a follower, who knows what would come out of this? — goodness and repair for the entirety of Yisrael and for the entirety of all the worlds completely, as understood from this story itself. For wasn't this Tzaddik also famous, and Yisraelite people were followers of him? for didn't the same people who advised this rabbi's son to travel to this Tzaddik belong to them? And specifically on this rabbi's son, because in him was a high aspect, for he merited to the aspect of the Minor Luminary — and if he would have become a follower of this Tzaddik who was the aspect of the Major Luminary, there would have been the repair of the world, as explained there — therefore on him the Accuser exerted great strength, and the main part of his assault was to prevent him from becoming a follower of this Tzaddik specifically. But even the Accuser wanted to draw close to other tzaddikim, and it could be that these tzaddikim that this Accuser told him about (when they first met him), that "there, there is a tzaddik, and there and there," there could be true tzaddikim among them as well, only without being on the degree and level of this Tzaddik on whom depended the perfection of the rabbi's son's soul and the completion of the whole entire world's repair.

It is also understood from this story how in these matters one cannot rely on testing whether it goes in orderly fashion, for on the contrary, in most cases, if the interest is a truly big thing then definitely at the interest's beginning the Accuser and prosecutors will be strong to summon some circumstances that are in the category of out of the ordinary, in order to prevent him thereby, God forbid. And one needs to pray a great deal about this to Hashem Yithbarakh to not summon him trials and circumstances, God forbid; and as King Dawidh a"h said, *"Ger anokhi ba'aretz al-taster memeni mitzvotheikha/* I am a sojourner on the earth; hide not Your commandments from me"* [Ps. 119:17] and many more verses like this on this topic. And if one sees that the obstacles wax strong upon him, then he needs to bring his strength up to the same level, with a will that is stronger, as explained in his words z"l a great about this. And the main thing is one needs to be strong against the brain's obstacles, for the Accuser exerts great strength to make the heart and brain crooked, with false and errant reasonings, for in this story as well wasn't the brain's obstacle the main thing? So at first the obstacle was from his father, who replied to him, "Aren't you more learned and pedigreed than him? It does not suit you to travel to him" etc., and then when he traveled he relied on a test, whether it will go in proper order etc. This too was from the side of the brain's obstruction. And similarly after the horse fell off the bridge and the carriage turned over, and similarly the second time, when the two axles of the wagon broke, was there really through this any real impediment from traveling to the Tzaddik? Only, thereby the brain's obstacle prevailed, and especially on the third trip, when they agreed to no longer rely on such tests, unless it will be a very detectable thing: and then they were held back by encountering the trader who spoke slander and lies about the Tzaddik. And is such a thing really a very truly substantial thing, such that one should be held back by it? Isn't it known that the whole entire world is full of lies, as stated in the scripture, *"Te'almanah sifthei-shaqer, hadoveroth `al-tzaddik `ataq/* Let the lying lips be dumb, which speak arrogantly against the righteous"* etc. [Ps.

31:19]; and as is known and publicized, that essentially most of the great ones of Yisrael, especially the special unique ones of the era, suffered a great deal of controversy, and they spoke a great deal of lies and falsehood about them. And then they were so held back by what the trader said "innocently." Who knows if it was "innocently?" — for perhaps he is one of his opposers and haters, and when they started talking about him he replied to them in his mode.

From all this it is understood by everyone that the main block in this matter in just the mental block. Therefore one needs to pray a great deal to Hashem Yithbarakh to be saved from this.

And the main thing is to minimize one's own honor and to increase the honor of the Omnipresent, and to let all his deeds be just for the sake of Heaven in truth. Then Hashem will be at his help, to withstand and overcome all the obstacles, and he will merit to walk in the way of truth for its own sake. And as discerned from this story as well, that the obstruction from his father the rabbi was only on account of decrease in honor, for he replied to him, "Aren't you more of a scholar and more pedigreed than him? So it's unseemly for you to travel to him." And in truth, the main perfection does not depend on being a scholar nor a pedigreed, but rather "on the preponderance of one's deeds," as Rabbeinu z"l also hinted in this story itself, in what is written there, that this son had performed a mitzvah through which he had come to reach the aspect of the Minor Luminary. See and be astonished at the depth of his words' holiness z"l, for he did not simply say that this son was the aspect of the Minor Luminary; rather, he clearly explained that he had *reached* this level through the mitzvah that he had done, for everything is according to the preponderance of one's deed's, as mentioned. And here is not the place to elaborate these matters further; and they are explained elsewhere.

And look some more there, that afterwards when the rabbi met the trader after his son's passing away and he recognized him that he was the trader he had seen before, he answered him, "Definitely you saw me," and he opened his mouth and told him, "If you want, I will swallow you down" etc. And even though this expression is common among people, nevertheless it is a surprising expression, for who is it that wants someone to swallow him? And also, if he can swallow him, he will swallow him even if does not give him permission. Rather, he circles around with his many strategies, incitements and deceits until he inserts desire in the man's heart to turn after him, and then he can really swallow him, God forbid, like also in this story he put it into the rabbi's heart at the beginning to not want his son to travel to the Tzaddik, for it seemed to him that it was a reduction of honor for him. And as it is explained also afterwards when he met the trader he was embarrassed to say that he was traveling to that Tzaddik, so automatically when the Accuser put it in his mind to turn after his will, it was definitely in his power to overcome him. And this is his hinting him, "If you want," that is: if your will will be drawn after my will, I will definitely swallow you, in the aspect of "*Bevala` rasha` tzaddik mimenu/* When the wicked swallows up the man that is *more righteous than he*" [Hab. 1:13] *specifically* — and not a complete tzaddik, as our Rabbis expounded, for he definitely wants to swallow down the man completely, God forbid, in the aspect of "*Tzofeh rasha` latzaddik umvakesh lahamitho/* The wicked watches the righteous and seeks to slay him" [Ps. 37:32]. And therefore the main advice for winning is to have no interest in him (for, does it make sense that a man should want his enemy to swallow him?), and then he will definitely overcome him, for Hakadosh Barukh Hu helps him and assists him, in the aspect of "*Hashem lo-ya`azvenu beyado/* Hashem will not leave him in his hand" [ibid. :33], as our rabbis z"l expounded on the verse, "*Ve'atah timshol-bo/* But you may rule over it" [Gen. 4:7]: if you want, you will defeat him — if you *want* specifically. And this is the aspect of what the scripture says, "*Beni im-yifattukha chata'im al-toveh/* My son, if sinners entice you, do not want" [Prov. 1:10] — "do not want" specifically, and then you will definitely overpower him. And this is the aspect of what is said regarding Yosef the tzaddik, "*Vayma'en/* But he refused" [Gen. 39:8] — *refused* specifically; and also as explained about this elsewhere.

And in truth, for the most part, the Accuser's sometimes swallowing down a man completely, God forbid, is by first inciting him to what he incites him — and then when he is listens to him, he himself comes and informs him the enormity of the damage that he has caused by this, until thereby he weakens his mind and makes him fall entirely, God forbid. And therefore here too, when he came to inform the rabbi the enormity of the damage that he caused by being drawn after his incitements and lures, he said to him first, "If you want, I will swallow you," that is, if now too he will want to be drawn after his advice and be extremely downcast [*vaychalesh da`atho*], then he can really devour him, God forbid, as there have already been many cases like this in the world; Hashem Yithbarakh save us.

Now look what else: explained and discerned from the beginning of this story is that it is needless to say that someone who does not delve in prayer and is entirely far from serving Hashem, such a person definitely needs to try to come and draw close to the True Tzaddik, for he will definitely wake up to make complete return through him; rather, even someone who delves in serving Hashem and is constantly studying and praying — nevertheless, to feel taste in his devotion, to serve Hashem in joy, and for his service to be perfect without any lacking, is only by following the True Tzaddik, as explained there, and more in many places in his words z"l. And see the lesson "*Emor el-Hakohanim/* Speak to the priests" [Lev. 21:1] in *Likutei Moharan* #2: it explains that the whole aspect of prayer-service is the aspect of the Minor Luminary, therefore one must tie it and bring it to the True Tzaddik, who is the aspect of Moshe, the aspect of the Major Luminary, in order to illuminate it and perfect it, which is the aspect of "*Lehaz'hir gedolim `al haketanim/* To make the big shine on the small" [a novel reading of Rashi on ibid. and *Yevamoth* 114a], which is the aspect of what is stated about the Tabernacle, "*Vayavi'u eth-hamishkan el-Moshe... vayakem* **Moshe** *eth-hamishkan/* and they brought the Tabernacle to Moshe... and Moshe (specifically) put up the Tabernacle" [Ex. 39-40], and as also explained in the holy Zohar (Pekudei 238b); see more there, and several more places from his words z"l in this matter, and you will be delighted.

(*Likutei `Etzoth 2/e Tzaddik* #86: Brought there is a summary in brief of all the aforementioned matter: the whole time a man does not merit to truly draw close to the True Tzaddik, then even though he is constantly studying and praying, nevertheless he does not attain feeling true taste in his learning and prayer. And if he paid good attention with his heart, he would feel it himself that something is lacking for him, without him knowing what (and in truth, the lack arises from not drawing close to the True Tzaddik who will truly illuminate him). So fortunate is one who merits to draw close to the True Tzaddik in this world, while alive in this lifetime, for the Accuser puts himself to this a great deal, to preclude the man from this all the days of his life, God forbid, since the essential perfection of his Judaic holiness depends on this. And sometimes there is a person who does such a mitzvah that through it he achieves the aspect of the Minor Luminary. And if this man would just merit to draw close to the True Tzaddik, who is the aspect of the Major Luminary, Mashiach would already come and the world's repair would already be in full. And this man, even though he has great yearning and hope, presumably, to draw close to this Tzaddik, the Accuser presents great challenge for this man and summons other great obstacles for him repeatedly, especially the mental block, as explained elsewhere (and as explained above). And the main blocking is by the $S''M$ himself clothing himself in some opposers and slanderers, "who speak arrogantly against the righteous" etc. Therefore one needs to very much ask from Hashem Yithbarakh to merit to break down all the obstacles and truly draw close to the True Tzaddik; see there.)

STORY #9 (THE WISE MAN AND THE SIMPLE MAN)

A wonderful and awesome story, and explained in it is how very lofty are the ways of simplicity, and how the simple man even during the time of his pressure and lowliness was constantly full of joy and cheer, and sufficed with what he had without ever lacking anything. And ultimately he merited through this simplicity and righteousness to rise to very great grandeur and heights, until the king made him minister over all the ministers; and he also became a great sage and very enlightened. And nevertheless even then he did not leave his simple ways. But with the clever man all this was the opposite, for he was always full of anger and pain, and even during the time of his stature and greatness, and even more so towards the end, when he became very poor and destitute, low and disgraced, nevertheless then too he did not leave his clever ways but disbelieved everything, God forbid, until thereby he reached hard and bitter torments for several, several years, God save us. And his ultimate hope and repair was only by means of the simple man, as is all well explained there. And also there, are things that are very wanted and needed for serving Hashem and living an everlasting life through them, as is understood and clear for whoever looks inside, aside from the great secrets that are in this story, as also understood at the end of the story, in the hints that hint that this secret touches the matter of the war and the suppression of the *qelipah*/husk of `Amaleq and Agag etc., to which the holy Torah alerted us a great deal and said, *"Zakhor eth-asher `asah lekha `Amaleq... lo tishkach*/ Remember all that Amaleq did to you... do not forget" etc. [Deut. 25:17-19]. And it says, *"Milchamah laShem ba`Amaleq midor dor*/ Hashem is at war with `Amaleq generation to generation" [Ex. 17:16], and our rabbis z"l said: until the generation of Mashiach. And similarly our rabbis z"l said [*Tanchuma Ki Tetze*, end]: The Name is not whole and the Throne is not whole (the aspect of the name of the Tzaddik, who is the aspect of the Ba`al Shem, whose name includes that of the Blessed One's name, as explained elsewhere [Josh. 7 and Rashi there; *LM II* #67], and the aspect of the *Kisse Malkhuth*/ Kingship's Throne) until the seed of `Amaleq is destroyed. And everything touches upon the secret of the interests that are explained and hinted to in this story. For, the whole essential repair of the world depends on this, that all the ways of the bad wisdoms be annulled from the world (which embitter the man's life exceedingly, making him constantly full of lackings and all his days he is full of anger and pains, God save us; and not only that, but all kinds of apostasy and blasphemy are drawn forth from them as well, God save us), and all the world's inhabitants reach the same perfect faith in Hashem Yithbarakh and His holy Tzaddikim and all their holy words that were stated in truth, great simplicity, and very wonderful and awesome wisdom, both spiritual and physical, as discerned from this story and more in many places in his words z"l.

And also discerned from this story is how much one needs to keep himself far from "sages" of the aforementioned wickedness, especially from listening to their evil words and their apostasies, God save us, because by the simple man sitting with the clever man at the same meal, when the clever man "proved" to him his opinion that there is no king whatsoever — even though the simple man, the minister, rebuked him etc. and was very upset at him about this, nevertheless he caused him some damage, to the extent that he was very frightened by the Devil (who is from the *qeliphoth*/husks) sending for him too (because just by him sitting with the "sage" of evil and listening to his words of apostasy, therefore he had some grip on him as well), and the Ba`al Shem had to give him *kamea*s (amulets with holy names) and protections etc., as explained there. And similarly, also understood from this story is how great the opposite is, the height of how dear is the connection and the love with the kosher and simple ones. For by means that the clever man had learned with the simple man during his youth, and he asked about his wellbeing in love and with joy, etc., then because of the love of youth that they had between them, the clever man drew him close and entered with him into the city, and the simple man brought him into his house afterwards, and he always opened his mouth to him and chastised him for always being full of suffering, until he told him with a full mouth, "If only you could reach my level" etc., as explained there. Thereby things circled around afterwards until in the final end the simple man, the minister, made effort with the tzaddik, the Ba`al Shem, until he took out the clever man from the mud and mire that he was engulfed in for so long, and made the truth clear to him, to his eyes, until the clever man also had to acknowledge the truth. So everything came about through the great love that he had with the simple man during the days of his youth, as mentioned.

And behold, it is illustrated there that when the simple man rose to greatness and became a governor and those who loved him advised him to also study wisdoms and languages, and the thing was accepted in the eyes of the simple man etc., discerned from this, somewhat, is the fact that there have been several great tzaddikim who were expert in wisdoms and languages, and it was perfumery and cuisine for them. This was because from the beginning they had served Hashem for many years in very extraordinarily great truth, wholesomeness and simplicity, and had really given their souls for the service of Hashem Yithbarakh from childhood to maturity, and themselves had fulfilled myriad times the scripture, "*Beahavatah tishgeh tamid*/ With the love of her [the Torah], be ravished always" [Prov. 5:19], as our rabbis z"l expounded [i.e. *tishgeh*, akin to *shogeg*/neglect, i.e. even to the neglect of one's own needs], and they made their piety precede their wisdom, even the wisdom of the holy Torah, for *"lo hamidrash hu ha`ikar elah hama`aseh/* not the exposition but rather the performance is the main thing" [*Pirkey Avoth* 1:17], and they excelled in their mitzvoth and good deeds, innumerably. And after they were extremely rooted in the ways of simplicity and the holy faith, then they were forced, for the benefit of the world, to sometimes enter into studying wisdoms/sciences. And due to their vast righteousness and the purity and cleanliness of their souls and bodies, therefore they did not need to spend a great deal of time on this study; just in a very short time they became expert in all the wisdoms. But still then they did not forsake or leave, God forbid, the ways of innocence, simplicity, and their holy faith. And therefore these wisdoms were not able to damage them at all, but just the opposite, etc. But those who are not yet thoroughly regular and rooted as needed, in the ways of simplicity and the holy faith perfectly, and enter into these wisdoms, it will definitely harm them very much, until it will be very, very hard for them afterwards to return and hold by the ways of the holy simplicity. For regarding this is said, *"Kol ba'eyah lo yashuvun velo-yasigu orchoth chayim/* None that go to her return, nor do they attain the paths of life" [Ps. 2:19], which are the ways of simplicity and the holy faith, which are the essence of the paths of life, as written, *"Vetzaddik be'emunatho yichyeh/* but the righteous shall live by his faith" [Hab. 2:4]. And this is the simple man saying to the clever man, "See, I have already reached your place, but you still have not come to mine. And I see that it is harder for you to come to my simplicity," that is, as mentioned. And see *LM II* #19 regarding that the essence of the ultimate purpose and perfection is to just serve Hashem in complete simplicity, etc.; this also pertains to this story, as explained there. And there, this whole matter is further elaborated and explained.

(*Likutei `Etzoth 2/e Temimuth* #4: The main cause of all declines is by means of cleverness. For, when a man walks after his wisdom, he can fall into very bad things. For, the wisdom makes him turn from one wisdom to another, and from one to another, until he is captured and lost in his own cleverness, until he becomes really insane, God save us. And he can fall into complete apostasy, God forbid, denying the king and his ministers, that is, denying the King of the Universe and all the true tzaddikim. And the whole world becomes nothing to him and he scorns the entire world, as if the whole world is mistaken, God forbid. And thereby he becomes very fallen, lowly and disgraced, spiritually and materially, aside from him being always full of very great afflictions and lackings. And everything that happens to him is all against his will, and he is constantly full of anger and pains, even when he is having great success. And all the more so afterwards when he declines from his height, and hard and bitter punishments come to him, God forbid, that are entirely unnatural, he still remains in his rebellion and errs with his wisdom, attributing everything to natural means, even though everyone discerns of his words then, that they are words of a really insane person. And discerned in there is that his cleverness and error is so great that he is resolute in his evil thinking then as well, and thereby automatically these afflictions and punishments themselves afflict and torture him and distress his soul exceedingly. For, since he does not believe, and he attributes everything to natural means, hence he has no way to console himself at all regarding his hard pain and afflictions, God forbid.

But one who is privileged to walk in the ways of simplicity in truth, he lives true life, truly good life, and whatever way it goes for him it is all good and right for him, and he is constantly full of joy. And even if he only has *"lechem tzar umayim lachatz/ sparing bread and scant water"* [Isa. 30:20], he delights in it a great deal and truly feels in the bread and water all the tastes of all the foods and drinks in the world. And similarly regarding clothing, even if he only has some very humble garment, he delights in it a great deal, as if he has all the good clothing in the world. And nothing at all is ever lacking for him, and he is never jealous of any man. He is just truly happy in his lot, spiritually and materially, and he does not look at others' affairs at all. And he is not affected by the mockery of the generation's mockers, and even when they mock him he replies to them in simplicity and truth, and speaks with everyone in great simplicity, without any cunningness at all. And by this itself he can merit to go up to a very high level, spiritually and materially, and be a ruler and a fair judge. Also he can later merit to be wise and enlightened in all the wisdoms on an extremely high level, spiritually and materially; but then too he does not forsake his ways of simplicity. Subsequently he is most important to the king, the King of the Universe, until He lifted him up to an even higher level (see *LM II* #5, the lesson *"Tik`u — Emunah,"* what we get by being simple). And in the end of ends, the final repair of these clever persons who were led astray after their wisdoms — after they will have very, very hard punishments and afflictions, God save us, in this world and in the next — the end of the repair will only be by means of these tzaddikim and kosher ones, those whose way is simple [Ps. 119:1; *LM* #1], who merited to truly go just in the way of innocence and simplicity all the days of their lives, as is fit, in truth.

Ibid. #5: The simple man went into his father's house and inherited it, apparently to hint that his father's house is the holy faith, which is the *nachalath avoth/* paternal inheritance [Prov. 19:14] (see *LM* #94, the lesson *"Zakhar chasdo/* He has remembered His mercy" [Ps. 98:3]). And therefore he had rest and residence in his *nachalath avoth*, because into the place that he was not able to reach with his intellect, he was planted in his *nachalath avoth*, which is the holy faith. But the clever man, his father's house became lost and destroyed, because he goes after his intellect and does not want to rely on the faith, and therefore he is shaken and torn and he has no house of rest, since he has no foundation of faith, which is the strongest foundation to rely on and rest in.

Ibid. #6: It is easier for the simple one to reach the clever one's level as well, that is, to be wise and enlightened in all the wisdoms more than the clever one, as we have seen with many, many simple ones and awesome tzaddikim who were wise and enlightened in all the seven wisdoms in ultimate simplicity. And not only that, but they attained a most lofty comprehension, from the aspect of *Chokhmah `Ila'ah/* Upper Wisdom, which is above all the wisdoms. But whoever goes after his intellect and strays after external wisdoms and philosophy, it is very hard for him to return to the ways of truth and the holy faith in entirety, as mentioned above.

Ibid. #7: The king does not want to appoint a clever person to be in charge over the treasuries, lest by means of his cleverness and intellect he squanders the king's treasury. Therefore the king (the King of the Universe) makes specifically a simple man in charge of the treasuries (see the lesson *"Tik`u — Emunah,"* LM II #5).

I bid. #8: The clever man was so prideful in his cleverness, wealth and greatness that the whole entire world was as nil in his eyes, and he had great afflictions in travel, for on account of his cleverness he had no one to talk with, as told in the story. And toward the end, when the king sent for him, the clever man thought cleverly with his cleverness, "What is this? That such a king should send for such a humble and lowly person as I?!" etc., until he came to complete apostasy thereby, as he completely denied the king and "proved" that the entire government was by means of seventy senators. And at first his entire "proofs" were only, "Who has seen the king?" etc.; but towards the end when the simple man, the minister, told him, "Haven't I myself seen the king?" he contradicted him as well and said, "From where do you know that this is the king?" etc. See and discern the depth of his blasphemy's evil; and especially regarding the Ba`al Shem Tov, who was the aspect of the True Tzaddik, he disbelieved to the utmost, as explained there. And all this is due to the nonsense of his wicked and disturbed wisdom, which overturns the straight paths to the total opposite. For, the ways of the holy intellect, which are the aspect of simplicity, are the opposite of all this. For, we need to hold fast in belief in the sages and the True Tzaddikim, and all the more so in the King of the World himself. And in truth, belief in the sages and belief in Hashem Yithbarakh are all one, as explained elsewhere [Ex. 14:31 and *Yalkuth* there; *LM* #61], and they are interdependent. And we also need to believe that even though Hashem Yithbarakh is very great, above all spirituality and high above all blessing and praise, and thought cannot conceive of Him at all, nevertheless He desires our service specifically, as written, *"Ve'abita tehillah migushei `afar um'krotzei chomer/* You desire praise from bodies of dust and from physical formations"* [Yom Kippur liturgy]. So he sends for us and calls us at all times and hints to us holy hints to draw us close to Him, Yithbarakh, and even though a man definitely needs to be lowly in his eyes in truth, nevertheless he needs to believe that Hashem Yithbarakh gets great pleasure from our service. And we need to fulfill, *"Al tehi baz lekhol adam/* Do not disdain any man"* [*Avoth*

4:3], and to know and believe that within each member of Yisrael there is a very good and precious point that is in no other, and we have to receive this point's revelation from him, as also explained elsewhere [*LM* #34]. And whoever goes on this path, definitely each and every member of Yisrael is very important and precious in his eyes, and when he meets even the least member of Yisrael, he will definitely have something to talk about with him and receive from him, or to illuminate him. And even when he meets an idolater, he can receive from him, as also explained in the lesson "*Mi ha'ish hechafetz chayim*/ Who is the man who desires life" [*LM* #33]. And all this we achieve through the ways of simplicity specifically.

Ibid. #9: The simple man, he knows his low [secular] worth, therefore he delves in his craft, the holy service and the service of Hashem, with perseverance, until he has not even free time to sit himself down to a meal, and so forth with his other worldly needs; just while he is occupied in his craft he snatches and eats his meal too, casually etc. And nevertheless if he sees that the project is not completely successful and it is only in the aspect of a "three-cornered shoe," on account of this he does not expect a large payment for his work, since he knows in himself that it is not a perfect state; but nevertheless he delights in this work, feels in it very wonderful pleasure and sweetness, and does not at all look at someone else's work being more perfect than his work, since the other is a very intellectual person and a perceptive person, and presumably also receives greater payment for his work. And the fact that there are many people who have become downcast and have fallen from their devotions due to things like this, that they were jealous of their peers, as they saw that their deeds and devotions were achieved more perfectly etc. — the simple man, however, that is, the one who serves Hashem in simplicity and truth, he does not look at this at all, for what is someone else's affair to him? That is the other's concern and this is his. And he is happy in his lot and has great pleasure from his labor, the service of Hashem, earning his profit handful by handful. And after all his constant work and toil, if he merits only that Hashem Yithbarakh receives from him some bit of satisfaction from a mere movement that he makes for the sake of Heaven in truth and simplicity, certainly this is very much dearer than all riches, to toil in this all the days of one's life. And certainly his reward is not withheld either, and "Better is an hour of cool spirit in the coming world" [than all the life in this world, *Avoth* 4:17].

And see *Likutei Halakhoth: Hilkhoth Pesach* #9, which connects this to the concept that this is the aspect of *"Echad hayah Avraham/* Avraham was one" [Eze 33:24], that a person should think as if he is the only person in the world, and should not look at someone else's affairs; that he should not feel bad even if he is greater than him. And this is the aspect of, *"Usfartem lakhem/* And you shall count *to you"* [Lev. 23:15] — to *yourselves* specifically etc.; look there and see wonderful ways in the service of Hashem.)

STORY #10 (THE BURGHER AND THE PAUPER)

An awesome and wondrous story. Its solution is unknown, but from the hints at the story's end it is discerned that it speaks of the secret of the future Redemption to come, soon in our days, and of the secret of drawing down the soul of Mashiach. And behold, from the story in general it is discerned and clear how the *Sitra Achra*/Other Side ambushes the holiness to hide it entirely, God forbid. And nevertheless *"`atzath Hashem hi takum/* the counsel of Hashem, it shall stand" [Prov. 19:21]; *"Ve'atah marom le`olam Hashem/* But You are on high for ever, Hashem" — Your hand is always on top [Ps. 92:9 and *Yalkuth*], and He, the Blessed One, finishes what is His. And specifically by means of the extreme surge of the hiding force, thereby is raised and exalted afterwards the horn of holiness all the more, as we saw in this story itself, that at first the burgher and the pauper (from whom afterwards emerged the holy couple who later ruled over the face of the earth) were entirely childless, and then the general grabbed the pauper's wife (who was very righteous and Heaven-fearing and merited that afterwards the holy emperor's daughter came from her), and the burgher's compassion was very aroused and he did a very reckless thing (and it was a truly insane thing, etc.), until he merited to take her out of there, and he took cover with her in the seven bodies of water, which are the pit, mikveh, pond, spring, stream, river, and sea (which is discerned by everyone, that this hints to very high and hidden things), and in each and every place she swore to him etc., as explained there. And specifically due to the force of the surge of such great concealment, they merited afterwards to bear children and from them descended the holy couple mentioned. But then too the concealment surged up greatly, and they wanted to separate this holy couple. And they stalked the emperor's daughter much more, and sons of nobility wanted to have matches with her. And similarly, the soaring success of the pauper, until he became emperor over the whole world, was also part of the surge and concealment, for thereby he further refused to have a match with the burgher's son, and he devised thoughts about him to remove him from the world entirely etc. But Hashem's counsel stands, and by the end all this was reversed into goodness, for the holy couple received the kingdom and they reigned over the face of the earth.

Also discerned from this story is how Hashem Yithbarakh conducts His world measure-for-measure. For just as the judges sentenced the burgher's son to have him put in a sack and thrown into the sea, Hashem Yithbarakh then brought it about that the murderer upon the sea put the emperor's daughter into the sack. And just as the burgher took cover with the pauper's wife in the seven bodies of water, and she swore to him etc., likewise later the murderer took cover with the emperor's daughter also in these places. And just as the burgher's son had to be exiled from his father's house, until he got lost in a wilderness, likewise the emperor's daughter too came to this very same wilderness, and so too the emperor himself was driven out of his house and also came to this wilderness. But in the final end Hashem Yithbarakh brought it about that specifically through this was the redemption, for the three of them met up together, and the emperor's daughter found the letter, and they all returned home, and the emperor too returned to his home, and the couple received the kingdom.

Also understood from the story is how it is completely forbidden for a man to despair, God forbid, for there is nothing in the world to despair of, as we saw with the burgher's son, that it did not at all enter his mind to find the letter which he had hidden in a tree, for there were millions of trees there, and it was already concluded in his mind that he would never get back to any settled area, but just live out the days of his life there in the wilderness, and he proved to the emperor and the emperor's daughter that it is good to live out all the days of their lives there. Nevertheless he still did not despair his heart entirely, but walked every day and made some sign on three trees, and looked for the document in them. "*Kulei ha'i ve'ulai*/ All this and only maybe" he would find the document (which contained the essence of the bond between him and the emperor's daughter, which hints to the core source of holiness of all Yisrael's hope). And when he sought and did not find it, he would cry a very great deal and return from there with cried-out eyes, and on the next day he did the same, as mentioned. And likewise each and every day, until later the emperor's daughter herself found her document and returned it to him. And this was certainly a great and wonderful joy, but nevertheless despair overcame the burgher's son and he said, "What good is the document for me? How can I find her... Here I will live out the days of my life." And he gave the document back to her, until she had to ask him to go with her too etc. And he agreed to go with her, and from this is discerned by every man how it is forbidden to despair, but to just look for the holiness at all times, even if it seems to him that according to what he knows in his soul, the plagues of his heart and his pains, it is very far-fetched that he should attain the holiness. Nevertheless he should do his part, and seek after it with all his might, and even if it seems to him that even after searching so many, many years without finding and without attaining any level of holiness at all — and he will definitely need to cry about this a great deal every day, nevertheless he should still search. "All this and only maybe? All this and just maybe!" (*kulei ha'i we'ulai, kulei ha'i we'ulai*). Until if the man is truly very strong in this all the days of his life, Hashem Yithbarakh will have mercy on him, and the source of holiness itself will assist and help him search as well, until, as it were, she herself finds the document and returns it to him. Only, since the thing must be in secret and concealment of the thing, for the sake of free will's existence, therefore the despair surges up on him then as well, until as it were she is forced to ask him to go with her, until they come to their home etc. Then they receive grandeur in perfectness.

But the inside of the story, and the holy lofty hints that are clothed in each and every interest in it, are very hidden, concealed and obscure. "`Amoq amoq, mi yimtza'enu/ Deep, deep, who can find it out?" [Eccl. 7:24] And see more in the new thoughts in *Chayey Moharan* pg. 5.

There, on the last page of the story, is written, "*Ha'hárah himmalét* (to the mountain flee for salvation, Gen. 19:17) — this is a burgher" [a play on words: Yid. *barg* mountain, pl. *berg* < Ger. *berg* mountain; ME *burgh* city < O. Eng. *burg* fortified town; O. High Ger. *burg* fortified castle, all from Indo-European root **bhergh*]. And apparently this is incomprehensible, for didn't he *not* flee to the mountain but only to Tzo`ar, as explicitly stated in the holy Torah? But the truth is: the angel who told him, "flee to the mountain," meant that — that in truth, Lot would not be saved except in the merit of Avraham, and as written, "*Vayhi beshacheth... vayyizkor Elohim eth-Avraham vayshalach eth-Lot/* And it came to pass, when God destroyed... and God remembered Avraham and sent Lot out..." [ibid. :29]. And the matter of his flight to Tzo`ar was by Hashem Yithbarakh's providence, as thereby were born `Amon and Moav; hence the essential salvation of Lot was in the merit of Avraham, which the angel hinted to him in his statement, "*Ha'hárah himmalét;*" and this is the aspect of the burgher.

(*Likutei `Etzoth 2/e Yir'ah Ve`Avodath Hashem* #35: It is known that the whole job of Yisrael is to extricate the holiness from the exile, from amidst the *qelipoth*/husks and the *Sitra Achra*/Other Side. And sometimes a man has a big arousal for some devotion and thing in holiness, when he might do a reckless thing that seems truly insane, and there is no human intellect that would agree to this, how he will be able to attain this thing. But nevertheless on account of his true arousal, Hashem delivers him success and he merits to get through all the boundaries and obstacles and break them all, until he merits to finish the thing and take the holiness out from them completely, while in truth it is above nature and human intellect entirely. However, all this is the aspect of *retz'o*/running, the aspect of entering [see *LM* #6:4 and Zohar II 213b: Fortunate is the lot of he who enters (to grasp higher perceptions of Godliness) and exits]. But the main trial is afterwards, when he is in the aspect of returning, when he returns to his mind and his existence; then the Sitra Achra pursues him and he has to take cover from it, with many, many strategies, and many, many kinds of waters change and pass over him, and

many, many trials etc. etc. And whoever merits to be strong, he
will merit then as well to pass through everything in peace; fortunate is he!

Ibid. #39: The root of Yisrael's holiness gives and transmits
signs to each member of Yisrael who makes an approach to
cleave to and bind himself with her, in order that through these
signs, the bond and the secluded unity [yichud] between them
will be whole, and no other party mixes in between them. Except,
the Accuser exceedingly attacks this, until he causes the man to
be distanced and driven out from his holiness to a place of wilderness, and then he attacks yet more, until a storm wind comes and
makes such confusion that he also loses the signs; and meanwhile
what happens to the man happens. And similarly, to the branches
of parts of holiness that pertain to each person happens a great
deal as well, for many waylay them to catch them with their
traps, and for the most part, the man himself causes this, and all
of them are like envoys from him, God forbid, and then the Accuser surges up even more on the pieces of holiness, until the aspect of a murderer comes and entirely catches it in its trap, and
wants to drown it completely, God forbid. But nevertheless
"`atzath Hashem hi takum/ the counsel of Hashem, it shall stand"
[Prov. 19:21]; "ve'atah marom le`olam Hashem/ but You are on
high for ever, Hashem" [Ps. 92:9]. And when the man is strong in
his mind and does not despair nevertheless, and fixes times every
day to search and dig after the signs of holiness that were lost
from him — and if he does not merit to find it, he nevertheless
lays out his conversation about this before Hashem Yithbarakh
and cries and pleads before Him Yithbarakh, "like a son implor-
ing his father" [Ta`anith 23a] — then in the final end everything
will be reversed to good, and specifically by means of this murderer who snatched the holiness into his trap entirely, through
him Hashem brings it about that the holiness draws close to the
man, really close to him. But only, they still do not know and recognize each other. Then Hashem Yithbarakh brings it about that
the first one who caused the man to be distant and drove him out
from his holiness, he too will turn out being there, and they all
help the man to search and seek the signs of holiness. And
Hashem Yithbarakh helps them that the holiness itself finds the
signs and returns it to its owner, that is, the man. And then there

is definitely a great celebration. But nevertheless the holiness still does not reveal herself to the man that this is she, in order that the approach and the secluded unification not be in the aspect of *harisah*/destruction, the aspect of *"pen-yehersu*/ lest they break through" etc. [Ex. 19:21], and not in the proper way, God forbid, in a place of wilderness, etc. And on account of this, even when she returns the signs to him, then the concealment and despair return and surge up on the man, for how can he seek out the holiness, knowing that to her as well has happened what has happened? so who knows where she is now? And then the holiness itself appeases the man and asks him to go with her, until both of them arrive and come back to their first place, to the source of the root of their holiness. And then they gather unto one another, and the reunion and joy is entire. *"Vehayah Hashem lemelekh `al-kol-ha'aretz*/ And Hashem will be king over the entire earth" etc. [Zech. 14:9]. Look some more there and discern further, according to what is hinted in [these] basic meanings of the things, aside from the awesome secrets that are in this story, as inferred in the notes following it.)

STORY #11 (THE EXCHANGED CHILDREN)

A very exceedingly awesome and wonderful story, as declared by his holy mouth himself z"l. And as explained at the end of the story, clothed in it are very holy and wonderful secrets, lofty hints. It speaks of the secret of `Olam haTikkun/ the World of Repair, and the repair of the holy souls and the holy sparks that have fallen where they have fallen and come to where they have come, by means of the force of the interchanges, from the secret of the *Heikhlei Hatemuroth*/ Interchange Palaces, until not only is the kingdom given to the servant's son, and the king's true son is given over to the servant and grows up in his house and becomes distant from royal manners (even though by his nature he is very much drawn after royal manners, as explained there), but also the interchanges become so strong that it is hushed to mention the affair of the interchange at all and to say about him that perhaps he is the true king's son; and whoever talks about it, they punish him and take revenge on him; and not only that, but they devise thoughts to entirely annihilate the king's son, God forbid, that his name be not mentioned at all, God forbid, in the aspect of

"*Lekhu venakhchidem migoy velo yizakher shem Yisrael `od*/ Come, and let us cut them off from being a nation; that the name of Yisrael may be no more in remembrance" [Ps. 83:5], God forbid; and to the extent that the king's son thereby has to be uprooted from his place and be a refugee and exile, traveling about and wandering. And behold, truthfully this matter itself, that the king (who is actually the bondmaid's son) attacks him so much that he has to flee, it is also only from the aspect of the sophistries and lies, the changes and interchanges of the *Heikhlei Hatemuroth*. For how can it arise in his mind to do such a great injustice against the bondservant himself, for maybe this is his father (as he actually was)?! Especially against the son — for not only are there those who say that he is the king's son and the whole reign belongs to him, and through the switch and interchange the reign was given to the servant's son, in the aspect of "*Tachath-`eved ki yimlokh*/ Because of a servant having the reign" [Prov. 30:22] — even devising thoughts to entirely eliminate the king's son himself from the world, God forbid, until he had to flee and be exiled. And anyhow, he did not deserve this, which the king himself actually realized later, and he pondered in himself that he had committed a great injustice in this, as explained there. But more than all this, the interchanges grew so severe in the heart of the king's son himself that he became very downcast in his mind, and he took to drunkenness and went after the dictates of his heart. This was worst of all. And this too was only on account of the fallacious sophistries and reasonings that are drawn from the *Heikhlei Hatemuroth*; thus did he himself meditate afterwards: "If it is so, that Hashem Yithbarakh can do such a thing... is it right what I have done?" And he regretted this very much, as explained there. But this very matter, that the king himself had thoughts of *teshuvah*/ return and regret, and also that such thoughts came to the king's true son, and also the matter that then came about thereby, until the repair was complete, was all only by the graces of Hashem Yithbarakh, in the aspect of "*Ve'atah marom le`olam Hashem*/ But You are on high for ever, Hashem" [Ps. 92:9], that He caused and drew down some revelation and flash of holiness from the place where it was drawn and revealed, until the *temuroth*/interchanges became cleared somewhat, until the world was repaired and Hashem Yithbarakh brought it about that the king got lost in the thick of the forest, by means of chasing after the horse that ran away from him, and the king's son got lost there by pursuing the beasts that ran away from him. And all this was measure for measure, because when the changes and interchanges grew so strong upon them here, to the same extent the king's son received his punishment by chasing after the beasts until he got so lost thereby. For this is also from the aspect of the change and interchange, because Hashem Yithbarakh created the man with intellect and knowledge, whereby the horse is subservient to the rider, for the man is in control with his mind over all the beasts and animals and he conducts them. But those who are drawn after the folly and the interchanges, thereby the thing is altered for them, that the beasts were drawing and conducting them, until they got lost where they got lost by chasing after them so much. And therefore in truth, when the king's son told the man of the forest that he is chasing the beasts, the man told him, "Leave off from chasing after your sins! For this is not beasts at all but rather your transgressions are what are making you go that way. Enough for you; you have received yours... so now leave off from pursuing them any more. Come with me and you will arrive at what befits you" etc. And specifically to the king's son he said thus, as also indicated in the text. All this is understood from the simplest of simple meanings of the things.

But the wonderful depth and the lofty secrets that are in each matter of this holy story, even in matters that seem to us to be according to their simple meaning, and especially with what is obvious to everyone's eyes that they are awesome secrets — for example the laughter that they heard in the forest, which the man of the forest later explained to them the secret of the matter, and the matter of the man of the forest himself, and the sack of bread that the king's son found in the forest, by means of which the king was sold to him as a slave, and how the man of the forest made them to pass over the place where there were snakes and scorpions and brought them into his house that stands in the air, and fed them and went away, and how the king himself told the king's son the reason why he arrived here, and how they heard the sound of the animals and birds and they inclined their ears and heard it is a wonderful melody, and how the man of the forest later explained to them the secret of this melody, and the matter of the instrument that he gave the king's son, and ordered him to go to the country that is called by this name, "The Foolish Country and the Wise King," and there he would come into his greatness, and all the matters of the story to the end — all of them are exceedingly awesome and wonderful, concealed, laid up, and covered from everyone's eyes, in the aspect of, *"Mah rav-tuvekha asher-tzafanta lire'eykha/* How abundant is Your goodness which You have laid up for those that fear You" [Ps. 31:20]. And fortunate, fortunate is he who merits discerning and attaining some flash in them!

(*Likutei `Etzoth 2/e Da`ath* #17: The fact that the world is so far from Hashem Yithbarakh, is only because they do not have *yeshuv hada`ath/* a mind that is settled with the correct mindset, as explained elsewhere. For in truth, when the *Heikhlei Hatemuroth/* interchange palaces wax strong, then not only do they exchange and alter bad to good and good to bad etc. in all the world, and give all the rule and the greatness to the bondmaid's son, and also in the core of the thought of the bondmaid's son's himself the *Heikhlei Hatemuroth* grew so strong that they turned over his mind and heart so much to cause great ills to his true father himself, and to drive out the king's son entirely, but also in the core of the thought of the true king's son himself the *Heikhlei Hatemuroth* prevailed and exchanged and altered his mind to the opposite of the truth, until he became so downcast in his mind by being upset at being driven out, until he took himself to drunkenness and walked after his heart's dictates (as explained above at length), and therefore in truth, afterwards even the bondmaid's son himself when he somewhat entered into the category of *yeshuv hada`ath* discerned in himself that he had made a grave mistake in driving out the king's son, for, "any way one looks at it" etc. And all the more so, the king's son, when he came to his senses, then he discerned the truth, that on the contrary, "If Hashem Yithbarakh can do such a thing etc., then is it right what I have done" etc.? And he was very regretful, and by means of these regrets the world returned to its proper state, as in the text. So behold, we see that everything depends just on honest *yeshuv hada`ath*, as mentioned.

Ibid. *Mamon Parnasah* #23: Sometimes a man chases after his livelihood, or after other things that it seems to him that he is very much forced to pursue after them, and he chases after them all his days and is unable to attain them, and because of this he is constantly full of anger and pains. And in truth, if he would put it to his heart and see in himself that he is only chasing after his sins, because his transgressions are what make him stray from one thing to another and from one reason to another, until he is chasing after actual thin air all his days, and it does not let him rest his spirit, and in truth perhaps he has already received his punishment for his sins — enough; he is released, and the time of his repair and rest has already come.

Ibid. *Teshuvah* #8: If a man would attain honest, complete remorse, then even though it may be that afterwards he will go back to his place and whatever happens to him happens, nevertheless his thoughts of remorse and return have already mixed him up anyhow, until in the final end he will merit to reach his true repair in entirety. And this is as we saw with him [the bondservant's son] afterwards too, constant regrets for the great evil and injustice that he did against the king's son, for driving him out etc., until by means of these remorses of both of them, the world returned to its repair, as explained in the text.)

STORY #12 (THE PRAYER LEADER)

An awesome and wonderful story, marvelous and wondrous, as noted and explained at the end of the story, which talks about the secret of *Mitath Hamelakhim*/ Death of the Kings and their repair etc. And according to its simple meaning too, explained in it, in each and every matter, are smart guidance and straight ways, and it tells in general about almost every kind of error and deceptive reasoning of falsehood and error that is found in the world, and their clarification and repair.

And behold, the Prayer Leader, all of whose interests, thoughts and deeds were just for the true and eternal ultimate purpose, and who was constantly involved in prayers etc., dwelled outside the settled areas, except that he regularly entered in the settled area in order to draw people into serving Hashem Yithbarakh. And whoever gave him consent, he would immediately take him out of the settlement, because most of civilizations, as they are presently, before completion of the repair, are very far from the true purpose, as in the statement, "*Ki rov*

ma`aseihem tohu/ For, most of their deeds are astonishingly void"
[morning prayers, Ashkenaz and Sefard; v. Eccl. 3:19]. So all the
practices of the Prayer Leader and his people were almost opposite the conduct of civilization, and therefore a big fast or deprivation was more a delight than all the pleasures in the world, as explained following this, the story of the world's settlements, most
of which are drawn after worldly vanities, pleasures and cravings,
and therefore the Prayer Leader and his people's place was outside of settlement. And so now as well, whoever wants to think
just about the true purpose, which needs a great deal of actual
isolated meditation, but even when he is in the settlement and is
forced to be mingled with creatures such as these that are entirely far from the purpose — nevertheless it is known that the
essence of man is his intellect and thought; therefore one must be
alert then too that in any case that his thought be outside of settlement, and to distance his thought, mind and all his conduct
from all the aspects of foreign practices, foreign mindsets and
false reasonings that are very much found and present among
most people in settlement. And it may be that this is also included in what is explained further on, that by means of the
storm wind all the world was mixed up and desert made into settlement etc. For, at present, due to our many sins, most people in
settlement are quite astray from the way of truth, and they are
really in the aspect of "*Ta`u bamidbar bishimon darekh, `ir
moshav lo matza'u*/ They wandered in the wilderness in a desert
way; they found no city of habitation" [Ps. 107:4], and not only
that but also they do not at all feel that they are astray in wilderness; on the contrary it seems to them that this is the essential
settlement. And therefore the Prayer Leader and his people were
forced to dwell outside of settlement etc. And regarding clothing
he was not particular at all, for most of mankind are very pas-
sionate about expensive clothes, and thereby they are more
caught in the Accuser's web, as explained elsewhere on the verse,
"*Vatitpesehu bevighdho*/ And she caught hold of him by his garment" [Gen. 39:12]. And the Prayer Leader paid no mind to this
specifically, at all. And nevertheless it is explained, further on,
that when the Prayer Leader would discern of one of his people
that he needed, for serving Hashem, that he be clothed in golden
garments, he would provide it for him. However, it is understood

that this was only for a few special people; but for most mankind the right way for them is to not be particular about clothes at all, especially as long as they have not reached a high level and great wealth; then if Hashem Yithbarakh wants for their benefit that they go dressed in expensive garments, because it is specially potent for them for serving Hashem, there is no limit for Hashem to deliver and bestow abundant riches on them. But they themselves need to be careful to thoroughly bind themselves in their minds that one does not need to be particular about clothes at all, as mentioned. And similarly regarding other needs of a man, such as eating and drinking: one also need not be particular, as explained there, that in this place where the Prayer Leader dwelled there was a river before him and trees and fruit, and they would eat from the fruit.

And behold, it is explained in the text that the people of the settlement lay in wait on the Prayer Leader to seize him. And this was on account of the world being confused and they were so lost in their distorted mindsets that whoever was drawn after the true purpose and talked against their errant reasoning and was involved in drawing people close to serving Hashem Yithbarakh, they lay in wait on him to capture and seize him, therefore he had to carry about this with great cleverness, as explained in the text the Prayer Leader's practices in this.

And behold, explained in the text are various kinds of bizarre ways and practices and bad mentalities by which people of the world were distorted after the confusion of the storm wind, and most extensively it explains the matter of the country that was very sunk in the craving of money etc. Aside from the great internal matter that is in each of these stories, and the roots of the things, from where have been drawn down and evolved all these kinds of errors in which the world has been so confounded — aside from all this the reader will rightly judge that all of this is not a story that ever happened, but rather, this is how the world behaves presently, with all the details explained there. For some people, the errors and distortions drawn from one sect that chose for them that purpose overtook them the most; and others, other distortions of another sect overcame them the most. And so there are many variations in this, according to the variation of place and time. For, sometimes upon one person, one bad trait and one foreign mindset prevails in him, and at another time a different trait, different mentality and different distorted mindset prevails in him. The rule is that by means of all this the world grows so very far from the true purpose, that our rabbis z"l have said, "*Ra'iti benei `aliyah vehema me'utim/* I have seen the elite members of Heaven, and they are few" [*Sukkah* 45b]. And therefore whoever looks into this story with an honest eye, discerning heart and straight and pure thought, will learn from all this, smart and righteous guidance how to be very careful with his soul, to not stumble and go astray on errant paths and distortion of his mind, by means of everything that is discerned in this awesome story, and from other words of Rabbeinu z"l haKadosh, which are faithful and stated in righteousness and judgment, truth and straightness.

Also discerned from this story is how much one needs to be strong and involve himself in this business, to talk with people regarding the true purpose and take them out from their error. And even if thereby he will have enemies and those who lie in wait to capture him, and even if it seems to him that he has accomplished nothing with them with his words and that they are not heard by them at all, nevertheless he should do his part and be strong and be busy with this, and talk with them once more, and very many times, even if he comes to exert great toil thereby and a vast amount of time will pass that he is involved with them and does not perfectly affect one thing in them at all.

But rather, in any case, it *will* be discerned from their words that they already have some doubt in their hearts: perhaps his words are true, that the main thing is to be involved for the true purpose? — even though in real actuality he will still not see anything in them that inclines toward this, but just the opposite, like their prior conduct. Nevertheless, these words too, that he will hear from them that they already have some doubt in this matter, this too will be very dear and precious in his eyes like one who finds a great prize, since it is discerned by him that the things have already begun to enter in their ears a little, confuse them, and make some doubt in them in any case, that they will not be so strong in their distorted mindsets, and he should trust in Hashem Yithbarakh that in the final end He will thereby finish every matter of the repair entirely.

And the rest of the matters of this story: particularly regarding the holy assembly of the King and his people, and how he showed each one of his people a way how to receive his power, and the matter of the Hand that the King had, which was a "*landkart*/land map" of all the worlds, and how they were all scattered by the storm wind, etc., and how afterwards they all gathered together and thereby the entire world was repaired, and the matter of the Warrior's path to the Sword hanging in the air, from whence he received his power, and only by this way could they remedy and extricate people from the craving of money, by means of the foods cooked in the *Kech*/Kitchen, by means of the pipes that extend to it from the Fiery Mountain, on which a Lion crouches, and the rest of all the details of the matter explained in the text, and how this entire story is hinted in Isa. 31 etc. — even though we have no concept and no glimmer in the mind about all this, nevertheless it is discerned and obvious to everyone's eye, really tangibly, that they are all very wondrous and awesome things; no thought can contain them; and there is awoken a wondrous desire for serving Hashem for everyone who looks into them. "*Mi-shama` kazoth, mi ra'ah ka'eleh*/ Who has heard such a thing? Who has seen such things?" [Isa. 66:8]

(*Likutei `Etzoth 2/e: Yir'ah ve`Avodath Hashem* #40: Everyone must admit that whoever makes more effort and is closer to the ultimate purpose, ought to be head and king over everybody. For, everyone acknowledges that the main thing is the ultimate purpose. But since the great storm wind happened and it confused and turned over the world entirely, water to dry land and dry land to water, wilderness to habitation and so forth, and the King and the Queen etc. and all his people were separated and scattered, and all the world's people were confused and separated and partitioned into many factions over speculation what is the ultimate purpose: Some of them said that the main purpose is honor, to be pursuing, God forbid, after honor and attain it; and they had demonstrations, proofs and reasons for this. And some of them said that the main purpose is murder, anger, cruelty and brazenheartedness; some said the main purpose is procreation; and similarly all the factions who were very confused and disrupted regarding the purpose, as all this is explained in the text. And each faction of them in each trait or craving that they chose for themselves as the purpose, certainly were very sunk in it, for aside from man's very nature being drawn after bad traits and cravings, apart from this the thing was for them like a religion, that this is the purpose, according to what each faction of them chose for themselves according to their confused opinions. And more than all, most disturbed and confused was the faction that chose for themselves that money is the purpose, until they made money a complete idol and god, God forbid; and they would offer themselves as sacrifices to the idol of money. And in truth, even though from all the bad cravings it is very hard to extract a man that is sunk in it, especially when he is rooted in them so much that they have become for him a religion and purpose — harder than all is to extract and repair these that are more fallen and sunken into craving money, for it is hardest to extract them from there, as in the text. And in truth, even though most people, each individual is composed of the evil of all the factions and his mind is disrupted and confused from all the kinds of the aforementioned disruptions, sometimes one trait and some craving challenges him more, and sometimes another craving and trait challenges him more. Nevertheless, in the generality of mankind there are also great differences from one man to another. This one is most excited about chasing honor; another, anger and murder challenge him the most by his nature, and so forth with all the aforementioned traits. So, fortunate is the holy faction whose mind honestly agreed with the true purpose and said that the main goal is just to occupy oneself with prayer and to be humble and lowly etc. (in the way that our rabbis z"l said the prayer of the lowly is not despised, *Sotah* 14), and they elected the Prayer Leader as king, who was an exceedingly great and holy tzaddik, and by means of the Prayer Leader and this faction of his, and in the merit of their many holy prayers, the King and his people were gathered together, and all the aforementioned factions went out from their nonsense and errors, and returned in repentance, and the whole entire world returned to its ultimate repair in entirety.

Ibid. *Mamon Parnasah* #21: One needs to be extremely careful to not be excited for the craving of money, because there are those who are so excited for money and extremely sunk in this, that all status and importance for them is only according to money, and whoever only has a little money, and especially someone who is entirely poor, is entirely not within the bounds of humanity, according to the nonsense of their mindset, and is considered among them just as an animal or bird. And accordingly whoever has a very great deal of money is in their eyes as higher than human bounds, and is instead in the category of a star, a constellation, an angel — and on up to those that have such abundant money that they are considered by them almost gods entirely and idols, God forbid. And many people in the world have so entered in this nonsense and error of craving money that the poor and those who lack money have so fallen in their own eyes and minds versus the rich and those who have money, until they virtually offer themselves as a sacrifice to them due to the self-deprecation they have in the presence of their big money. And in truth it is not so, as the scripture has said, *"Mah-le`oni yode`a, lahalokh neged hachayim/* What [advantage] has the poor man that has understanding, in walking before the living"* [Eccl. 6:8], for the [wise] poor person is considered in the category of mankind just as the rich, and also the rich are only humans, and are cut down like grass, and silver, gold and so forth do not follow a man [to the grave]. And in truth there are people that are so sunken in craving money that someone who comes to demonstrate to them that craving money is nonsense, and that money is not a purpose at all, then not only are his words not heard by them at all, but also he is for them like someone that talks against the religion, because money for them is the essential goal and the religion, God forbid. So in truth these that have fallen into craving money, it is much harder to take them out of this than all those that have fallen into the rest of the cravings, God save us, and only by the way explained in the text.

Ibid. #22: There exist such foods (presumably they are spiritual, we infer), that when a person merits to eat and taste of these foods, he immediately throws away the craving of money, and feels the great stench of money, which stinks like actually feces, to the extent that one is very embarrassed to have money, and money is the greatest shame of all shames, and whoever has more money is more ashamed, and even those of low level and who lack money are very ashamed of themselves for being so small in their eyes on account of lacking money. For, now it is revealed to them that on the contrary, money is the main embarrassment, and therefore the wealthy are much more ashamed, and they bury themselves in holes in the dirt due to the great embarrassment that one person feels before another, until they cannot raise their faces at all due to the shame. For, these foods have the special power that through them a person is repulsed by money with the utmost repulsion, and throws away his idols of silver and idols of gold [Isa. 2:20], as will happen in the future, soon in our days.

I bid. *Tzaddik* #80: The True Tzaddik who occupies himself with drawing mankind to serving Hashem Yithbarakh dwells with his people outside the settlement, meaning: because all his abode and practices are definitely the real opposite of the ways of the settled area, whose deeds are empty and they chase after waste and weary themselves with the vanities of the time. But the Tzaddik and his people are far from all this entirely, and they suffice with what they have, and especially regarding their clothes they are not at all particular, so they are as people who really live outside of civilization entirely, in all their mindsets, practices and occupation only in prayer, songs and praise to Hashem Yithbarakh, and repentances, confessions, fasts etc. And for these people, all the great devotion in serving Hashem that seems to most of the world like a hard thing to accept upon themselves such devotion, especially deprivations, fasts etc. — for them, all this is more precious than all the world's pleasures, for they have more pleasure from the great deprivation, fast, etc. than from all the world's pleasures. But nevertheless even though they dwell outside of settlement, anyway they still go into settlement repeatedly, in order to draw more people into serving Hashem, and they carry about this with great cleverness, as explained in the text.

I bid. #87: This Tzaddik can "suffice" for each and every person who follows him what he needs. If he discerns of one of his people that in accord with his brain he needs for serving Hashem to go dressed in very expensive garments, he provides him; and likewise sometimes the opposite, that is, some rich person draws close to him and he takes him out of settlement as mentioned, and leads him there in lesser garments. And the rule is that he knows the need of providing for each and every person, and thus he provides him and conducts him, as mentioned.

Ibid. *Tefillah* #24: How very lofty is the sanctity of prayer, which is beyond everything, for wasn't the Prayer Leader, who was very great and holy in all the good traits and in all the levels of charity, nevertheless only called by the name "Prayer Leader?" And he compiled many books regarding prayer and arranged for his students a ready path for this, and he, specifically, merited passing by the places of all the King's people; and all the King's people themselves — each of whom was an awesome and wondrous novelty, each one according to his aspect and trait — nevertheless they all acknowledged and said that the fact that the King and his people were gathered together and the world was repaired in entirety, it was all only in the merit of the Prayer Leader and in the merit of his abundant holy prayers; and similarly the purification of the whole world and its repair, each and every sect according to its aspect, was only by means of this Prayer Leader.

Ibid. *Tochakhah* #7: This person who occupies himself with drawing mankind to serving Hashem, even though in truth the main thing is to try to draw great people, notable people, that is, the wise, the rich and the pedigreed, for such people have an additional, higher level also with regard to their souls; and also because when one merits to draw such people, then those of lower level draw close anyway, as this is discerned and explained elsewhere. But nevertheless, since the Accuser waxes very strong against this, and mainly against drawing great people, and summons against this many, many obstacles, therefore this True Tzaddik as well who begins to be involved with this, drawing people to serving Hashem, is also forced at the first beginning to be involved with people of low level, namely with the poor and so forth, talking to their hearts to wake them up to Hashem Yithbarakh and thoroughly explaining to them that there is no other purpose in the whole entire world except being busy in serving Hashem all the days of one's life, and so forth such words, until his words enter in their ears and they consent with all their hearts and all their souls to be connected with him, and then he takes them and brings them to his place which is outside of settlement (and as explained above, the explanation of the matter of outside of settlement). And later when these who have become followers merit to truly receive his words and they delve only in prayers etc. and fasts etc., until there are found among them as well, some people who are also fit to draw people to serving Hashem, then the Tzaddik gives them permission to also enter into settlement and be busy with this matter, until the Tzaddik's gathering increases and grows and it makes a big impression on the world.

Ibid. #8: This Tzaddik, who pertains to the Prayer Leader who draws people to serving Hashem, he conducts himself very cleverly in this, altering and changing himself for each and every person with a different change, as explained in the text. And so too when he discerns that he will have no effect he goes around with other words and hides his good intention, as explained there. And all this is in order that they do not recognize that this is he, because then it is possible that his words will not at all enter the ears of the listener and he will be unwilling to talk with him and hear his words at all, on account of the strength of the bad venom that is rooted in the heart of many mankind, by means of which as soon as one starts to talk with them and draw them close to the good, then the evil stirs up, God forbid, to the same degree, until thereby they not only do not listen to his pleasant words, but also sometimes they stir up against him in hatred and great warfare, as also discerned from the words of Rabbeinu z"l. And because of this the Tzaddik is forced to alter himself and hide his good intention, as in the text.)

STORY #13 (THE SEVEN BEGGARS)

An awesome and wonderful story including many interests, and each and every interest is a wonderful story, wondrous and marvelous, full of wonderful secrets and lofty hints, aside from the wonderful *mussar*/practical guidance that is discerned from each and every story, even according to its simple meaning.

And behold, from the start of the story, about the king who transferred the reign to his only son, it is discerned there how a man needs to constantly prevail in being strong in joy, even during the time of his fall from reign, God forbid (and whoever cannot prevail in joy even when he has a fall, then it is very right and fitting that he falls from his level, since he cannot prevail in joy during the decline, God forbid).

And similarly it is discerned there how even the greatest of great men need to be very careful to not stumble, God forbid, by too much cleverness, such as what happened with the king's son and his wise men, that by their over-cleverness they fell into heresy, God save us; and the king's son himself, even though on account of having good in him and reflecting occasionally where he is in the world, and moaning and sighing a great deal for having fallen into such confusions — as soon as he began to use his intellect, the cleverness of apostasy came back and prevailed in him. And thus it happened several times, as explained in the text. Discerned from this is how one needs to be careful and guard himself against entering in this at all. And regarding this was said, *"Ve'al-tithchakam yother/* Neither be overly wise" [Eccl. 7:16]. And many warnings about this are already explained in his words z"l.

(*Likutei `Etzoth 2/e Chaqiroth* #4: Sometimes there are people who delve a great deal only in wisdoms, and for the most part, their intention in this is only for the sake of the futilities of this world, that is, for the sake of prestige, honor, money and so forth. And because they delve only in wisdoms, thereby they completely forget the strategies of war (that is, how to fight the greatest war that a man needs to fight in this world, which is the war with one's *yetzer/* evil inclination). And sometimes they arrive at complete heresy by the wisdoms, as explained above; therefore one needs to be very careful about this.)

And behold, after this story of the son (which is also an incomplete story and still not finished), he begins to talk about the matter of the children who are the boy and girl who got lost during the fleeing of people that passed through the forest, and how the beggars came to them and gave them bread and blessed them. Then he tells about their wedding, how they longed for the beggars; and they [the beggars] came again to them and gave them *derashah geshenk*. And each and every story is a very awesome and wonderful matter and extremely wondrous, as discerned by whoever looks into it.

And behold, the story of the beggars as a whole encompasses almost the entire *Shi`ur Qomah* ["measurements" of the Divine "image"]. For, the first one was blind, the second was deaf, the third was speech-impaired, the fourth was crooked-necked, the fifth was hunchback, the sixth was armless, and the seventh was footless. But in fact they were intact in all these limbs of theirs, in such great perfection that has no greater perfection beyond it; just the opposite: on account of the greatly exceptional perfection of their height and their very lofty, enormous and awesome level, and also on account the great strength of the world's concealment, therefore they appeared in the world's eyes like blind, deaf and so forth. Similarly discerned there as well is the power of the strength of this world's concealment and hiding, until the aspect of such a holy, wondrous and awesome wedding that is made up of such wondrous and awesome stories as these, had its place of *chupah*/wedding-canopy and wedding inside a big pit that they covered with reeds, dirt and garbage, and the feast was from their collecting bread and meat from the *myenines* (birthday) of the king. But this wedding was such a big, awesome and wondrous joy and with such awesome and wondrous revelation. Also discerned there is the great loftiness of holy longing and hope, for by means of the holy children longing, crying and yearning each time how to bring the beggars here etc., they merited one beggar from these beggars revealing himself to them each time, and revealing new, wondrous, awesome things to them; and not only that, but the children merited that the beggars conferred and gave to them all these aspects in the legality of a *derashah geshenk*. And accordingly, also discerned is the great high level of the holy children, who merited receiving such gifts; but in any case everything was by means of their holy longing, yearning and hope.

Also discerned there is how when some time of celebration comes to a man (for instance, a wedding celebration and so forth), he needs to remind himself of the great charities that Hashem Yithbarakh has done for him from the time he came to exist until this day, and to give Hashem Yithbarakh praise and thanks for all this from amidst his joy, and to wake up from within his joy with great hopes and yearnings for Hashem Yithbarakh who has bestowed and performed such kindnesses, specifically — because it is all only in the legality of a charitous gift from Him, Yithbarakh.

And behold, the first Blind Beggar boasted of his long life, and said about himself, "I am very old and still I am entirely a suckling babe" etc.; and that he has a consensus on this from the Great Eagle, and he told, regarding this, about the people who journeyed a great deal by ships on the sea, and a storm wind came and broke the ships etc., and the matter of the elders, where each one told an old story, what he remembers from his first memory etc. And behold, all of this story is awesome and wondrous even according to their actual simple meanings, for who has heard such a thing, that a man boasts of such a memory, that he remembers even when they cut his umbilical cord, which is really right after birth when he emerges from his mother's womb? (And even though we have found in the *Yerushalmi Ketuboth*, chapter "*Af `al pi...*" [*perek* 5 *halakhah* 6 *Gemara*, *daf* 36] that Shmuel boasted that he recognizes his midwife from the time of his birth, and Rabbi Yehoshu`a ben Levi said he recognizes the mohel from when he was circumcised, and Rabbi Yochanan said he recognizes the women who accompanied his mother when he was born — in truth they too were prodigious at a very extraordinary level, as the greatness of their level is well known throughout all of Shas.) And here the first elder boasted of the aspect of this memory, and the second elder was surprised at him and replied in astonishment, saying, "That is an old story?! ... But I remember also when the candle was burning" etc., and thus it is inferred that the first elder's aspect of boasting of memory has no value at all compared to the second elder's aspect of memory. And similarly with the second elder's memory compared to the third elder's aspect of memory, and so forth, higher above higher, with no bound or limit at all. And similarly even the eighth beggar's memory has no value at all compared to the Blind Beggar, who was altogether a suckling babe then, and he spoke up and said to them, "I remember all these memories — and I remember 'Nothing At All' (*Un ikh gidenk gar nit*)!" Who has heard boasting of such wonders and awesome things as these, even according to the things' simple meaning?

But in truth, from what the Great Eagle concluded and said to them, "Go back to your ships, which are your bodies, that were broken, which will be rebuilt" etc. — from this it is inferred that these people who went by ships a great deal, are souls of tzaddikim who came to this world clothed in bodies, which are the aspect of ships, in the way that is explained in the holy *Zohar P.*

Vayak'hel 199, "Yonah who went down into the ship, this is the soul of man, which went down into this world to be in a man's body... And now, a man goes out in this world like a ship in the great ocean, which is thought to be broken, as stated (*Yonah* 1), 'And the ship was thought to be broken...' And then Hakadosh Barukh Hu picks up a powerful storm wind... and this is what shakes the boat" and so forth. Also discerned in the *Tikkunim*, *Tikkun* #18, which is the aspect of what is explained in this story, is how a big storm wind came and broke the ships (implying that the bodies broke and died, God save us), and the people were saved and came to one tower and went up on the tower etc., and all good and all the worldly pleasures were there. (We infer that Rabbeinu z"l's apparent meaning is the souls of the tzaddikim, which were clothed in those bodies, and which ascended to their place of rest in the Lower Gan `Eden, and perhaps in the Upper Gan `Eden.) There each one of them told what he remembers from his first memory. And anyhow we discern that there, it is irrelevant to say that any of the boasting of these aspects of memory are according to their actual simple meanings, but rather are much higher than high above; altogether inestimable and boundless. And in accord with this, it is discerned, by the way, that the Great Eagle who came and knocked on the tower etc. and explained to them all the stories that all the elders told etc. and said to them, "Go back to your ships, which are your bodies, which were broken, which will be rebuilt; now go back to them" — this Great Eagle, apparently he is the aspect of the one in charge of awakening those who rest in the dirt for revival of the dead, and therefore he said of himself that he is old, "but yet I am a suckling babe," as also discerned in the holy Zohar *Vayeshev* pp. 181-182, that of him was said, "*Na`ar hayithi gam zaqanti*/ I have been young, also I have been old" [Ps. 37:25]; see there. But there are many aspects in this, higher above higher, and higher above those; but in truth in matters such as these we are merely as blind ones groping in the dark, and we have no inkling of knowledge or concept at all in any of this, and all our words here are merely to somewhat alert the one who looks into it. And see the wonders in this in *Likutei Halakhoth: Hilkhoth Tefillin* #5 and in *Hilkhoth Milah* and *Avadim veGerim*.

(*Likutei `Etzoth 2/e: Tzaddik* #88: Insofar as the Tzaddik renews himself more in his devotions each time, and makes himself as if he has no knowledge, and as if he is entirely a suckling babe, and has still not begun living at all, and begins each time anew, as explained elsewhere — by means of this specifically he merits to go up, each time, to higher perceptions and levels, "eye has not seen" etc. [Isa. 64:3], until thereby even though he is most infantile as mentioned, nevertheless he is older, up above, than everyone, and he attains such long life that all the world's time in entirety does not count by him so much as an eyeblink. And on account of this he has no looking at this world, since all the world's time does not count by him as much as an eyeblink.)

And similarly, on the second day, about the deaf one who boasted of his good life etc., it is also a very awesome and wonderful story. And in it is also discerned how even among the greatest tzaddikim on extremely exceptional levels there are also levels and degrees, higher above higher. For, even the country of wealth, where they had great treasuries and they lived good lives, and each one boasted of his good life — anyhow it is also inferred that they were awesome tzaddikim and they had great treasuries in great spirituality and on a very high and wondrous level, until through them they truly lived the aspect of good life, as also discerned further on in the text regarding the country that had a garden through which they lived a good life and the gardener became lost etc. (and behold, the matter of the garden and the gardener hints to what it hints, as somewhat discerned in the *Zohar Terumah* 166b and other places); and they came to the decision, inasmuch as there is a country of wealth, that it appears to them that their gardener that was lost is from the same root as those people of the wealthy country that also live a good life. Also discerned from this is: the people of that country were great and awesome tzaddikim and they lived truly good lives; and nevertheless the good life of the deaf one was on a level higher than and above their aspect of good life, with no bound or measure at all. And the proof is: when they came close to that country, in which their good life had become spoiled, the taste and the other things were spoiled for them as well, and when the deaf one gave them from his bread and water, they felt in his bread and water all the tastes etc., and everything that was spoiled for them was repaired, and then the deaf one also repaired that whole country with the garden, until the gardener through whom they lived a good life came back and was revealed to them.

And behold, the holy inner things and the lofty hints that are in this story are also very awesome and wonderful; and according to the simple meanings of the things one can also learn from them a great deal of smart guidance: How one very much needs to guard against tipping a judgment or sentence, favoritism, or taking bribes, for by means of this the eyes were darkened and the aspect of sight was spoiled. And similarly one must guard against all kinds of obscene language, even in a very fine manner, and even just hearing such speech and having some enjoyment from it at all, for by means of obscene language was spoiled the aspect of taste, until all the tastes were of rotten flesh. And all the more so, one needs to guard against any sort of aspect of adultery: real or even in a very fine degree, for by means of this, the aspect of smell was spoiled, that all the smells would be like the smell of galbanum. All this is aspects of total blemish and spoilage of the aspect of good life. And also discerned, by the way, is that the intention is not just spoilage of sight, taste and smell in physicality, but presumably the main intent is regarding spoilage of all these three aspects also in spirituality, as they are the essence of the aspect of truly good life. And when one merits to return in complete repentance from all these three transgressions and distance oneself very far from all people that stumble in it, thereby not only are the taste, sight and smell repaired, but also the gardener by whom they lived a good life and was lost — presumably also by some aspect of fine blemishes that came about in his countrymen, and now specifically after the cruel king came over them and spoiled their good life entirely, by means of the three factions of agents, who introduced these sins among them — now when they merit to return and repair all this, thereby they merit that their gardener also returns to them, and they merit to live a good life through him in entirety. And everything is repaired by means of the deaf one, who merited to live a good life that has no lack in it at all. For, all the sounds in the world are all only from lackings etc.; but for this deaf one, the whole entire world does not count as anything for him, that they should bring into his ears its lack (and therefore he appears deaf, as explained in the text). For, he lives a good life that has in it no lacking at all, and his good life is that he would eat bread and drink water etc. From this whole story is also discerned smart and wondrous guidance for whoever truly desires. And see regarding this in *Likutei Halakhoth: Hilkhoth Ishuth.*

(*Likutei `Etzoth 2/e Tzaddik* 89: All the voices in the world are all only due to lackings. For, each and every person cries out for his lack, and even all the celebrations in the world are only on account of the lacking that was missing for him and now has been filled for him. But there is a True Tzaddik who merits to live a good life that has in it no lacking at all. And he appears like a deaf person because the whole world does not amount to him as anything, that he should hear their lackings. And his good life is bread and water; but in his bread and water one can feel all the tastes, all the smells, and all the pleasures in the world, until through them one truly lives a good life with no lacking at all.

I bid. #90: There is an aspect of such a garden, in which grow wonderful fruits and crops that have all the tastes, all the smells and all the sights in the world. And the whole world would be able to live a truly good life through this garden. And over this garden there is a gardener, which is called *"agradnik,"* that is, such a holy and supernal Tzaddik who is in charge over it and constantly exerts himself with all the garden's repair. And sometimes due to the generation's transgression, the gardener is lost, that is, the light of this Tzaddik is hidden and covered up and the world is not privileged to know of him that he is this gardener through whom they can all live a truly good life through the garden and this gardener. Even though he goes about and says he is the gardener, the world, however, regards him as an insane person, God forbid, and they throw rocks at him and drive him away. And subsequently he cannot exert himself with the garden's repairs, and thereby whatever is in the garden definitely must end and be cut off, since there is no one in charge there, that is, the gardener. But nevertheless they would be able to live from the after-growths in the garden; but the Accuser challenges this a great deal as well, and brings into the world such bad traits that spoil the good life that they were able to live through the garden. For, through these traits, every kind of taste is spoiled to the point that is the aspect of rotten flesh flavor, and every kind of smell

until it is in the aspect galbanum smell, and also the eyes are
darkened by the aspect of clouds that cover the eye, until thereby
all the kinds of sights and colors in the world are damaged. And
behold, even though there are definitely such tzaddikim in the
world that have great wealth and large treasuries in spirituality,
who also boast that they live a good life — and verily they live a
good life through their holy treasuries — nevertheless those
spoilages that spoil the world can also spoil for them the taste,
the smell and the other things mentioned. And all the more so,
they have not the power to repair the world and return to them
the good life that they were able to live through the holy garden.
And therefore sometimes when their good life is also spoiled then
their whole repair is by the great Tzaddik on the aforementioned
level, who is the aspect of deaf; who lives a good life that has in it
no lacking at all, and he gives them to taste from his bread and
water, in which they feel all the tastes, as mentioned, and also
thereby is repaired what was spoiled for them. And this Tzaddik
can repair also the good life of all the world, and he makes it
known that the essence of the spoilage of their good life comes to
them from the bad traits that the Accuser introduces to them,
that is: through lewd speech is spoiled for them the taste, that all
the tastes are of rotten flesh; and by actual adultery the smell is
damaged; and by them not having truth, tipping the judgment,
showing favoritism, and taking bribes, thereby the sight is spoiled
for them. And he warns them direly to purify themselves from
these transgressions, and then not only will the taste, sight and
smell be repaired for them, but also they will thereby merit to
find the gardener who was lost. So they attain all this through
this deaf Tzaddik.

Ibid. #91: When people begin to open their eyes to what they
are busy with, that is, thinking thoughts how to repair the
good life that has become spoiled for them, then they first come to
these tzaddikim who live a good life though the wealth and treasuries of holiness that they have. Only if the world is meritorious
and the time of their repair has already arrived, then these tzaddikim acknowledge the truth and inform the world that all the repair is by these tzaddikim themselves. And likewise the repair of
all the world's creatures depends only on this deaf beggar.)

On the third day of the wedding is the extremely wondrous and awesome story about the speech-impaired one, who boasted how he is a very wonderful orator and speaker, and is able to say such wonderful riddles and poems that there is no creature in the world that will not want to hear him (examine and discern from this wording, "no creature," that it includes all creatures in the world, which are: inanimate, plant, animal, speech-capable; and also all the spiritual entities up to the top-top, for they are all creatures, in the aspect of *"ki hu tzivah venivra'u/* for He commanded, and they were created" etc. [Ps. 148:5]). And within these riddles and poems are all the wisdoms, except that since the world's speech that is not praise of Hashem Yithbarakh does not have perfection, therefore he appears speech impaired (and from this is discerned even from its simple meaning, smart guidance on guarding one's speech). And then he tells how he has approbation of his boasting from the great man, the Truly Gracious Man etc. And the whole matter there is very awesome and wonderful, and speaks of Dawidh haMelekh a"h, and somewhat hints to Tehillim Ch. 61, as explained at the end of the story, what was heard from his holy mouth himself z"l, aside from what we somewhat inferred when this holy story was heard from his holy mouth. For, he told it with awesome and wonderful passion, enormous awe, and enormous and awesome wondrous attachment. From this we also discerned that in this story are enormous awesome things in the extreme. Fortunate are the ears that merited hearing such awesome stories from his holy mouth and merited gazing on and delighting from the bliss of his holy face's radiance then, in the aspect of, "Vehayu `eineikha ro'oth eth-moreikha/ Your eyes shall see your teacher" [Isa. 30:20]. Happy is their lot. And see *Likutei Halakhoth Hilkhoth Tzedakah*.

(*Likutei `Etzoth 2/e Tzedakah* #8, *Tzaddik* #92: The essence of how time is generated, which is the essence of how the Spring and the Heart maintain existence, as explained in the text, through which is the essence of how the whole entire world exists, is by means of the true kindnesses (and from this is discerned that a man has to be very careful to do some true kindness every day, in order that he also has some part and pertinence in all this). And each and every day, when it emerges from the place where it comes from, it goes forth with very wonderful riddles and songs that have in them all the wisdoms. And there are differences between the days, for no day is like another, as in the text. And there is a big and wondrous Tzaddik who involves himself in this. That is, he goes and collects all the true kindnesses and brings them to the Truly Gracious Man, who is truly a very great man, and that is the essence of how time is generated. And this Tzaddik who involves himself with this, collecting the true kindnesses, he is definitely a very great and wondrous sage, and he too is a very wondrous orator and speaker, and can speak riddles and songs so wonderful that there is no creature in the world that will not want to hear him, and in these riddles and songs are contained all the wisdoms. And all this is understandable as a matter of course, since the essence of the existence of the world, the Spring, the Heart, and all the creatures in entirety, is only by means of him collecting all the true kindnesses. Similarly, all the riddles and songs of each and every day, which these songs contain all the wisdoms — it is all through him. Thus he knows very wondrous riddles and songs, as mentioned. But since the world's utterances that are not praises to Hashem Yithbarakh do not have perfection, therefore this Tzaddik specifically appears in the world's eyes as a speech-impaired, for he is "speech-impaired" from these worldly utterances that are imperfect. But in fact he is not speech-impaired at all, rather just the opposite: he is a very wonderful orator and speaker, as mentioned.

I bid. *Ratzon* #5: The essence of the world's vitality and existence is only by means of holy yearnings and hopes, as discerned in the text, that the world's Heart, on which all the vitality and existence of the world depends, with all of creation in entirety — the essence of this very Heart's vitality is by it standing facing the Spring that is at the world's edge, constantly hoping and yearning very passionately, to come to that Spring, even though it is impossible for it to go and get close to the Spring due to the reason explained there; nevertheless the essence of its vitality is only by means of it standing, looking out, glancing and gazing at the Spring from very far away, from the end of the world, and longing, hoping, and yearning with great passion, with exhaustion of soul, and constantly crying out to come to that Spring; and also this Spring yearns for it, and thereby is the essence of the Heart's vitality, on which the essence of life and the existence of the whole entire world depends, as discerned in the text.

Ibid. *Tefillah* #25: When the day comes to be ended and terminated (which is the time of the Minchah and Ma`ariv prayers) then a man needs to wake up with great arousal and remind himself how the world's Heart and the Spring (by which is the essence of the world's existence) begin to take leave of each other (which is called *gizeginen zikh*), and say wonderful riddles and songs to each other with great love and very great passion; therefore he too needs to participate with them, and wake up with great passion and hope towards Hashem Yithbarakh, and pray with great attachment. For, the creation of the entirety of this day is already ended and cut off, and who knows what a day will bring? — as discerned in the text. And similarly afterwards one needs to prepare himself to receive the holiness of the new creation of the coming day, and remind himself well, that each and every day, when it comes from where it comes, then it comes with wonderful riddles and songs that contain all the wisdoms. And there are variations among the days, for each day differs from another, especially sanctified days, which are Shabbath, Rosh Chodesh and Yamim Tovim. Therefore a man must also involve himself in this and pray each day and say before Him Yithbarakh songs, praises etc. with new desire and very great holy fervor, and with entirely new brains, and bind himself to and draw upon himself the merit and the power of the one who occupies himself with this, collecting the true kindnesses and bringing them to the Truly Gracious Man, whereby is the essential generation of time, the riddles, the songs, and the wisdoms mentioned above, and also the essence of the existence and vitality of the Spring and the Heart and the whole entire world, as in the text.)

(And by the way understood from this in particular is: when the year comes to its end and term, that is, in the last month of the year, the month of Elul, which are days of holy favor and hope, one definitely needs to remind himself of all the aforementioned, and wake up more at that time with great aspirations to Hashem Yithbarakh, and prepare himself to receive the holiness of the new creation of the coming year, and remind himself on the holy day of Rosh Hashanah, that such a holy day comes from where it comes, with very wondrous riddles and songs; therefore a man needs to also make himself part of this, and pray then with great desire and holy fervor, and draw on himself the merit and power of the Truly Gracious Man who is supreme on a very high level; especially the merit and power of the one who occupies himself with collecting the true kindnesses, whereby is the sustenance of the world and the creation in entirety which is created then, as written, "*Zeh hayom hatchalath ma`aseikha*/ This is the day of the beginning of Your works;" and as mentioned.)

On the fourth day of the wedding is the wondrous and awesome story of the one whose neck was crooked, and his telling that on the contrary he has a very even and handsome neck, but rather there are *hevlei `olam*/ worldly vanities-vapors and he twists his neck because he does not want to emit any vapor or wind (which is called *dukh*/breath) into the worldly vapors. (See and discern from this, smart guidance for your soul, and contemplate the vast enormity of the awes of this one's righteousness.) But in truth he has a very wonderful neck and very wondrous voice, and he has a consensus on this, and the whole matter there is very awesome and wondrous, as discerned by whoever looks into it honestly. And see regarding this in *Likutei Halakhoth H' Nedarim.*

There, regarding that crooked neck boasted he can produce with his neck all the sounds in the world and can throw voices afar, and he has consensus on this from the country that was very expert in the wisdom of music, and he showed them that he is more expert than them in this, and that he can throw voices, and he told them an entire matter in this — actually it is not understood there. For, his boasting against them that he can quiet the sound of wailing and crying that the two countries have that are one thousand *parsah*s apart, namely, by his being able to throw voices and draw together the birds that are lost from each other, by throwing voices at them — in truth, it is not clear there that he did so and quieted the sound of wailing. Rather, he told a different matter, showing them that he *can* throw his voice; see there. Instead, the matter seems to me another thing that our Rabbis z"l said regarding the redemption's appointed daybreak (which is the aspect of drawing the birds close to each other, which is the aspect of union of Kudsha Berikh Hu and His Shekhinah, and to quiet their yelling) is that it has two aspects, the aspect of *be`itah*/in its time, and the aspect of *achishenah*/I will hasten it [Isa. 60:22; *Sanh.* 98a]. And behold, the aspect of *achishenah*, which depends on the whole world repenting, it is understood of course that it is impossible to repair this until everyone returns in repentance, so it is understood that he must be talking of the drawing the birds close that will be *be`itah*, so therefore he was unable to finish the thing immediately, since it is not yet *be`itah*, so he is forced to still hold back until it will be the period and time for it, except that then too the repair will only be completed by the aforementioned voice throwing. Therefore he was unable to finish the thing presently, and he showed them this thing, that he can throw voices of things that are somewhat external, for instance a house that was open and the door being shut, and also the shooting of a gun etc. And all this is on account that then the matter of throwing voices was still clothed in external things, except nevertheless they discerned that his words were true and he *can* throw voices and finish the repair perfectly, except that the time has not yet come, therefore he only informed them of their lack of perfection, that they have not yet arrived at the perfection of the matter in this, and they all have to just receive perfection from him. And then when they all attain this, perhaps the time will come to complete the repair by this in perfection, even in the aspect of *be`itah*.

Likutei `Etzoth 2/e Tzaddik #32: There are two birds, one male and one female, and they are just one pair in the world. And these two birds have gotten so lost and far from each other, that one cannot find the other. And when night arrives then they wail with a very great voice of wailing, for each one wails for his mate. And these two birds hint to what they hint to (as somewhat discerned by those who know, and as written, "*Ketzipor nodedeth min-kinah*/ As a bird that wanders from her nest" etc. [Prov. 28:7], and the scripture, "*Sha'og yish'ag `al-nawehu*/ He roars mightily because of His fold" [Jer. 25:30], and there it is written [ibid. 31:14] "*Meanah lehinachem `al-baneyah ki einenu*/ She refuses to be comforted for her children, because he is not" — specifically, as our rabbis z"l have explained [i.e. he is missing in exile and she does not see him, the male bird — thus the explanation is perfect, and by the way, explains the verse's seeming contradiction, "*baneyah..einenu*"]). And there is one Tzaddik who has a very beautiful and wondrous neck, and a very wonderful voice; and all the sounds in the world, which are voice without speech, he can emit all of them with his voice, that is, he can project in making his voice like all the kinds of sounds that are in the world, of all the kinds of animals and birds, and of all the kinds of instruments, and so forth, and also he can throw voices. That is, in the place where he emits the sound, the sound will not be heard at all; only at a distance will the sound be heard. And thereby he can draw these two birds close and unite them with each other, as in the text. However, since there are *hevlei `olam*/ worldly vapors-vanities, and this Tzaddik does not want to emit any spirit or breath (which is called *dukh*) into the world's vapors, therefore he specifically appears in the world's eyes like his neck is bent, because actually he bends his neck altogether from the worldly vapors and does not want to emit any vapor and wind into the worldly vapors. But in truth his neck is not bent at all, but rather just the opposite, as mentioned.)

On the fifth day of the wedding is the wonderful and awesome story of the one whose back was hunched, and his telling them that on the contrary he has such shoulders (*pleytses*) that have the aspect of the "little holding the much." And they were laughing at and mocking one of the others [who boasted of this], who bragged that his brain is the little holding the much, because he carries in his mind thousands and myriads of people with all their needs and all their existence and movements etc., and therefore he is the little holding the much. And they laughed at him, and told him that his people are nothing and he is nothing. One of them spoke up and said a very minor, inferior and contemptible analogy to this person's little holding the much etc. — and by the way, it is understood that this man too was very great, since he has connection with thousands and myriads of people, such that he thought he could boast of this aspect — nevertheless they replied to him as mentioned (and from this is discerned by anyone who looks into it, great guidance for his soul, how his days are consumed with futility and emptiness, and all his thoughts and ideas which he goes into a great deal for the sake of the management and the needs of himself and all his household who accompany and rely on him, while it appears to him that he carries all of them on his heart and mind — in truth if his intention in all this is not in the utmost perfection of intent, only for the sake of Heaven alone and to do the will of the Blessed One in this, then it is all vanity, as discerned from this story by whoever looks into the text). And the rest of them who boasted in this aspect had their words accepted, and there it is also discerned how also on the level of great tzaddikim there is higher above higher, and then higher above them, as discerned from this story in the text. And the matter of the story of the group that was investigating the wondrous and awesome tree explained in the text, and how even after they all attained all the traits of the tree, which are truth and steadfastness, humility and awe, nevertheless they were not able to come to the tree, since it is the aspect of above space, until the hunchbacked one brought them there. So the whole entire story is very wondrous and awesome. (And see *Likutei Halakhoth H' Tzitzith* #3 and *H' Sefer Torah* #3.)

There, regarding their laughing at the one who boasted that his brain is the little holding the much — and see there in the text, what they compared him with — discerned there is that in this they informed him the enormity of his error, the polar opposite. For behold, he imagined that he carries all of them on his brain, that is, because their existence, their uses, and all the good within them is all only from his brain; and ultimately it is the total opposite, that all the garbage and waste that is in each of them, it is all by him carrying them on his brain and leading a person according to his mind, whereby he adds a great deal of waste to them and makes the smell of their soul putrid; his are all these who hold on to him and are called by his name (and see in *LM II* the lesson "*Tik`u — Tokhachah* #8), and they are just like the parable of the garbage that was abundantly scattered on the mountain and the man that was sitting on the mountain boasting that it was all from him.

(*Likutei `Etzoth 2 / e Tzaddik* #94: There is someone who boasts that his brain is the aspect of "the little that holds the much," in that he carries in his mind thousands and myriads of people will all their needs and practices and all their existence and motions; everything in entirety he carries in his brain, and therefore he boasts of himself that his brain is the little that holds the much. And in truth he is nothing and his people are nothing, and they all altogether from *hevel*/vapor-vanity; and there are many things that increase *hevel*. On the other hand, there exist truly great tzaddikim who each have the aspect of the little that holds the much, each one according to his aspect. There is one whose speech is the little holding the much, and there is one whose silence is the little holding the much. And there is one who moves the lunar orbit, even though the lunar orbit is very large, and he is what sustains the entire world, for the world needs the moon; hence he is truly the aspect of the little holding the much. But there is a further aspect of the little holding the much, that is above all of them entirely. And this Tzaddik who attains this aspect of the little that holds the much at the utmost highest level that has nothing above it, he specifically appears hunchback (which is called *hoykir*), and in truth he is not hunchback at all, rather just the opposite: he carries on him everything; see the text.

Ibid. #99: There is a tree in the shade of which all the animals would dwell, in its shade; and on the branches of which all the fowl and all the *tziperei shemaya/* birds of the sky [Dan. 4] would dwell. And the wondrous delight that is there at that tree is unfathomable. And sometimes there is a group of people who perceive that there exists such a tree in the world and they want to go and arrive at it. However, there is no one among them to make the decision, which direction to go to reach that tree, and a dispute falls among them about this, as one says to this side they must go, and another says to that side, and there is no one to decide between them, until a sage arrives and informs them that is impossible to merit to come to that tree except for someone who has the characteristics of the tree. For, the tree has three roots, which are: faith, fear, and humility; and truth is the body of the tree. And then when they all manage to reach these traits, then they all agree with one mind that this is the way they need to go to get to the tree. But this tree has no place at all, for it is entirely above space, and therefore even these tzaddikim who attain the traits of the tree, it is nevertheless impossible for even them to go up and come to it, except by means of this Tzaddik, the aforementioned hunchback, who attained the ultimate highest level in the concern of the little holding the much, and he is on the end level of the aspect of space, for immediately above him is above space entirely, and therefore he can carry and raise them from within the aspect of space and bring them up to the tree, which is above space.)

On the sixth day of the wedding is the awesome and wondrous story of the one without hands, and him saying that in truth he has power in his hands, only he does not use this power in his hands in this world, because he needs this power for a different interest, and he has a consensus on this from the Watery Castle (has such an expression ever been heard in the world? especially with what is explained further on in the text, that there are ten walls, one within the next, and they are all of water, and also there are trees and fruits, and it is all of water, and the beauty of the castle and the greatness of the marvel of this castle is needless to say, etc.), and all the matter there, how the king's daughter fled into this castle, and passed through the gates of the walls of water, until she arrived inside (after they shot her and all the ten kinds of arrows hit her), and she fell down faint there, and he heals her, etc.

(And also from this story is discerned how with the levels of the greatest tzaddikim as well there is higher above higher, for all of these who are explained in the text who boasted of the power that they have in their hands, each one was a wondrous and awesome novelty on a very extraordinary level, as discerned in the text, and nevertheless the handless one replied to each of them, "If so, you cannot heal the king's daughter.")

And the whole matter of the story in detail, as explained in the text, it is all very wondrous and awesome; no thought can contain it, and fortunate is he who can attain some true spark in the holy, awesome, and enormous stories explained in this whole book of stories, especially this holy story which he himself extolled its vast praiseworthiness and sanctity, as somewhat explained at the end of the text.

And see regarding the story of the Sixth Day in *Likutei Halakhoth H' Rosh Hashanah* and at the end of *H' Pesach* and in *Hilkhoth Tola`aim* and in *Hilkhoth [P"U] Ishuth.*

Regarding the boasting of the Sixth Day's beggar, it was also in the manner explained above regarding the Fourth Day, that he still has not finished the repair perfectly, but rather he involves himself presently in healing the king's daughter; and when they will merit to feel their deficiency, how they are far from the great power he has in his hands, then it is possible for the king's daughter's healing to be finished perfectly, more speedily; so be His will, soon in our days, Amen.

(*Likutei `Etzoth 2/e Tzaddik* #96: The essence of the king's daughter's complete healing is only through the very great Tzaddik who: [1] has such a power in his hands that he can go back and remove all the ten kinds of arrows even after they have reached whom they were shot at; [2] and also has the power in his hands that from whom he receives, he gives to, until thereby he has in his hands all the ten kinds of charity; [3] and also knows the ten kinds of pulse-beats, by means of having such a power in his hands that he can give to whomever he lays his hands on, all the ten measures of wisdom; [4] and also has such a power in his hands that he can hold back and grasp with his hands all the ten kinds of winds, and make weight for the wind with his hands, whereby he knows to play the ten kinds of melody. And the melody is the king's daughter's healing. Hence he has such power in his hands, but nevertheless he appears like one who is hand-less, since he does not use the power in his hands in this world, for he needs to use the power in his hands for the aforementioned interest.

Ibid. #97: You, reader, stand and contemplate from all the above, that the massive concealment of the light of the greatest tzaddikim is at so extreme that their light is hidden in this world, as this world is so very far from the awesomeness of their holiness that they appear as blind, as deaf, and as having defects in all the above; and not only that, but they are called "beggars" because this is the lowest and ignoblest of levels in this world. And also the matter of the holy wedding, where the whole matter was the revelation of their awesomenesses and wonders, was also in the very humblest and lowest place in this world, namely in a big pit covered with reeds, dirt and garbage. And thus it goes presently as well, in each and every generation, until the world comes to the completion of its repair, and then "the tzaddikim will see and rejoice" etc., and then the holiness of the True Tzaddik's light will be revealed, that shines in all the worlds, especially in this world, as explained elsewhere.)

(Copyist's and arranger's note: I also heard that Rabbeinu z"l hinted, in his calling them beggars, that these awesome Tzaddikim did not reach the awesomeness of these wonders except by being beggars, that they constantly asked and entreated Hashem Yithbarakh to be privileged to serve His Blessedness, until they attained high lofty levels as these; and as brought in his words z"l elsewhere [*LM II* #25], that all the Tzaddikim did not reach their levels except through prayer. So may Hashem Yithbarakh let us merit to constantly be involved in prayer, until we merit to be in accord with His will, and according to the will of the holy ones who fear Him; may their merit protect us, Amen.)

D one and finished, the book *Rimzei haMa`asiyoth*, praise to God, Creator of the universe!

Rimzei haMa`asiyoth — Hashmatoth
(Hints of the Stories — Appendices)

on

Sipurei Ma`asiyoth

published by
R' Avraham ben R' Nachman of Tulchin z"l
in the 1902 Lemberg printing of S"M

THE LOST PRINCESS

Found in the sack of one of the Rebbe's followers*, a summary from the book Biur haLikutim *about the torah* Pathach Rabbi Shim`on *[LM #60] which is an explanation of the first story, the Lost Princess:*

> **probably R' Avraham Peterburger z"l, who was the only one other than R' Nathan to record the Rebbe's teachings*

According to what is understood from his holy words, that the Nefesh/soul of Malkhuth/Kingship, Dawidh [I Sam. 18:1 nefesh Dawidh; Arizal on Sifra deTzni`utha comments that the nefesh of Gen. 1:20 is nefesh Dawidh, Malkhuth], is the aspect of the king's daughter that was lost [Malkhuth is "feminine"], and it is also the aspect of the hithbonenuth [deep contemplative understanding] of the Torah, as understood in the Second Preface to Sipurei Ma`asiyoth: Understood, by the way, is that from the time of Creation, his nefesh descended into the place of the qelipoth/husks, that is, to Sedom/Sodom in the qelipah of Moab, and therefore it is said about him, "Matzati Dawidh `avdi/ I have found my servant Dawidh" [Ps. 89:21], and our Rabbis explained in Midrash Rabbah, "And where did I find him? In Sedom, as it says, 'Ve'eth-shetei venotheikha hanimtza'oth/ and your two daughters, that are found'" [Gen. 19:15], that is, the aspect of finding the king's daughter. Also understood, by the way, in accord with this, is the count of his lifespan being seventy years, and his need for guarding against being overtaken by sleep, as brought in the words of Chazal, that he never in his life slept sixty breaths. Also understood, by the way, in accord with this, is the Admor z"tzl's not telling us *how* he took her out; "Even from my heart to my mouth I did not reveal this" [*Sanhedrin* 99a on Isa. 63:4; *Shivchei haRan* #31]. And it is impossible to take her out except secretly and with cleverness and cunning, as it were. And behold, the matter of the cleverness and the slyness that one needs in order to take her out, perhaps it is the matter brought in the torah "*Pathach Rabbi Shim`on*" [*Likutei Moharan* #60], that when one wakes up a man from his sleep, then he needs to show him the faces of the Torah that he lost during his sleep, and needs to clothe the faces for him in order that the forces outside of holiness should not have any grip on him and not let him leave, in the aspect of "*Meshaneh panav vateshalchehu*/ You change his face and send him away" [Job 14:20], as mentioned there in that torah.

Also according to what is explained in that torah is that by means of reverence, one attains length of days on the side of holiness, whereby one attains riches of holiness, whereby one attains contemplation of the Torah, which is the aspect of the king's daughter, as mentioned. Understood, by the way, is that the princess is the aspect of "*ishah yir'ath-Hashem*/ a woman who fears Hashem* " [Prov. 31:30] explained there; and thereby is subdued and nullified the promiscuous woman, the aspect of the king's daughter of the *Sitra Achra*/ Other Side that is in the *qelipah* of *hevel hayofi*/ futility of beauty, whereby comes poverty, the aspect of, "*Al-tachmod yofyah bilvavekha*/ Do not covet her beauty in your heart [whereby a man is] `*ad-kikar-lechem*/ brought down to a loaf of bread" [Prov. 6:26], quoted there, whereby one does not attain finding her and repairing her. For, the essence of finding her is by the golden mountain and the castle of pearls [as in the story], which are the aspect of wealth on the side holiness, as explained in the Second Preface.

And understood in accord with this, by the way, is the Pelishtim taking over Sarah and Rivkah, in their *qelipah* of *hevel hayofi*, which this is the matter of the loss of the princess to the place of *qeliphoth*, until Avraham and Yitzchak had to be involved with this in all the holy repairs explained there in that torah, until they managed to take her out of there. Also discerned in accord with this is what Chazal explained (*Bava Bathra* 16b) about the verse, "*VeAvraham zaqen ba bayamim vaShem berakh eth-Avraham bakol/* And Avraham was elder, advanced in *yamim*-days-years, and Hashem blessed Avraham with everything" [Gen. 24:1], quoted there in that torah: he had a daughter etc. (the aspect of finding the princess); Rabbi Shim`on ben Yochai says he had a gemstone (the aspect of the aforementioned castle of pearls, whereby he merited to find her). And even though the main repair depends on the special persons of the era, nevertheless there are aspects of these repairs found with each man and woman, and every person needs to involve himself in these repairs, each one according to his level, until he merits to find his mate, for she is what he has lost, whom he goes about searching for, as Chazal said, "The one who has lost the object goes searching for it" [*Kiddushin* 2b]. And understood, by the way, according to this, is the concept of the marital relations explained there in the torah *Pathach R"Sh*. Also discerned from this is how Yitzchak and Ya`akov came to meet their mates at a well and an `*AeYN*/source [of water], whereas the viceroy [in the story] did not attain this but drank from a spring (*ma`yan, kval*) [of wine] and became poor and destitute of the riches of holiness, and thereby the princess became more hidden from him; but they merited that the well and source became for them a head and brains in the clarification of the `*AYN* (i.e. seventy) faces of Torah in its contemplation, which is the aspect of the princess. Also understood, according to this, is the concept of Ya`akov Avinu being forced to take out Rachel and Leah, who are from the aspect of the princess on the side of holiness, from the place of *qelipoth*, the house of Lavan, by means of trickery, deception and cleverness. And also understood by the way and in accord with this is the matter of Leah having six boys and one girl — who also descended into the place of *qelipoth*, the house of Shekhem, and again there was no possibility of taking her out except by trickery and cleverness.

And behold, during the time when sleep overcomes a man — which is when the princess of holiness and the contemplation of the Torah is lost from him, as explained in that torah and the story, and in accord with the rule of *zeh le`umath zeh* (each thing in Holiness has its counterpart on the Other Side, and viceversa) — then is when the princess of the Other Side comes to dwell by him. And in accord with this is understood what Chazal said regarding *netilath yadayim/* the ceremonial hand washing three times alternating right-left when a man awakens from his sleep: [The bad spirit that remains on the hands after sleep] is a princess and insists [on remaining on the hands until washed it is washed off in that manner: *Kaf haChayim* 2:9 on *SAOC* #4; *Shabbath* 109a].

Also explained by the combination of that torah and the story, is concerning the soul of the *tevunah/*understanding and the kingship of the Davidic son, mentioned above, which descended from the day of Creation to a place of *qelipoth/*husks like Sedom, mentioned above, and became concealed and hidden among them, until it is not known where she will be found, and what kind of place of gemstones and pearls and golden-earth mountain is at where she is dwelling. For she is not at all found in civilization, in the land of the living. And all these pearls and gems are worth nothing more than introductions and scrap in compare to her. And also all the land animals and birds of the sky replied and said they have not set foot on it and not seen it and they do not know of it at all. Only upon gathering the winds, then it was made known by the spirit of God which arrived to him at the last end-time, by the great strength of his faith, as he destroyed and killed himself with his enormous effort and exertion in order to look for her. Gaze upon and see the wonders of the scripture's language (Job 28:4): *"Hanishkachim mini-ragel/* Those who caused the foot [of wayfarers] to be forgotten," which the Admor z"l quoted, regarding the corruption of Sedom, where they wanted to eliminate commerce and the "one-third of one's wealth a person should apportion in commerce" [*B"M* 42a] in order to overcome the aforementioned spirit of understanding and the kingship of the Davidic son. So discern from afar the loftiness of the whole matter that is there (in Job 28), from all the aforementioned, as this is the language of the scripture there, immediately after the aforementioned *"hanishkachim mini-ragel."*

- 6 *"Mekom-sapir avaneyah, we`afroth zahav lo/* Its stones are a place of sapphires, and its dust is gold" (which is the mountain and the castle mentioned).

- 7 *"Netiv lo-yeda`o `ayit, welo-shezafato `ein ayah/* The path, no bird of prey knows, nor has the falcon's eye seen it" (which are the birds mentioned).

- 8 *"Lo-hidrikhuhu venei shachatz, lo-`adah `alav shachal/* The proud beasts have not trodden it, nor has the lion passed by it" (which are the animals mentioned)...

- 12 *"Wehachokhmah me'ayin timatze, we'ey zeh meqom binah/* But the wisdom [Hei-Chokhmah i.e. the princess!], where shall it be found? And where is the place of understanding?"

- 13 *"Lo-yada` enosh erkah, welo-timatze be'eretz hachayim/* No mortal knows her value; nor is she found in the land of the living..."

- 17 *"Lo-ya`arkhenah zahav uzkhukhith, uthmurathah kelifaz/* Gold and glass cannot equal her; neither shall her exchange be vessels of fine gold."

- 18 *"...U'meshekh chokhmah mipnimim/* But the price of wisdom is above pearls" (for they are but scrap in compare to it)...

- 21 *"Wene`elmah me`einei khol-chai, ume`of hashamayim nistarah/* As she is hidden from the eyes of all living, and concealed from the fowls of the air."

- 22 *"Avadon wemaveth amru, be'ozneinu shama`nu shim`ah/* Destruction and Death [which describe Malkhuth having descended into qelipah; perhaps referring to the viceroy going out to seek her] say: 'We have heard a rumor of her with our ears,'"

and so forth, that is, as mentioned.

Also the matter of the verse *"Pethach pikha le'ilem/* Open your mouth for the mute" [Prov. 31:8] that is quoted there in that torah, regarding when one awakens a man from sleep, then he [the one who was awoken] opens his mouth and speaks holy speech before Hashem Yithbarakh, with great power etc., until one merits thereby to arrive at contemplative understanding of the Torah, which is the aspect of the princess. Discern from afar, in this scripture stated in the cry of *BATH SHEVA`* [which can be read "daughter of seven," i.e. the aspect of the princess] about Shelomoh haMelekh, who is the aspect of the viceroy (for he reigned over the upper and the lower worlds, as our rabbis explained) as she said, *"Al lamlakhim shetho-yayin/* It is not for kings to drink wine" [ibid. :4] (for at that time he married the princess daughter of *Par`oh*/Pharaoh, of the Sitra Achra, and slept up to the fourth hour of the day, as our rabbis expounded: *V. Rabbah* 12:5). And thereby the princess on the side of holiness became more hidden from him, for *"keshezeh qam zeh nofel/* When one side (impurity) rises, the other side falls (holiness, and vice-versa)." And she wakes him up with her screaming and crying and says to him, *"Pethach pikha le'ilem,"* which hints to the repairs of finding her, as in the text [*LM* #60]. And immediately he wakes up, feels remorse, and cries [Prov. 31:10], *"Esheth-chayil/* Woman of ('valor' or 'soldier': for she traveled with the soldier to the place of the pearl castle) — who can find" her, now that her price is far above *peninim*/pearls. But by means of *"Batach bah lev-ba`alah, veshalal lo-yechsar/* Her husband's heart is sure about her, so he hath no lack of (booty, or something that is carried off)" [ibid. :11]: even today there is hope to find her, for this scripture hints to the confidence on the side of holiness, which is the aspect of the tie with an Yisraelite woman, which is drawn, at its root, from the aspect of the princess on the side of holiness, as explained in the torah *Pathach Rabbi Shim`on*. And she is in the aspect of, *"Sheker hachen vehevel hayofi, ishah yirath Hashem hi tith'hallal/* Charm is deceitful and beauty is vain; a woman who fears Hashem — she is to be praised" [ibid :30], which Shelomoh haMelekh concluded at the end of the matter.

And this verse is quoted at the beginning of that torah, regarding finding the contemplative understanding of the Torah, and also in the matter of the scripture, *"Beshuv Hashem eth-shivath tziyon/* When Hashem brought back those that returned to Tziyon" etc. [Ps. 126:1], which is mentioned in the Gemara at the beginning of the story of Choni Ham`agel. It seems clear that the Babylonian exile, seventy years, is the seventy years that the Admor z"l mentioned in this story, and the Redemption and the construction of the Temple is the aspect of wak-

ing up from sleep. From this it is understood that Rabbeinu z"l
also hints to the matter of the Holy Temple, which is built on the
mountain where there is all the wealth of sanctity of the land of
Yisrael, which is the aspect of the golden mountain. And the Holy
of Holies is the aspect of the pearls, as our rabbis z"l expounded
on the verse, "*Yeqarah hi mipnimim*/ She is more precious than
pearls" [Prov. 3:15], and there specifically, were laid the Testimonial Tablets, which are the aspect of the contemplative understanding of Torah, as in the text, and Dawidh HaMelekh a"h merited to find the Temple Mount by means of sleeplessness specifically, the aspect of, "*Im eten shenath le`einai*/ I will not give sleep
to my eyes... `ad emtza maqom laShem*/ until I find the place for
Hashem" etc. [Ps. 132:4].

A lso by what is explained in that torah — that the whole entirety of being asleep from the seventy years is considered
one particular face of the contemplative understanding of the
Torah (which is the aspect of the princess, as mentioned), and in
accord with the known rule that every aspect is made up of all
other aspects — understood from this is the princess's advice for
finding her, that the viceroy should sit and tarry a complete year.

A lso by what is explained in that story, that on the last day of
sleep, if he would withstand the test, he would merit to find
her, that is, at the very last moment, for then the waning of the
moon (which is also drawn from the utterance that was spurted
out by the high king, unintentionally, "*Lekhi um`ati eth `atzmekh*/
Go and reduce yourself" etc. [*Zohar Chadash Sh"HSh Ma'amar
Mi`ut HaLevanah*]) will be reversed, toward the birth and head of
the year, which at that time, "*Dirshu Hashem behimmatzo*/ Seek
Hashem when he may be found" [Ps. 55:6], as known [i.e. these
are the ten days between Rosh Hashanah and Yom Kippur, *R"H*
18a] — be**Himmatzo** [when finding *Hi*/Her] specifically, the aspect of finding the princess: thus behold, it is clear from this that
on Rosh Hashanah is repaired the damage of her being lost, if one
merits to withstand the test. And understood, by the way, in accord with this, is what is explained in that torah, about the repair
of Rosh Hashanah, that it revolves around all these repairs.

THE BURGHER AND THE PAUPER

I heard from my father z"l that after the Admor z"tzukl told the story of the Burgher and the Pauper, then there was a big enormous celebration among his followers, and during it they sang the scripture, "*Ki nicham Hashem [eth] Tziyon*/ For Hashem has comforted Tziyon" etc. [Isa. 51:3]. For, then they realized from his holy comments that he said after it, which are explained at the end of the story, that the matter of the young man [the Burgher's Son] and the emperor's daughter that is discussed there, hints to the soul of Mashiach and Kenesseth Yisrael, who are presently apart from each other. And all of Kenesseth Yisrael and the Malkhuth on the side of holiness that is drawn from her, fell under the hand of the *qelipoth* of the murderer's anger, such that a man dreads and is afraid to shout out to Hashem Yithbarakh, and he tells him, "If you shout I will strangle you right away." And also, they fell under the hand of the *qelipoth* of pride of the [emperor-pauper] who was poor of *da`ath*/knowledge etc. And as it were, he [the young man] is also bound in fetters, as is known, for the soul of Mashiach as well is also subjugated in exile under the *qelipoth* in a place of wilderness and desolation, where no man passed by; and the storm wind went around, mightily, and mixed things up with such disturbances, that lost from him were even the signs that were given to him from the roots of souls of Yisrael, until it is impossible for them to in any manner recognize him, because due to the great events that happen to him, it subjugates him under their hands, and due to their enormous feeding off of him, transmitted to them too are some of the signs, markers, and wonders, until there have been, from them and among them, those who were as a monkey imitating a man, calling themselves by the name of "Mashiach," which is the whole matter of the false mashiachs who have been in the world. And afterwards when their lies and recklessnesses became known, it was very hard to then believe in the light of his identity's truth when he is revealed to them, for behold, also regarding the first one they imagined it clear as day that this is he, and likewise regarding the second one, and likewise regarding the third, as described there in the story. And now, "Where shall their help come from" to recognize him himself, since the liars who wanted to connect with her, also each had such signs and wonders (and this matter was an indirect cause of damages [*garma benizkin, B"K* 60a *B"B* 22b] also in the controversies and fights that were on the true great tzaddikim as the Ba`al Shem Tov z"tzukl and our Admor z"tzukl, such that the whole world has not been privileged to recognize the level of their greatness, and if all Yisrael were to follow them, there would definitely be a complete Redemption). And from then and till today, the descent of Kenesseth Yisrael has grown even stronger, to be caught by murderers and desperados who have removed from her all the glory of her precious garments [and see *CM* #422], until her appearance [lit. face] has been so altered as to be totally unrecognizable, as in the story. But over all this, the Cause of all Causes and the Prime Mover rises up, exalts Himself and reverses even such declines as these into ascents, and brings it about through His chains of causes that specifically by this they will be convened together and will join together, and she herself will find the signs, to recognize them eye to eye that they are genuine, until they rise up and return to their place, and the Kingship is given to them for ever and ever, "*Ki nicham Hashem Tziyon...*"

A nd even though it is clear, there, from his holy words, that those who approach to make an effort for her, hint to the truly great ones of Yisrael — see there — yet there is double, infinitely much more, to his holy stories. And it is also possible to explain that his words revolve around this as explained earlier, regarding those who make an approach to have a match with her, that to some of them she sent a reply by a messenger, and to some of them she sent a reply by herself from behind the wall; and of those who strove for this the most, such that she showed them her face, some looked and went insane, and some looked and fainted (the aspect of looking and dying) [v. the four who entered Pardes, *Chagiga* 14b] and it is of course understood that some apostatized entirely, God forbid. And finally, in the aspect of entering in peace and leaving in peace there are many aspects, and the essence is the aspect of the chosen one among the choicest for this [*habachur shebamuvcharim*; in the story, the burger's son is called the *bachur*, which also means young man]. "*Ashrei hamechakeh veyagi`a*/ Fortunate is he that waits and arrives" [Dan. 12:3].

THE EXCHANGED CHILDREN

On the subject of entering *Pardes* ["Garden"], which is the *Ma`aseh Merkavah* [The Work of the Chariot, Eze. 1], wherein one of them looked and was stricken, one looked and died, and only Rabbi `Akiva entered in peace and left in peace, and Chazal said that we do not transmit the *Ma`aseh Merkavah* to anyone but a wise person with a discerning mind: Understood, by the way, is what is explained in the story of the exchanged children, that all the people who entered the garden were so chased about that they were forced to flee out of the garden, but the king's son, because he became able to extrapolate, entered in peace and left in peace. And everything depends only on the man standing next to the garden and Pardes, who is of one aspect with the throne, as explained there at the story's end, for "*`al demuth hakisse demuth kemar'eh adam `alaw milema`elah*/ upon the likeness of the throne was a likeness as the appearance of a man upon it above" etc. [Eze. 1:26]. And therefore even Moshe Rabbeinu was not spared from the jealousy of the angels who chase a man who wants to enter the garden of the Torah so they envy him, except by the advice of, "*Echoz bekisse kevodi*/ Hold on to My Throne of Glory" [*Shabbath* 88b; Job. 26:9], upon which stands the aforementioned "as the appearance of a man," as also explained in *LM II* in the torah *Tik`u — Memshalah* #1, and he too entered in peace and left in peace in the utmost degree, by means of him being wise and discerning and adding one day of his own understanding, as Chazal explained [*Shabbath* 87a; Ex. 19:10-15].

But the rest of the people, devoid of these vessels, were forced to stand from afar, "lest they break through" [ibid. :21], and come there without those vessels, and then they would be "stoned-stoned, or shot-shot" etc. [ibid :13]. And behold, the whole change of the throne as explained there [i.e. the rose that was missing from the top etc.], and also the change of the garden from the placement of the likeness of the man, the king to whom peace belongs, and also the change of the country's name [to] "The Wise Land With the Foolish King," in the aspect of "*Ei-lakh eretz she-malkekh na`ar*/ Woe to you, land, when your king is a fool!" [Eccl. 10:16] — it is all drawn from the interchanges of the king's son and the bondservant's son. And when the animals of the chair sang the song and the melody when they were clarified of the changes, everything was clarified, and everything changed over into the aspect of "*Ashreikh eretz shemalkekh ben-chorin/* Fortunate are you, land, when your king is a free man," and he said, "Now I know that I am the truly the king's son." And by the way, it is clear that the animals' song and melody, this is that melody and song that Moshe himself will sing in the future, until all the earth's inhabitants will recognize and know: who is the bondservant riding on the horse, and who is the prince who is the true ruler. who is included in the rule and kingship of the Blessed One Himself, Who shall reign forever and ever. And this is, "*Ashirah laShem ki-ga'oh ga'ah, sus verokhevo/* I will sing unto Hashem when He is exalted-exalted, the horse and its rider..." mentioned above (namely, the bondservant's son, who rode a horse) "*ramah vayam/* He has thrown into the sea" [Ex. 15:1]. So be His will, soon in our days, Amen!

THE PRAYER LEADER

It is clear from the words of the Admor z"tzl that the ten people along with the King are the aspect of the ten *Sefiroth.* And by the way, we discern from this that the Warrior corresponds to the attribute of G*evurah/* Stricture and *Din-*Judgment. And he, in his hard strictures, wants to demolish the world if they do not subdue their uncircumcised heart to return in complete repentance, as explained in the story of the Prayer Leader, that the Warrior wanted nothing else but subdual, and if not, he would destroy them. And in like fashion did our teacher the great tzaddik Rabbi Nathan z"tzl once talk about this, that this is the matter that after the curses in *Torath Kohanim,* who are from Hakadosh Barukh Hu's traits of stricture and judgment, is said, "*O-az yikana` levavam he`arel/* If then, their uncircumcised heart will be subdued..." [Lev. 26:41]. And this is the scripture concluding the end of Malakhi with, "*Hineh Anokhi sholeach lakhem eth Eliyah hanavi, vehashiv/* Behold, I send you Elijah the prophet, and he shall bring back" etc. [Mal. 3], that is, they will return in complete repentance, "*pen-avo vehikeithi eth-ha'aretz charem/* lest I come and smite the land with utter destruction," that is, as mentioned. But the tzaddikim with their awesome prayers sweeten the judgments, and they cause Him to lengthen His temper and extend time for them; perhaps they will turn around, as explained in the story, that the Prayer Leader and the Warden over the treasuries had an effect on the Warrior, that he should extend time for the country that was sunk in craving money. And Hashem Yithbarakh helped, in the merit of the kosher Prayer Leader's prayers, that the end of the repair was made complete and they were all repaired. And behold, it is known from the kabbalists that *Techiyath Hamethim*/ Resurrection of the Dead will be from the aspect of the attribute of *gevurah*, which is the matter that in the blessing "*Atah gibor...*/ You are Mighty" we mention resurrection of the dead. And this is what is explained at the end of the story, that afterwards at the end of the repair the Warrior came and took them out from the holes and graves, which is the aspect of "*befithchi eth-qivrotheikhem*/ when I open your graves" [Eze. 37:13] which refers to resurrection of the dead. And then everybody will throw away their idols of silver and gold [Isa. 2:20], and all the world will involve itself just with Torah, prayer, repentance and good deeds. So be His will, soon in our days, Amen!

And see in the *Tikkunim*, *Tikkun* #70 [daf 123b]: "*Dawidh, shiv`ah minei dehava havah bese`aroi*/ Dawidh had seven kinds of gold in his hair... *kelil kol givunin*/ including all the colors" etc.; see there; and understand regarding the seven golden hairs that had all the colors, of the Child, which the Warrior took. Also, the faction that chose for themselves merriment as a purpose, accepting over them the Trusty Friend as king: look in the book *Yiqra deShabta* regarding this story; explained there is that in truth, joy on the side of holiness is sanctified and intertwined with love on the side of holiness; the aspect of "*Veya`letzu vekha ohavei shemekha*/ Let them also that love Your name ecstasize in You" etc. [Ps. 5:12]; see there.

♦ ♦

Sichoth Haran #147-151:
Regarding the Tales

147

I heard one of his followers say that before Rabbeinu ob"m told the tale of the King's Son Who Was Made Entirely of Gemstones which is printed [in Story #5], he said before telling it, "I know a story that contains the entire Divine Name of 42 letters," and then he told this story. But nonetheless we do not know if this is the story of the 42-Letter Name. And I too heard from his holy mouth several years ago, saying that the Baal Shem Tov obm knew a story that contained the 42-Letter Name, and he spoke with me then regarding the 42-Letter Name. And he asked me to find an explanation in common language [i.e. Yiddish] regarding the two Letters *waw* and *tzaddi* that are in that name, and I could not find [one]. And according to [my] understanding it was because he already knew the secret of that name, but only these two letters *waw* and *tzaddi* he was still unable to insert into the matter that he wanted to clothe this Name in.

148

When he told the tale of the Prayer Leader that is printed in *Sipurei Ma`asiyoth* he asked us afterwards, "Who told the story that there were factions in their chronicles?" — regarding the factions that were made when there was a storm wind in the world, etc. We replied to him that one of the strongmen of the Warrior told this to the Prayer Leader, as explained there. And he nodded his head that it was so, and we understood from his words that there is a very profound intention in this, why specifically one of the guards told this. And from this, learn that in each and every utterance of the stories there is a very, very profound intention, impossible for the mouth to speak or for the heart to ponder.

149

[Rebbe Nachman] told the Tale of the Seven Beggars printed in *Sipurei Ma`asiyoth* [Story #13] over several days, and each time, he told a matter related to what people were telling him, that caused him to start telling the story.

I n the beginning, on the night of the holy Sabbath it began because of snuff-tobacco which he received from one of his people and which was mentioned in a letter that I sent to my friend [R' Natfali], that he, of blessed memory, had received it; and I wrote to him, [telling him] to be happy. Then he commented on this; he spoke up and said, "*I'll* tell you how they were once happy!" (I [R' Nachman Goldstein] heard that he said it in these words: "What do *you* know about how to rejoice from out of melancholy?! *I'll* tell you how they once rejoiced!" — <u>Chayei Moharan #63</u>) And he began to tell the story. He told the whole introduction of the story through the end of the First Day pertaining to the beggar who was blind. And all this was on the night of the holy Sabbath, and I [Rabbi Nathan] was at my home in Nemryov [while Rabbi Nachman was in Breslev].

A fterwards on Tuesday my friend [Rav Naftali] came to my house and told this story and I stood trembling and astounded, for indeed I had already heard from him many awesome stories, but a story like this I had never heard from his holy mouth. Afterwards I went there and I came to the house of our Rabbi of blessed memory when he was already closed in his room. In the morning, which was Wednesday, I entered and approached him and spoke with him a great deal, and I told him stories of the world that I had heard recently, and afterwards he spoke with me regarding the said story which he had told on the night of the holy Shabbath, and he said that he greatly desired to know (i.e. tell) the end, that is, what happens on all the rest of the seven days of celebration; and also the whole conclusion of the ending of the story of the king's son who had received the kingdom from his father during his lifetime, with which the story began. And he told me, then, that similarly, each day of the seven days of celebration, each day one of the Seven Beggars would come and bless them and give them a wedding gift etc. And he also told me about the order of the story of the elders with the memories, which this matter I did not hear in completely clear order from my friend, and he, of blessed memory, himself explained me a little of it in order. And he also spoke with me regarding the Blind One who boasted that he does not remember anything at all (in Yiddish, *Ikh gidenk gar nisht*) that the explanation of *Ikh gidenk gar nisht* is that he remembers when he did not yet have any existence etc.; and he found this a wonder.

Afterwards I greatly yearned that he should start telling about the Second Day, but I did not attain it, for meanwhile his attendant came and said, "Rabbi, it is mealtime." And he set the table before him to eat and I had to leave from his presence. Afterwards, after he slept a little after eating, afterwards I returned and went in to him, and stood before him, telling him several things from worldly affairs, and mostly from Berdichev, where I was close to at the time. And I spoke with him regarding that everyone is full of many worries and lackings, that all the big rich people lack severely, each and every one, etc. And afterwards I spoke up and said to him this verse (Eccl. 3:11): "He has set the world in their heart, yet so that man cannot find out the work that God has done from the beginning even to the end;" see the comment of Rashi. He, of blessed memory, replied, "Isn't this our story?" And immediately he asked where we are in the story. And I was immediately frightened due to my great yearnings I had for hearing this, and I answered him in trepidation that we are on the Second Day. He answered and said, "On the second day they again yearned" etc. And he then told on Wednesday the whole story of the Second Day, and afterwards on the night of the Holy Sabbath the story of Third and Fourth Day, and afterwards on Sunday the story of the Fifth Day, and afterwards on the following Tuesday the story of the Sixth Day. And after he told the story of the Sixth Day, we were standing before him, and one of his people told him some story. He replied and said, "Isn't this exactly related to the story of the Seventh Day?" And he said it seems the world is telling his story and he very much wanted to tell it, but we did not merit it being told then, and he did not tell any more of it.

150

One time he said, "To whoever I get and receive money etc. from, I give, for by receiving I give." (And this is the concept explained in the story of the Sixth Day in The Seven Beggars, where someone boasted of the wonders of the power in his hand; see there.)

151

The story of the Third and Fourth Day, he told on the night of the Holy Shabbath, as mentioned above. And then at that time his baby grandson was on his sickbed, and he had great affliction from this, for his illness was very serious, specially since his daughter the righteous Mrs. Udel, may she live long, the mother of the child, had great pain in child raising; God save us. Hashem keep her now.

He, of blessed memory, went in on the night of the holy Shabbath and sat at the table in great pain and did not take his time at this meal at all. We blessed right away [reciting] the Grace After Meals before people started entering in to him as they always did. Afterwards, after the Grace After Meals he remained sitting at his holy table and opened his holy, pure and awesome mouth and then said this wonderful and awesome discussion, which had holy Torah as always in most of his holy discussions, and the whole discussion pertained to the great pain he had. To the best of our recollection, he spoke then of "the Heart that is pursued" etc.

And then during that conversation he spoke up and asked where we were in the story. Immediately we were startled and answered him in panic, awe and fear that we are on the Third Day. Immediately he replied saying, "On the third day again the couple remembered, 'How can [the speech-impaired beggar be brought here]..." (as printed there) and he told the whole story of the Third Day, and explained there a little resembling what he told earlier. Then he finished the story of the Third Day, that a celebration was made there etc.; then he said in these words: "Zei haben a Hilva gitan [They had a ball]." Right afterwards he told the story of the Fourth Day, and as soon as he finished it, he immediately and right away left the table in haste.

And because I was very busy in my mind going over the two awesome stories of the Third and Fourth Days and I immediately reviewed them with the people who were there so no word would be lost from them, because of this I forgot the whole holy discussion mentioned that he spoke before it. A pity it is lost. Honor and praise to the Living God for letting us be privileged to remember and record these stories that even according to the limited inspiration in my heart I have no vessel of speech and writing to speak of the high awesomeness of their level. [See _Chayei Moharan_ #64 regarding the inception of telling the Fifth Day.]

Afterwards on Tuesday it was close to Pesach and he left his house because they were plastering his house for Pesach. And he went to the house of the Rav [of the city], and there we stood before him. And I do not remember what matter they discussed in his presence that had some little connection to some matter of the story of the Sixth Day, but because of it, he told the story of the Sixth Day, and afterwards someone told him etc. as mentioned.

And behold, then it was close to Pesach as mentioned, and in my opinion the secret of the parting of the Sea of Reeds is hinted in the matter of the ten walls of water. And see _Likutei Halakhot_ in _Yoreh Deah hilchoth tola`im_ (_halakhah_ ד) and explained there is the matter that Hashem enlightened my eyes with in this.

The rule is that with each story that he told, the story came about via some conversation that he had and spoke with us regarding worldly stories, and in the midst of them he began to tell the story by means of the story having some utterances with relation to the story in his heart. And this was like _ith`arutha diltatha_ [arousal from below], to draw down perceptions of Godliness that he clothed in that story. And so it was with each and every story.

And so it was with several Torot he revealed that were not at a fixed assembly time. And in all this we always saw the wonders of Hashem and the greatness of the Tzaddik's level, that all the utterances in the world were for him Torah and revelation of Godliness. But much more did we see this with this awesome story of the Seven Beggars which is wonderful awesome high revelations without bound. As an understanding person will understand by himself if he puts his heart to them with an honest eye to understand and perceive holy wonders of the boastings of each one mentioned there each day, and in particular the greatness of the holiness of the boasting of the seven beggars themselves who boast each day: that the Blind One boasted that he doesn't look at the world at all, therefore he is actually blind to this world; and likewise the deaf one who doesn't hear any sound of this world etc., therefore he is deaf etc. etc. And likewise with each utterance of this story which are all wonderful revelations even according to meager minds even though we do not understand them at all. And all this revelation, it is all through stories of worldly matters; through them it came about that he had pity on us in such extraordinary compassion and revealed to us all this, in order to benefit us and our children forever.

He said regarding the tales that he told, that it would be better to not reveal of them what any of the clues hint to, for when the thing is hidden, more can be accomplished with it that is needed. But he was forced occasionally to just reveal some hint, in order that people should know there are hidden things in them.

♦ ♦

Chayei Moharan: Rabbi Nachman's Biography, written by Rabbi Nathan and published, after the latter's passing, by the Tcheriner Rav, R' Nachman Goldstein z"l. Notes of "the Copyist" are those of R' Nachman of Tcherin. Notes that are enclosed in <pointed brackets> indicate text that was not included in earlier, censored versions.

Chayei Moharan #25:
"Today I Have Said 3 Things Contrary..."

Pertaining to the essay *"Pathach Rabbi Shimon"* (<u>Likutei Moharan #60</u>): After Rabbeinu of blessed memory said this lesson he said plainly, "Today I have said three things contrary to what the world says:

1. The world says that telling stories induces sleep; but I said that by story tales we awaken people from their sleep.

2. The world says that from talking words no one conceives [a child]; but I said that by the Tzaddik's telling of words, through which he arouses people from their sleep, conception comes to barren women.

3. The world says that the true Tzaddik of towering stature does not need much money, because why should he need money? But I said that there is such a contemplative understanding [of the Torah] for which one needs all the fortune of the world."

[Copyist's note:] I heard from one prominent follower of Rabbeinu, of blessed memory, that he heard from his holy mouth regarding his will being that they print the Story Tales also in the Yiddish language that we speak; and he said at that time that it can easily happen that a woman who is barren would read some story from them and thereby conceive goodly offspring and be privileged to have children; this is the extent of what I heard. (And there is support for this from what is explained in that aforementioned essay, that via these story tales a barren woman becomes impregnated.)

Chayei Moharan #59:
Dates of Lessons

The dates when teachings were given, where known to us:

Likutei Moharan

№	Heading	Date
1*	Ashrei Temimei-Darekh	Medvedevka, year unknown (*Tovoth Zikhronoth*)
2*	Emor el-haKohanim	Zlatipolia (*Tovoth Zikhronoth* 2)
3	Aqruktha	I heard that it was given on the first Shabbath when Rabbeinu z"l entered Breslev, at the end of 5562/1802.
4	Anokhi	in Zlatipolia on Shavu`oth
5	Bachatzotzerot	Rosh Hashanah 5563/1803
6	Qera eth-Yehoshu`a	the following Shabbath Teshuvah
7	Mishpatim	winter 5563/1803
8	Ra'ithi Menorath Zahav	Shabbath Chanukkah 5563/1803
9	Tehomoth Yekhasyumu	Shabbath Shirah 5563/1803
10	Mishpatim	the same winter in Terhovitza before Purim
11	Ani Hashem Hu Shemi	Shavu`oth 5563/1803
12	Tehillah leDawidh	Shabbath Nachamu 5563/1803; includes an explanation of the verse, "Nachamu Nachamu" etc.
13	Ashrei — Hashgachah	Rosh haShanah 5564/1803
14	Tik`u — Lehamshikh Shalom...	Shabbath Chanukkah 5564/1803
15*	Ohr Haganuz	Zlatipolia (*Tovoth Zikhronoth* 6)
16	Rabbi Yochanan Mishta`ei	Shabbath, at the morning meal, summer 5563/1803

17	*Merikim Sakeihem*	*Shabbath Chanukkah 5566*/1805
18	*Kartalitha*	It appears this was said in winter of *5564*/1803-4 in Terhovitza.
19	*Tefila Lechabakuk*	*Shavu`oth 5564*/1804
20	*Tish`ah Tikkunim*	*Rosh Hashanah 5565*/1805
21	*`Atika*	*Shabbath Nachamu 5564*/1804
22	*Chotam Betokh-Chotam*	the week after Rosh Hashanah
23	*Tzivitha Tzedek*	Winter *5563*/1802-3
24	*Emtza`itha de`Alma*	Shabbath night meal, summer *5563*/1803
29	*Hai Gavra...*	*Shavu`oth 5566*/1803
30	*Meishra deSakina*	*Shabbath Chanukkah 5567*/1806
38	*Markevoth Par`oh*	*Shabbath Shirah 5562*/1802
44	*Atem Nitzavim*	end of *5562*/1802 on the Shabbath before Rosh Hashanah
48	*`Al-Asher-Me`altem*	*Isru Chag Sukkoth 5563*/1802
49	*Lashemesh*	Shabbath, 3 Nissan *5563*/1803, after the marriage of his daughter Sarah z"l which was on Rosh Chodesh Nissan in Medvedevka
51	*Amar Rabbi Akiva*	after *Shavu`oth 5563*/1803
52	*Hane`or Balailah*	beginning of *5563*/1802
54	*Vayhi Miketz — Zikaron*	*Shabbath Chanukkah 5565*/1804
56	*Uveyom Habikurim*	*Shavu`oth 5565*/1805
58–59	*Telath Nafkin* and *Heikhal haKodesh*	Rosh Hashanah *5566*/1805

60	*Pathach Rabbi Shim`on*	Rosh Hashanah *5567*/1806
61	*Chadi Rabbi Shim`on*	Rosh Hashanah *5568*/1807
62	*Vayasev*	*Shabbath Shirah 5565*/1805
63	*Sod Kavanath Hamilah*	the Shabbath before the *berith milah* of his holy son Shelomoh Efrayim z"l, who was born close to Rosh Chodesh Nissan *5565*/1805
65	*Vayomer Bo`az*	Summer of *5566*/1806, shortly after the passing of his aforementioned holy son Shelomoh Efrayim, which was in Sivan *5566*/1806. And that is when this lesson was given, on Friday at day. And prior to this he taught the lesson, *"Da` ki yesh arikh anpin...*/ Know that there is an *arikh anpin* of the *Klipah,"* #242. And on the preceding Thursday he cried in our presence. And *"Weshiquvai Bivkhi Masokhti*/ I have mixed my drink with my weeping,"* #262, he taught on the following Shabbath.
66	*Viyhi na pi shnayim*	After Chanukkah *5567*/1806: on Shabbath, regarding breaking obstacles, as explained there; and on *Motza'ei Shabbath*, regarding drawing forth the spirit of Mashiach, as explained there. And at the same time, that is, on the same night that he began to teach that lesson at the night meal, he told before the meal the story of the birds and "Mazal tov!", as explained elsewhere [*Chayei Moharan*: New Stories #82].
67	*Vayiven Eth-Hatzela`*	Zaslav on Shavu`oth *5567*/1807
72	*Lehithchazek Bekhol Pa`am Neged Hayetzer Hara`*	when his holy son Shelomoh Efrayim was born
78	*Viyten-`Oz Lemalko*	Zlatipolia on Rosh Hashanah *5561*/1800
96	*Zomem Rasha` Latzaddik*	a long time before his trip to Eretz Israel
112	*Tzohar ta`aseh latevah*	start of winter *5563*/1802

132 – 132	*Ma`yan Denafek Me'athar Chad and We'orach Tzaddikim*	after Pesach 5563 / *1803* upon his return from travel to his daughter Sarah z"l's wedding
175	*Beshimkha Yegilun*	*Motza'ei Shabbath Teshuvah 5565*/1804
177	*Vayomer Hashem Salachti Kidvarekha*	Shabbath Rosh Chodesh Cheshvan *5565*/1804, which is when the *forshpiel* [bridal party] of his daughter Miriam z"l took place.
197	*Lashon Hara` Pogem `Anavah*	before Shavu`oth *5565*/1805
205	*Tikkun Lemikreh...*	After Shavu`oth *5565*/1805. Revealing the ten Tehillim was in *5569*. [That is when R' Nathan glimpsed a manuscript where the Rebbe had written down the ten Tehillim. Public revelation occurred later: according to an unnumbered letter from Rabbi Nachman Goldstein of Tulchin dated Monday 18 Adar, 5633, at the end of *Alim Litrufah*, R' Nachman revealed the ten Tehillim to R' Aharon and R' Naftali between *LM II* #74 and the tale of the Seven Beggars, shortly before the Rebbe left Breslev for Uman. As that torah, regarding Parashath Parah, was most likely given that Shabbath, 18 Adar II, 5570, and the tale was begun a week later on 25 Adar II, therefore the Tehillim were revealed that week. See *CM* #141.]
206	*Ta`ithi Keseh Oved*	I heard from the rav, R' Nathan z"l, that when Rabbeinu z"l revealed this lesson in front of him, he told him that this lesson was his *hithbodedut* presently at that time.

211	the practice of traveling for Rosh Hashanah	close to Rosh Hashanah *5568*/1807; and on Rosh Hashanah, *Chadi Rabbi Shim`on*, #61, was given, and there it explains more fully the concept of traveling to Tzaddikim for Rosh Hashanah and the concept of "*kulehu bemachshavah ithbereru*/ all are purified in thought," except that here in #211 there is also allusion to traveling to gravesites of Tzaddikim, in the aspect of, "*Vayikach Moshe eth-`atzmoth Yosef*/ And Moshe took Yosef's bones...*"
277 – 278	*Bekamim `Alai* and *Da` She`al Chalef Tov* — *Bekan'o Eth-Kinathi...*	Shemini `Atzeret
282	*Azamera*	same; and after Sukkoth during his trip to Lviv as they escorted him from Krasne he revealed the idea of the Mishkan and the children, which is the end of that lesson *Azamera*

Likutei Moharan II

№	Heading	Date
1	*Tik`u — Memshalah*	Rosh Hashanah *5569*/1808, and before this he told an awesome vision, as explained elsewhere [*CM* #84, the chair]
2	*Yemei Chanukkah*	Shabbath Chanukkah *5569*/1808
4	*Uveyom Habikurim*	Shavu`oth *5569*/1809
5	*Tik`u — Emunah*	Rosh Hashanah *5570*/1809
7	*Ki Merachamam*	Shabbath Chanukkah *5570*/1809
8	*Tik`u — Tokhachah*	Rosh Hashanah *5571*/1810
10–17		end of *5568*/1808 after his return from Lviv
32	*Yesh Tzaddikim Genuzim*	Shabbath Parashath Yitro *5569*/1809

66	*Hatzaddik Mukhrach La`asoth Teshuvah*	between Yom Kippur and Sukkoth 5570/1809; at the same time, the lesson *"Lefi Hayamim Nora'im..."* was given [in *SH* #87]
67	*Bereishith — Le`einei Kol-Yisrael*	Shabbath Bereishith 5570/1809. There it hints to the passing of the holy rav of Berdichev and the passing of Rabbeinu z"l himself, as inferred from his repeating this lesson close to his entry into Uman.
68	*[Ikar Shelemuth haTzaddik Sheyuchal Lihyoth Lema`alah Ulmatah]*	Before Chanukkah 5570/1809
71	*Chavalim Nafelu Li Bane`imim*	Shabbath Shirah
72	*Chayim Nitzchiyim*	Shabbath Parashath Yitro 5570/1809
78	*[Be`Inyan Hanhagath Hapeshituth Shel Hatzaddik haEmeth]*	Shabbath Nachamu in Uman

Sipurei Ma`asiyoth

Nº	Story	Date
1	["The Lost Princess"]	summer 5566/1806
7–8	"The Fly and the Spider" and "The Rabbi and His Son"	summer 5567/1807
9	"The Clever Man and the Simple Man"	winter 5569/1809, before Purim
10	"The Burgher and the Pauper"	5569/1809, after Purim
11	"The Exchanged Children"	*Motza'ei Shabbath Parashath Noach 5570/1809*
12	"The Prayer Leader"	*Motza'ei Shabbath Va'era* and *Motza'ei Rosh Chodesh Shevat 5570/1809*

| 13 | "The Seven Beggars" | its beginning was on the night of Shabbath Kodesh, *Parashath Shemini*, 25 Adar II 5570/1810 |
| Comments Following the Stories | "The Horse and the Pump" | Shavu`oth 5567/1807 in Zaslav |

Sichoth Haran

№	Topic	Date
7	The *Sichah* regarding pouring out one's speech like a child pleading before his father, and the story of his grandfather, Rabbi Nachman	after Shavu`oth 5569/1809
24	The benefit of being privileged to give money to true Tzaddikim	summer 5569/1809, and afterwards on RH 5570 the lesson *Tik`u — Emunah* was given, and included there is the concept of "*Tzaddik okhel lesova` nafsho*/ A tzaddik eats to satisfy his soul" (Prov 13:25) and "*Wehisbi`a betzachtzachoth nafshekha*/ He will satisfy your soul with splendor" (Isa. 58:11)
32	"One needs to strengthen himself in faith..." and that by means of faith one merits to arrive at the aspect of *ratzon*/ desire...	winter 5570/1809-10, after the lesson, "*Ki Merachamam...*" [*LM II* #7] which was given on Shabbath Chanukkah.
40	Regarding religious philosophers' books, and the idea of the dreidel	the same Chanukkah 5570/1809 as well

51	From "This world is nothing..." to "we already know what to do, from the Torah"	first night of Shavu`oth, *Motza'ei Shabbath* 5569/1809. And then during that *Sichah* he spoke regarding "*Tenu Levavkhem Li*/ Give Me Your Hearts..." as explained elsewhere [*Hishtapkhuth Hanefesh*, Preface]. There he spoke up and said, "... the sediment of the mind stands still and remains quiet..."; summer 5569/1809
60	Regarding construction	winter 5570/1809-10
86	Regarding wedding concepts and practices	*Shemini `Atzereth* 5563/1803
87	"In accord with the *Yamim Nora'im*..."	between Yom Kippur and Sukkoth 5570/1809
91	A *segulah* for continued diligence in learning	`Erev Rosh Hashanah 5571/1810
93	"Know: that there is a light that shines in a thousand worlds"	winter 5567/1806, before Chanukkah, in the week of the *Berith Milah* of his son Ya`akov z"l

Chayei Moharan #60-66: *Sipurei Ma`asiyoth*

60

The tale of the burgher [#10] he told after they first told in his presence of the matter of a document written with golden letters [and such a document is mentioned in the tale], and this was after Purim [5]569; before Purim he told the story of the Clever Man and the Simple Man [#9].

61

In the evening after *Shabbath Parashath Noach* year [5]570 after he had said on the night of Shabbath the torah [*LM II* #67] which begins, "And this is the aspect of the eulogy over the passing away of the Tzaddik," and in the evening after Shabbath we entered to him in our usual way and he tipped with his hand that we should go from him, and we immediately went from him, and it was wonder to us because our usual way was to always talk with him a great deal after Shabbath, and we had some pain because of it, and we went in to the house of the local rav. After some hours he sent his attendant and called us that we should enter to him, and we entered to him — I and my friend Rabbi Naftali. And he told us to tell him news, the way he always did, asking [us] to tell him news specifically, and Rabbi Natfali told him what he heard then regarding the French war that was then. And then in that conversation we were astounded and astonished over the enormity of [Napoleon's] rise, that he had risen suddenly to such heights, for at first he was a simple servant, and he became emperor. And we talked with him regarding this matter. He spoke up and said, "Who knows what kind of *neshamah/* soul he has, for it could be that he was interchanged, for so it is in the *Heikhlei haTemuroth/* Interchange Halls, that sometimes the souls are interchanged" etc. And afterwards he began to relate that there had already been a story like this, that one time the queen gave birth and at the same time etc. and he told the whole story of the King's Son Who Was Exchanged [#11].

After he told the story of the King's Son and the Bondmaid's Son then I had an argument with my friend Rabbi Naftali over the fact that it is written there when he [the king's son] went to the fair, that he took everything he had and laid it down for the lodging. And it seemed to one of us that he put it down for the sake of what he owed for the lodging, and the other said it is not so but that he put it down *stam*/ for no reason. And we made a bet on this and we went and asked his holy mouth. And he was involved in his devotions, pacing to and fro in his home in his holy manner, and he replied to us as per the words of the second person, that he just plain laid down [his belongings], and not for debt.

Afterwards present with him was one of his most important followers and Rabbeinu z"l related to him and said to him that in these stories when one alters one utterance from according to what he himself said, much is missing from the story. And he told him: Doesn't it seem that these two who made a bet on this matter — it seems apparently that it's a small thing and there's not so much *kefeida*/ what to mind about this, whether it is as this one says or like that one says? But actually much depends on this and there is great *kefeida* and *dikduk*/ precision/ fine detail in this. And from this you can understand a little, `ad heichan `ad heichan/ how far, how far these stories reach, for his "thoughts are extremely deep" [Ps. 92:6]. Fortunate is he who will be privileged to conceive of them a little, according to his level.

62

The tale of the Prayer Leader began after he told it with the local *chazzan* [cantor, lit. visioner] Rabbi Yossi, and we were standing before him and the chazzan's garment was ripped. He spoke up and said to the chazzan, "Aren't you the *ba`al tefilah*/ leader of prayer, through whom everything is drawn down (that is, all the influxes)? So why should you not have a garment (which is called a *kaftan* [a long robe-suit])?" And amidst this he began to tell, in these words, "There was already a story like this, that there was a Prayer Leader," and he told the whole story. And at the beginning of his telling we did not know that he's telling his stories, but rather we thought that he's telling a plain event that happened that way. Only afterwards when he got into the things did we discern the awesomeness of the matter, that he's telling an awesome story from his tales, which are *sipurei ma`asiyoth shel Shanim Qadhmoniyoth*/ Stories of the Ancient.

63

Pertaining to the inception of telling the Seven Beggars, printed in the *Sichot* #149 q.v., after the words, "*I'll* tell you how they were once happy:"

It should say, "I heard that he said it in these words: 'What do *you* [plural] know about how to be happy from within the midst of melancholy?! *I'll* tell you how they were once happy' etc." It was heard from his holy mouth explicitly that the tales he tells are extremely wonderful and awesome novelties and are fit to be lectured in public, standing in the synagogue and telling a story from these tales he told, for they are extremely high and awesome novelties. (Copyist's note: I heard from the mouth of Rav Naftali z"l that after Rabbeinu z"l told the legend of the Seven Beggars he extolled its loftiness exceedingly and said [we] are permitted to travel to Brod and enter the synagogue and say to the *shamash/* attendant that he should assemble the public for a lecture and knock on the table (as is done before a lecture to quiet the murmur of the people) and tell them this story).

64

Pertaining to the *Sichot* #151 after the words "...loftiness of their level:"

Then on Sunday afternoon we stood before him and he talked with us, and during the conversation he spoke some quip which is called a *vartil/* wisecrack regarding that sect etc. Then he spoke of the concept of wide shoulders. Then from that same conversation it came about that he asked where we are standing in the story and we replied to him: on the Fifth Day; and then he told the story of the Fifth Day and he told it in joy.

65

I heard from one of [Rabbeinu z"l's] most important followers, who said that he heard from the mouth of Rabbeinu z"l, the story regarding the tzaddik who fell one time into great sadness, where he enlivened himself by reminding himself of the profound kindness of Hashem Yithbarakh, "*shelo `asani goi/* for not making me a heathen," which is already printed in *Sipurei Ma`asiyoth* [Comments Following the Stories] q.v. — which was written according to what I myself heard from his holy mouth z"l himself.

And this man said that he heard this story from the mouth of Rabbeinu z"l in a slightly different style.

And he said that Rabbeinu z"l told that there was one tzaddik of supreme level who was of the *ma'rei d'chushbena/* "masters of accounting" who would measure himself every day whether he had performed the service of Hashem in entirety on that day, as was his constant practice. And he reckoned the things that he needed to do on that day and found that he had not fulfilled his obligation entirely on that day. For example, he needed to go to and fro in his house a certain number of times according to what he needed in relation to his lofty perception, and on that day he did not pace to and fro in his house as much as he ought to, and through this he became so downcast that he could not revive himself until he revived himself from the fact that he was privileged "*shelo' `asani goi/* that He has not made me a heathen." And also in the story tale there was a slight variation and I do not remember more. And from this matter discern the loftiness of the great exaltedness of that tzaddik, how great a level he was, that he had a high service in walking to and fro in his house, to the extent that by falling short in this service in his estimation he became so afflicted that he almost could not revive himself if not for reminding himself *shelo' `asani goi*. See, discern and look at the service of the tzaddikim, that their pain over their shortcoming in their service — how far, how far it extends; fortunate are they!

66

Pertaining to the matter that is printed at the end of *Sipurei Ma`asiyoth* which begins, "Know that there are two kinds of palaces: in one dwells the king and in one dwells the `*eved/* servant" etc.:

When one serves Hashem and he is still in the aspect of `*eved*, he is still in the aspect of *arur/* cursed, God forbid; but there is an aspect of `*eved bikdushah/* servant in holiness, aspect of *Moshe `eved Hashem*. And know that there is a mitzvah through which one goes out from the aspect of `*eved* and it is the mitzvah of *pidyon shivuim/* redeeming captives. [Consider his holy purpose of repairing and freeing the naked souls in the mass graves in Uman, *CM* #151 etc.; his Tikkun haKlali, etc.]

Chayei Moharan: Additional Selections Having Special Relevance to *Sipurei Ma`asiyoth*

[#1-59] Pertaining to the Torahs

46

Before revealing the matter printed in *LM II* #68 regarding the tzaddik, that he needs to leave children and students, which pertains to the torah *"Ki merachamam yenahagem"* [*LM II*] #7, he said that there have been many great figures who each accomplished and repaired what they repaired and then it stopped. And his meaning was regarding the illumination with which they lit up the minds of their students, drawing many men to Hashem Yithbarakh, but afterwards their illumination stopped. But we need to do something that will never stop; that these men will make other men, and they will make more men, and thus for ever.

And something similar I had already heard: that it is obligatory that our followers illuminate their friends and students. And each one is obligated to perform some action and illuminate his friend, and his friend his friend. For, the tree has branches, and out of these branches emerge more branches, and so on, etc. And his statement is already recorded elsewhere [*LM* #229], where he said, "My fire will burn forever without going out." And he said it in Yiddish in these words, *"Mayn fayeril vet shoyn tluen biz Mashiakh vet kumen/* My fire will burn intermittently all the way until Messiah comes!"

And the beginning of that conversation, regarding a son and pupil, began by him entering from his room [of his beit midrash] to the other room, toward his larger house, and he stood by the doorway from where he came out of his room, and found us standing before him, namely I, my friend, and his son in law Yoske a"h. And he began to speak with his son in law and said to him, "I heard that you learned today," and he began to chide him lovingly that he should hold fast to his studies, and he said, "Isn't it good and beautiful to learn first and then afterwards go to the market to trade" etc.

And later he spoke up and said, "Don't I also learn as well? And my learning is a novelty! And he began to speak gloriously of himself, declaring, "I can learn; I can show the biggest lamdan of the biggest that he still can't learn at all and doesn't know at all. And conversely, I can show the little ones that they are close to Hashem Yithbarakh and the Torah etc." And he entered from this conversation to that one, and revealed the whole matter stated there, regarding a son and student, that those who reside above ask specifically, "*Ayyeh meqom kevodo*/ Where is the place of his glory?" and conversely those who reside below say, "*Melo khol-ha'aretz kevodo*/ The whole world is full of His glory;" see there and understand thoroughly. Fortunate is the time and the second when we were privileged to hear this from his holy mouth himself. If we had not come into the world except to hear this, *dayenu*/ it would be enough. And thus regarding each and every utterance that I heard from his holy mouth. "With what shall I come before Hashem, after all he has bestowed on us? What shall I return to Hashem for all his benefits to me?"

[#67-73] Pertaining to Sichot Haran

67

Pertaining to the *sichah* [*Sichoth Haran* #3] that is printed at the end of *Sipurei Ma`asiyoth* which begins, "He greatly emphasized the greatness of Hashem Yithbarakh," and a little is missing there and it is not written as it ought to be, and this is how it should be:

While he was sitting on the carriage at the time when I traveled with him from here, Breslev, to Uman, [for him] to pass away there, he spoke up and said, "Hashem Yithbarakh is extremely great and [we] know nothing whatsoever" etc. And he said it in Yiddish in these words, "**Gott iz groiss**," (and he pulled the word "*groiss*" upward in a wonderful pleasantness, and it is impossible to describe this in writing whatsoever), "*men veyst gor nit; se tuen zikh oyf der velt a zelkhe zakhin, men veyst gor nit*/ We know nothing; such things are happening in the world yet we know nothing whatsoever." And I asked him, "Didn't you already say that now the concept, "*Takhlith hayedia`ah asher lo-neda`*/ The ultimate knowing is that [God] is unknowable," is known to you? He replied, *"Zint ikh bin aroys fun Breslev biz aher veys ikh shoyn oykh nit/* From the time that I left Breslev until here, I already [i.e. again] still don't know." (All this he said at the time of that conversation, and at that time it was no more than a short amount of time since he left Breslev. And if you are a little adept in the depth of his holy conversations you will understand from this a little of the amazingness of his greatness, for he had already said that his *"eino yode`a/* not knowing" is the maximum, and now he boasted that in such a short time once again he doesn't know whatsoever.)

68

Pertaining to the *sichah* regarding doctors, that one must distance oneself from them to the utmost extent; see there [*Sichoth HaRan*] #50: [Translator's note: in Rabbi Nachman's times and environs the doctors were extremely harmful.]

And he said that whoever has an ill person in his home, God forbid, if someone would come to him and would say to him that he will deal the sick person a great blow with a thick wooden club which is called a *druk*, he would definitely be panicked at this. And behold, when one gives the sick person into the hands of the doctor, behold he is like one who gives him to an actual murderer. For his treatments will certainly harm him more than a murderer's blow, and why would one want to kill the sick person with one's hands? And really, just because he has to do something for the sick person, to make effort for his deliverance, should he then give him over to the doctor? If so, let him call someone to beat the sick person immediately with deathly blows; understand this well.

(And the fact that Rabbeinu himself traveled to Lemberg and got involved with treatments there, there are very secret and hidden things in this, for his intention was not at all in going there for treatments, but rather for other things known to him, and just as all his travels were hidden and lofty wonders, such as the trip to Kaminitz, Navritch, Sharhorod and so forth, which are somewhat mentioned in our words. For, he had very wonderful secrets in this that are hidden from the eye of all living. And just as one time when he came from those aforementioned ways, he told some awesome tale (of the Fly and Spider) that is explained in

Sipurei Ma`asiyoth, and he said that this story explains the matter of his trip — but actually the thing is very closed up and sealed, for who can stand in the secret of the tales he told, or in the secret of his wonderful and hidden trips and conducts? — that is just how his trip to Lemberg was, and after he set out and arrived there he was forced from Heaven to be involved in treatments due to reasons and secrets known to him. But when he returned from there, then specifically he spoke a great deal more about keeping distant from treatments, and he said at that time several Torot from *Sichoth Haran* about this. And also before he traveled to Lemberg he would speak of this matter, but afterwards he would speak very much about it, to keep distant from them to the ultimate extent.)

[#81-103] New Stories

84

What he told shortly before Rosh Hashanah 5569, at the end of summer 5568, at which time the *shochet* of Teplik brought him a wonderful chair: close to this time he told this, that he saw it in a vision or a dream that they brought him a chair, and it was surrounded by fire:

And the whole world, men, women and children, went to see it, and when they returned from there then immediately they became interconnected and matches were made amongst them. And all the leaders of the generation also went to see it. And I asked how far is it, and why matches were immediately made. And I went around them to get there, and I heard that Rosh Hashanah was fast approaching. And I had doubt whether to turn back or to remain there, and I was confused in mind, and I said in my heart, "How shall I remain here for Rosh Hashanah?" but in my mind I said, "Considering the frail body that I have, why should I turn back?" So I was there, and I came to the chair and I saw there Rosh Hashanah — the real Rosh Hashanah. And also Yom Kippur, the actual Yom Kippur. And also Sukkot, the real Sukkot. I also heard that they were shouting, "*Chodsheikhem umo`adeikhem son'ah nafshi/* My soul hates your new moons and your festivals" [Isa. 1:14]. "What [place] do you [plu-

ral] have to judge the world? Rosh Hashanah itself will judge."
And they all fled; they fled with all the leaders of the generation.

And I saw that engraved on the chair were the forms of all the
world's creatures, and each one was engraved with his mate
next to him, and for this reason matches are immediately made,
for each one found and saw his partner there. And because I had
studied it during in the preceding days, the verse came to my
mind, *"Korsyeh Shevivin Di-Nur/* His throne was fiery flames"
[Dan. 7:9] — acrostic for *ShaDKhaN*, matchmaker. For, by means
of the chair, matches were made, as mentioned; and also, *Ko-
RSYeH* is acrostic for *Rosh Hashanah, Yom Kippur, Sukkoth*. And
therefore on Shemini `Atzeret is the "marital union" of the "Su-
pernal Matron" [v. Zohar III 96b-97a].

And I asked "What shall be my livelihood?" And they told me
that I would be a matchmaker.

And the fire surrounded it in a ball, for in truth, Rosh
Hashanah is a big favor, for it is a appointed time when the
moon is hidden, of which is it said, "Bring atonement for Me"
[*Chullin* 60b]. And it is a big favor for the world, because through
this we can request atonement on Rosh Hashanah.

And see all this in the torah *"Tik`u Vachodesh Shofar —
Vayiven Hashem Elohim eth-Hatzela`,"* which speaks of the
roots of the souls that are included in the Throne; see there thoroughly in *LM II* #1, for it is an explanation of this story, for, that
torah was given on the Rosh Hashanah following this story. And
the things and very closed up and hidden; also a little is missing,
for it was not written in full.

And one time he spoke regarding these stories, and he mentioned this matter, the connection of this story with that
torah. How very awesome, wonderful and exalted is this matter
for one who has a heart to discern. Then he said, "If you [plural]
are not happy, I don't know what is with you!" In other words, it
is proper for us to anyway be extremely happy at all times now
that we have been privileged to taste such awesome lights, etc.
And after he told this story, he said that "You [plural] will be able
to say Torah teachings about it all the days of your lives," and he
scolded us for not being happy and he said that we ought to be
very, very happy.

90

On Purim, wonders became known to me. Rabbeinu z"l spoke up and said, "*Oraita shema deKudsha Brikh Hu*/ The Torah is the name of the Holy One, Blessed be He [*TZ* #10 p. 26; *Zohar Yithro* p. 90] — *satum vegalia*/ hidden and revealed [*Zohar III* 73a]:" First, the Torah reveals its face to a man, and then it hides. And whoever is a master of his soul, goes around and pursues it and sacrifices his life for it, and has great yearning and vigorous passion, with self-sacrifice, until he merits that the Torah is revealed to him. For, at first the idea of Purim was revealed to me limitedly and in concealment [that is, the matter was not revealed to him in complete revelation, but only in a mere hint of flashing], and afterwards Hashem Yithbarakh helped me, for Hashem Yithbarakh always helps me, and this matter was revealed to me. And the matter of Purim that was revealed to me then was closed up and hidden from all the worlds; only in the uppermost worlds that are very, very distant, only there do they know this. For, my work on that Purim was to repair the damage of Qorach, and when this was revealed to me, it was very far in my eyes, what connection Purim has with QoRaCh, until Hashem Yithbarakh helped me etc. For, there are very closed up things in the holy Torah; and it was revealed to me that the letters of *PURIM* are acrostic for "*Ve'im Mipe'ath Panav Yimaret Rosho... QeReaCh hu*/ And if his hair be fallen off from the border of his face, he is bald" (Lev. 13:40-1) [and the rest he did not explain]. Later Rabbeinu z"l said he was unable to sleep all that night that he told this, because he was sorry he revealed this. But he said his consolation was that he still did not reveal it at all. Also, in actuality it is not written that way in the Torah, but rather it is written like this: "*Ve'im Mipe'ath Panav Yimaret Rosho, gibeach hu;*" [forehead-bald, v. 41] only before it is written "*Ve'ish ki yimaret rosho, qereach hu*" [v. 40]. So the things are very closed up and hidden. Fortunate is he that waits until the coming of the Redeemer; then they will grasp his holy utterance!

100

I heard, in his name, on the subject of famous miracle workers, that he told a parable of a king who had two sons. One was intelligent and one a fool, and he put the fool in charge over the treasuries, and the clever one had no position at all; he just always sat by the king's side. The public found it quite hard to understand why this one who is not clever has all the responsibility, and everyone comes to him to make a deposit or withdrawal from the treasuries, while the clever one has no position at all. The king replied to them, "And is this a big deal, that he brings out treasures that are already prepared, and distributes them to the world? For, this clever one sits by my side, and devises new thoughts and counsels that I cannot arrive at. And by means of these advices I conquer countries that I would not have known about at all; countries that are the source of all my treasures. But this appointee takes ready treasures and distributes them to the world. So the role of the clever one is definitely much greater and higher than the appointee, even though it may appear he has no position. For, he is the source of all the treasures."

[#104-128] His Place of Birth and Residence, and His Trips and Excursions

123

Before traveling to Berdichev he assembled a minyan of ten men and argued in their presence with the *Ba`al Davar*/ Accuser. And I do not entirely know this matter in detail. But he said that from that time on, whatever he wants to do, the *Ba`al Davar* lets himself span the length and the width [of the universe] to ruin it, and on account of this it is very hard to carry out his instructions, but nonetheless Hashem Yithbarakh is at his help. And whoever has been privileged to draw close to him has seen a little of this. And all his days Rabbeinu z"l had no peace, even one moment. For he was constantly waging Hashem's war every single moment.

ודע שיש בידינו כתיבת יד רבינו ז"ל שכתב בעצמו, וזה לשונו: דעו אחי ורעי, אגלה לכם סוד, ותצניעו את הסוד הזה להיות כמוס ביניכם, כדי ...שלא להרבות מחלקת בישראל "and I am the true Elder on the side of holiness."[64]

Copyist's note: I heard that one time Rabbeinu z"l and that elder were brought together, as the public wanted to make peace between them.[65] The Zeyde asked the Rebbe, "How is it possible that an old man like me, with no teeth, could want strife?" And he took Rabbeinu z"l's finger and put it in his mouth to prove to him that he hadn't any teeth. "I will just ask you about a few things that you have said. Is it true you said there is a city of Zlatipolia in Heaven?" Rabbeinu z"l said, "Isn't this the explicit statement of our Rabbis z"l? — *"Arim gedoloth uvtzuroth bashamayim/* Great and fortified cities in Heaven" [Deut. 1:28] — as there are cities down below, so are there cities above [see *Ta`anit* 5a]. Then he asked Rabbeinu z"l, "Is it true that you said that [when you were] in Zlatipolia you were remedying Yerov`am's error?" He answered, "True," and told him the concept that he explained [in *LM II* #64] which speaks about repairing the fault of `avodah zarah/ foreign mode of service, repairing ***"Eleh eloheikha, Yisrael/* These** are your gods, O Yisrael" [Ex. 32] by fulfilling [self-inflicted wanderings as in] ***"Eleh mas`ei venei Yisrael/* These** are the journeys of the sons of Yisrael" [Num. 33]; and there this is understood implicitly. Then he continued and asked, "Is it true that you said that you have been in Mashiach's palace?" Rabbeinu z"l replied, "And what of it? Were you there and did not find me? But since you are asking me — if you come with me to my house to drink a tea or coffee together with me, and inform the public that you go back on your words and regret the strife, I will explain the thing's inner meaning and concept." The Zeyde answered him, "I'll have to first go home and then come to you." As the Zeyde was leaving from Rabbeinu z"l, Rabbeinu z"l heard him say: And how would I appear in the eyes of my wealthy supporters, if I go to him and make peace with him, etc.?

R abbeinu z"l said, "If he would have first come to my house as I had said to him, I might have had peace with him, but now there will be no peace between me and him and he will carry on with the conflict. But — I am not afraid of him at all, for didn't he show me he has no teeth?" Copyist's note: See the tale of "The Fly and the Spider" [*Sipurei Ma`asiyoth* #7] which relates to this matter, as explained there, that the enemies of the mountain, before they wanted to go up on the mountain their teeth fell out and they were unable to go up.

I have such an enemy! *Ikh hob azoy a soneh vas er kilt zikh andersh nit in mir, saydin er zeyt mayn blut/* His anger and wrath at me is not cooled off except by seeing my blood!" [Rabbi Nathan adds:] But he did not say who this enemy was. This he said on his last Rosh haShanah, when he gave the lesson *"Tik`u — Tokhachah/* Blow the shofar — Rebuke" [*LM II #8*], when he coughed up a great deal of blood, as explained in *Chayei Moharan* and *Yemei Moharnat*.>

When that elder began to oppose him he said, "I knew that the Samekh-Mem <and his agents> would rise up against me etc., but I am surprised that they handed this off to him. And he said, then, a pun: For, our Rabbis z"l have said that it is "better for a man to cast himself down into a den of lions [and snakes] and not be given over to his enemies" [*Y. Reuveni, Vayeshev*] — but what does one do when his enemy himself is an *Aryeh/* lion? <Then he said this is the explanation of, *"Va'ani er'eh ve'son'ai/* And I will gaze upon those that hate me" [Ps. 118:7], for apparently it is surprising: surely Dawidh Hamelekh a"h knew that Shaul hates him, so how could he want to see his downfall: didn't Hashem Yithbarakh tell him (*Mo`ed Katan* 16:2), "If you were Shaul and he were Dawidh [I would have destroyed many Dawidhs for him etc.]?" Rather, Dawidh said thus: Master of the Universe, give me eyes that I may see in my enemies how he is standing presently, on what level he is now standing, and thereby I will know my level with clarity. And then he said a pun:> But *"Raboth machashavoth beLeibish [beLev-ish] ve`atzath Hashem hi takum/* Many are the contrivances in Leibish [a man's heart], but it is Hashem's counsel that shall stand" [a pun on Prov. 19:21]. He said in the future to come there will be a nice little game with him: *"Oyf yener velt vet zayn asheyn shpilkhen mit ihm."* Then Rabbeinu z"l spoke several Torot that touch upon the subject of the controversy of that elder; see there and discern. Blessed is Hashem Who has delivered us from him and let us be in the portion of Rabbeinu hakadosh z"l.

[#151-166]: His Journey to Navritch, Zaslav, Dubna and Brod

151

In the year [5]566, which was the fourth year of his residence here in Breslev, which was the fourth year of my drawing close to him, for when he entered here I drew close to him immediately after, as mentioned above — then in the summer of [5]566 in the month of Sivan his baby son Shelomoh Efrayim z"l passed away. And [statements] regarding the interest of this dear holy child have already been described elsewhere, that Rabbeinu z"l said: that he was already fit <to be *Mashiach*>. And then after the boy died, when we came to him afterwards he began talking with us regarding *tikkun haneshamoth* / the repair of souls; regarding the *Ba`al haSadeh*/ Master of the Field, that there is a field wherein souls grow, and they need the Ba`al haSadeh to repair them, and he who girds his loins to be the Ba`al haSadeh has countless many afflictions upon him, as explained in the torah "*Wayomer Bo`az el Ruth*" (in *Likutei* I:65); see there.

And from that time on, he spoke very much regarding the repair of souls, and especially when he returned from Lemberg when he entered Uman; that his whole going in there and his choosing to pass away there and lie there — it was all on account of this, for the sake of *tikkun haneshamoth* which need repair since several hundreds of years back. For, there in Uman, countless many souls were murdered, including many children, thousands and myriads, who were killed before their time. [His intentions] were evident from things he said in Uman, and some of them are written elsewhere (below, #190, 191, 205, 217).

Then in that same year he began telling the *Sipurei Ma`asiyoth* which have now been printed and he said, "Now I will start telling story tales" (*Ikh vil shoyn anheyben maysiyos dertzeylen*). And then on that Yom Kippur there was a fire, the Merciful One spare us, here in Breslev during the prayer time of Kol Nidrei when the chazzan began the *piyutim* that follow `Arvit, which are *Ya`aleh* etc. And we each scattered to save his house and possessions and the prayer got mixed up; only after the fire was over did we assemble approximately a minyan and also Rabbeinu z"l was with us and we completed the piyutim.

And then on *motza'ei* Yom Kippur Rabbeinu z"l said that on that Yom Kippur he wanted to elicit something from Hashem Yithbarakh, <namely he wanted Hashem Yithbarakh to again tell him the Torah as he told it before Moshe a"h>, and he had several arguments for this which if written would have filled several *bogin* (sheets), and I made a big arrangement of this for him. Alas, by means of the fire the thing was mixed up. And also after he returned from Lemberg he talked about this matter and it was understood from his words that from that time onward when he wanted to elicit this on Yom Kippur, on account of this he has great accusation against him on high and that the illness and afflictions which he had and which he still has are on account of this. And he said, "Even though my intentions were definitely for the sake of Heaven, nonetheless" etc. — and then he told the story of the son of the rav of Shpitivke who had an illness and he knew that it was on account of a mistake where he made a blemish in the honor of father, but yet he does not have regret. And he said that Rabbi Shmuel Yitzchak, who is presently rav of Tcherin, informed him before the fire that it would happen. Also in Medvedevka there was a fire, and then too Rabbi Shmuel Yitzchak informed me beforehand. "Shmuel Yitzchak" is gematria SeReiFaH / burning [585] as written in the Torah, chasser [without a yud].

And then in that same year I was expelled from my place by force, from Nemryov to Mohyliv, and in that same year several of our people got mixed up; Rabbi Avrahamtchi was in Peterburg and many were mixed up. And Rabbeinu z"l himself was wandering and exiled that year on his big trip when he traveled to Navritch, Brod, etc. and tarried on that trip approximately half a year.

And that winter when he was in Tcherin for Shabbath Shirah and then in Krimenchuk as he went every year, then his grandson Rabbi Yisrael z"l was born, son of his daughter the tzadeket Mrs. Sarah, and his birth was before Rabbeinu z"l went on that big trip, and right after he came from Krimenchuk he took that trip. Before his birth he remained several weeks in Kremenchuk and waited until she give birth, and during that whole time before she gave birth he never smiled and he got upset when they gave him two foods at a meal, for he was entirely uneasy until she give birth in peace, may she live long; so he remained in great affliction that whole time until that birth that his daughter gave.

And then after the birth he was immediately filled with joy and ordered to light candles and make the drink called "punch" and he was in great joy, and then on the eighth day he circumcised his grandson boy in the proper fashion and after the *berith milah* he was in joy that day and said that he had satisfaction from hearing from people etc. who mentioned him, that his name, Yisrael ben Sarah, is like the name of the Baal Shem Tov z"l. But then on the third day of the *berith* his daughter who gave birth became weak and he had great affliction and fled in great haste from Krimenchuk. And he said that his vitality was cut off due to the severe pain. And the man who was with him, Rabbi Shmuel of Teplik, tarried a bit, and he left him there without waiting for him and rode off without him, and Rabbi Shmuel was forced to hire a carriage and run after him.

And then when he came from Krimenchuk he went to Navritch and on that whole big trip etc. And that winter I was sick three times in Moyhliv and my wife-partner and children as well, and Rabbeinu z"l had great pain from this, and by God's mercy and the strength of his holy prayer I remained alive, praise God.

And in this whole matter there is a great deal to tell, for there are extremely hidden things in all this, *genizaya deMalka*, which he merited to perceive in all these matters, for the sake of which he was forced to travel around and suffer afflictions so much. And it was all for the sake of *tikkun ha`olamoth* / repair of the worlds, *tikkun haneshamoth vehanefashoth* / repair of souls and lifeforces, of the living, and especially the souls of the dead, in which he was most involved at the end of his days, as he said explicitly there, that what he does for us is a minor thing for him and it is something that we should do, but he must involve himself in repair of the souls of the dead, for there are *neshamoth artila'in* / naked souls etc. as described elsewhere.

And even though we never heard or knew more than a drop in the ocean of all this — and even the slightest bit that he informed us of in compassion, even this is impossible to describe except more than the slightest bit in hints — nevertheless I have not held back from recording what is possible, for it is a great benefit for those who seek in truth and haste to his doors, when they come to know what they know of what he endured and what came out of his holy mouth regarding these matters. And those who are smart enough to look into our words with an honest eye will understand a little of the greatness of the Creator, Blessed Is He, through this, and the greatness of the tzaddikim and how many sufferings and troubles they suffer for the sake of repair of our souls. Maybe we will be awoken by all this to go in his holy ways which he showed us in his holy books and we will truthfully return to Hashem, soon in our days, Amen.

152

In that year of [5]566 when he began to talk with me regarding *tikkun haneshamoth* / repair of souls which he was involved in, which is the matter of the *Ba`al haSadeh*/ Master of the Field etc., as mentioned above, then he said to me, "In Zlatipolia I got to know a bit of this," for then he began to know a little of this matter of the *Ba`al haSadeh*. And what is understood from his words is that is when he *began* to know [i.e. in Zlatipolia], but now he knows the essence. And he said that Rabbi Shimon Bar Yochai hinted a little of this in the holy Zohar, and the inference was that the way he now knows about this matter of the Ba`al haSadeh, <no tzaddik had ever yet> known.

153

In the year [5]567 before Purim he traveled from here, Breslev, and no simple explanation was known to any man regarding that trip. And he traveled then to Navritch and wanted to travel further on but became held back there during the days of Purim in the house of the local rav who was somewhat of an in-law. And from there he resumed traveling to Ostroh and from there he sent people to bring his wife to Dr. Gardin, of there, to get involved in treating her, for she had a critical illness, which is the illness of *hust*/ tuberculosis, and he z"l remained there alone except that they hired one man there to attend to him. And his wife arrived there for *Shabbath haGadol* and did not want to get treatment from Dr. Gardin; she only wanted to go to Zaslav to the doctors there, and he traveled with her on Sunday which was four days before Pesach, and also Rabbi Shmuel of Teplik was with him there, and they all went and arrived in Zaslav close to Pesach. And *Erev Shavu`oth* his wife passed away there, and we gathered together to him and came to him for Shavu`oth, to Zaslav. And Hashem Yithbarakh had compassion on us and we were privileged then too to hear wonderful Torah from his mouth, and it is already printed in the book, [*LM* I] #67.

154

I heard in his name that he said that when he traveled to Navritch and the rest of the communities and then he spoke about his travel, no man knew about it. Explanation and clue: for he traveled under cover from the world and did not accept any money along the way, and he said at that time, "And I — my hands are dirtied with blood, placenta and umbilical cord in order to purify a woman [i.e. Yisrael] to her husband" [i.e. Hashem Yithbarakh; see *Berakhot* 4a], and this was a faint hint that this was the concern of his travel.

155

B efore this aforementioned trip he said, "I am like a little boy who does not want to go to school but when he enters the schoolroom is able to learn. If the world would know why I am traveling they would kiss my footsteps at each and every step of mine. I tilt the whole world [to be] judged to the side of merit."

156

H e said, "My place is only the Land of Israel. The fact that I travel, I travel only to *Eretz Yisrael*; and temporarily I guide people in Breslev and so forth."

157

B efore he made the aforementioned trip he clapped palm on palm in joy and said, "Today I begin a new thing," and then he said, "We are like someone playing music and everybody dancing, and whoever does not discern and hear the melody, it is a wonder in his eyes what they're running after and why they're dancing like that; it's a wonder to the world why you are running after me. When I return from my way I will be able to play and you will be able to dance. And then he traveled to Navritch and he was in Zaslav, Ostroh, Dubna, Brod and other additional places, and he was looked for and they did not know his whereabouts. And he was in the house of the big opposers in Brod and he had involvement with each and every one of them. When he entered Brod the whole city came out to him. (Explanation: for they did not at all intend to honor him, for they did not know about him at all, but rather, anyhow it was ordained that way from Hashem Yithbarakh.) And I heard a voice of shouting of their cravings, craving and shouting, "Money!" etc., which was a big shout from their cravings. At that same time, on *Erev Shavu`oth,* his wife passed away and we gathered to him for the festival of *Shavu`oth* and he taught us Torah, as mentioned.

158

On that festival of *Shavu`oth* he studied much during the morning meal, and between dishes before they placed the food on the table he would study in the meantime (and he learned then the *Idra*). And then they placed the food and he paused and ate a little and then went back and delved in his study; and thus it was each time between each and every food. And he thought that each time they would not bring another food, but they placed several more dishes, and he would study between each and every food, as mentioned.

After the meal he spoke up and said, "They [were] arguing with me, for I was of the mind that each time they would not give another dish again, but they gave more foods each time. And they [were] arguing with me, because I would have wanted that meal end with study, and they wanted greater — that the meal end with eating. For, there are simple people who eat in order to have strength to study, and there are people higher above and they study in order to have knowledge how to eat. And I wanted it to be in its simple manner, that the end of the meal would be in study after eating, which is the aspect of simple service, where one eats and then studies, that is, eating in order to have strength to learn. But they hold me to be on the greater [level] so they each time place more food, wanting the end to be with eating which is the aspect of the higher service, where one studies and then eats, that is, studying in order to have knowledge and a brain and intellect how to eat. Understand.

159

While he was in Zaslav he had severe pain and illness, and he wrote a letter to all his followers, very much requesting that we pray for him, and then he returned to his strength. And then he wrote another letter to all his people, that his efforts that he made with each and every one of us to extract him from the teeth of the *Samekh Mem* ought not be in vain, as explained. A copy of the letter appears elsewhere [*CM* #166]. And when he came home he said that we had accomplished by our prayers that he returned to his strength in Zaslav from that sickness.

160

After the passing of his wife in Zaslav, later he was matched in Brod, and when he came home to Breslev he told on Shabbath the tale [in *Sipurei Ma`asiyoth* Tale 7] of the king whom the book's page saved, etc. And he said before telling that story, "I will tell you my trip," and regarding this he told that story. And there in that story the conclusion about a beautiful woman who bore children is missing.

161

As he returned from his big trip to Navritch that summer, tuberculosis befell him. Then Rabbeinu z"l urged us direly to pray for him very much. But due to our many sins, *"gavru ha'erelim/ the angels prevailed"* [*Ketubot* 104a] and he passed away three years after contracting that case of tuberculosis. And he said that he lived these three years by miracle as well, etc., and regarding this there are numerous stories to tell, aside from countless things hidden from us.

162

He said that as soon as tuberculosis befell him, as soon as he coughed the first time, he immediately knew that he would die. And he immediately started talking about the matter of his passing away, even though Hashem Yithbarakh in his great charity did His exceptional miracles for us, that he lived afterwards for three years and a bit more. Nonetheless, in the summer of 5567 when the tuberculosis struck him while returning from his big trip that he took to Navritch, Zaslav, etc. as mentioned, etc., as soon as arriving at his home from that trip he started talking about his passing.

And he said, then, that he has great fears and he said that it was necessary for sixty *gibborim,* mighty men, to be with him, as were with the Ba`al Shem Tov of blessed memory. And he spoke a great deal regarding this [but I myself was not privileged to hear these matters from his holy mouth, for I was not with him, and much of this has been forgotten]. And one time he was crying on Shabbath and Rabbi Naftali was with him them, and at that time he told the story of the king who had great wars up against him, in the tale of "The Fly and the Spider." And then he made his usual annual trip in the Ukraine — he always traveled to Tcherin for Shabbath Nachamu — and on the way, in the community of Ladyzhyn he spoke with our people, his followers that are there, that he is forced to pass away, and he also spoke with them regarding the sixty gibborim whom he needs, and how the Ba`al Shem Tov of blessed memory had sixty gibborim: "And they will definitely grow up and there will be of my people sixty gibborim, but they are still youths and tender in years and the war is exceedingly heavy and harsh on them, 'and I have no one to lean on' [cf. *Sotah* 49b]," etc. And he spoke more of this numerous times, and a little of it I heard: that even if he had sixty gibborim it would not avail him to be healed from his illness.

And he said that he would have wanted to go to the land of Israel, that is, travel once more to the land of Israel and pass away there; however, he fears lest he will not be able to reach there. Also, if he should pass away there, followers would not come to his grave and they would have no involvement or activity with his grave site. But when he will lie in our country, we will definitely come to his grave to learn and pray there, and he will have great delight and pleasure from this.

And from that time on, he spoke a great deal regarding his passing and spoke a great deal regarding his grave. And he expressed his will numerous times, in numerous wordings, that they should constantly come to his grave, saying Tehillim at his grave, learning there, and performing a great deal of prayer and supplication there. And he spoke with numerous followers regarding this. Also when he came from Lemberg he said that it would be well for him to pass away there and lie there, since numerous, numerous great tzaddikim lie there; however, for the following reason he was not comfortable with passing away there: because there, not one of his followers would come to his grave.

And he said that when one will come to his grave and say a chapter of Tehillim with arousal of the heart, he will have great pleasure from this, and he made movements with his body and his bones then, and hinted that he would have *chilutz* `atzamoth/` renewed energy in his grave when they will say Tehillim at his graveside. And he talked more about this numerous times. And later he revealed the ten chapters of Tehillim [i.e. *Tikkun haKlali*], and he said that whoever comes to his grave, gives a token to charity and says these ten chapters of Tehillim, he will let himself span the width and the breadth [of the universe] to help this man, even if what has happened to him has happened, etc., and he designated two witnesses for this, as explained elsewhere [#225].

[#185-229] His Journey to and His Residence in Uman

188

As I was traveling with him to Uman at the end of his days, he spoke with me aboard the carriage, consoling words, many extremely beautiful and holy words, invigorating the soul a great deal. And I discerned from his holy words: the abundant compassion of Hashem Yithbarakh, and at the end of it all Hashem Yithbarakh will reveal the truth and make the end good for us, etc. Then I spoke up and said in his presence, with excitement of heart, "Nevertheless Hashem Yithbarakh will finish according to His will!" He replied to me, with an expression of surprise, "What is this that you say Hashem Yithbarakh *will* finish? Isn't Hashem Yithbarakh constantly finishing?!"

189

On the road, during his trip to Uman, he spoke up and said, "Despite this, Hashem Yithbarakh helps Yisrael always, and there is no orphaned generation." And similarly did Rabbi Shimon Bar Yochai say, when a certain Tanna said, "The Torah will end up forgotten by Yisrael," and Rabbi Shimon said "No! But via this Zohar they will go out from exile. '*kI loA tishakhaCh mipiY zar`O/* For it shall not be forgotten out of the mouths of their offspring' (Deut. 31:21; the end-letters spell YOChAI)." And therefore he stood himself on this verse and revealed the secret printed in Likutei [Moharan] in the beginning there, regarding the greatness of Rabbi Shimon Bar Yochai. I answered and said to him, Rabbi Shimon certainly also has enjoyment from this, that is, from this wonderful revelation. He replied, "Yes." Afterwards he spoke up and said, "Rabbi Shimon in his uniqueness is a different matter, because Rabbi שמעון/ **ShiM'ON** is [alluded to in the acrostic of] "עיר וקדיש מן שמיא נחית" `*Ir Vekadish Min-Shamaya Nachith*/ A watcher and a holy one came down from heaven" [Daniel 4:10], as printed there, but now there is [myself, נחמן/**NaChMaN** alluded to in] "נחל נבע, מקור חכמה" / *Nachal Nove`a Mekor Chokhmah*/ The gushing stream, the wellspring of wisdom [Prov. 18:4]!" <And even the `*Ir Vekadish Min-Shamaya Nachit* must receive from there. Understand well.> And it has already been heard that he said of himself, "I am a river that cleanses from all stains" [below, #322].

218

In Uman before the last Rosh Hashanah he talked to his followers about his passing away, that he considered it to be already three years since he has passed away, for since the illness befell him he regarded himself in his own eyes as already passed away from the world. And he said he does not know by what merit he miraculously remains alive all these years, etc. Then his followers told him things and groaned a great deal: What shall we do? Who are you leaving us to? And he replied: You just hold yourselves together; then you will be kosher people, and not just kosher but even tzaddikim and good [Jews] you will be. For Hashem Yithbarakh will definitely help me that it will be as I wish, as I have long desired, for by Hashem's help I definitely have finished and will finish according to my desire. And he said that whoever makes contact with and connects with one of his followers will definitely be a kosher man in truth, and not just a kosher man but even a total tzaddik, as I would want. See below [#291-339] regarding his followers' stature.

225

Our Rebbe of blessed memory already assured us during his lifetime, and designated two kosher witnesses on this, that when he passes away, when [people] come to his grave and give a token to charity* and say these ten *Tehilim*/psalms that we have recorded for remedy of nocturnal emission, Heaven spare us, then our Rebbe himself will span the length and width [of the universe], and will surely save this person. And he said that he will pull him out of Gehinom/hell by his peyot/sidelocks, even regardless of how that person be, and even regardless of what happened, only from now on he must accept on himself to not return to his wicked ways, Heaven forbid. And the night before he passed away he said: "What do you have to worry about, since I go before you; and if the souls who did not know me at all, look forward to my *tikunim*/remedies, all the more so [should] you" etc. (And likewise even those who were not privileged to know our Rabbi of blessed memory during his lifetime, when they come to his holy grave and rely on him and learn his holy books and accustom themselves to walk in his holy ways that are mentioned in his holy books, surely they have on what to rely. Fortunate are they! Fortunate is their portion! "And none of them that take refuge in Him shall be desolate" [Ps. 34:23], for he already revealed his mind in several terms, explicitly and by hint, that all that he is involved in with us is not for us only, but "with those who are here... and with those who are not here" [Deut. 29:14], as explained further below (see Sichot Haran 209).)

* Copyist's note: I heard from Rabbi Naftali z"l, who was one of the two witnesses whom Rabbeinu z"l designated for this matter, namely Moreinu haRav Aharon z"l and haRav Rabbi Naftali as mentioned, that Rabbeinu z"l said it then in these words: "When they come to my grave and give a token to charity for my sake (he means, for remembrance of his holy soul, as commonly practiced), ..." and in Yiddish: *"un vet gebin a pruta tzedaka fon maynit veygin*/and will give a token of charity for me" etc.

229

One time I asked him, "What about the things you said?" Namely, how we had previously heard from his holy mouth several statements that it appeared that he would live a long life and finish as he wished, etc. He spoke up and said, "Did you hear what he's asking? I too have this question." But nevertheless he said, "I haven't finished?! I've already finished, and I *will* finish!" as above [#218].

Also when he was traveling to Uman and I traveled with him he spoke with me regarding that Hashem Yithbarakh is constantly finishing, as mentioned above [#188]. And to explain all these matters would take much telling, for which many sheets would not suffice. The generality is that initially it arose in his thought when we became his followers that he would finish the repair immediately, and he made several statements indicating this; but afterwards, due to our many sins and the sins of the generation, and because of the vast determination of the Satan, to the extent that he made the opposition to him very great, by means of all this the world became out of order and he was not able to finish in his lifetime what he wanted. But nevertheless he said that he finished and will finish, as mentioned. For, after he returned from Lemberg, he attained such a way, and spoke such words, that his lamp will never, ever, go out, like we heard it stated in his name, in these words: *"Mayn fayeril vet shoyn tluen biz Mashiakh vet kumen/* My fire will flicker all the way until Messiah comes!"* Soon in our days, Amen!

[#241-290] The Enormous Awesomeness of His Attainments

243

Regarding worldly conversation, even jesting, which the great tzaddikim are able to lift up and perform a great devotion from their telling of secular affairs, and as somewhat inferred from the methods and practices which are told of the Ba`al Shem Tov z"l and other awesome tzaddikim from recent eras, and also in the holy Zohar a little is hinted about this, as is related there about Rav Hamnuna Saba "who was arranging three sections of silly material." But the eminence of the greatness of his wisdom and the enormity of Rabbeinu z"l's holiness and attainment in this matter of worldly talk etc. was most exceedingly high. And a little bit of this was discerned and hinted at for whoever was privileged to stand before him and speak with him, for all the kinds of stories that exist in the world etc. which people tell, were all brought to him, and also all the affairs that are printed in the world were all present with him. And he always wanted people to tell him news from world affairs, for he was able to elevate and to perform extremely awesome and hidden devotions with all the stories of the world. And whoever was privileged to stand in his presence regularly, even though there was no one who understood the concepts of his practices even one drop in the sea — nevertheless it was possible to discern some scant hint how far the secret of his conversation in worldly affairs reached. For, many times we were privileged to hear wonderful Torah in the line of the conversation and the affairs that we told in his presence beforehand. And it is impossible to explain all this in writing, regarding conversation and stories with him in secular matters. And whoever was privileged to stand in his presence saw wonderful and awesome novelties in this, and many, many messages that were revealed though this, aside from hidden things, for he did not reveal so much as even a drop in the sea, for it was extremely closed up and hidden, in ultimate concealment. And still his great light is extremely closed up and hidden from the world, until Mashiach Tzidkeinu comes — soon in our days; then they will know his greatness and splendor.

And more and more, before his passing way, from the time he returned from Lemberg until he passed away, which was a span of two years and more, during which he had his severe illness, then they told in his presence more and more of the worldly affairs. And always he requested that they tell news in his presence, and he said that he does not know how it is possible to live without news. And his way was, in general, that most of the day he was closed off and shut away, and afterwards he would talk with people, whether it was someone who needed to talk with him for some advice in some business, and especially advices in the fear of Heaven, which was the bulk of his involvement with his followers, or whether it was other conversations and stories, whatever came to our mouths. And almost always he would come from that conversation to wonderful talks of Torah, prayer and fear of Heaven. And it was always the way with him that even when he would talk about worldly matters with people, his leg and most of his body would shake vigorously. And his leg would actually be quaking a great deal, and if he was against a table, the table and all the rest of the people against the table would also shake on account of him, for his leg and body were always shaking and trembling a great deal. And whoever was not privileged to see the awe that was constantly upon his face, has never ever seen awe. And all the kinds of worldly charm were upon him, and he was full of the most wonderful fear and love in the world.

And he was full of wonderful and awesome fear, love and sanctity in each and every limb, and was devoid of all bad traits and cravings in such ultimate simplicity and ultimate nullity that are impossible for the human brain to conceive of at all, that there has never been anyone like him in the world. He was such an extremely wonderful and awesome novelty that the mouth cannot speak and the heart cannot think it.

< One time I heard from his holy mouth that whatever speech presents itself before him becomes something else entirely — even [words of slander]: once they were said in his presence, they became entirely different matters. And I asked him about this, "Haven't our Sages said: A covenant was cut regarding [striking with *tzara`at* whoever speaks] slander? [*Tanchuma Vayikra* 14:1], from which even Dawidh Hamelekh did not come away unscathed [v. *Shabbath* 56]?" He replied, "So what? Must we all now succumb in this matter?" I understood him to mean that nevertheless there was someone who could stand up to this because when he heard slander, he could turn it into something else. Nevertheless he said it would be better for us not to speak [words of slander] even in front of him. However, when it did happen that someone told it in front of him, it became an entirely different matter.>

245

I heard this from his holy mouth during Chanukkah *5563*/1802: He spoke up and said, "I am an extremely fine and wondrous tree with extremely wondrous branches, while underneath, I am laid in the ground *mamash*/ really/ tangibly."

249

In Kremenchug he said, "*Men vet amal zogn, Ay, iz das geven a Reb Nachman*/ In the future they will say, 'Ay, was that a Reb Nachman!' For they will yearn for me a great deal." He also said that in the future it will be a big wonder that he had opposition, and they will say, incredulously, "This is who they were opposed to?!" He also said that when someone will have opposition they will say, Didn't they also oppose him? — so as to say that therefore the opposition proves nothing.

260

He said a parable, that one time a big merchant traveled with fine Hungarian wine. One time the attendant and carriage driver said to the master, "Aren't we traveling on this way with this wine — and we're suffering so much. Give us to taste a little." And he gave them to taste from this good wine. After some days it came about that this attendant was together with wine drinkers in a small town, and they were drinking wine and praised it a great deal and said that it is Hungarian wine. The attendant said, "Give me to taste," and they gave him. And he said, "I know that this is not fine Hungarian wine at all, and they berated him and expelled him. But he said, "But don't I know that this is not Hungarian wine at all? For, after all, I was with a big merchant who" etc.; but they paid him no mind. And he said, "But in the future when Mashiach comes, then they will know when they give them the *Yayin Hameshumar*/ Wine Stored Up [for the Righteous]. Others they will be able to deceive and they will give them Wallachian, Zdravetsian [סטראוויצטיר] wines and tell them that its good *Yayin Hameshumar*, but my followers they will not be able to fool, for we have already tasted the good wine" etc.

261

On the night before the *berith milah* of his son Shelomoh Efrayim z"l, he sat with us a long time and spoke with us a great deal regarding his greatness and the true eminence of his stature, and we heard several things then. And he said, then, that it is hard to enter into the heart of the matter of his greatness and impossible to talk about it because others also speak with such expressions; and whatever the mouth is able to speak, the other says the same thing. However, each person, in accord with what he reckons in his heart, can discern a little, where the real points of truth are. Discern this.

262

Many times he repeated about himself that which people say about him, that "there is no middle way here:" either he is, God forbid, as his opposers fabricate about him etc., "*hadoveroth `al-tzaddik `atak*/ who speak arrogantly against the righteous" [Ps. 31:19], the Merciful One spare us, etc. — or in fact it is the opposite, that he is a True Tzaddik, in which case he is a wonderful, awesome and exalted marvel that cannot be fathomed by the human brain at all. For, so did most of the public routinely say about him z"l, and he z"l repeated about himself these words many times, and hinted to us that the truth is so, that "there is no middle here." So as a person is given choice he must choose for himself the truth, for "ha'emeth hu echad/ the truth is one" [v. *LM* #51]. And from this very discussion one can discern a little of his greatness, for through the enormity of the opposition and controversy one can discern the truth by its real opposite and be stymied at the enormity of his immense greatness, for "there is no middle here," as stated. So, discern well the real truth.

266

He [Rabbi Nachman] said "All the benefits that Mashiach can do for Yisrael, I can do; the only difference is when Mashiach decrees, he will say and it will happen, but I —" and he stopped and did not say more. An alternate version has: "...but I cannot finish yet." And another version is like this: "...with me there is *bechirah*/ free will, but with Mashiach there will no longer be any free will."

267

I heard in his name that he said that he had ascertained the [Divine] *Yechidah* at the utmost top level. For as is known, the *Nefesh*/ vitality of the *Neshamah*/ soul is higher than the *Yechidah* of *Ruach*/ spirit, and so forth with the rest. And he ascertained the *Yechidah* at the utmost highest level. And he said, "Thus, I know 'a little,' and I stand on a high level; nevertheless I still want more. For, who knows? Maybe there is more, [as there are] heights above heights up to the Ein Sof.

He said, "I will sing a song, in the future, that will be the `Olam Haba/ Coming World of all the tzaddikim and chassidim. Copyist's note: See *LM* #64 "*Bo El-Par`oh*" and *LM II* #8 "*Tik`u – Tokhachah.*"

One time he lifted his hands up to his shoulders, then brought them down from his shoulders and said, "All the tzaddikim are from here to here on me," that is, from his shoulders down. Then he raised his hands above his head and brought them down alongside his head, down to his shoulders and said, "and I am from here to here," that is, from the head to the shoulders. *"Vehadevarim `Atiqim*/ These {words, records} are ancient" [I Chron. 4:22]. [That is, "These are towering words." Or, in following with the meaning of the verse there {namely, Yokim etc. are much earlier than the men mentioned in the preceding verses; in other words, this verse is out of chronological order}: He, Rabbi Nachman, is more "ancient" i.e. higher than all other tzaddikim even though he has come after them chronologically.] And look in the writings of the Arizal — if you have keen eyes to understand from there — regarding the greatness of the man who merits to perform the will of his Creator to the extent that he completes the "image of God" in entirety.>

268

He said, "I could receive endless amounts of money and there would be no change in me: For, the usual way with a man is that when money comes to his hand, especially a great deal of money, his face changes and other things change in him; but with me, even if I will receive an enormous amount at once, there is no change in me at all." And I heard in his name that he said that his way of receiving money is a novelty among the novelties that Hashem Yithbarakh has. For Hashem Yithbarakh has many novelties, and his way of receiving money is a novelty by Hashem Yithbarakh [even] among His novelties.

269

The fourth of Elul 5569, Breslev. He said, "I am more humble than all the well-known figures, for each one has his way of service, and I — am humble, for they are considered by me as nothing. For, the attribute of humility is to not consider oneself anything, but to be nothing and non-existent in his eyes. And since they are not considered anything by me, hence I am their humble one." Meaning: From all the well-known figures, I am the humble one, for this one does this and that one does that, and I do not hold of them at all; hence in the combination of all of them, I have the trait of humility among them. "However, whom do I maintain as being more nothing: myself or them?" etc. And nevertheless it appears that it is himself whom he maintains as being more nothing and zero. And similarly, regarding Moshe Rabbeinu a"h, what is written about him does not sit right with me, that he was "'*anav me'od mikol-ha'adam*/ very humble above all man" [Num. 12:2]: How can this apply, since they all were his pupils? How could he be humble versus them? Rather, one must say the same as above, that he was "very humble, above any man" insofar as he had everyone's attribute of humility, namely, the humility of every man was with him, for all of them were, in his estimation, the category of humble, in the aspect of null and non-existent, as mentioned; but he held himself to be more null and non-existent, more than the category of nullity and non-existence that he maintained of them. Discern this well.

Copyist's note: It appears, to my humble knowledge, that his desire was to say: [Moshe Rabbeinu a"h was "very humble, above all man"] because he so much ascertained the greatness of the Blessed Creator — so much that the service of every man was considered to be in the category of nullity and non-existence versus His Blessed greatness. And he himself, even though he was the maestro of all Yisrael, for he ascertained more than them all, nevertheless he maintained himself as more null and non-existent than them all. For, specifically by his perception being so high, thereby he perceived that in relation to his level and understanding, his service is considered the most nothing, versus His Blessed Creator. And this is easy to understand.

272

One time [a statement] came out of his holy mouth regarding himself and he said, in these words, "I am the Elder of Elders (*Saba deSavin*)." And if you look into it and infer from the awesome tale of the Seven Beggars — in the story of the first beggar, who was blind, to whom the Great Eagle said that he is very old but yet he is a suckling babe and has not begun living at all, etc., but yet he was old compared to all the all the elders mentioned there — you will understand a little of this matter. And similarly with the rest of the interests of that story you can discern a little of the greatness of Rabbeinu z"l; the wise will get the hints.

281

In *5569/1808-9* on *Motza'ei Shabbath* he spoke up and said, "Even if a great soul were to come to us, we would still be seen as important figures. And in truth, they are not making opposition against me; rather, they make up some person they imagine," as explained elsewhere [*Sichoth Haran* #182] etc. etc. while he sits in his house.

And this has already happened before, where they were opposing someone and he built a high tower and sat inside it. And they waged war on him and were sending and shooting arrows and fire at him, but they could not do a thing to him. However, there are precious stones which are formed from gasses and vapors, and there was a precious stone which was growing in the air, but it did not yet have its complete perfection. And by means of their firing arrows at him, as mentioned, they thereby cast down the precious stone and it fell on the tower. And this precious stone was of *chen/* grace-charm-favor, and as soon as it fell on the tower they immediately fell down before him and said, "*Yechi hamelekh, yechi hamalekh/* Long live the king, live the king!"

But small souls, such as you, which fall down by means of the war, they are in the aspect of, "*Tishpachena avnei kodesh/* The holy stones are poured out" (Lam. 4:1), and it is called "pouring" because they do not yet have all their completeness and they fall down before they are complete. But the great soul, the precious stone [prob. a ref. to R' Nathan] — its aspect of *chen* was perfect. Albeit, other perfections it still did not have, but by means of the *chakham/* sage [pr. a ref. to R' Nachman] it achieves perfection.

282

After Pesach *5565/1805* he told this to us: he said that now he knows two things, but he is not able to verbalize them, for they appear to be *peshutim/* the simple meanings, for the simple meaning of the thing appears identical; however, now he knows these things.

Namely, he knew what our Rabbis z"l said: "*Adam `over `averah omer shelo' yir'eni adam/* A man who commits [lit. passes] a transgression says 'No man will see me [alternately: Let

Adam (the image of God) not see me].'" And said nothing, but just emphasized the words, *"Shelo' yir'eni Adam,"* and did not explain at all what became known to him, for he had already prefaced that he cannot explain the things, for the simple meaning of the thing appears the same. But nonetheless, now the *sod/* deepest meaning has become known to him.

And the second: the statement, *"Takhlith hayedi`ah asher lo'-neda`/* The ultimate end of knowing is that a person does not know [Hashem]" [*Bechinath `Olam* 33:13] became known to him — *asher lo'-neda` mamash/* actual "Not Knowing" (here too he explained nothing at all, but also just pressed on the words, *"Asher lo'-neda`"* — *lo'-neda` mamash*); and even though its simple meaning is thus, nonetheless only now has this thing become known to me, that the ultimate knowing is *"asher lo'-neda`"* — *lo'-neda` mamash.* And he said that since he now knows *"Takhlith hayedi`ah asher lo'-neda`"* — *asher lo'-neda` mamash,* therefore he knows that since he has merited the end of knowledge, still, nonetheless he knows nothing at all: For, did it not seem to me, previously, that I was at this ultimate knowing, *"asher lo'-neda`,"* and now I see how far I was from this end? (And he said it, then, in disparaging terms about himself, for he held this end from the earlier time to be foolishness, that it seemed to him then that he had attained *takhlith hayedi`ah asher lo'-neda`.*) For, now it has become known to me that *"Takhlith hayedi`ah asher lo'-neda`"* — *asher lo'-neda` mamash!* And this thing as well he cannot express or explain, for it appears like its simple meaning; but in truth, it is only presently that this has become known to him, and so too with the first thing.

283

After a long time, in the summer of *5570/1810,* while traveling to Uman, he once again spoke about the aforementioned matter, and said that [he] knows nothing at all, that is, [he] knows absolutely nothing. And he extolled the greatness of the Blessed Creator, which is impossible to explain, and said that [he] does not know, as mentioned. And I asked him, "Haven't you already said all this and talked about this — regarding *"Takhlith hayedi`ah asher lo'-neda`"* — and already explained all this, that even though one merits this knowledge, *"asher lo'-neda`,"* nonetheless one still knows nothing at all, for it had already appeared to you that you had attained this ultimate end etc. as mentioned?

He spoke up in reply, "Who knows regarding what 'knowing' this 'end' was?!" That is, because also at the time when he told this, after Pesach, he also had not merited the aspect of actual "*lo'-neda`*" except in some knowing. That is, in that knowing, he merited the ultimate of "*asher lo'-neda`.*" And what he meant was that there are knowings above knowings, and *hasagah/* perception-attainment above hasagah, higher and higher. And at each knowing and hasagah, all the way up, the ultimate end is, "*Asher lo'-neda`.*" And he said, then, that even from the time when he left Breslev until now [which was on the same day; it had been no more than a span of a few hours, for at that time we had traveled no more than approximately three parsahs], again he does not know. That is, within these hours as well, he had merited the aspect of not knowing. Now discern these matters, for they are extremely deep, high and lofty things. Fortunate is a man born of woman who has merited such attainments, the utmost truth. And see above regarding this, that in this regard, in the aspect of "I do not know," he was a novelty, quite apart, as we heard from his holy mouth. And even though there is no one who will understand this matter, for it rises higher and higher, nonetheless I have not held back from writing it, for if a person merits it, he will discern and see inside a little, each according to what he estimates in his heart, and will be able to discern thereby a tiny bit of the greatness of the Creator, Yithbarakh Shemo.

289

I heard it from his holy mouth, saying, "*Ani kankan chadash maleh yashan/* I am a new container full of old [wine]" [*Avot* 4:7]. Also, there was found among his holy manuscripts, "*Ani zaken shebikdushah... shemegaleh devarim shekisah `Atik Yomin.../* I am the Elder on the side of holiness... [see Isa. 9:14] who reveals things that the Ancient of Days concealed."

[#291-339] The Stature of His Followers

294

I heard in his name that he said if he wanted to reveal and show his awe [of Heaven], people would not be able to stand within four amot of his house, however, he hides his awe purposely. And I too heard from his holy mouth, that he said, "I am a treasury of the fear of Heaven, from whom anyone who wants can receive." And truthfully, it could be seen, tangibly, that whoever became his follower was immediately filled up with great, enormous awe and developed such enthusiasm in serving Hashem Yithbarakh that one does not see. And now, too, his great awe is embedded in his holy books and whoever wants to delve in them in truth and wholesome simplicity, receives great awe and becomes very aroused for Hashem Yithbarakh, for all his words are as fiery coals.

295

I heard in his name that he said, "If we would see a treasure we would certainly run to it and dig and dirty ourselves in soil and mud to strive for it and find it. And am I not a treasury of the fear of Heaven? So why should people not be eager and running after me to receive it? And I asked him, "How is it possible to receive." He replied, *Mitn pisk un mitn hertz/* With the mouth and with the heart one must strive and request; [It is very close to you,] 'in your mouth and in your heart, so that you may do it [Deut. 30:14].'"

322

He said to one of his followers to whom he was talking about serving Hashem, "Aren't my eyes run out all day as I stand, look out, hope, long and wait the entire time, that Hashem Yithbarakh should let me be privileged to see in you [plural] what I desire, that you should be servants of Hashem in truth as I wish? And I hope with Hashem's help that it will definitely be so. And not only those who follow me, but even those who will follow my followers, and even someone who just touches them will definitely be a kosher man in truth, and not just a kosher man, but even a very great tzaddik" — whoever will be privileged to follow his followers. And I heard that he said it in these words, *"Ikh hab mikh shoyn mayne oygen oys gikukt oyf eytlikhen bazunder/* With my own eyes I have already spied out each one separately... and I hope to Hashem" etc. as above. Also on that occasion he said, "I have already finished and will finish — *Ikh hab oys gifirt un vel oysfiren."*

332

He said, "I am a river that cleanses from all stains." <And he extolled himself further, saying, *"Mi sheyiga` bi afilu be'etzba`, hu kevar ya`avor afilu shiva` meymoth beli lehiratev/* Whoever makes so much as the touch of a finger on me [i.e. whoever makes some contact with him or his teachings, his followers etc.], will already pass through even seven waters without getting wet [i.e. without harm]." Alternately, "Whoever so much as harms my finger will already pass by even seven waters without getting wet [i.e. without being cleansed]."\>

[#392-402] Regarding His Opposition

393

He said, "Even if the Baal Shem Tov were on earth he could not compare with me."

400

Rabbeinu z"l's holy discussion regarding the way of the world in present times: It has always been this way, many times, that the world had it this way, that those of low grade were extremely great and esteemed in the world, so the world did not work in a truthful way. But nevertheless there was one person tucked away in a lowly place, and who laughed at the whole world, and who sustained the entire world with his merit, and who had great yearnings for His Blessedness, and who lived absolute Life that is truly called "Life." ...

[#403-406] The Great Preciousness of His Rosh Hashanah

403

He said, "My Rosh Hashanah is above everything. And what has been a wonder to me is that if my followers believe me then why are not all my followers heedful that they should all be [present] on Rosh Hashanah; no man should be missing! For, my whole thing is Rosh Hashanah." And he ordered to make an announcement that whoever turns to his sound and follows him should be at Rosh Hashanah by him, no man missing. And whoever is privileged to be at Rosh Hashanah is entitled to be very, very happy; "*Ikhlu [ma`adanim] ushthu mamthakim... ki chedvath Hashem hi ma`uzekhem/* Eat [delicacies] and drink the sweet... for the joy of Hashem is your strength" [Neh. 8:10] — this refers to Rosh Hashanah.

[#407-425] To Distance Oneself from *Chaqiroth*/Philosophical Probings and Strengthen Oneself in *Emunah*/Religious Steadfastness

422

He spoke up and said, "This, you are not aware of: that in Germany, the books of the holy Zohar are not available. Even though books of the holy Zohar have been printed there, nevertheless they are not found there, but rather, are sold to our lands. And since there are no books of the holy Zohar there, therefore they go about dressed in *Daytch* [*Deutsch*, i.e. German] clothes. For, clothes are the aspect of *makifim*, and therefore one needs to be very particular to maintain his clothes in cleanliness and honor them properly. (And he stopped in the middle and did not at all reveal what relevance German clothes [which are characterized by the jacket, "*yekke*," cf. Ger. *Jacke*, which clothes only the torso, as opposed to longer outerwear worn by Jews in the east] have to the fact that books of the holy Zohar are not found there.)

[#444-615] His Devotion to Hashem

536

One time his followers were standing in his presence when this uncut man from the idolaters' troops that are stationed in our midst came, knocked on the window and asked: Is there a soldier here? They answered him: No, none of them are here. And he went his way. Later, after some time, he came back and knocked on the window some more and asked if there is a soldier here. Rabbeinu z"l spoke up and said, "That is how your *Yetzer Hara`* is: at first it comes and knocks on the man, and when he turns his back to him and replies, There are none of his soldiers here, and makes him go away and then he goes away, nevertheless afterwards he comes again and knocks on the man, even though he already made him go away and answered him, None of his soldiers are here, as he and his soldiers have no place here. Nevertheless he does not hold back from coming again and again, and one needs to drive him out each time, until he is driven out completely." And see elsewhere regarding this, that one must be very persistent against him, time after time, even a hundred times and more, and then if he will be strong against him, many, many times, he will merit to drive him away completely. "*Umechala'im ra`im verabim vene'emanim/* And from many evil and faithful illnesses [You have saved us]" ought to be said with much concentration, because God forbid if He did not save us...

568

The main source of hope is by means of the concept of "above time," which the Tzaddikim, who are in the aspect of Mashiach, attain. This I understood from Rabbeinu z"l's holy mouth saying, close to his passing away, that now he is going with the lesson that he revealed on the verse, "*Ani hayom yelidh'tikha*" [*LM II* #61], which concerns the aspect of above time etc. And it is impossible to explain this matter in writing at all, except, what I understood from his words is that he said this regarding the fact that he is involved in such enormous efforts to draw many souls to Hashem Yithbarakh, and has still not achieved it as he desired, and the opposition and the obstacles, physical and spiritual, were getting much, much, more powerful and widespread, in general and in particular, for every individual, to the extent that the power to endure was faltering, and many had fallen as a result... And regarding this he said that he revives himself with this principle of *"Ani hayom yelidh'tikha,"* namely that Hashem Yithbarakh should help us to skip over everything, and in the final end the truth will be revealed, and we will all return to Hashem Yithbarakh in truth, and the former days will fall away, for, all of time will be nullified, and everything will be merged into the aspect of "above time," and there, everything will be set right.

597

I heard in his name that he said that Mashiach will come all of a sudden, and there will be a big uproar that Mashiach has come, and everyone will cast away his commerce that he is engaged in: the banker will throw away his table, and another will throw away his wax, as written in Isaiah, *"Vehishlikh ha'adam eth elilei-khaspo ve'eth elilei-zehavo/ And the man will cast away his idols of silver and his idols of gold"* [Isa. 2:20]. This is unlike what some people believe, that when Mashiach comes, the world will be [altogether] different from now; rather, it will be as mentioned, each person being ashamed of the nonsense of his deeds, each person according to his actions. And probing and questioning are still needed as to who heard this conversation from his holy mouth.

Likutei Moharan #60: Pathach Rabbi Shim`on

The holy *Idra Rabba* ["The Great Assembly:" a part of the Zohar where Rashbi and nine other sages gather together and they explain deep secrets of the Divine "Anatomy." This torah is an explanation and commentary on this beginning passage from it]:

Rabbi Shim`on opened [the discourse] and said: "`*Eth la`asoth laShem...*" [Simply read, "Time for Hashem to act," but which the Sages read midrashically as: It is time (for us) to act for Hashem, Ps. 119:126]: Why is it "time to act for Hashem"? Because "...*heferu Toratekha/* they have annulled your Torah." What is, "They have annulled your Torah?" The Supernal Torah [which is the secret of the *Ze`ir Anpin*], for it is nullified if it is not carried out with these repairs of it [which follow]; and this [verse] is said concerning the `*Atik Yomin/* Ancient of Days. One verse states [Deut. 33:29], "*Ashreikha Yisrael, mi khamokha/* Fortunate are you, Yisrael; who is like you?" whereas another verse states [Ex. 15:11], "*Mi khamokha ba'elim Hashem/* Who is like You among the mighty, Hashem?" He called to Rabbi El`azar his son [whose soul was rooted in *Chokhmah*] and sat him in front of him, and Rabbi Abba [whose soul was rooted in *Binah*, he seated] from the other side [while R. Shimon's soul was rooted in *Da`at*] and said, "*Anan klala dekhola/* We are the embodiment of everything! `*Ad kan ith'taknu kayamin/* Up until now the Pillars have been repaired." They were silent, heard a sound, and their knees [*aRKuVatan*] trembled [lit. kissed each other]. What was the sound? The voice of the supernal assembly assembling [*kenufaya `ila'ah de'mithkanfei;* namely, the *meRKaVoth* of HK"BH]. [Zohar Nasso 128a]

1.

Know that there are pathways of the Torah which contain very profound *hithbonenut* [contemplation; understanding; insight; discernment]; that it is impossible to come to this *hithbonenut* except by way of wealth. Just as with the simple teachings of the Torah, "*Im ein kemach ein Torah/* If there is no flour, there is no Torah" [*Avot* 3] — and in any case a person needs sustenance — so accordingly for this *hithbonenut* which is extremely great it is necessary for him to have very great riches; to have great *hon*/wealth without any lack in it whatsoever. For, one needs all the abundance of the world for this *hithbonenut*.

And the children of Yissakhar, who had this *hithbonenut*, in the aspect of, "*Umibnei Yissakhar yod`ei vinah/* And of the children of Yissachar, [people] knowing discernment..." [I Chron. 12:33], were not privileged to this except by way of wealth, as in, "*Yissakhar chamor garem/* Yissakhar is a {bony, strong} ass" [Gen. 49], and its Targum is: "rich in property." Therefore Moshe and all the prophets had very great riches in order to come thereby to this *hithbonenut*. And on account of there being this *hithbonenut* in the Torah therefore the Torah is called *hon/* wealth [see *Eruvin* 54b].

And similarly, whoever the Torah passed through their hands had very great riches: namely Moshe Rabbeinu who brought the Torah to Yisrael had great riches as our rabbis z"l have said [see *Nedarim* 38a], and so too were Rebbi [Yehudah haNassi] who arranged and sealed the mishnayot and Rav Ashi who was the sealing of the Talmud and organized the whole Talmud as well, who also were extremely wealthy, as our rabbis of blessed memory have said (*Gittin* 59a; see *B"M* 85a), for on account of them arranging the entire Oral Torah and the Torah passing through their hands, therefore they were also wealthy, as mentioned, for one needs great riches for this *hithbonenut*.

And this is the aspect of, "*Pesol lekha/* Hew for yourself" (Ex. 34:1) — and our rabbis obm expounded, "*hapesoleth yihyu shelkha/* the discards shall be yours (*Yerushalmi Shekalim* 5:2), for just as with simple teachings of the Torah, before one brings out a new *peshat*/ basic meaning, one must first say prefaces and afterwards one throws away the introductions and comes to what

[he] intends to say — for the essence is what one intends [to say], and all the words and introductions before are an aspect of *pesolet* which shed off and are discarded around the intended thing — likewise in *hithbonenut* of the Torah one needs to walk around first and go around in several turns until coming to the intended thing. And the essence is the intended thing, and all these turns are an aspect of *pesolet* and they are the aspect of riches, through which one comes to the *hithbonenut*. And this is the aspect of, "*Pesol lekha* — *hapesoleth yihyeh shelkha*:" that is where Moshe became rich from, for these discards of the Tablets are the aspect of surroundings, which fall down and are discarded around and around the *hithbonenut*; and they are the aspect of riches as mentioned, through which one comes to the aforementioned *hithbonenut*.

And this is the letters of "ממון / *MaMON*" being acrostic for, "*Misham Nith`asher Moshe*/ from there Moshe became rich" [Rashi on Ex. 34:1], and the *Vav* [=six]" is the aspect of the tablets from whence Moshe became rich, for the tablets were six long and six wide etc., as our rabbis z"l have said [*B"B* 14a].

2.

And arriving at this prosperity is by means of the aspect of "*tikkunei `Atik*/ repairs of the `*Atik*/ Ancient/ Everlasting One," the aspect of "*arikhuth yamim*/ length of days/ longevity," the aspect of *zaken*/ elder, for *arikhuth yamim* is needed in order to receive into it the riches of the *hithbonenut*.

And the *arikhuth yamim*/ length of days is namely that a person needs to see to it to lengthen and expand his days, because each and every day from the place where it begins for each person is definitely short initially; that is, in the beginning of the day the service that he needs to perform on that day is very hard upon him, for example to pray, study and so forth, and therefore the day initially is short, for he needs to begin little by little and then progressively broaden in his service. And the man needs to see to it to expand, widen and lengthen each and every hour which comes afterward, expanding and widening it with additional *kedushah*/ sanctity/ separation. And likewise when the second day comes, he should continually broaden with the addition of extra *kedushah*, and thus at each and every moment his days should widen with the addition of *kedushah*; and this is the aspect of *arikhuth yamim*.

And Avraham, who merited to the aspect of *zaken*/ elder, the aspect of *arikhuth yamim*/ length of days, by means of this merited riches, in the aspect of, "*VeAvraham zaken ba bayamim vaShem berakh eth-Avraham bakol*/ And Avraham was *zaken*/ old, advanced in *yamim*/ days/ years, and Hashem blessed Avraham with everything" [Gen. 24:1]. And this is the aspect of, "*Mizekenim ethbonan*/ More than my elders [or, From elders] I will discern" [Ps. 119:100], that through this aspect of *zaken*/ elder he comes to the *hithbonenut* which comes via riches, which is drawn down into *arikhuth yamim*/ length of days, which is the aspect of *zaken*/ elder as mentioned.

3.

And the aspect of *zaken*, that is, to widen and lengthen his days by adding *kedushah* each moment, as mentioned, is via *yir'ah*/ awe/ fear, as the *yir'ah* brings additional *kedushah* each and every day, by which the days lengthen and widen, in the aspect of "*yir'ath Hashem tosif yamim*/ the fear of Hashem will increase days" [Prov. 10:27]. "*Yir'ath Hashem hi otzaro*/ The fear of Hashem is His storehouse" [Isa. 33:6], in the aspect of: He [God] made her [Eve] like a storehouse, as she is narrow on top and wide below" [*Berakhoth* 61a], for at their beginnings the days are short and then they go and widen with additional *kedushah* via *yir'ah* as mentioned.

Hence by *yir'ah*/ awe one merits *arikhuth yamim*/ length of days, which are the aspect of *zaken*/ elder, the aspect of *tikkunei `Atik*/ repair of the Ancient One, by which one merits riches. For *yir'ah* guards against the opposite of wealth, namely poverty, which comes through the aspect of, "*Sheker hachen vehevel hayofi*/ Charm is deceitful and beauty is vain" [Prov. 31:30]. For there are several kinds of *chen*/charm-grace of falsehood which people do, in how a person stands, eats, talks with people and likewise in other things, and each thing has a particular different *chen*. And all these deceptive *chens* come by means of *hevel hayofi*/ the vanity of beauty, in the aspect of *sheker hachen vehevel hayofi*, that is, whoever does not guard from the beauty of women has craving for these deceptive *chen*s. And *yir'ah* is the opposite of this, as it is written, "*Sheker hachen vehevel hayofi, ishah yirath-Hashem hi tith'hallal/* Charm is deceitful and beauty is vain; a woman who fears Hashem — she is to be praised."

And therefore Avraham and Yitzchak, when they came to places where there were no *yir'ah*s and as soon as they wanted to enter there they felt this by means of starting to feel — in accord with the extent of their great holiness — the beauty of women and thus they detected that there is no *yir'ah* there, so therefore they prohibited for themselves relations with their spouses as with his sister, as it is written, "*Ki amarti rak ein yir'ath Elohim bamakom hazeh/* For I said, there just is no fear of God in this place" etc. [Gen. 20:11].

And afterwards Avraham repaired this and drew *arikhuth yamim/* length of days, as it is written, "*Vayagar Avraham be'eretz Pelishtim yamim rabim/* And Avraham dwelled in the land of the Philistines many [or vast] days" [ibid. 21:34], the aspect of, "*Yir'ath Hashem tosif yamim/* The fear of Hashem will increase days," as mentioned. And afterwards the Pelishtim spoiled all the repairs which Avraham had accomplished, the aspect of "*Vekhol habe'eroth... sitmum Pelishtim/* and all the wells... the Pelishtim closed them up" [ibid. 26:15]. And therefore when Yitzchak came there he also needed to proscribe his wife like his sister as above, until he drew *arikhuth yamim* to there, which is the aspect of *yir'ah* which protects from this, as mentioned. And then she became permitted to him, as written, "*Vayhi ka'asher arkhu lo sham hayamim vayashkef Avimelekh/* And it came to pass, as the days prolonged for him there, that Avimelekh peered out" etc. [ibid. :8]. And by his drawing down *arikhuth yamim*, there he became privileged to riches, as written, "*Vayizra` Yitzchak ba'aretz hahi vayimtza bashanah hahi me'ah she`arim/* And Yitzchak sowed in that land and produced in that year a hundred-fold" etc. [ibid. :12] as mentioned.

For whoever does not have *yir'ah* is not protected from the aspect of *hevel hayofi*; thereby he comes to poverty, as written, "*Al-tachmod yofyah bilvavekha/* Do not desire her beauty in your hearts... *ki ba`ad-ishah zonah `ad-kikar-lechem/* for on account of a promiscuous woman a man is reduced to a loaf of bread" [Prov. 6:25-26]. For riches and the vanity of beauty are two opposites, for prosperity is from *arikhuth haneshimah*/ elongation of the breathing, and beauty is from interrupted breathing. For at the time of emission of the seminal droplet there needs to be an interruption of breathing for two reasons: one, so that the droplet does not cool off by breathing, which is the cold air which one receives each moment from outside, for it needs to exit with warmth in order that it be fit for conception; and the other, because the force of pressure is occupied in emitting and pushing out the droplet, therefore the interruption of breathing is obligatory, for the breath emits spirit and takes in spirit, and since the expelling power is occupied in pushing out the droplet it is impossible to exhale, and thus there is an interruption of breathing.

And this breath and vapor which enters before and remains there is clothed in the force of expulsion, and by means of it the droplet goes out. And in accord with the purity and cleanness of the breath so is the offspring made bright and vigorous, for if the breath is pure and clean then the droplet which goes out, in which this breath is enclothed, is also pure and clean, and then the offspring is also made bright and vigorous. But if there is turbidness inside the breath then the droplet becomes turbid as well, and this is, *"Adam lahevel damah*/ Man is like a breath"* [Ps. 144:4]. For in accord with the breath so is the makeup of the fetus, and this is the aspect of, *"Akh hevel benei-adam*/ Mankind are but a breath"* [Ps. 62:10], for the breath polishes/ brightens and invigorates the offspring, as mentioned.

And therefore whoever desires women's beauty, hence he receives the aspect of interrupted breathing, and therefore he is in the opposite of riches, which is the aspect of lengthened breathing. For, all kinds of riches, that is, all kinds of grain, all the fruit trees and herbs, and all kinds of metals, they are only by means of *geshamim*/ rains, and also all the treasures are by means of rains, as written, *"Yiftach Hashem lekha eth-otzaro hatov... leteth metar-artzekha*/ Hashem will open up for you His good treasury... to give the rain of your land"* etc. [Deut. 28:12]. And the rains are from the aspect of breathing, as they bring in and receive air [*avir*] from the outside, as written, *"Minishmath-El yiten-karach verochav mayim bemutzak*/ From the breath of the Almighty is the giving of ice, and breadth of waters in flood"* [Job 37:10]. And this is the aspect of *"Hon `ashir kiryath `uzo*/ The rich man's wealth is his city of strength" [Prov. 18:11], that is, the richness is by means of the aspect of the breathing which is the cold [*kar*] air which one receives each moment from the outside, as mentioned. Thus, "*kiryath `uzo*/ his city of strength [or, the calling-meeting-cooling-occurence-emission of His strength]," the aspect of "*geshem mitroth `uzo*/ shower of the mighty rains of His strength" [Job. 37:6].

And this is what is written [Jer. 14:22], "*Hayesh behavlei hagoyim magshimim*/ Are there any, among the vanities [lit. vapors, fig. vain idols] of the gentiles, who can cause rain?" For, "in the vapors of the gentiles," who are the aspect of interrupted breathing, the aspect of the aforementioned "*hevel hayofi*," there is no aspect of rain there, for rain is only by means of the breathing, as mentioned. And this is an aspect of, "*Hon mehevel yim`at*/ Wealth gotten by vanity shall dwindle/ Wealth shall be diminished by vanity" [Prov. 13:11]: by means of the aforementioned *hevel* the wealth is diminished. And this is the aspect of "*vekar-ruach ish tevunah*/ and he that cools his spirit is a man of discernment" [Prov. 17:27]: by means of cool spirit, which is the cool wind of the breathing, thereby one attains the aforementioned *hithbonenut*, which comes via riches, as mentioned.

And this is an aspect of, "*Venishmath Shaddai tevinem*/ And the spirit of Shaddai [that] gives them discernment" [Job 32:8], for the essence of the *hithbonenut* is via breathing, the aspect of cool spirit as mentioned, for the main repair of the intellect is by way of the breathing, for the main thing for the intellect to be in its proper state so that he can *lehithbonen*/ reach contemplative understanding is by means of the lipids that are in the body. For the intellect is like a lamp that burns, for it burns by way of the lipids that are drawn to it and they are like oil that is drawn to the lit wick. And when there are no lipids in the body the intellect cannot burn in the *hithbonenut* and from this come insane people, by the bodily moisture drying up, and by this the brain is spoiled, by it not having oils to light. And all the moisture and the lipids in the body are by means of the breathing, for, "*Il-male kanfei re'ah denashvin `al-liba havei liba oked kol-gufa*/ If not for the lobes of the lung which blow over the heart, the heart would incinerate the entire body" [*Tikkunei Zohar* 27a]. Hence the essence of maintaining the oils and moisture in the body is by way of breathing, that the lung receives cool air from outside to cool the heart, and by way of breathing is the preservation of the intellect, that it should be able to light in the *hithbonenut* as mentioned.

And this is the aspect of, "*Ner Hashem nishmath adam*/ The soul [the breath] of man is the lamp of Hashem" [Prov. 20:27], that the main sustenance and repair of the *ner Hashem*, which is the intellect, is by means of the breathing, as mentioned. Hence through *yir'ah* one attains *arikhuth yamim*/ length of days and through this the wealth is drawn down, through which they come to the aforementioned *hithbonenut*.

4.

And the completion of the *yir'ah* is in the aspect of three lines: the aspect of *mora' shamayim*/ fear of Heaven, *mora' rabakh*/ fear of your rav, and *mora' av va'eim*/ fear of father and mother. And when there is a *chakham hador*/ Sage of the Era who is privileged to worthy students and worthy children then the *yir'ah* is in completion, for: the *yir'ah* of the *chakham* and the rav of the era is the aspect of *mora' shamayim*, his students have *yir'ath harav* in the aspect of *mora' rabakh*, and his children have *mora' av va'eim*, so that the *yir'ah* is complete through these three *yir'ot*.

And the aspect of the *yir'ah* of each of these three needs to be of threefold makeup. That is, fear of one's rav, which is *mora' shamayim*, needs to include all three brains, *chokhmah, binah,* and *da`at* (wisdom, discernment, and knowledge), for the fear of one's rav comes mainly by means of the *hithbonenut* of the greatness of the Creator, *yithbarakh Shemo*, which he probes and seeks with his mental faculties. Hence the fear of his rav is by means of the intellect; therefore it is necessary that the *yir'ah* be filled with all three brains, with his *chokhmah, binah* and *da`at*; all of them should be filled with *yir'ath Hashem*.

And *yir'ath hatalmid*/ the pupil's fear, that is, *mora' rabakh* which is by means of the learning which he receives from the rav, needs to be drawn into all parts of the learning, which is also an aspect of the three lines, that is, the aspect of *oraitha tlita'ah*/ the Threefold Torah [*Shabbath* 85a].

And *yir'ath haben*/ the son's fear, which is *mora' av va'eim*, one needs to draw it forth in the aspect of *nachalath avoth*/ paternal inheritance, the aspect of, "*Bayith vahon nachalath avoth*/ A home and riches are the inheritance from the fathers" [Prov. 19:14]. And it is necessary that the *yir'ah* spreads out on all parts of the wealth, which are the *nachalath avot* as mentioned: "*Le'olam yeshalesh adam ma'otav: shelish bifrakmatia, ushlish bekarka`, ushlish beyado*/ Always a man should apportion his money into three: one third in trade, one third in land, and one third in [cash in] his hand" [B"M 42a].

And these three components in wealth correspond to the three times that riches are mentioned in the Torah. For, riches are not mentioned in the entire Torah except these three times: regarding Sedom, as written, "*Velo-tomar ani he'esharti eth-Avram*/ So that you should not claim, 'I made Avraham wealthy'" [Gen. 14:23], and regarding Rachel and Leah, as written, "*Ki khol-ha'osher asher hitzil Elohim*/ For all the wealth which God has delivered" etc. [ibid. 31:16], and regarding the *shekalim*, as written, "*He'ashir lo-yarbeh*/ The rich person should not contribute more" [Ex. 30:15].

For, the one-third in trade corresponds to the wealth that is mentioned regarding Sedom, for about Sedom it is written, "*Hanishkachim mini-ragel*/ those who caused the foot [of wayfarers] to be forgotten" [Job 28:4], for they wanted to abolish trade, which is an aspect of *regel*/ foot, as written, "*Semach Zevulun betze'thekha*/ Rejoice, Zevulun, in your going out" [Deut. 33:18], and therefore one must specifically have commerce; and this is: "one-third in trade."

And the "one-third in land" corresponds to the wealth that is mentioned with Rachel and Leah, for in truth the essence of wealth is only for the *hithbonenut*, but without this the wealth is only for women and those who have internalized wisdom to a lesser extent [*katanei-da'at*] like them. And this is their statement of, "*Ki khol-ha'osher asher hitzil Elohim me'avinu lanu hu ulvaneinu*/ For all the wealth which God has taken away from our father is for us and for our children" [Gen. 31:16], that is, all the wealth is only for women and the *katanei-da'at* such as us. But you [*Ya'akov*] — "... *ve'atah kol asher amar eleikha Elohim `aseh*/ and now whatever God has said to you, do," that is, you need the wealth for the sake of the *hithbonenut* of the greatness of Hashem. And corresponding to this is the aspect of one-third in land, the aspect of *"ishah karka` `olam/* woman is compared to the earth" [*Sanhedrin* 74b; *Kli Yakar* to Gen. 24:63].

And the one-third in [cash in] his hand corresponds to the wealth mentioned regarding *Shekalim*, as stated there: *"lekhaper `al nafshotheikhem/* to atone for your souls" [Ex. 30:15], the aspect of *"asher beyado nefesh kol-chai veruach kol-basar-ish/* in Whose hand is the soul of every living thing and the spirit of all human flesh" [Job 12:10].

5.

And the revelation of the *yir'ah* is by means of barren women being visited/remembered with conception [*pekiduth `akarot*], for *yir'ah* is revealed by means of giving birth, the aspect of, *"ra`adah achazatham sham, chil kayoledah/* trembling took hold of them there, pangs, as a woman giving birth" [Ps. 48:7], for by giving birth, bloods and strengths go out, which are the aspect of *yir'ah/* fear, and especially when a barren woman is visited, as the bloods and strengths had been stopped up until now, therefore afterwards when they go out the *yir'ah* is most revealed.

And in accord with the birth, so is the revelation of the *yir'ah*. For when one barren woman is visited, the *yir'ah* is revealed, and when many barren women are visited, the *yir'ah* is revealed much more. And this is the aspect of, *"chil kayoledah/* trembling one who gives birth:" in accord with the birth so is the revelation of the *yir'ah*.

Therefore the birth of Yitzchak was on Rosh Hashanah, for he is the epitome of the extreme revelation of the *yir'ah*, the aspect of "the fear of Yitzchak." For when Sarah was visited many barren women became visited along with her, as our rabbis obm have said [Gen. R. 53]. And this is the aspect of, *"Ki-yaladeti ben lizkunav/* For I have borne a son in [lit. to] his old age" [Gen. 21:7], for by means of Yitzchak's birth, who is the revelation of the *yir'ah*, thereby *arikhuth yamim/* longevity was drawn down, the aspect of elder, as mentioned, in the aspect of *"Yir'ath Hashem tosif yamim/* The fear of Hashem will increase days," as mentioned.

6.

And the visitation of barren women is accomplished by means of awakening mankind from their sleep, for there are mankind who sleep through their days: even though it appears to the world that they are serving Hashem and are involved in Torah and prayer, nonetheless all their devotions — Hashem Yithbarakh has no satisfaction from them, for their service remains down below and cannot get high and ascend up. For, the essence of life is the mental faculty, as written, "*Hachokhmah techayeh eth-ba`alei'ah*/ The wisdom preserves the life of him that has it" [Eccl. 7:12]. So when the service is with the mental faculty, one puts life into it so that it can go up. But when one falls in to the aspect of *mochin de'katnuth* / constricted consciousness, the aspect of sleep, it [the mental faculty] cannot rise up.

And there are those who have fallen into the aspect of sleep by means of cravings and evil deeds. And there are those who are fine and decent people except that their downfall is through eating. For sometimes when the man eats a food that has not yet been refined into human food, thereby his brain falls into the aspect of sleep. For just as physically there are foods that induce sleep and there are foods that diminish sleep, likewise spiritually there are foods that have not been refined, which bring [a person] down into the aspect of sleep. But when one eats in *kedushah*/ sanctity/ separation and *taharah*/ purity, then it is the aspect of, "*lechem hapanim*/ showbread [lit. face bread, Ex. 25:30]. For, the intellect is the face, as written: "*Chokhmath adam ta'ir panav*/ A man's wisdom illuminates his face" [Eccl. 8:1]; but when his eating is not with sanctity then he loses his face, that is, the mental faculty, and falls into the aspect of sleep.

For the main [purpose] of food is to give life to the heart, as written, "*Vayochal... vayeshth vayitav libo*/ And [Bo`az] ate and drank and his heart was merry [lit. made good]" [Ruth 3:7], as our rabbis z"l have said, "*Pita sa`ada deliba*/ Bread strengthens the heart" [Gen. R. 48]. But when the food is not refined or when one does not eat in holiness then he brings badness to the heart, and by means of heart-badness his face is damaged, as written, "*Madu`a paneikha ra`im*/ Why do you have a bad face? ...*Ein zeh ki-im ro`a lev*/ This is none other than badness-sorrow of heart" [Neh. 2:2]. And conversely, seeking his face, that is, recovering his face, depends on proper condition of the heart, as written, *"Lekha amar libi, bakeshu panai*/ On Your behalf my heart says, 'Seek My face'"* [Ps. 27:8].

Hence sometimes by means of unrefined food, whereby the heart is damaged, thereby one loses his face and falls into the aspect of sleep and must be awakened from his sleep. But it is impossible to awaken him except when he has begun to rouse on his own, for there must be *ith`arutha dil'tatha*/ awakening from below. However, when he has started to wake up by himself, if *they* had not awakened him he would have remained sleeping more. Therefore as soon as he is roused he must be shown his face and enclothed with his face that had departed from him during sleep. And this is the concept of being awakened from sleep.

And when we want to show him his face and awaken him from his sleep, we need to clothe his face for him in story tales. For there are seventy *panim*/faces-facets to the Torah [*Bamidbar R.* 13:16], and they are the aspect of "seventy *ShaNim*/ years/ differences," for each one is *meShuNeh*/ different from the other. And it is necessary to enclothe specifically the face, for three reasons: One, for it is like healing a blind person: he must be enclosed so that he should not see the light suddenly, and one needs to restrict the light for him so that he should not be harmed by what he sees suddenly. Likewise for this person who was in sleep and darkness a long time, when one wants to show him his face and awaken him one must clothe his face for him in story tales in order that the sudden light should not harm him. And this is the aspect of, *"Ani betzedek echezeh paneikha*/ I will behold Your face justly-temperately..."* [Ps. 17:15]: *tzedek*/ justness is the aspect of clothing, the aspect of *"tzedek lavashti*/ I don righteous-ness"* [Job 29:14]. And then: *"...esbe`ah vehakitz temunathekha*/ I shall be satisfied, whilst awake, with Your image,"* for then he can see afterwards while awake, that is, when he has been roused and awakened from sleep, for the sudden light will no longer harm him. And the second reason is that it is necessary to en-clothe [his face] in order that the *chitzonim* [forces that are out-side of holiness] should not take hold of him. And the third reason is that the *chitzonim* which do have a grip on him will not release him, therefore it is necessary to enclothe his face in order to alter it so that they do not recognize him, in the aspect of *"Meshaneh panav vateshalchehu/* You change his face and send him away" [Job 14:20].

N ow, there are several aspects in this enclothing the face. For sometimes his face is clothed in a story tale. And sometimes it is impossible to awaken him with his face and he needs to be shown a higher face. And sometimes one also enclothes [it] in words of Torah, that is, saying a high Torah that is impossible to convey as-is, so one clothes [it] in a Torah that is lower and lesser than it. And this is the aspect of, *"Hashem, pa`alekha bekerev shanim chayehu/* Hashem, revive Your work in the midst of these years" [Hab. 3:2]: *chayehu/* revive it — Rashi explains, "awaken it." And this is, *"pa`alekha"/* Your work [lit. Your deeds], namely story tales — *"bekerev shanim/* within *shanim/* years/ versions," namely the aspect of stories of the seventy facets, which are the seventy years, as mentioned. That is, one awakens him by means of story tales that are *bekerev shanim/* within the facets, that is, the stories of the seventy [Torah] facets, as mentioned.

B ut sometimes a person has fallen from all the seventy faces to the extent that it is impossible to awaken him with any face, other than by means of *"sipurei ma`asiyoth shel Shanim Qadhmoniyoth/* Stories of the Ancient Years-Faces," as all the seventy faces, seventy years, receive life from there [i.e. from something more Primal than mortal life and experience]. And this is the aspect of the `Atik/ the Ancient One, the aspect of *zaken/* elder, the aspect of *Hadhrathh Panim/* honorable face, as all the seventy faces receive life and honor from there. And this is the aspect of *"verav-chesed/* and abundant in kindness" [Ex. 34:6]. For, one who teaches his student one *halakhah/* Torah conduct has acted kindly toward him, as our rabbis obm have said, *"Kol ha-mone`a talmido mileshamesho, ki'ilu mone`a mimeno chesed/* Whoever does not permit his student to attend on him, acts as if he deprived him of [an act of] kindness" [*Ketubot* 96a]. And attending on sages is the aspect of *halakhoth /* Torah ways which a student receives from his rav. Hence what the rav teaches his student is an aspect of *chesed/* kindness. And therefore when one awakens him with some face from the seventy faces which he enclothes in the aspect of *Hashem pa`alekha bekerev shanim chayehu"* as mentioned, this is the aspect of ordinary kindness.

But when he awakens him by means of *sipurei ma`asiyoth shel Shanim Qadhmoniyoth* it is the aspect of *"verav chesed*/ and utmost kindness,"* for all the faces and all the kindnesses receive from there.

7.

And when one is involved in awakening people he needs to guard himself from students who are not worthy, in order that their badness should not cling to him, so that it should not harm him, as our rabbis o"bm have said, *"Kol hamelamed latalmid she'eino hagun*/ Whoever teaches an unworthy student"* etc. Similarly our sages obm forbade writing on the hide of a non-kosher beast, as written, *"Lema`an tihyeh Torath Hashem befikha*/ So that Hashem's Torah be in your mouth" [Ex. 13:9] — from that which is permitted to [enter] your mouth [*Shabbath* 108a]. And teaching someone is like writing, for the tongue is the aspect of, *"Leshoni `eth sofer mahir*/ My tongue is the pen of a ready writer" [Ps. 45:2], for the heart of the student is engraved and written on, as written, *"Katevem `al-luach libekha*/ Write them upon the table of your heart" [Prov. 3:3]. And therefore his words must not be written on the aspect of a non-kosher beast, that is, an unworthy student.

However, it is impossible for flesh and blood to guard itself such that unworthy students should not hear from him. And for this, he needs that his study should be, *"lilmod ulelamed, velishmor vela`asoth* / to learn and to teach, and to keep and to do-make,"* that is, by means of his study with his student, it should be as if he made the person and as if he made the words of Torah, as our rabbis obm have said, "Whoever teaches someone else's son Torah, is as if he made him... and as if he made the words of Torah" [Num. 3:1 and Rashi; *Sanh.* 99b]. And when he studies with this intention, then Hashem Yithbarakh guards him so that his words should not be written in the memory of a student who is not worthy, but only be forgotten by him.

And when one is involved in awakening others by means of story tales, his conversations and stories also need to be in this aspect of study, that is, *"lilmod vela`asoth* / to teach and to author/ make"* as mentioned. And this is the aspect of, "The conversations of Torah sages require study" [A"Z 19b], that is, whatever is needed in his studies is needed also in his conversations, which are the aspect of story tales, as mentioned. And this is, "Ve`alehu litrufah/ And its leaf for healing" [Eze. 47:12]: "Its leaf" is the aspect of the Torah sage's conversation, as our rabbis obm have said, "Ve`alehu lo-yibol/ And its leaf shall not whither" [Ps. 2]: even the conversation of a Torah sage" etc. [A"Z ibid.].

And this is, "liTRuFaH": leHaTiR PeH/ to permit-release-open the mouth, that is, the aspect of "from that which is permitted to your mouth." For when his conversations are in the aspect of, "Torah sages' conversations require study," that is, lilmod ule-lamed, lishmor vela`asot as mentioned, then he will be protected from unworthy students, which is the aspect of "from that which is permitted for your mouth" as mentioned, from whence we learn that we do not write etc. as mentioned.

8.

And this is the aspect of what our rabbis obm taught regarding the verse, "Ve`alehu litrufah/ And its leaf for healing: lehatir peh ilemim/ to permit-release the mouth of the mute... ul'hatir peh `akaroth/ and to open the mouth of barren women" [Sanh. 100], for by awakening people from their sleep by way of story tales, which is the aspect of, "ve`alehu litrufah" etc. as mentioned, thereby is accomplished the aspect of "releasing the mouth of the mute," for previously when they were in the aspect of sleep and were not hearing the sage's rousing and his words were not heard by their ears, for [Zohar II 186b], "Zaka'ah man demallel `al udna deshama`/ Fortunate is he who speaks to an ear that hears!" — but these were like deaf people and did not hear whatsoever, and on account of this it was impossible for them to speak, for, "a regular deaf person can neither hear nor speak" [Terumot I:2; Chagigah 2b], that is, on account of his deafness he cannot talk. And now, when the sage wakes him up and he hears his words, then he can talk. And this is the aspect of, "lehatir peh ilemim," and this is the aspect of, "Pethach pikha le'ilem/ Open your mouth for the mute" [Prov. 31:8].

And by means of this is the aspect of, "ul'hatir peh `akaroth/ and to open the mouth of barren women," for this speech, which had been so constricted within them for such a long time that they were [like] the deaf and the mute, now that this speech emerges, it emerges with great force, in the aspect of [Ps. 103:20], "*giborei koach `osei devaro*/ those who are mighty of strength, that fulfill His word;" and this strength enters into the vessels of procreation, in the aspect of [Gen. 49:3], "*Kochi vereishith oni*/ My strength and the first of my virility;" that is, the *BaTChanei hador*/ guarantors of the epoch, who are the aspect of the procreative organs, they receive this power, in the aspect of, "*Vekavei Hashem yachalifu koach*/ Those who trust in Hashem will have renewed strength/ The pillars of Hashem will wax strong" [Isa. 40:31]. And therefore the *kelayoth* / kidneys/ testicles are called *BaTuChoth* / guarantors/ inward parts [see Ps. 51:8 and commentaries; Job 38:36; cf. "testicles"], for the *kelayot* are procreative organs. [Translator's note: Chazal believed that the seed originates in the brain, takes physical shape through the various organs, especially the kidneys, and is then emitted. In Aramaic, כליא/ *Kolia*, denotes either a testicle or a kidney, and its etymology denotes something "round-shaped;" cf. גל/ *gal*/ round. Chazal may have had a concept of *kelayot* as relating to the entire uro-genital tract. Furthermore, the adrenal glands which sit upon the kidneys are known to secrete sex hormones.] And when the *batchanei hador* receive this power of speech they receive it lawfully and justfully; each according to his *bitachon*/ trust receives this power.

And this is the aspect of, "*Pethach pikha le'ilem, el-din kol-benei chalof*/ Open your mouth for the mute, in the cause of all who are appointed to destruction" [Prov. 31:8], the aspect of, "*kavei Hashem yachalifu koach*/ The pillars of Hashem will grow strong," as by means of "*pethach pikha*" etc., the power of speech goes out to the procreative organs which are the *batchanim*/ guarantors, which receive it lawfully and justfully, as mentioned.

And one must see to it that one's speech organs be interrelated with his procreative organs in order that they be able to receive the power of speech, as mentioned, so that they should not be in the aspect of, "*Karov atah befihem verachok mikiliyotheihem*/ You are near in their mouths but far from their *kiliyoth*/ thoughts-kidneys" [Jer. 12:2; Chazal viewed the kidneys (adrenals?) as a source of `etzah/ advice-motivation]. And therefore the speech organs and procreative organs have the same structure, for these are full of sinews and nerves as those are, for they are one aspect, for by means of the power of speech, procreation is accomplished, as mentioned. And this is the aspect of, *"Ve`alehu litrufah/* And its leaf for healing: *lehatir peh ilemim/* to permit-release the mouth of the mute... *ul'hatir peh `akaroth /* and to open the mouth of barren women,"* for they are interdependent, as mentioned.

And this is the aspect of the kissing relations and the bodily relations, as the kissing relations precede the bodily relations, as brought in the [kabbalistic] texts. For by means of the power of speech, the aspect of *"lehatir peh ilemim,"* which is an aspect of the kissing relations, thereby the bodily relations come about, the aspect of *"lehatir peh `akarot,"* as mentioned.

And this is the aspect of the breaking of an earthware vessel which is broken when couples make their ties, to teach that now the tie has been made, which is for the sake of procreation, which is the aspect of *bitachon/* trust, the aspect of *kelayoth /* kidneys, which are procreative vessels, as mentioned. And this is the aspect of, *"Batach bah lev ba`alah/* Her husband's heart trusts in her"* [Prov. 31:11]: by means of this, the aspect of *bitachon/* trust of the *sitra achra/* Other Side is annulled and broken, and it is for this that we break the earthware vessel, in the aspect of, *"Vativtechu be`oshek venaloz/* You trusted in fraud and corruption... *ush'varah keshever nevel yotzrim/* and He shall break it as a potter's vessel is broken... *velo yimmatze vimkhitatho cheres/* so that a sherd shall not be found among its pieces"* etc. [Isa. 30:12-14]. For, the trust of holiness which is accomplished by this tying, as mentioned, is the opposite of the trust of the *sitra achra*, which pertains to breaking the earthware vessel, as mentioned. And it also hints to them that if they do not conduct themselves in holiness but betray, God forbid, the aspect of trust, the aspect of procreation, then they will be in the aspect of breaking the earthware vessel, which comes about by trust in an unfaithful person, as mentioned [Prov. 25:19]. And this is, *"Al tivtechu be'aluf, mishokheveth cheikekha shemor pithchei pikha/* Do not put confidence in an *ALuF/* familiar friend; from she that lies in your bosom guard the openings of your mouth"* [Mic. 7:5], that is, [then] it is impossible for confidence, that is, the procreative vessels, to correlate with speech, which is the aspect of *ALuF/* taught/ trained/ accustomed, which is acrostic for *"Lehatir Peh Ilemim/* To open the mouth of the mute." And this is, "*Mishokheveth cheikekha*/ From she that lies in your bosom..." — that is, so that procreation comes about from this, the aspect of, "*Veshokhva vecheikekha*/ Let her lie in your bosom" [I Kings 1:2 — Dawidh did not "know" her, ibid. :4] — this is not possible except by way of, "...*Shemor pithchei pikha*/ Guard the openings of your mouth," as mentioned.

And this is, "*Yiten be`afar pihu, ulai yesh tikvah*/ Let him place his mouth in the dust; perhaps there is hope" [Lam. 3:29]. `*Afar*/ dust is the aspect of absence of speech, as written, "*Ume`afar tishach imrathekha*/ And your speech will be low out of the dust" [Isa. 29:4]. That is, the aspect of speech must be placed in, "*Lehatir peh ilemim*," as mentioned, and thereby the power of speech comes to *KoVei Hashem*/ Hashem's pillars, who are the procreative vessels, as mentioned. And this is: "perhaps there is *tiKVah*/ hope:" in order that speech reaches the *KoVei Hashem* as mentioned. And this is, "*Vehayah zar`akha ka`afar ha`aretz*/ Your offspring will be like the dust of the earth" [Gen. 28:14], for procreation depends on the aforementioned aspect of, "*Yiten be`afar pihu*/ Let him place his mouth in the dust."

And this is the aspect of, "*Verabim miyeshenei admath-`afar yakitzu*/ And many of them that sleep in the dust-earth shall awake..." [Dan. 12:3], that is, they will awaken and stir them up, as mentioned. And this is, "*miyeshenei admath-afar*/ of those that sleep in the dust-earth," of the aspect of absence of speech as mentioned. And this is, "...*eleh lechayei `olam*/ these, to everlasting life," that is, the aspect of speech, as written, "*Vayhi ha`adam lenefesh chayah*/ And man became a living lifeforce," the Targum of which is, "*leruach memallela*/ a talking spirit," that is, the aspect of "*lehatir peh ilemim*/ opening the mouth of the mute;" "...*ve`eleh lacharafoth*/ And these to reproaches," etc., that is, the aspect of, "*Cherpah shavera libi*/ Reproach has broken my heart" [Ps. 69:21], the aspect of forgetting; breaking of the heart, which is the aspect of breaking of the Tablets, as written, "*Luach libekha*/ The tablet of your heart" [Prov. 7:3]. And by the breaking of the tablets comes forgetfulness, as our rabbis z"l have said, "*Ilmale lo-nishtabru luchoth harishonoth, lo-haytha shikhecha*/ If the first Tablets had not been broken there would not have been any forgetfulness [of Torah in Yisrael]" [`Eruvin 54]. That is, those who are not worthy to receive, who are the aspect of the hide of a non-kosher beast — it is forgotten by them, as mentioned.

9.

And this is the aspect of the *shofar*/ horn, for shofar is the aspect of awakening from sleep, as brought in the [kabbalistic] books, that the shofar alludes to the aspect of, "`*Uru yeshenim mitardemathkhem*/ Wake up, sleepers, from your sleep" [*Mishneh Torah: Teshuvah* 3:7]. And thereby it is the aspect of, "*ul'hatir peh `akarot*" as mentioned.

And this is the aspect of, "*Teki`ah*/ sustained shofar blast, *shevarim*/ [three short] broken blasts, *teru`ah*/ [nine of the very short] tremulous/ shouting blasting:" *TeKi`Ah* is the aspect of the absence of speech, the aspect of, "*Taka`ta lazar kapeikha: Nokashta be'imrei fikha*/ [If...] you have struck hands for a stranger: You are trapped in the words of your mouth" [Prov. 6:1-2]. *TeRu`Ah* is the aspect of speech, the aspect of, "*Siftei tzaddik yiR`U rabbim*/ The lips of a righteous tzaddik/ righteous man will feed many" [ibid. 10:21]. *SheVaRim* is the aspect of *bitachon*/ confidence, the aspect of, "*SiVRo `al-Hashem Elohav*/ Whose hope is in Hashem his God" [Ps. 146:5], the aspect of procreative organs, as written, "*Ha'ani aShBiR velo olid*/ Shall I bring to the birth [lit. cause to break out], and not cause to give birth?" [Isa. 66:9]. For by means of the shofar, which is an aspect of the awakening from sleep, thereby it is the aspect of "*lehatir peh ilemim... ul'hatir peh `akarot*," as mentioned. That is, the power of speech which emerges forcefully out of these who have awakened from their sleep, who initially were in the aspect of absence of speech, for they were like deaf and mute people, as mentioned. And now when they wake up to Hashem Yithbarakh from their sleep, to the extent that they hear the rousing of the true sage — then they begin to speak, as mentioned.

And this speech goes into the procreative organs, which are the aspect of *batchanei hador*/ guarantors of the era, as mentioned. And thereby the visitation of barren women is accomplished, which is the aspect of Rosh Hashanah, which is when Sarah etc. were visited, as mentioned. And all this is the aspect of the shofar which we blast on Rosh Hashanah, the aspect of, "*tek-i`ah, teru`ah, shevarim,*" as mentioned [i.e. lack of speech, speech, and confidence-procreation]. And by means of the visitation of barren women, the fear/ awe is revealed, as mentioned. And this is the aspect of shofar, as written, "*Im-yitaka` shofar be`ir ve`am lo-yecheradu/* Shall the horn be blown in town, and the people not tremble?*" etc. And this is the aspect of the shofar, which is narrow below and wide above, which is the aspect of, "*Min hameitzar karathi Y-h, `anani vamerchav Y-h/* Out of my straits I called upon the Y-h; He answered me with great enlargement" [Ps. 118:5] as is brought, for by means of shofar is the revelation of fear, as mentioned, by means of which they merit *arikhuth yamim/* length of days, that is, to widen and lengthen one's days with additional extra holiness at all times, which is the aspect of "narrow above and wide below," the aspect of, "*Yir'ath Hashem hi otzaro/* The fear of Hashem is His treasure house," the aspect of "He made her like a treasure house" etc. as mentioned.

A nd this is the aspect of *tikkunei `Atik/* repairs of the Ancient One, which is the aspect of the *arikhuth yamim/* length of days/ longevity mentioned earlier, the aspect of the *zakan/* beard, as mentioned. For the beard is also narrow above and wide below, as brought in the *Kavanoth,* that *tikkunei dikna/* proper states of the beard are aspect of, "*Min hametzar karathi... `Anani vamerchav*" etc., as initially it was narrow and then progressively widens, namely as mentioned. For the beard is the aspect of *arikhuth yamim* mentioned earlier, namely, that one lengthens and widens his days at all times with additional holiness, as mentioned, which one merits through fear as mentioned, which is all aspect of shofar as mentioned. Hence by means of the shofar, which is the aspect of awakening from sleep, and whereby the visitation of barren women is accomplished, as mentioned — thereby the fear is revealed, as mentioned, and fear suppresses the vanity of beauty as mentioned. And this is the aspect of the breaths of the shofar, for they are an aspect of "*hevel hayofi/* the vapors of beauty," for "*shofar*" is a term for beauty, the aspect of "*shipru ma`aseikhem/* improve your deeds," [*Midrash Rabbah Emor* 29], that is, by means of the shofar's *hevels/* breaths, the *hevel/* vanity of beauty is subdued, for the shofar is the aspect of the revelation of the awe, as mentioned.

And this the explanation of: **Rabbi Yochanan said, "Throughout all of that tzaddik's [Choni Ham`agel's] days... he asked, 'Is there someone who sleeps for seventy *shanim*/ years?' One day he was going along the road and saw a man planting a *charuva*/ carob tree. He said to him, 'Doesn't a carob not bear until seventy years? Is it plain to you that you will live seventy years and eat from it? He said to him, 'I found the world with [lit. in] carobs; just as my forefathers planted for me so too do I plant for my descendants. He [Choni] sat down to wrap bread [i.e. have a meal], became drowsy and fell asleep. A grotto formed around him and concealed him from every being [lit. no creature knew] and he slept seventy years. When he got up and awoke, he saw a man eating from that carob, and said to him, 'Do you know who planted that carob?' He said to him, 'My father's father.' He said, 'Surely I have slept seventy years.' He saw his she-donkey which had given birth to hinnies and more hinnies"** etc. [Ta`anit 23a]

For, Choni Ham`agel was exceedingly great, as they stated in this passage, that "when he went to the study hall, he would answer all the questions that the rabbis had," for no facet of the Torah was hidden from him. Thus he asked, **"Is there somebody who sleeps seventy years?"** That is, how is it possible to fall into the aspect of sleep from all the seventy faces? For although it is possible to fall from one face or more, is it nonetheless possible to fall from all of them?

❝ **He saw this man planting a carob and said to him, '...Is it plain to you that you will live seventy years and eat from it?"** *Charuv*/ Carob is the aspect of *zaken*/ elder, the aspect of `*Atik*/ the Ancient One, for the carob is the "*beroshim*" [Isa. 55:13 and Metzudat Tziyon; *Kil'ayim* 6:5], which is the aspect of Mordekhai, as our rabbis obm have said: "*Tachath hana`atzutz ya`aleh verosh*/ Instead of the thorn, the *berosh* shall come up" [Isa. 55:13] — this is Mordekhai [*Megillah* 10b]. Now, Mordekhai is the aspect of *rav chesed*/ abundant in kindness, for they are numerically equivalent [274=רב חסד=מרדכי], which is the aspect of `*Atik*. That is, [Choni] saw someone involving himself with *sipurei ma`asiyoth shel Shanim Qadhmoniyoth/* Stories of the Ancient, which are the aspect of `Atik as mentioned, and asked him, "Is it plain to you that you will live seventy years?" "Live" is the aspect of arousal from sleep, the aspect of speech, as mentioned. That is: Have you tried to awaken [people] by means of story tales of *bekerev shanim/* that are within *shanim* [i.e. within the 70 years and 70 Torah facets, i.e. within the realm of human experience]?

...And eat from it?" That is, the aspect of, "From that which is permitted for your mouth," that is, that his words should be heard; that his students be worthy. (That is, he asked him: How do you involve yourself in such sublime Stories of the Ancient? — for perhaps students will hear who are unworthy, who are not in the aspect of, "From that which is permitted for your mouth," as mentioned. Have you already tried and tested to arouse by way of story tales from within the years, which are within the seventy years, which are the seventy faces of the Torah, and did you succeed in arousing them from their sleep thereby, your words having reached worthy students who are the aspect of, "From that which is permitted to your mouth," the aspect of "...*ve'akhleth minaihu/* and eat from it," as mentioned? To the extent that now you want to delve further in story tales that are loftier, which are Stories of the Ancient?! So how are you not afraid to tell such lofty story tales, lest unworthy students hear [them]?)

He said to him, '**I found the world with carobs (or, I caused the world in carobs to be forgotten: `Alma becharuva eshkachteih),'** that is, even though I tell Stories of the Ancient which are the aspect of carobs, as mentioned, I can bring the aspect of forgetting, so that the unworthy students will forget it, as mentioned. [That is, as explained above, that the tzaddik who involves himself in arousing the world from sleep by means of story tales, Hashem Yithbarakh protects him so that his words will be forgotten from the heart of unworthy students, as mentioned.] '**Just as my forefathers planted for me so too do I plant for my descendants.'** That is, just as they begot me by means of the aforementioned story tales, in the aspect of, "*Lehatir peh ilemim... lehatir peh `akaroth,*" as mentioned, '**so too I plant**

for my descendants,' that is, our children as well are born by these same means, as mentioned. (Explanation: He said to him that he must tell such story tales for the sake of barren women's conception, for: just as my fathers were involved with story tales and thereby drew down procreation, the aspect of barren women's conception, as mentioned, by which means they bore me, so too I need to bear my descendants by means of this. For procreation is mainly drawn down by means of story tales, as mentioned. And this is: **Just as my forefathers planted for me so too do I plant for my descendants.**)

He sat down to wrap bread [i.e. have a meal], became drowsy and fell asleep.** That is, he ate a meal, and by eating he became drowsy and fell asleep. That is, he fell into the aspect of sleep, relative to his level, by eating, as mentioned above, that sometimes through eating, a person can fall into the aspect of sleep, as mentioned. ***Meshunita*/ A grotto** [<*shen*, tooth] ***hadra `aleh*/ formed around him/ came back,** that is, the aspect of the turns and the imaginations which return and surround about during sleep; **and no creature knew,** for the world does not recognize someone who is in the aspect of sleep, for it appears to them that he is involved in Torah and devotions while in truth is all the aspect of sleep, as mentioned. **When he got up and awoke,** that is, the aspect of awaking from below, **he saw a man eating from this carob,** that is, he saw him involved in the aforementioned story tales, and eating from them — that is, from the aspect of, "From what is permitted for your mouth."

And said to him, 'Do you know who planted that carob?'** — that is: From what time is this story tale? For it is possible for someone to tell a story which has already taken place but actually was no more than four years ago. **He said to him, 'My father's father,'** that is, the aspect of *zaken*/ elder, the aspect of `*Atik*/ the Ancient One. That is, he answered him that the story tales which he is involved in are Stories of the Ancient, which are the aspect of *zaken*/ elder, the aspect of `*Atik*/ the Ancient One, as mentioned. **He said, 'Surely I have slept seventy years,'** that is, surely he has fallen to the aspect of sleeping from all the seventy faces, which are the aspect of seventy years, as mentioned.

He saw his she-donkey, which had given birth to hinnies and more hinnies, that is, the aspect of wealth, the aspect of, "Yissakhar is a {bony, strong} ass," for thereby great riches are drawn down, as mentioned. For by means of the aforementioned story tales, by means of which one rouses from sleep, as mentioned, thereby "to open the mouth of the mute... to open the mouth of barren women," as thereby the awe is revealed, and by means of awe, *arikhuth yamim/* length of days/ longevity is drawn down, the aspect of *zaken/* elder, the aspect of *tikkunei `Atik/* repairs of the Ancient One, as mentioned; and thus the riches are drawn into the *arikhuth yamim*, as mentioned.

And this is, **Rabbi Shim`on opened [the discourse] and said: "`Eth la`asoth laShem..."** [This is] the Supernal Torah, which is nullified if is it not carried out with these repairs of it; and this [verse] is said concerning the *Atik Yomin/* Ancient of Days: that is, the Supernal Torah, which is the aspect of the aforementioned *hithbonenuth/* contemplation-understanding, which is nullified and cannot be carried out if it is not accomplished by means of the aforementioned tikkunim, which are the aspect of *Tikkunei `Atik/* Repairs of the Ancient One, the aspect of the aforementioned *arikhuth yamim*. **One verse states [Deut. 33:29], "Ashreikha Yisrael, mi khamokha/** Fortunate are you, Yisrael; who is like you?" This is the aspect of arousal from below, which is the praise of Yisrael who awaken from below, the aspect of *"Ashreikha Yisrael, mi khamokha."* And afterwards it is the arousal from above, as mentioned, which is the aspect of, **"Mi khamokha ba'elim Hashem/ Who is like You among the mighty, Hashem?" He called to Rabbi El`azar his son... and to Rabbi Abba... and said, "Anan klala dekhola/ We are the embodiment of everything!"** That is, the aspect of the completion of the *yir'ah/* fear, which is by means of the aspect of the three pillars, mentioned above, the aspect of fear of Heaven, fear of one's teacher, and fear of father and mother. Hence by means of Rabbi Shimon, his son Rabbi El`azar and his student Rabbi Abba, the fear is made complete, whereby *arikhuth yamim* comes about, the aspect of *tikkunei `Atik/* repairs of the `*Atik.* **They were silent and heard a sound,** that is, those who were in the aspect of keeping silent, the aspect of the mute, and were unable to speak because of the sleep, as mentioned, **heard a sound,** that is, the aspect of awakening from sleep, the aspect of, "Fortunate is he who speaks to an ear that hears," as mentioned. **And their knees [*aRKu-Vatan*] trembled [lit. kissed each other]:** this is the aspect of procreating, the aspect of bodily relations, for by means of awakening from sleep, which is the aspect of, "To open the mouth of the mute," thereby is the "opening the mouth of barren women," as mentioned, which is the very aspect of the kissing relations which precede the bodily relations, as mentioned. **What was the sound? The voice of the supernal assembly assembling.** That is, the aspect of story tales in which they clothe the faces of the Torah, as mentioned. For the clothing is the aspect of *kanaf/* cover: *"Velo-yikanef `od moreikha/* Yet your Teacher shall no longer hide himself"* [Isa. 30:22]. And by means of this clothing, one rouses [people] from sleep and they begin to talk, in the aspect of, *"Uva`al kenafayim yagid davar/* And that which has wings shall speak the word"* [Eccl. 10:20].

♦ ♦

Likutei Tefilloth #60: Hashem, Shama`ti

[This prayer by R' Nathan corresponds to LM #60 above]

7 32   "*Hashem, shama`ti shim`akha yare'thi; Hashem, pa`alekha bekerev shanim chayeyhu, bekerev shanim todi`a, berogez rachem tizkor*/* Hashem, I heard your sound and feared. Hashem, your works, in the midst of these [bad] years, revive it. In the midst of these years make it known. In wrath remember compassion" [Hab. 3:2]

❝ *Yir'ah vara`ad yavo vi wattekhaseni palatzuth*/ Fear and trembling come upon me, and horror has overwhelmed me" [Ps. 55:6]

❝ *Samar mipachdekha vesari, umimishpateikha yare'thi*/ My flesh shudders for fear of You; and I am afraid of Your judgments" [Ps. 119:120]

❝ *Mi lo-yir'akha melekh hagoyim ki lekha ya'othah, ki vekhol-chakhmei hagoyim uv'khol-malkhutham me'eyn kamokha*/ Who would not fear You, O king of the nations? For it befits You; forasmuch as among all the wise men of the nations, and in all their royalty, there is none like unto You" [Jer. 10:7]

❝ *El na`aratz besod-kedoshim rabbah, venora `al-kol-sevivaw*/ A God dreaded in the great council of the holy ones, and feared of all them that are about Him" [Ps. 89:8]

❝ *`Al-ken mipanaw ebahel, ethbonen we'efchad mimenu*/ Therefore am I affrighted at His presence; when I consider, I am afraid of Him" [Job 23:15]

7 33   Master of the Universe, Almighty, Great and Awesome! Holy are You and Awesome is Your Name; the awe and fear of You is on all the hosts of heaven and on all the Serafim and Ofanim and Chayoth haKodesh, and on all the worlds, upper and lower, and all its inhabitants, upper and lower; they all shudder and fear from Your terrifying name. Be charitous and kind to me in Your great compassion and bestow and draw upon me the holy awe of You, that I may be privileged to fear, revere and tremble before You constantly, in truth. In fear and trembling let us make You king over us, and let us be privileged to feel the awesome fear of You in all our 248 members and 365 sinews, and let the fear of You be over our faces, so that we commit no error or transgres-

sion at all, neither unintentional nor deliberate, from now until forever. And let the fear of Hashem hover over us constantly, in complete truth and steadfastness, till we merit through the fear of Hashem to prolong and expand our days and to add, every day, every period, and every hour, an addition of extra holiness. And let all our days widen, lengthen, and expand, each time more and more, with additional holiness every day, every period and every hour, till we be privileged to the length of days and years that is in holiness, in truth, according to Your good will. And let us not spend our days in vain, God forbid, but only merit to guard all our days and hours, periods and moments, adding, every time, a supplement of added holiness through the fear of Hashem. And let be fulfilled in us the scripture, *"Yir'ath Hashem tosif yamim/* the fear of Hashem adds days" [Prov. 10:27]. And have compassion on us, and see our lowliness and pressure; and in affliction-constriction, widen for us. For You know the astounding greatness of our afflictions, pressure, lowliness and toil that we have each and every day at its beginning, for it is very, very tight for us, and we cannot begin any devotion, Torah, prayer, tzedakah, or any holy deed; and each and every day our inclination overcomes us, God forbid, and makes serving You very, very difficult, without bound or measure, and presses us rigorously and confuses our mind and tires and suppresses our lifeforce, spirit and soul, and shuts and closes all the gates and paths of holiness from in front of us, and wants to confine us, God forbid, in shackles of oppression and iron, and subdue our heart in toil, until we stumble and are left helpless.

7 34 Full of compassion, Lord of all, You alone know the tightness of our hearts, yea, it is bad, yea, it is bitter, yea, it reaches unto the vitality; You have known all the travail that has found us. See our poverty and fight our battle; please be charitous and compassionate to us. Turn to us in compassion, for You are the Master of compassion. And give us power and strength, day by day, moment by moment, hour by hour, time by time, that we constantly be privileged to push off, drive out, and annul our evil inclination from inside us and to receive upon us the yoke of Heaven in love and truth at every hour and time, and to lengthen our days and years by means of the fear of Hashem in truth, adding holiness and purity hour by hour, day by day, week by

week, month by month, and year by year, until we merit to genuine length of days and years, to old age and seniority of holiness,
and let us not lose one day or one hour from all our days, for ever,
such that we merit, when the time comes for us to be gathered to
You in peace, to come and rise up and appear before You with all
our days and years; that they should all be complete, holy and
pure, with additional holiness on top of holiness, "and let us never
be ashamed or embarrassed forevermore."

7 35 And therefore grant it to me in Your great compassion and
guard and deliver me always from deceptive charms and from
the vanity of beauty, and let me neither covet nor crave within my
hearts the vanity of feminine beauty, and let me not gaze upon
them, and let me not stray after my hearts and eyes at all, in accord with the scripture, "*Al-tachmod yofyah bilvaveikha... ki
ba`ad-ishah zonah `ad-kikar-lechem/* Covet not her beauty in your
hearts... for on account of a promiscuous woman [one is brought]
down to a loaf of bread" [Prov. 6:25-26].

7 36 Please, Hashem, in compassion and pity give us a free gift
and charitous donation; have pity on us in Your great compassion, in Your vast compassion, and do not act with us according to our mistakes, and judge us not according to our deeds. Let
us be privileged to turn from evil, and deliver us from such evil;
let us be privileged from now on to perform "sit, and act not,"
truthfully. Have pity on our holy vitality and deliver us from destruction. "*Hatzileni mitit we'al-ethba`ah, inatzelah mison'ai
u'mima`amakei mayim/* Deliver me out of the mire, and let me
not sink; let me be delivered from them that hate me, and out of
the deep waters. *Al-tishtefeni shibboleth mayim, we'al-tivla`eini
metzulah, we'al-te'tar-alai be'er piyah/* Let not the water flood
overwhelm me, neither let the deep swallow me up; and let not
the pit shut her mouth upon me" [Ps. 69:15-16]. For, "*Mah-betza`
bedami, beridh'ti el-shachath; hayodekah `afar, hayagid
amitekha/* What profit is there in my blood, when I go down to the
pit? Shall the dust praise You? Shall it declare Your truth" [Ps.
30:10]? For I do not know how to be alert and guard against what
I need to guard against; just on You alone I cast my lot. Here I am
before You full of shame and disgrace: do with me what You will
do in your great compassion and Your vast kindness and bring me
back in complete repentance before You in truth, and deliver me

from blemish of the Covenant and let no evil musing or bad thought at all come upon me. And sanctify me with Your highest holiness constantly, and guard me and deliver me always from the deceit of charm and the vanity of beauty, and let me be privileged to not conduct myself with any false charm, not in sitting, standing, walking, eating, talking with people, or in any of the rest of the movements and involvements with people, which people are very much trapped in, in these deceptive charms, and conduct themselves with a special charm for each and every movement.

7 37 Please, Hashem, have pity on me, and guard me and deliver me from all sorts of deceptive charms, and let me not be trapped in them at all, in no movement and no enterprise, but just let all my actions be for the sake of Heaven, with no turning to self-aggrandizement to find favor in the eyes of people, God forbid. And let all my intentions and all my movements and endeavors be only for Your fame alone, for Hashem alone, and let me draw upon myself complete fear, always, from before You, in truth, and let the fear of Heaven be on me as much as the fear of flesh and blood, until I merit through the fear to lengthen, widen and expand my days and years in upper holiness. And let us merit to illuminate and draw upon us and all Yisrael a great illumination and holiness from the "repairs of the Ancient One," which are accomplished and drawn down through the true Tzaddikim and the Elders in holiness; and thereby let us merit to great wealth of holiness. And guard us and deliver us always from promiscuous craving, and help us that we should be privileged to have compassion on ourselves, to guard the moisture and lipids in our body, that they should go up to the brain to complete and expand our mind in great holiness; and let them not go out, God forbid, by excessive relations, God forbid, and deliver us from the spirit of folly and insanity which comes by sexual craving, God forbid, through which the moisture and lipids of the body dry up, and from which all the insane people in the world arise. Have pity on us and deliver us from this, and let us have mercy on our bodies, lifeforces, spirits and souls, and let us very much guard the lipids in our bodies. And deliver us from short-spiritedness and interrupted breathing, and let us be privileged to length of breath, that we should merit to draw upon us always the spirit of

life that is in holiness at all times, all hours and each and every moment. And guard our intellects always, and let us be privileged to always and at all times draw holy oils to our intellects, until our intellects blaze in great contemplative discernment [hithbonenut] of holiness, and let our brains and intellects progressively increase in great holiness in truth. And let us merit to the great holy wealth that is drawn from the discards of the Tablets, wherefrom Moshe was enriched, until we merit thereby to the highest hithbonenut, very great, holy and awesome, that is drawn down via great riches of holiness.

7 38 And let us merit to complete awe in all its aspects, in all its parts, specifics and details, and let the three lines of fear be drawn upon us, which are each composed of three, which are: fear of Heaven, fear of one's rav, and fear of father and mother, in all their parts and aspects. "And put the awe of You, Hashem Eloheinu, on all your works, and the fear of You on all that You have created, and let all Your works fear You and let all creatures prostrate before You, and let them all make one band to perform Your will with whole hearts."

7 39 And therefore have compassion on us with Your great compassion and Your great and enormous lovingkindness, and wake us up from our slumber, for due to our great transgressions the sleep has overcome us, with great strength, until it has been many days and years that true Tzaddikim have been involved with us to rouse us and awaken us from our sleep and lethargy, and with many great ways and aspects and turns and great and enormous exertions they have toiled and labored for us and focused His Blessed Godliness toward us, and illuminated the faces of the holy Torah for us, and clothed the faces of the holy Torah for us with many, many faces, in Torah expositions and Stories of the Ancient, as with everything we have seen in their holy books and heard from their holy mouths, things high, vast and awesome up to the Ein Sof, things that stand at the peak of the summit of the universe, things drawn down from You in truth, things that have in them power to rouse and awaken all the people of the world, all of them, from their great sleep, big and small alike — and still we have not awakened and not turned back from our error. And now do we have more charity to shout for to the King? What is there to do for us that He has not done

for us, through his holy and awesome Tzaddikim and sages who were in each and every era from the giving of the holy Torah until today, who all, united, rouse and awaken us with great arousal, *"ve'ein ish sam `al-lev/* and no man takes it to heart"* [Isa. 57:1], and I am poor, aching and exhausted; I have no escape and deliverance except I cry out and shout: *"Qoli el-Hashem ekra, veya`aneni mehar kodsho, Selah/* With my voice I call out to Hashem, and he answers me out of His holy mountain, Selah. *Ani shakhavti va'ishanah, hekitzoti ki Hashem yismekheni/* I lay me down, and I sleep; I awake, for Hashem sustains me" [Ps. 3:5-6].

7 40 Answer, Hashem, before Whom there is no sleep and slumber, as written, *"Hineh lo-yanum welo yishan shomer Yisrael/* Behold, He who guards Yisrael neither sleeps nor slumbers" [Ps. 121:4]. And You rouse the sleeping and awaken those who slumber; "You revive the dead and heal the sick; You make the blind see and make the bent erect; You give speech to the mute and release the bound" — answer, in Your great compassion! Rouse me please! Awaken me please! Please raise me up in Your great compassion! *"Peneh-elai wechoneni, ki-yachid we`oni ani/* Turn Yourself to me and be gracious to me, for I am solitary and afflicted. *Tzaroth levavi hirchivu, mimtzukothai hotzieni/* The troubles of my hearts are enlarged, bring me out of my distress. *Re'eh `onyiy ve`amali, wesa lekhol-chatothai/* See my affliction and my travail, and forgive all my sins. *Re'eh-oyvai ki-rabu, wesin'ath chamas sene'uni/* See how many are mine enemies, and the cruel hatred wherewith they hate me. *Shomerah nafshi wehatzileni, al-evosh ki-chasiti vakh/* Keep my soul and deliver me, let me not be ashamed, for I have taken refuge in You." [Ps. 25:16-19]. Help me and be gracious to me, from now on, that I should be privileged to wake up from my great slumber which has overcome me by my evil deeds, and also by craving food and drink. Help me wake up in great arousal and return to You in truth for truth's sake, very expediently, and save me from now on from all kinds of errors, sins and transgressions, and be always with me, and keep me and deliver me from the blemish of craving food and drink, and let me be privileged that my eating should always be in great holiness and purity without any physical craving at all, and let my eating and drinking always be from food that has been refined for human consumption, and shield about me

and guard me and deliver me, that into my mouth should not come any food or drink that has not yet been refined for human consumption, whereby one can destroy, God forbid, the face of holiness, and fall into sleep, God forbid. Just let me merit to eat, in great holiness, foods that have been refined, foods that are in the sanctity of the *Lechem Hapanim*/ Shewbread, so that I may attain through them a good heart, a happy heart, and faces of holiness; and deliver me from foods that bring badness upon the heart.

7 41 Master of the Universe! Deliver me from badness of heart, deliver me from crookedness in the heart, grant me goodness of hearts in truth. Do free charity for me, and order, in Your great compassion, to bring back and return to me, soon, all the lost things that I have lost until now, and draw upon me the faces of holiness that are drawn from the Ancient, from the Splendor of the Face, wherein are rooted all the seventy faces of the Torah. "*Kechasdekha chayeni we'eshmerah `eduth pikha*/ Quicken me according to Your lovingkindness, and I will observe the testimony of Your mouth" [Ps. 119:88]. "*Chanun werachum Hashem, erekh apayim ug'dol-chased*/ Hashem is gracious and full of compassion; slow to anger, and of great mercy" [Ps. 145:8]. "*Lekha amar libi, bakeshu fanai; eth-paneikha, Hashem, avakesh*/ In Your behalf my heart has said: 'Seek My face;' Your face, Hashem, will I seek. *Al-taster paneikha mimeni, al-tat be'af `avdekha; `ezrathi hayiytha al-titesheni we'al-ta`azveni, Elohei yish`i*/ Hide not Your face from me; put not away Your servant in anger; You have been my help; cast me not off, neither forsake me, O God of my salvation" [Ps. 27:8-9]. "*Ha'ira faneikha `al `avdekha, hoshi`eni vechasdekha*/ Make Your face to shine upon Your servant; save me in Your lovingkindness" [Ps. 31:17]. "*Paneikha ha'er be`avdekha, welamedeni eth-chukeikha*/ Make Your face to shine upon Your servant; and teach me Your statutes" [Ps. 119:135]. "*Peneh elai wechoneni, tena `uzekha le`avdekha wehoshi`ah leven amathekha*/ Turn unto me, and be gracious unto me; give Your strength unto Your servant, and save Your handmaid's son" [Ps. 86:16]. Hashem, "*Elohim-Tzeva'oth, hashivenu; weha'er paneikha wenivashe`ah*/ O God of hosts, restore us; and cause Your face to shine, and we shall be saved" [Ps. 80:8]. "`*Ura khevodi, `ura hanevel wekhinor; a`ira shachar*/ Awake, my glory; awake, psaltery and harp; I will awake the dawn" [Ps. 57:9].

7 42 And have compassion on me and save me and let me be privileged to be in the category of fit and proper scholars, that I should be privileged to thoroughly hear and remember the sound of the true Tzaddikim's words: all that they have performed and done for us, all the holy words that we have been privileged to hear from their mouths and from the mouth of their writing, all the big and awesome things, all the great work of Hashem which they have done for us, who left after them a blessing, their holy books, "*Hanechemadim mizahav umipaz rav, umthukim midvash venofeth tzufim*/ More to be desired are they than gold, yea, than much fine gold; sweeter also than honey and the honeycomb" [Ps. 19:11], which illuminate the eyes and bring back the soul from the ways of death to the ways of life. And let me be privileged that their words should enter in my ears and my heart, and let me listen well to their holy words and not forget a word from my reviews.

7 43 Please, be gracious to my lifeforce, so very weak and wretched, and have pity on me with Your great pity, and give me hope and let me not perish, and give me a goodly end and be gracious to me from now on, that I should merit from today to remind myself of all the words of Hashem which we have heard from our holy rabbis z"l, in such a way that I should be privileged to really wake up from my great sleep. For I go about, wandering, like a sheep without a shepherd, like a mast on a mountaintop, and like a ship in the heart of the sea. "*Shakadh'ti we'ehyeh ketzipor, boded `al-gag*/ I watch, and am become like a sparrow that is alone upon the housetop" [Ps. 102:8]. Establish, please; rise up, please; be aroused, please; wake up, please; stand up, please; rise up, please; "please supplicate before God with the best pleas;" my soul, my soul, lay flat on the dust, and lay prostrate to Him, and put your mouth to the dust. "*Veshafalth me'eretz tedabri, ume`afar tishach imrathekha*/ And brought down you shalt speak out of the ground, and your speech shall be low out of the dust" [Isa. 29:4]. Maybe there is hope, maybe Hashem Tzeva'ot will give freely, maybe Hashem will do as per all the wonders which he did with our fathers. "*Mah-lekha nirdam, kum kera el-Eloheikha, ulai yith`asheth haElohim lanu velo-novad*/ Why should you slumber? Arise, call upon your God; maybe God will think upon us, that we perish not" [Jonah 1:6]. "Maybe He will be gracious to

a poor and destitute people; maybe he will have compassion."
Awake, my brother, from the slumber of your folly; awaken and
start up. "`Ad-mathai `atzel tishkav; matai takum mishenathekha/
How long will you sleep, sluggard? When will you arouse out of
your sleep? Me`at shenoth, me`at tenumoth, me`at chibuk-yad-
ayim lishkav/ Yet a little sleep, a little slumber, a little folding of
the hands to sleep..." [Prov. 6:9-10]. "Al-titen shenah le`eineikha,
uth'numah le`af apeikha/ Give not sleep to your eyes, nor slumber
to your eyelids. Hinatzel kitzvi miyad, ukh'tzipor mipach yakush/
Deliver yourself as a gazelle from the [hunter's] hand, and as a
bird from the hand of the fowler" [Prov. 6:4-5]. "Zekhor al-
tishkach eth asher-hiktzafta eth-Hashem Eloheikha/ Remember,
forget not, how you have made Hashem your God wroth" [Deut.
9:7] these many days and years, and nevertheless the mercies of
Hashem have not ceased from you, and at all times He is involved
in rousing you up and waking you up from your sleep in His great
generosity. Remember this; how much have they roused you and
woken you up with many kinds of rousing? — without bound,
measure or count, which would not be believed if it were told that
it were possible to sleep from the sound of such shouting, arousal,
proclamation, hinting, flashes, in the revealed and in the hidden,
"Qol gadol welo-yasaf/ With a great voice, and it did not cease"
[Deut. 5:19]; "Veqol shofar chazak me'od/ and the voice of a horn
exceeding loud" [Ex. 19:16], progressively increasing its sound every day and at all times and all hours. "Hen yiten beqolo kol `oz/
Lo, He utters His voice, a mighty voice" [Ps. 68:34], effectively
saying, "`Uru yeshenim mitardemathkhem, wenirdamim hakitzu
mitnumathkhem/ Wake up, sleepers, from your slumber, and
drowsy ones, start up from your dozing!" — and still you have not
ceased from your error; still you roll around in the street, amidst
the mire and mud, amidst the deep mire of vanities. Do you still
not return, do you still pave over your lifeforce and not set it free,
that it should return to do the will of He who formed you and created you, which is its entire strong and enormous desire, yearning
and longing?

744 And do not despair, God forbid, and say that your sins are
with you, and that you've become spoiled in them, God forbid,
and that it is impossible for you to still return from your folly and
nonsense, for your sins have gone past your head, to the point

that, God forbid, your victory and hope are lost, alas, alas — be gracious and have compassion on yourself and on your few days that you still have allotted for you to tarry a little in this world which passes as an eye blinks, and do not say such things, God forbid, for this is worse than before, for thoughts, conceptions and confusions such as these are grave and harmful, and make angry your Creator more than all the mistakes, sins and transgressions that you have done from your inception until this day, for you still have great hope at any time, any hour and any moment. "*Chasdhei Hashem ki lo-thamnu, ki lo-khalu rachamaw/* Surely Hashem's mercies are not consumed, surely His compassions fail not" [Lam. 3:22]. Eternal and concealed from you is — and you will not know — the enormous vastness of His great compassion and kindness that is upon all items to return in truth, even though they have not yet returned, and His entire Blessed salvation and desire is to return to and to have compassion on all those who wait upon, look out for, yearn for, and strive with resilience to find, deliverance and escape to Hashem Yithbarakh, even though [circumstances] wax stronger upon them at all times and do not leave them many days and years to return to their Father's house; nevertheless, His lovingkindness has been very, very strong upon them and us, without bound, measure or number, which the mouth cannot speak and the heart cannot conceive. If all the seas were ink and all the lakes quills, and all mankind scribes and tongues full of praise, it would not suffice to describe and explain one thousandth or ten-thousandth of His vast lovingkindness which He practices generously in every era, and especially on those who are groaning, crushed, waiting, and expectant to return to Him, Yithbarakh, in truth. "*Halo' me`ata karatha [lo] avi, aluf ne`uraim atah, hayintor le`olam, im-yishmor lanetzach/* Did you not just now cry unto [Him]: My father, You are the friend of my youth. Will He bear grudge for ever? Will He keep it to the end" [Jer. 3:4-5]? Be strong and be strengthened! And renew yourself at all times, and begin from now on to serve your Creator in truth, and forsake your bad ways, and your indecent thoughts and the remnants of your vanities and nonsenses — "*vehaser ka`as milibekha veha`aver ra`ah mibsarekha/* therefore remove vexation from your heart, and put away evil from your flesh" [Eccl. 11:10]. Tie yourself truly to Hashem Yithbarakh and return no more to folly. Draw your eyes on high and remember your love of old; wake up, wake up, arise, my lifeforce, arise! "*Uri uri dabri-shir*/ Awake, awake, utter a song" [Judg. 5:12]. "*Al-techerash we'al-tiskhot*/ Hold not Your peace, and be not still" [Ps. 83:2]. Lift up your sweet voice, open your mouth and bring out your pleasant utterances before Hakadosh Barukh Hu, open your mouth and let your words shine!

745 And therefore privilege me in Your great compassion that I should merit, through awakening from sleep, strong speech of holiness, that I should merit in Your compassion to speak holy words continually, with great power, true devotion and with a whole heart, and let me merit to put all my power into the words of prayer and all the holy words, and let be fulfilled the scripture, "*Barekhu Hashem mal'akhav giborei koach `osei devaro lishmo`a beqol devaro*/ Bless Hashem, [you] angels of His, mighty in strength, that fulfill His word, hearkening unto the voice of His word" [Ps. 103:20].

746 And let me be privileged to great *bitachon* [trust, confidence] of holiness, for You know the enormous lack of sustenance at this time, for the money is no more and there isn't a coin in the pocket, and the needs of Your people are extremely great, for the necessities alone are also very great: the necessities of food, drink, clothing, shelter and the rest of the mandatory needs. "*Wa'anachnu lo neda` mah-na`aseh, ki `aleikha `einenu*/ Neither know we what to do; but our eyes are upon You" [II Chron. 20:12], for "*lo'-itanu yode`a `ad-mah*/ there is no one among us that knows how much" [Ps. 74:9], for we are unable to know to what extent, from where, to request sustenance, and we have no hope or surety except in You alone. Our eyes are only turned to You, therefore we have come to ask of You, full of compassion, that You be gracious to us in Your great kindness, and bestow on us the trait of *bitachon* in entirety, that we should merit to trust in You honestly and in complete steadfastness, with a strong and courageous trust that You will fill all our lackings and You will give us our sustenance completely, and You in Your compassion will fill up compassion upon us at all times, and You will give us all our needs and all the needs of your households with great expanse, and You will summon to us our sustenance before we need them, in permissible means and not forbidden, honorably and not

shamefully, generously and not meagerly, from under Your wide and full hand, in such a way that we can merit to do Your will all the days of our lives forever.

7 47 And let us be privileged that our words should be in great sanctity, such that we will have power to make barren women conceive by means of our words, and let our speech organs be in akin to our reproductive organs, and let us produce, through our sanctified speech, sanctified progeny, and let Your people Yisrael grow numerous like the sand on the seashore and like the stars in the sky in multitude, and let none be a barren man or barren woman among us; and visit with child all the childless, with enduring progeny, for Your service and Your fear. And through this let us merit that complete awe, great awe, will be revealed in the world, and bestow the awe and fear of You on all the inhabitants of the world, "and let every work of creation know that it is You that have made it, and let every formation discern that it is You that have formed it." And let us merit to all the parts of awe, in entirety, and through awe let us merit to subjugate, break and annul deceptive charm and the vanity of beauty, as written, "*Sheker hachen vehevel hayofi, ishah yirath-Hashem hi tith'hallal.*" And let us merit to lengthen our days and years in great sanctity, adding sanctity and purity at all times, so that "we should not toil in vain and not beget chaos," and let us merit to repair of all the worlds, anew, and to continually draw upon us the illumination of "the repairs of the Ancient One" which are drawn by the true Tzaddikim and the holy Elders. And in their merit let us be privileged to great bounty and wealth of holiness, to all the worldly good, such that we merit through this wealth, the very greatest and highest *hithbonenuth /* contemplative discernment-understanding in Your Torah, devotion, and perception of Your Godliness in great sanctity and purity, truthfully and in whole faith, according to Your good will, in truth, from now and forevermore.

7 48 *Elohim yechonenu wiyvarekhenu, ya'er panaw itanu, Selah/* God be gracious unto us, and bless us; may He cause His face to shine toward us, Selah [Ps. 67:2]. *Nora Elohim mimikdasheikha El Yisrael hu noten `oz weta`atzumoth la`am, barukh Elohim/* Awful is God out of Your holy places; the God of Yisrael, He gives strength and power unto the people; blessed be God [Ps.

68:36]. *Yir'ei Hashem haleluhu, kol zera` Ya`akov kabeduhu, veg-uru mimenu kol-zera` Yisrael/* Ye that fear Hashem, praise Him; all ye the seed of Ya`akov, glorify Him; and stand in awe of Him, all ye the seed of Yisrael. *Ki lo-bazah velo-shiketz `enuth `oni, velo-histir panaw mimenu, uv'shav`o elaw shame`a/* For He has not despised nor abhorred the lowliness of the poor; neither has He hid His face from him; but when he cried unto Him, He heard [Ps. 22:24-5]. *Yevarekhenu Elohim weyir'u otho kol-afsei aretz/* May God bless us; and let all the ends of the earth fear Him [Ps. 67:8]. *Reishith chokhmah yir'ath Hashem, sekhel tov lekhol-`osei-hem, tehilatho `omedeth la`ad/* The fear of the Hashem is the beginning of wisdom; a good understanding have all they that do thereafter; His praise endures for ever [Ps. 111:10]. *Barukh Hashem Elohim, Elohei Yisrael `oseh nifla'oth levado, uvarukh shem kevodo le`olam, weyimale khevodo eth-kol ha'aretz, Amen ve'amen/* Blessed be Hashem-Elohim, the God of Israel, who alone does wondrous things. And blessed be His glorious name for ever; and let the whole earth be filled with His glory. Amen, and Amen [Ps. 72:18-9].

Likutei Moharan II #61: H"Y is Above Time

Hashem Yithbarakh is above time, as has been written. And this matter is truly a very wonderful and hidden thing, and it is impossible to understand this through human intellect. But know: the essence of time is only because one does not understand: that is, because our intellect is small. For, the greater one's intellect, the more time is reduced and nullified. For, in a dream, when one's intellect goes away and he has nothing but the power of imagination, then in a quarter-hour one can experience an entire seventy years, the way it appears in the dream, as many, many periods pass by in a very short time. And then when one wakes up from sleep, he sees that all these times and the seventy years which passed in his sleep are really a very short period. And this is because afterwards, when awake, then his intellect returns to him, and in the intellect, all these seventy years that transpired in the dream are just a quarter-hour for him.

Except, an actual seventy years are also considered seventy years at our intellect; but in truth, at a higher intellect above our intellect, what is considered seventy real years by us is also only a quarter-hour or less. For, as we can see, that a person can pass seventy years in a dream, and in truth we know afterwards in our intellect that it is but a quarter hour — just the same way, that which is considered seventy real years by our intellect is, at a higher, loftier intellect, only a quarter hour. Except, we do not discern this, for in a dream too, if someone would come to him and say to him that all of this, which appears to him that days and years are transpiring, are nothing, and it is all just a quarter hour, he certainly would not believe him at all, for according to his imagination, it appears in the dream that real days and years pass by. Just the same, even though by us, according to our intellect, it seems that *this* is the period of seventy years, at a greater intellect it is only a quarter hour. And thus higher and higher, so that at an intellect that is even higher up further, even the time that is at an intellect higher than ours is only considered a very little and minor span, there at the further higher intellect. And thus higher and higher, to the extent that there is an intellect so high that there, all the time in its entirety does not count at all, for on account of the great enormity of the intellect, all the time is entirely null and zero completely, just as by us, the seventy years that transpire in a dream are only really a quarter hour, as mentioned. Thus there is intellect above intellect, until time is nullified completely.

And therefore, Mashiach, who experienced what he experienced from the creation of the world and endured what he endured — after all this, at the end, Hashem Yithbarakh will say to him, *"Beni atah, ani hayom yelidh'tikha/ You are my son, this day have I begotten you"* (Ps. 2). And the thing is very astounding and wondrous, apparently, but this is all due to great astoundingness of Mashiach's intellect, in accord with the greatness of his level which he will hold by at that time; and due to the exceeding enormity of his intellect's level, which will grow very, very great at that time, therefore all the time which has transpired over him from the world's creation until that time, will all be null and zero, tangibly, as if he was born today, for all time will be nullified in his intellect, which will be very vast. And therefore Hashem Yithbarakh will say to him, "Today I have begotten you" — today, tangibly, as all the time which has transpired is entirely null and zero, as mentioned.

And thus too we see in space, how a strong person can traverse a place in a short time; hence for him all this space is small, while for weak people this place is considered vast and one needs to walk a long time until passing through that place. And thus higher and higher: the greater one's strength, the smaller space is for him. And thus higher and higher, until space is nullified completely, except that in our intellect it is impossible to discern all this; just as it is impossible to discern in a dream the truth, that all that time that appears to him in the dream is truly nothing at all, so too with us: we cannot discern that all our time is nothing, above, in the upper intellect, as mentioned.

Likutei Tefilloth II #32: Asaperah El-Choq

[This prayer by R' Nathan is based on the above torah LM II #61]

347 "*Asaperah el-choq, Hashem amar elai beni atah, ani hayom yelidh'tikha/* I will tell of the decree: Hashem said unto me: 'You are My son, this day have I begotten you'" [Ps. 2:7]. Master of the Universe! Ever Live and Eternally Enduring! "It is You Who were before creating the world, and it is You after You created the world," for You are above time. And all of time in its entirety, whatever was and whatever will be, doesn't count by You so much as an eyeblink. Have compassion on me in Your great compassion, and give me a true and complete knowledge and intellect, such that I may merit to go out from the restriction of time; that I should merit to know, discern, and perceive that all of time is nothing, "*ki hakol havel/* for all is vaporous," and our days pass like a shadow, and truthfully time does not exist at all for someone who has true intellect and knowledge. Rather, all of time stems from lack of consciousness, that in Your wonders and awesome things, You conceal this knowledge from mankind in order that time should exist, and it is all for the sake of free choice. But really, in true consciousness, there is no time at all. Let us be privileged to connect ourselves and be subsumed, truly, in True Tzaddikim, who attained this completely, subsuming themselves with their entire consciousness into the aspect of above time, exiting out from time completely, and escaping in entirety from all the evil doings done under the sun and within time. Let us be privileged to walk in their footsteps, go in their ways, and fulfill their counsels, without gazing whatsoever at the things that are within time, wherein are included all the cravings and evil traits. And let the impacts of time not panic us at all, but let us just merit each day and at all times and hours to remind ourselves of the nullification of time, that in truth, time is null and void, and connecting ourselves at all times with the aspect of above time, where all the cravings and traits and all the confusions, which all derive from the impacts of time, are annulled.

348 Master of the Universe! Master of the Universe, Primal of all primalities, Head of all headings, and Final of all ends, You have let us known, from afar, such lofty things, such awe-

some clues, and have hinted to us from afar, ways of Your awesome wonders, to enliven us "as sure as it is today," to restore our
vitalities in the depth of this long exile's bitterness, to remind us
the greatness of Your awesomenesses, to strengthen, encourage
and console us in all our afflictions, insofar as we have already
suffered many afflictions, bad and uncountable, since the day of
the Destruction until here, insofar as nearly "the power to endure
has faltered," for this exile has been extended for us very, very
much, and already all the final times have passed, "*ve'lo'-itanu
yode`a `ad-mah/* nor is there any among us that knows how long"
[Ps. 74:9], "`*Ad-mathai ketz hapela'oth/* How long will it be until
the secret end?" [Dan. 12:6]; and many of Your people have stumbled and fallen thereby, by the prolongation of this so bitter exile.
But in truth, You long consider to make our end good, with awesome and wonderful goodnesses which have never before been
heard, and "there is hope for [our] future" [Jer. 31:16], therefore
You have hinted to us from afar and informed us even now, a
wonderful glimmering from the aspect of above time, in order that
we should know and hold firm that all the protraction of the exiles' and sufferings' time — what has happened to Yisrael since
the day of the exiles in generality and in particular, everything
that has happened to each and every one — it is all reckoned as
nothing and will all be forgotten and nullified completely at the
time when the whole consciousness will be revealed through our
righteous Mashiach, who should come quickly in our days, so that
we may be privileged to attain this consciousness of the aspect of
supratemporality.

3 49 Therefore have compassion on us even now, and shine on
us an illumination of this holy consciousness, which is
Mashiach's light, in such a manner that we should merit to subdue and nullify all the cravings and bad traits by constantly remembering the obliteration of time. For, time runs and drifts and
dissipates a great deal, and does not tarry or stay put even one
moment, and there is no grasping it at all, for in truth time does
not exist at all. Be nice to us with Your great compassion and deliver us from the impacts of time, and let us not exchange the
world that stands for eternity for the passing world, God forbid.
Give us freely, from You, true consciousness and intellect in such
a way that we shall merit to discern and see the annulment of

time. And let time not deceive us at all, and let us begin anew in Your service each day and at all times, and let whatever should happen to us not confuse us at all, until that hour comes. And let us merit at all times to sanctify ourselves, truthfully, and to connect and subsume all of time into the aspect of supratemporality, until we merit to go out from under time and space, to the aspect of above time, above space, according to Your will and the will of Your True Tzaddikim, who attained this in entirety, in truth.

> *Hashivenu Hashem eleikha venashuvah,*
> *chadesh yameinu keqedem/*
> Restore us, Hashem, to You, and we shall be restored; make our days new as before" [Lam. 5:21].

Likutei Halakhoth O"C Tefillin
Halakhah 5

1   According to the most awesome story of the Seven Beggars..

2   Let us return to our subject. Behold, it is explained there..

3   And this is the aspect of tefillin, for tefillin are the aspect..

4   And the essence of tefillin Brains are the aspect of life of..

5   So behold, the main intent... for practical application..

6   For, the essence of tefillin is the flashing of the brains..

7   The rule is that any man who wants to consider the..

8   And this is the aspect of "Long-Tempered (Erekh Apayim)..

9   And all of them get strength from the aspect of the Elder..

10   And all this is the aspect of tefillin, which are the..

15   And this is the aspect of, "Sanctify to Me all firstborns..
Renewing Life~Kohen~Supratemporal Aspect of the Blind One~Tefillin Knot

18   And this is the aspect of Hashem Yithbarakh's extolling..
Tefillin Straps~Navel~David-Mashiach~Adam's Mistake~ Everlasting life after death~Long Life of the Blind One

23   And this is the aspect of Rosh Hashanah..
Day of Remembrance~The Blind One's Memory~Renew life

34   And therefore it is necessary to write tefillin on the hide..
Hide~Imagination~Straps Descend to the Navel~All the Elders Receive from the Blind One

36   And this is "And it came to pass, when the midwives..
Receiving the Repairs and Making Housings via Fear~ Aharon~8 Tikunei Diqna~Moshe~the Supernal Elder~Young and Old~Priesthood, Royalty, Mashiach

The interest of the mitzwah of tefillin of the arm and of the head, and that they must be made from the hide of a clean animal specifically, and written on the *Qelaf*/inner skin; and the interest of the straps, the tunnel, and the rest of their most holy and awesome details; and the interest of Rashi's tefillin and Rabbeinu Tam's tefillin:

POINT #1

Accrding to the most awesome story of the Seven Beggars printed in the book *Sipurei Ma`asiyoth*: See there, on page 96, the interest of the first beggar who was blind, who came to the groom and bride at the wedding after the canopy, and said to them that he gives them a wedding-discourse present, that they should be "old as I... that you should live a long life as I do. And you think that I am blind? Actually I am not blind at all. Only, the whole entire world does not amount to me so much as an eye-blink... for I am very old, but yet I am entirely *yanik* [lit. suckling, nursing] (that is, young), and I have not yet begun living at all. But nevertheless I am very old... And I have a consensus on this from the Great Eagle..."

Take a very thorough look there at all this, and if you have intelligent eyes, you will discern from afar how utterly deep his thoughts are; and it is impossible to fully explain this at all. But whoever truly desires will see and discern from there the greatness of the true great tzaddiqim; the enormity of their greatness, as each and every one had attained what he boasted of there. For everything that is explained there in the story of each one, is regarding the boasting of some utterly great and awesome tzaddiq boasting in the upper worlds, in the place where he boasted that he attained what he attained in this world. How fortunate is he! How fortunate is his lot!

For example, in the interest that will be explained below, that the elders boasted, and each one told what he remembers from his first memory etc.: The youngest of all was most utterly high, the enormity of his greatness and the validity of his sanctity inconceivable. For example, insofar as one of them boasted that he remembers what was happening to him when they cut his umbilical cord — look, discern, and see: is there even one person in the era who can boast like this one, that his material body is so pure and sanctified that he manages to remember what was happening to him then at the beginning of birth, when he emerged into the world's atmosphere, when they cut his umbilical cord? And he was merely the least of them.

And from him, see how high is the sanctity of the second holy elder, in whose eyes the level of the first elder was laughable, and he said in surprise, "That's an old story?! I remember that story, but I also remember when the light was shining," and the Great Eagle later explained that this is his remembering even what happened to him when he was in his mother's womb, when a light was kindled over his head, as explained there. So behold, the level of the second is higher than the first.

One can understand a little, from afar, even though we are most utterly far from this. For, the major difference in a person, before he emerges in the world's air versus afterwards, is explained in our Rabbis z"l's words in the Gemara (*Niddah* 30), and is explained in the holy Zohar. For during pregnancy when he is in his mother's womb, a "candle" is alight over his head, and he can look and see from one end of the world to the other; but when he has emerged into the world's air immediately an angel comes and strikes him on his mouth and he forgets it all. And regarding this said Iyov (Job 29), "O that I were as in the first months, as in the days when my God watched over me" etc., as explained in our Rabbis z"l's words (there). And a man's entire work is to manage to know and attain what he knew before whilst a light was blazing over his head, which is when he gazed at the Light Stored Up From the Seven Days of Creation, with which the man saw from one end of the world to the other, as is brought.

So, now see and discern how much greater is the second elder's level than the first; like the heavens are high above the earth, etc. And similarly the third more than the second, and so all of them. For, the least of them was so very utterly high that there is no one like him but one person in many generations, and nevertheless in compare to the second who is greater than him he is considered a mere speck, and similarly the second versus the third etc. etc., on and on — up until the one who boasted that he was altogether a suckling babe then, who is the Blind Beggar himself, insofar as he said that he recalls all these stories, plus he remembers "Nothing At All" etc.; see there.

For, this is a big rule and is explained and understood in Chazal's words and the Arizal's writings, that even the highest level of all, nevertheless compared to the even higher level, everything is considered but a mere point, as written in the holy Zohar (*Tikkun* #70 p. 123). Even the *Kether `Elyon* is paltry in compare to the `Ilath ha`Iloth etc., and all these greatnesses and wonders are explained in the story of the First Day, and similarly each Day many, many wondrous things that each person boasted of are explained, for example on the Second Day regarding the good life, and similarly on the rest of the Days, regarding the Little Holding the Much, and regarding the Pair of Holy Birds, which he is able to reunite etc. etc. Open your eyes and see what a man can attain in this world, that a man born of a woman can attain such high things that Hashem Yithbarakh himself glories in them (and see more in our words in *Even ha`Ezer Hilkhoth [P"U] Ishuth* [#3], where we also talk a little regarding the holy story of the Sixth Day regarding the Power in the Hands; see there).

And our holy Rabbi z"l knew about all of them, and had the knowledge to tell the story that happened at the place where it happened with all of them, and verily said of himself when he told this story, that if the world knew nothing else but this story, he would still be a most original person. But here is not the place to prolong discussing this. (See below at the end of the *derush*, what is brought there from the *Yerushalmi Kethuboth* regarding the aforementioned marvels of the elders' memories.)

POINT #2

Let us return to our subject. Behold, it is explained there that he said that each one should tell an old story, what he remembers from his first memory etc.

- and the first person among them told that he remembers even when they cut the apple from the tree, that is, when they cut his umbilical cord etc.
- and the second one told that he also remembers the light shining, that is, what happened with him during pregnancy, when a light was blazing above his head etc.
- and the third one told that he also remembers when his body began taking form etc.
- and the fourth told that he also remembers when they were bringing out the seed to plant the fruit, namely when the droplet emerged during relations
- and the fifth one told that he remembers even the sages who were bringing out the seed, that is, he remembers when he was still in the brain etc.

- and the sixth, seventh and eighth remembered even the appearance, the taste and the smell before they were infused upon the fruit, which are the aspect of *Nefesh-Ruach-Neshamah* etc.

And the *yanik* [infantile, lit. suckling], who is the Blind Beggar himself who is telling all this, said he remembers "Nothing At All," for he is above everything and remembers even what was before *NR"N*, which is the aspect of *EYN*/Nothingness etc. etc.. Take a good look there, and if you wish to look with an honest eye, you will see from afar the wonders of Hashem, the likes of which have been never heard or seen since the creation of the world.

POINT #3

And this is the aspect of tefillin, for tefillin are the aspect of memory, as written (Ex. 13), "*ulzikaron bein `eyneikha*/and for remembrance between your eyes" — *and for remembrance between your eyes* specifically, for memory depends mainly on *Tikkun `Eynayim*/Proper Repair of the Eyes, as discerned in this story, as this "blind" one — who was entirely blind to this world, who had no sight of this world at all, to the extent that he attained that the whole world did not amount to him so much as an eyeblink, which this is the essence of Tikkun `Eynayim — he attained the ultimate perfection of memory that has no perfection beyond it, as explained above, as this Blind One remembers more than all of them etc., as written there in the story.

Hence, memory depends mainly on the eyes, and thus it is explained in the torah "*Wayhi Miqetz — Zikaron*" (*LM* #54), that memory depends mainly on the eyes, see there, and he brings there the verse, "*ulzikaron bein `eyneikha*", see there, for tefillin are the aspect of *Mochin deGadluth*/Brains of Grown Maturity, which is the essence of memory on the side of holiness, for memory is the aspect of consciousness and awareness, as explained in the torah "*Dirshu Hashem*/Seek Hashem" (*LM* #37), and this is the aspect of head tefillin and hand tefillin, amongst which there are eight *parshiyoth*/text-passages, four of the head and four of the arm, corresponding to the eight holy elders who are masters of memory, which is the aspect of tefillin — "and for remembrance between your eyes" as mentioned.

For, it is known in the Qawanoth that the head tefillin are in the Male aspect and the arm tefillin are in the Female aspect, and all together the tefillin are in the aspect of *Mochin de`Ibur Sheini deGadluth*/Second-Embryonic Mature Brainphase, and this is the aspect of these holy elders, who attained such Mature Brains that each one attained remembering and reaching more of the beginning; what happened with him before in the beginning. And the more that one of them attained, the earlier the beginning that he could remember and reach, as explained above. And behold, they are eight elders partitioned into two fours, corresponding to two fours of parshiyoth of arm and of head. For the first four elders who first boasted of their memory, their whole concern was with what happened with the baby in its mother's womb: the emergence of the droplet until the cutting of the umbilical cord when it goes out into the world's air. Namely, the one boasted he remembers them bringing the seed to plant the fruit, which is the passage of the droplet etc., the second remembers the beginning of the fruit's formation, the third remembers when the light was shining, which is all the days of the embryo, and the fourth, the last, remembers the essence of birth's conclusion, which is the cutting of the umbilical cord, which is the beginning of his entering this world. (And these four are written here from top to bottom, the opposite of how they are written in the book of stories, and this is because here I have to begin from the fourth, so due to the flow of language the order is reversed, but the intention is the same).

Hence all these four stories tell of the great wonders of the Creator, Blessed Is His Name; what happens with the embryo in its mother, and so all these Brains and perceptions that these four elders attained are in the aspect of Female Brains, which are the aspect of the four parshiyoth of the arm tefillin which are the Female Brains as mentioned. And these aspects that these four elders told about are the aspect of Light-Water-Firmament mentioned in the holy Zohar and the *Qawanoth*. For, at the beginning of the droplet's emergence, which is the aspect of the one who tells that he remembers them bringing out the seed etc., this is the aspect of Light, for it still has no Form, and then when it began to initially take form it is like Water, and then the embryo changes every day of pregnancy; this is the aspect of Firmament, as is known. And then when the aspect of Firmament is finished he goes out in the air of the world and is born, and all this is the aspect of tefillin, which are the aspect of incubation and birth, which is the aspect of Yetziath Mitzrayim, as is known.

And the first four elders, all of what they told was what happened before the droplet descended into its mother's womb. For, they told that they remember when the droplet was still in its father's brain, and the Look, the Taste and the Smell which are the aspect of Nefesh-Ruach-Neshamah, which is where is the beginning of drawing the thought from where it is drawn from the place where it drawn, from cause to effect, from world to world, from intellect to intellect, which are the aspect of Neshamah, Ruach and Nefesh, until the thought is generated, whereby the holy progenitive droplet is generated. And all these four aspects occur with the father, in the Male aspect, as mentioned. And so they are in the aspect of the head tefillin which are the Male Brains as mentioned.

For tefillin are drawn from the aspect of *Tiqunei Diqna*/Features of the Beard, as known, which is the aspect of these elders in holiness, who are all in the aspect of the Holy Beard's Features, which is the root of elderliness on the side of holiness, the aspect of, "*wehadarta penei zaqen*/and you shall honor the elder's face" [Lev. 19:32], as is known. And the essence of the holiness of the tefillin's Brains are drawn from the Most Supernal Elder, the oldest of them all, who is the most suckling babe of them all, who is the Blind Beggar, who was "altogether a suckling babe" etc. as mentioned. For, from him is the essential holiness of elderliness, and all the eight elders who are the aspect of the eight parshiyoth in the tefillin, they all receive from this Most Supernal Elder, who is the Blind One. But his aspect of Brains itself is impossible to enclothe even in the tefillin passages, so there is no parashah corresponding to him, for he is above it all and is the root of it all, as they receive all the tefillin Brains from him, which are the aspect of all the elders in holiness, as mentioned. For he is merged with the Ein Sof, as mentioned, so his Brain is not called memory at all, which is the aspect of tefillin as mentioned, for he said that he remembers all this and remembers "Nothing At All." That is, even though he remembers everything that they remember, for he is composed of all of them and they all receive their Brains and

Memory only from him, nevertheless his Brain is impossible to call by the term "memory" at all, for he is above memory and is the root of memory, for he is united in the Ein Sof, as written there, and so he is not alluded to in any parashah, for he is above all and is the root of all, as mentioned.

POINT #4

And the essence of tefillin Brains are the aspect of life of Holiness, which one attains through tefillin, for the Brains are the Life, as written (Eccl. 7), "*Hachokhmah tichyeh*/Wisdom preserves alive," as our Rabbis z"l said (*Menachoth* 44), "One who lays tefillin attains life, as it says, "*Adonai `aleihem yichyu*/Adonai, by these things men live" (Isa. 38:16), as brought in the Qawanoth, that tefillin are the aspect of the three names *Ehyeh H' Eyheh* [21+26+21=68] which are gematria *ChaYIM* [68], which are the Brains, see there, for the Brains of the tefillin are drawn from the aspect of Tiqunei Diqna Qadisha, as brought in the Qawanoth, as they are the entirety of these holy elders, who have their root in the aforementioned Most Supernal Elder, who is the Blind One, who boasted that he lives truly long life, for he is very old and yet he is an utmost suckling babe, and still has not begun living at all, but nevertheless he is very old, and all the world's time does not amount to him so much as an eyeblink etc. And behold, although these are things that the `Atiq Yomin has covered and thought cannot grasp it at all, and there is no man on earth who can make this interpretation and explain this mystery, nevertheless since by Hashem's compassion on His people these words of his have come out of his holy mouth and they have taken form and been printed in a book, it behooves us to dig and find in them some Remez relevant to the story, such that we may merit waking up from our sleep, which this was his holy intention with these stories that he told, in order to wake up all people who sleep away their days etc., as explained in the torah "*Pathach R' Shim`on*" (*LM* #60), and there you will see and understand the great wonders of these stories, for they are the aspect of stories of *Shanim Qadhmoniyoth*/Ancient Years-Faces, the aspect of `Atiq/Ancient, the aspect of *Hadhrath Panim*/Splendor of the Face, from which all the seventy faces of the Torah derive etc.; take a good look there.

POINT #5

So behold, the main intent of the above words, for practical application, is what I saw and heard from the mouth of Rabbeinu z"l himself, many times, that he lived new life all the time; like I heard from him many times saying, "I lived life today, such life as I have never experienced" etc. And also I heard him other times speaking a great deal about life — that the world calls everything life etc., but even in regards to miserable lives there are many differences etc., see there in the *Sichoth* [*CM* #400] — but actually the essence of life is True Longevity, which is the aspect of the Long Life of the Blind One, who really lives long life, for he boasts that he is utterly old and yet utterly a suckling babe and still has not begun living at all. For this is the essence of life: when one starts serving Hashem anew all the time, as if he has still not started serving him at all, as written (Deut. 6), "*Asher anochi metzawekha hayom*/Which I enjoin you today." And our Rabbis z"l (*Sifri* there), commented, "Every day let them be new in your eyes;" and (ibid. 27) "*Hasket ush'ma` Yisrael, hayom hazeh nihyeytha le`am laShem Eloheikha*/Pay attention and listen, Yisrael: this day you are become a people to Hashem your God," and our Rabbis z"l explained (brought in Rashi): every day let they be in your eyes as if today you have entered the covenant with Him.

And like I saw from Rabbeinu z"l innumerable times, that even though he had previously boasted of big and wondrous things, and revealed wondrous Torah never before heard, as he usually did — and then afterwards we saw him in great pain, and many times he laid out his pain and conversation before us from the depth of his heart, that he is extremely afflicted over how to attain being a Jew, like someone who has never before smelled the spirit of serving Hashem. And whoever did not see this, it is impossible to describe it to him in writing, but a little about this is already explained in this *Shevachim* that are printed, and every time he would say that now he knows nothing at all, nothing at all etc., even though earlier he had revealed what he revealed and boasted that he attained what he attained that is impossible to reveal; nevertheless immediately after he would say that he knows nothing at all.

S o the rule was that he never stood on one level, but just always quickly went from level to level in the apex of uppermost and loftiest levels, and even when he reached what he reached etc., his mind still did not grow cool to this etc. But here is not the place to prolong discussion of this, and it will be explained elsewhere.

A nd this is truly the essence of life, when one attains always beginning anew in serving Hashem, which is truly the essence of life, as written (Deut. 30), *"Ki hu chayeykha*/It, precisely, is your life."* So the essence of serving Hashem is to always perform one's service anew, and to not fall into old age of the *Sitra Achra*; that his service not become old for him, God forbid, as Rabbeinu z"l warned us against and said it is forbidden to be old: not an old tzaddik and not an old chassid; old is not good!" etc., as explained in his holy *Sichoth* appended to *Sipurei Ma`asiyoth*, namely, one needs to always begin anew.

A nd this is the essence of the long life of the Holy Elder who is the Blind One, for he was most old and most *yanik* [infantile, lit. suckling], that is, the more he grew and became subsumed into holy elderliness which is the aspect of `Atik de`Atikin/Ancient of the Ancient of Days, the more yanik he became. For, every time he perceived that he is utterly far from Hashem Yithbarakh, for "there is no probing His greatness," therefore the more he was subsumed into holy elderliness, the more he saw and perceived that he still has not begun living at all, until he attained the aforementioned Long Life where elderliness and infancy are merged, which is totally impossible to comprehend.

A nd this is the aspect of tefillin which are drawn from the aforementioned Elder, who is the root of the tefillin, Brains, as mentioned, which are the aspect of life, as mentioned, the aspect of (ibid. 4), *"We'atem hadeveqim baShem Eloheikhem chayim kulkhem hayom*/And you that cleave to Hashem your God, all of you are live this day,"* which is said of tefillin, as is known, for this is the essence of tefillin-Brains, in order to attain, through the mitzvah of tefillin, living new life of holiness, to renew his days like an eagle, to begin serving Hashem Yithbarakh anew all the time, and not fall into the Sitra Achra's oldness, to not view his devotion be as old; on the contrary, tangibly new, as if he has never ever begun.

For in truth, even one who is a very great tzaddiq and has labored and toiled many years in His Blessed devotion, nevertheless in accord with the Every Day Renewal of Creation, he still has not begun at all. For Hashem Yithbarakh does new things all the time, as written, "and in His goodness renews every day constantly the work of creation," and no day is like another, and no time is like another, and each and every moment there are changes in the rising of the worlds and their order and position and conduct, in unfathomably wondrous and awesome variations. And all their vitality derives from the work of the man in this world, on which it all depends, from the head up to the Ein Sof. Therefore one must always serve Hashem Yithbarakh anew, in accord with the renewal of the work of creation in all the worlds needed now, and in accord with the revelation of the greatness of the Blessed Creator that needs to be revealed now. For, "Day unto day utters speech, and night unto night reveals knowledge" [Ps. 19], as every day, every night, every time and every moment, His Blessed Greatness is revealed in a new consciousness and awareness that never before existed. Therefore one needs to begin in His service new every time, in the aspect of, "Let them be like new in your eyes every day." And this is the essence of vitality, this aforementioned aspect of long life, and as explained in Rabbeinu z"l's words, that the essence of longevity, the aspect of long life, is to see to it to extend the day with additional sanctity and consciousness, every next day that comes. For, the day, at its beginning when it comes to a man, is very narrow, and one needs to see to it to widen and lengthen it with additional sanctity all the time. And so every day one needs to see to it that each day be longer than the other, with additional sanctity and purity etc. (as explained in the torah *Pathach R' Shim`on* in *LM* #60). And this is the essence of length of days, the aspect of long days, namely always beginning fresh in new service, much greater. For, all the service he has performed until now, he needs to forget entirely, and now begin new, as mentioned.

And by tefillin we attain this, as mentioned. And this is the essence of the mitzwah of tefillin that we lay every day, in order to attain life, the aspect of, "You who cleave" as mentioned, that is, to attain the aforementioned long life, to renew his life of holiness at all times, beginning new all the time. And this is the essence of Brains and life generated being drawn from the aforementioned Most Supernal Elder, where the source of tefillin is, as mentioned, as he lives the aforementioned long life, as there, elderliness and infancy are united together, which this is the aspect of (Ps. 103), "That your youth be renewed as an eagle," as our Rabbis z"l said (brought in Rashi there), "The eagle, the older it gets... " — that is, the older it gets, the more it renews its vitality and begins new, all the time beginning new life. And therefore he had approbation from the Great Eagle specifically, for such vitality is the aspect of "renewing oneself like an eagle" as mentioned. And the aspect of tefillin, which are the aspect of this life, is from there, as mentioned.

POINT #6

For, the essence of tefillin is the flashing of the Brains in the face, which is the aspect of Light of the Face, which is drawn from the aspect of *Tiqunei Diqna Qadisha*/Repair or Features of the Holy Beard, which is the essence of Honoring the Face, as is known, which is the aspect of the aforementioned Elder in Holiness, as mentioned. And the *Tiqunei Diqna* are the aspect of the Thirteen Attributes of Mercy, the essence of which is the aspect of subjugating anger and sweetening harsh decrees and the *Charon Af*/Burning Anger (Nose), which is the aspect of *Erekh Apayim*/Extending Patience (Nose), which is the main thing, and therefore Chazal said (*Sanh.* 111) regarding the verse "*Waymaher Moshe wayqod artzah*/And Moshe made haste and bowed his head toward the earth" etc. [Ex. 34:8]: What did he see? He saw Erekh Apayim. For, the essence of the Thirteen Attributes are the Thirteen Tiqunei Diqna which H"Y [Hashem Yithbarakh] revealed to him then, the essence of which is Erekh Apayim, which is the aspect of subjugating the *Panim*/Interior (Face), and therefore Moshe became excited by this specifically, as also explained regarding the loftiness of Erekh Apayim in the words of Rabbeinu z"l (*LM* #155, see there), in the lesson that begins, "Sadness is a very worst trait" etc., see there the entire interest until the end, for it is a wondrous path in serving the Creator, and if you gaze and look thoroughly there, you can get very wondrous advices and great encouragement, endlessly, for His Blessed service.

And the rule is that a man needs to cling to Hashem Yithbarakh's attributes, as explained in the words of our Rabbis and in all the holy books. Therefore one most see to it that he should have the trait of Erekh Apayim, that is, extending his patience for everything, not getting angry, not being annoyed at anything, not looking at any obstacle or confusion in his devotions, whether they be confusions, obstacles and trials that he has from people of the world, such as his father, father-in-law, wife, relatives or the rest of mankind. As is known and seen tangibly, that every time some person wants to enter serving Hashem, to begin praying with intent etc. and so forth, immediately he has great obstacles, without end, and then every one needs to "be bold as a tiger... and strong like a lion to perform the will of his Heavenly Father, to prevail against the obstacles and get through them, to not look at them at all, and to fortify himself a great deal for his part, to delve in Torah and prayer with intent and power etc.

And this is the aspect of Arikhath Apayim, to not be short spirited, God forbid, to stop his devotion, God forbid, due to the obstacles and trials he has from them, but only strengthen himself and extend his patience for everything, and not gaze at any obstacle at all. And the same even with the obstacles he has from himself, his evil and strange cravings and thoughts pursuing him constantly every moment, especially during prayer time, causing him much trial. And the main thing is the Erekh Apayim, which is the aspect of Emunah, as explained there, that the essence of Erekh Apayim one attains through Emunah, that is, having perfect Emunah in Hashem Yithbarakh and the True Kosher Tzaddiqim, and to strengthen himself in His service and not fall from anything, and to be easy-going, and not become short tempered on account of the evil deeds and faults he has committed until now. For, one needs to not look at this at all, as explained in the words of Rabbeinu z"l and in our words many, many times regarding this, just how much a man needs to be strong. For, there is no despairing at all in the world, and however it is, even though he has already fallen such a descent in himself many times, without bound, nevertheless there is no cause for despair at all in the world, and all the days he is alive on the face of the earth he needs to strengthen himself and each time begin new, and not fall into the Sitra Achra's oldness at all. For, all the descents in the world are the aspect of the Sitra Achra's oldness, as it seems in his eyes that he is already old in his mistakes and deeds that he is accustomed in, such that he cannot get out of them in any fashion, God forbid. But in truth, he needs to know and believe that every day, moment, and time, the power is in a man's hand to be new and be an actual new creation, for Hashem Yithbarakh is "doing new things" at all times, and no day or hour is like another etc. as mentioned. Therefore one needs to every time strengthen himself and begin every day anew, and sometimes even in one day one needs to begin many times, as explained elsewhere. And even if it will be that way for a long time, however it may be, every time and every hour he needs to remind himself of Hashem Yithbarakh and completely forget all the past until now, and really begin now from new, as much as he can, and not look at any confusion or weakness of mind at all.

And all this is the aspect of Erekh Apayim, that one needs to extend his spirit and pass over the confusions and obstacles and not look at anything and let nothing affect him, and not let his heart grow soft and not let his temper get short from anything that happens to him, but only strengthen himself in Hashem Yithbarakh in whatever he can. For Hashem Yithbarakh is always full of compassion, and Hashem's mercies are never finished and His compassion never ceased. And we have already spoken about this many times — but such a matter needs to be repeated many times, without bound, for "it is your life," for the majority of the world being far from Hashem Yithbarakh and losing what they lose, true everlasting life, is virtually all only on account of weakness of mind, being downcast, on account that most of them have experienced many times that they began a little in serving Hashem and then fell in what they fell, each person according to his fall, the Merciful One save us, and thereby they became discouraged from beginning again. And some of them once or a few times became somewhat aroused and began anew, but then when they saw they nevertheless fell afterwards, they became discouraged, since they saw themselves trying so much to get into serving Hashem and then falling in what they fell, the Merciful One save us, thus it seemed to them that their strength is exhausted to now begin any more. But really all this is the work of the Ba`al Davar himself, who is the aspect of the elder of the Sitra Achra, for he is called the "old and foolish king" [Eccl. 4], as he wants to cast a man down into oldness and exhaustion, God forbid, as if he is already so aged in his mistakes and deeds that he can no longer change. And really it is not so, for every day a man is a new creature, just as we say the benediction every day over Netilath Yadayim and the rest of the benedictions, "Who has not made me a heathen.. a slave.. a woman" etc., where the codifiers have written the reason being because a man is made like a new creature every day, as explained in the *Shulchan `Arukh*. And similarly the benediction, "Who gives strength to the weary" we say over renewal of the brains and vitality every day, as brought in the *Qawanoth*. And therefore a man needs to be very careful to not fall into this Sitra Achra's oldness, but only be strong and renewed all the time, as mentioned. So let it seem in his eyes every day and every hour that he is born today, and as if today he receives the Torah anew, as our Rabbis z"l have said, "every day let them be like new in your eyes," as mentioned, which all of this is the aspect of Erekh Apayim, as he extends his patience for every thing, obstacle, and confusion in the world, and passes over everything, and strengthens himself each time in His service etc. as mentioned. And this trait of Erekh Apayim is the essence of the aspect of Tiqunei Diqna, which is the aspect of the *Zaqen*/Elder in holiness, who is truly old, for he truly lives long life, for every time he begins living anew. And precisely this is the aspect of holy elderliness, the aspect of long life, for when one falls in the Sitra Achra's oldness, that is, when his devotion becomes old for him, and all the more so when he falls from his devotions, God forbid, since it seems that he is so old in his mistakes that he can no longer go back, God forbid, such "elderliness," God forbid, is the essence of shortness of days, as mentioned in Rabbeinu z"l's words, that "elders" like this who do not add vitality and additional service all the time, are called "short of days and full of trouble" etc. (Job 14). (See the torah *"Uv'yom haBiqurim," LM II* #4).

POINT #7

The rule is that any man who wants to consider the ultimate purpose needs to very much guard against being old at all. That is, to not fall into the Sitra Achra's oldness, God forbid, whether he is a tzaddik, a chasid, or any other kind of man. Even someone who is the lowest of the low in some regard, needs to guard against falling in this oldness, for even a great tzaddik is forbidden from being old in his service even if he has attained perfect devotion on a high level; he still needs to be strong in going from level to level and each time beginning anew. For this is the essence of Judaism, to be strong in ascending each time from level to level, as I heard from the mouth of Rabbeinu z"l when he began teaching the torah *"Tesha` Tiqunin Yaqirin Itmasru Lediqna"* (LM #20), as he said then in these terms: "Whoever wants to be an Israelite man, that is, going from level to level, cannot do so except by Eretz Yisrael," and from his words in general we hear that one is not called a true *Ish Yisra'eli* unless he goes from level to level. And one attains this through Eretz Yisrael etc.; see there in that torah *Tesha` Tiqunin Yaqirin*. And this is the essence of long life, the aspect of the Torah which is called life, when one always begins anew etc. as mentioned.

And conversely, even one who did what he did and transgressed what he transgressed, nevertheless is forbidden to be old, God forbid, and he needs to guard more and more against this aspect of oldness, to not get into any despair, God forbid; to not say in his heart that he is so old already, God forbid, in his deeds etc., that he cannot change. Rather, be strong and begin with whatever he can, and do any little or great thing that he can, even if he can really say no more than one utterance in prayer or secluded meditation-conversation, or learn the least of the least bit, anyhow he should do what he can and fortify and enliven himself in the least of the least that he still manages to strive in the sanctity of Yisrael. For, any way it might be, he definitely does many mitzwoth each day, for even "the transgressors of Yisrael are full of mitzwoth like a pomegranate," so one needs to find good points in himself and enliven himself each time, as also explained in the torah *"Azamera Lelohai Be`odi"* (LM #282), as brought in our words many times, and to be strong and begin anew each time, and to not lose himself entirely, God forbid. And "whatever your hand finds to do, do with your strength." And the main thing is the aforementioned Arikhath Apayim, that he should have a very great deal of Arikhuth Apayim, without bound, which is the aspect of long spirit/temper, that is, to extend his spirit, to wait and to anticipate Hashem's salvation, and to not gaze at any confusion or obstacle as mentioned.

POINT #8

And this is the aspect of "Slow of Angers [*Erekh Apayim*, Ex. 34:6, which is pl. rather than sing. *Erekh Af,* implying:] for both tzaddikim and the wicked" (*BK* 50a-b), as tzaddikim do need this trait of Erekh Apayim, which is the aspect of holy elderliness, the aspect of a*rikhath yamim weshanim*/prolonging days and years, the aspect of *Chayim Arukhim*/Long Life, mentioned above. That is, to not fall in the Sitra Achra's oldness, God forbid, that his service should not old be and weak for him, but just "renew his youth like an eagle" all the time, and every day begin new with additional sanctity and service, and never get tired or weary, and not be confused by anything, which this is the aspect of Erekh Apayim. For, sometimes one who serves Hashem gets weary on account of having suffered so many trials etc., and thereby he could fall into Sitra Achra's oldness and exhaustion, God forbid. Therefore he needs to strengthen himself a great deal with the trait of Erekh Apayim, all his days, extending his temper and spirit for all the toils and burdens, beginning new every time. And this is the aspect of Erekh Apayim for tzaddikim.

And likewise there is the aspect of Erekh Apayim for the wicked, as Hashem Yithbarakh also extends his temper for them all the days of their lives, in order that they return, as written, "Until the day he dies You wait for him; if he turns back [You receive him immediately]." Therefore the wicked themselves also have to bolster themselves in this trait of Erekh Apayim, that their wickedness should not confuse them from returning to Hashem Yithbarakh, and that their hearts should not falter nor their minds be downcast from the amount of their transgressions, especially if they have already begun a few times and fallen from it etc. Nevertheless they should be confident in His great mercy and prolong their patience and spirit over all that happens to them, and strengthen themselves each time to begin anew. Perhaps he will manage from now on to have compassion on himself, to leave his previous ways and thoughts, and never ever be old or weak in his eyes. For the essence of repentance has to do with renewing one's life whenever it is necessary to renew his days that have passed in darkness, in the aspect of (Lam. 5), "*Hashiveinu H' eleikha wenashuvah chadesh yameynu keqedem*/Return us, Hashem, to you, that we may be restored; renew our days as before."

Hence everyone needs the aspect of this trait of Erekh Apayim. And this is, "Long-Tempered (Erekh Apayim) for tzaddikim and for the wicked." And the rest of the levels of other people in the world are included in them, for the whole upkeep of their service and vitality is by this trait of Erekh Apayim, as mentioned.

POINT #9

And all of them get strength from the aspect of the Elder in Sanctity, who is the aforementioned Blind One, who is the aspect of the Elder of Elders, *Saba deSavin* [Zohar I:22a etc.], who has attained such holy elderliness that he said that he is "extremely old yet extremely *yanik* [infantile, lit. suckling]" etc. and as mentioned, as from him all the tzaddiqim receive strength to fortify themselves in their devotions to renew their strength and service all the time. And through these great tzaddiqim who begin anew every time — and even reach the highest of all levels, even the level of the greatest *Benei `Aliyah* [*Sanh.* 97b], nevertheless not sufficing themselves with this, but rather saying, "Who knows what else there is to attain?" and beginning every time anew, and like I heard from Rabbeinu z"l a great deal regarding this as explained elsewhere, until they each time arrive at perceptions new, wondrous, awesome etc. etc. — therefore with the strength of such tzaddiqim in all this, those who have fallen can renew themselves every time. As is very common presently in the darkness of the this exile, that the Sitra Achra and the Ba`al Davar have surged up a great deal upon anyone who wants to begin to delve in serving Hashem; and they cast him down every time, each person in accord with what they cast him down, God forbid, the Merciful one save us; and they need to be strengthened and revived each time with many kinds of encouragement, so that they never despair, and that they begin anew each time as mentioned. And they receive all this strength from these tzaddikim.

For the more ill a person is, the greater a doctor he needs, as explained elsewhere (#30), for due to the enormity of the power and perceptions of these tzaddikim, who every time began anew and each time perceived more and more the greatness of Hashem's kindness, how He, Blessed be He, devises considerations so that no one be flushed away from Him etc. And thereby they have power to draw new vitality and strength to all the fallen, to strengthen and awaken them every time, to never fall down due to anything, but only extend their patience and spirit for everything and be steadfast in Hashem and the power of the true tzaddikim, for His mercies have never ceased, and they should be strong and start following Hashem Yithbarakh anew each time in whatever they can etc., and as mentioned. For, by the power of these tzaddikim who every time began anew, that even when they reached the highest of high levels, that it seems there is no higher level that this, and really it is an extremely wondrous and awesome level and state, that, many great and wondrous tzaddikim never attained it — still even though they reached this and more and more etc. etc., nevertheless they never sufficed with this, but devised considerations every time to begin anew. Even though they never knew any more report of a higher level, nevertheless they said, "Who knows, what else there is?" etc., just like I heard from Rabbeinu z"l, as one time he was very afflicted before me and said, "How can one achieve being a Jew?" etc., and it was a big wonder to me on account that he had just revealed wondrous and awesome things etc.; he spoke up and said, "Who knows what else there is to attain?" etc. For, behold, did it ever occur to me to seek and yearn for such a perception and such a level? So who knows now too what more there is, etc. This was his way every day of his life. And it is impossible to elaborate and relate this here.

Hence there are such great tzaddikim that even when they reach the highest of high levels, that it seems there is no higher level than it, still they yearn, request and seek, and begin anew entirely. For, who knows what more there is? Even though their present perception and level is truly very high, still they say, "Isn't Hashem Yithbarakh infinite? So who knows what more one can reach in this world!" Therefore they begin anew every time, until they truly reach an even higher level. And then they say, "Who knows what more there is?" — and again they begin anew etc., and thus continually.

Thus by the power of these tzaddikim there is hope for all the fallen, and there is nothing in the world at all to despair about. For even though it seems to him that from such a descent he cannot get up, God forbid, nevertheless who knows the greatness of Hashem's kindness? For there is such kindness by Him, Yithbarakh, that even from there one can get up. And similarly even if, God forbid, he fell again many, many times without count, still any move whereby he wants to pick himself up each time from the fall, and each and every cry that he calls out even from the lowest depths, is also never lost. Like Rabbeinu z"l said, even a yell from the lowest underworld is never lost, regardless of what happens after. For Hashem Yithbarakh and his Torah are infinite and unbounded. As just as there is no getting high in the world, in accord with His greatness — heights above heights, and heights above that etc. and as mentioned — similarly there is no descent in the world, as for every descent, God forbid, there is a worse descent. And since there is a worse descent, God forbid, one needs to be strong and not fall any further, God forbid.

And the main empowerment is by the strength of the aforementioned tzaddikim, who never stayed put but every time rose higher etc. as mentioned. For they attained the perception that just as there is never an ascent, likewise there is never a descent from which one cannot rise up. For in truth it is all one, for the more a tzaddik rises to a higher level, he perceives more the generosities of Hashem, which this is the essence of Hashem Yithbarakh's greatness. For the trait of *Chesed*/Generosity is called *Gedulah*/Greatness, as is known, as written, "Yours, Hashem, is the Greatness" [I Chron. 29:11], which is kindness, as is known. Hence the trait of Chesed is called Gedulah. Therefore the more one perceives Hashem Yithbarakh's Greatness, the more one perceives His Generosity, for His Blessed Generosity is the essence of His Greatness as mentioned. Therefore these tzaddikim who never stay put but each time go up further and further, and each time further perceive His Blessed Greatness, that is, the vastness of His Generosity, thereby they attain perceiving that there is no fall or descent in the world and no despairing in the world whatsoever. For they perceive such Kindnesses each time, which are the essence of the Creator's Greatness, whereby everyone can have an ascent. And this is what Rabbeinu z"l said in the torah *"Mishra deSakina"* (*LM* #30), that a person needs specifically the greatest tzaddik on the utmost high level. For, the more ill a person is, the greater a healer he needs, that is, as mentioned. For the greater the tzaddik, the more he can raise up even those who are so very fallen, until by the power of the aforementioned tzaddikim [who receive from him], there is no fall or descent from which one cannot get up by their power, if they manage to believe and follow them; and as mentioned.

And all this is the abovementioned [#8] aspect of Erekh Apayim, the aspect of Erekh Apayim for tzaddikim and Erekh Apayim for the wicked, that these people on a high level, the aspect of tzaddikim, need to prolong their temper, that their temper not fall short, and they not stop having extra spirit and vitality, on account of the great ascent and level they have attained. For in spite of this they need to extend their spirit further, and to look to reach an even higher, higher level, and to begin anew etc. as mentioned. And these people on a low level, and even the wicked that have fallen in total evil, God forbid, nevertheless as long as the soul is in them, as long as they can still move one body member, need to extend their temper and spirit, to look out for salvation constantly, and prevail and begin anew each time, as much as possible — whatever will be will be — for there is never a move in sanctity, nor a groan, cry or aspiration in sanctity etc., that is ever lost, for "Hashem will not cast us off forever" [Lam. 3].

POINT #10

And all this is the aspect of tefillin, which are the abovementioned aspect of Arikhath Apayim, which is the aspect of the new brains and vitality that we draw by the mitzwah of tefillin, from the elders in sanctity who receive from the highest elder who is the Blind One.

POINT #15

And this is the aspect of (Ex. 13), "Sanctify to Me all the first-born, whatsoever opens the womb among the children of Israel," which is the beginning of the first passage in the tefillin. For the essence of the tefillin are drawn from the sanctity of the firstborn, which is the first birth, which is the aspect of Yetziath Mitzrayim, which is the aspect of birth, as is known, as on account of this we need to sanctify the first birth that is a male firstborn, as written there, "And it came to pass, when Par'oh would hardly let us go... therefore I sacrifice" etc. And all this is in order to draw on oneself the sanctity of birth of the brains which is the essence of birth, that is, to manage to renew one's vitality and brains at all times as if he was born today, as mentioned. Which, this is the essence of long life, which is the aspect of tefillin as mentioned.

And therefore one needs to give the firstborn to the Kohen or redeem him from him, for the Kohen is the aspect of the Elder in Holiness, in the aspect of (Ps. 133), "It is like the precious oil upon the head, coming down upon the beard; even Aharon's beard" etc., the aspect of the Eight Tikkunim of the Kohen Gadol, as is known. And this is what our Rabbis z"l said (*Shabbath* 151), "And let your head lack no oil (Eccl. 9:8) — this is head tefillin." For the essence of tefillin are drawn from the aspect of "like the precious oil upon the head..." of the elder, Aharon, as mentioned. And therefore by means of giving the firstborn, who is the first birth, to the Kohen, we draw the sanctity of the birth of the brains and vitality, to remember to always renew oneself as if he was born today, which this is the essence of tefillin, which are the aspect of Brains and Longevity that we receive from the aforementioned Elder in Holiness, who said that he is extremely old and yet has not begun living at all, as if he was born today. For, one needs to each time begin anew as mentioned, and this is the aspect of Mashiach, of whom it is said (Ps. 2), "Today I have borne you." For Mashiach will attain this aspect perfectly, which is the aforementioned aspect of long life, as each moment he will begin living anew as if he was born today, in the aspect of "I have borne you today." For Mashiach will attain the aspect of above time, as explained in Rabbeinu z"l's words on this verse, "I have borne you today;" see there [*LM II* #61].

For this aspect that the Blind One boasted of, who is old yet infantile etc. and the whole world does not amount to him so much as an eyeblink etc. All this is the aspect of above time, which this is the aspect of long life that Mashiach will attain, the aspect of (Ps. 21), "He asked life of You; You gave it to him," which is the aspect of "David King of Yisrael is Live and Well." For David is Mashiach. And this is the aspect of tefillin; that is where is the root of the Mashiach's soul, as is brought, as the root of Mashiach's kingship pertains to the tefillin's knot, as Rabbeinu z"l also said (*LM* #54), which this is the aspect of (Sam. 1 25), "Yet the soul of my lord shall be bound in the bundle of life," which is said of David, who is Mashiach. "The bundle of life" is the aspect of the knot of tefillin, which are the aspect of life as mentioned, the aforementioned aspect of long life, as mentioned.

POINT #18

And this is the aspect of Hashem Yithbarakh's extolling Kenesseth Yisrael (Song 7), "Your navel is like a round goblet that lacks no mingled wine," and our Rabbis z"l explained it (*Sanh.* 37) regarding the seventy Sanhedrin who sat in a semicircle like the moon etc. "Your navel" is the aspect of the tefillin straps which descend from the head knot to the navel, which is drawn from the aspect of the kingship of David-Mashiach who is live and enduring, who is the aspect of the head knot as mentioned, as from there is drawn the strap unto the navel which is the aspect of "your navel like a round goblet," the aspect of the seventy Sanhedrin who correspond to the seventy facets of the Torah, where David sat at the head, as our Rabbis z"l explained (brought in Rashi) on the verse, "Yoshev-Basheveth, a Tachkemonite, head" etc. (2 Sam. 23), for all the seventy Sanhedrin who are the aspect of the seventy faces of the Torah all receive from David-Mashiach, as all his vitality is from the aspect of the aforementioned elders, who are the aspect of Tiqunei Diqna Qadisha, the aspect of Splendor of the Face, the aspect of Stories of Ancient Times, as all the seventy faces of the Torah are drawn from them, as explained in the torah "Pathach R' Shim`on" (*LM* #60), see there; as thereby one can wake up from sleep, which is the absence of the brains. And by means of these elders, the aspect of the stories, are drawn all the seventy faces of the Torah and we wake up from sleep. Which, this is the aspect of the seventy years that David a"h lived. And therefore he minimized sleep to the utmost, as our Rabbis z"l said (*Sukkah* 26), that David never slept sixty breaths, so as to not taste the taste of death. For sleep is one sixtieth of death, which is drawn from Adam haRishon's mistake, by eating from the Tree of Knowledge Good-and-Bad and blemishing the Tree of Life which is the aspect of the light of the tefillin, as is brought. For tefillin are the aspect of life, the aspect of the Tree of Life, of which is said (Gen. 3), "and he eat and live forever." And by causing this damage, death was decreed on him for all generations.

B ut actually, after the mistake, death and sleep are a great benefit, for had Adam not erred he would have attained true life which is everlasting life, long life, whilst still in the body. That is, in his body he would have been able to be merged in the Ein Sof forever, running and returning, and to live long life, that is, renewing his vitality forever, in the aspect of renewing life of the Highest Elder, who is the Blind One, who lived long life, as he is ever old and ever infantile etc. as mentioned. But after the mistake and having eaten from the Tree of Knowledge Good-and-Bad and being driven from Gan `Eden, and the Serpent's filth taking grip on his body, the aspect of the "Serpent's bite," it is impossible for him to live long life in his body forever.

S o it is impossible to attain everlasting life except by death, which is a great benefit, as written (Gen 1:31), "*Wehineh tov me'od*/And behold, *me'od* is good" — this is death (*Ber. Rab.* 9), for by means of death, which is sleep, his brain is renewed. And then his body and life are renewed, and then he comes back to life in a body clean and pure that is entirely cleaned and purified of the Serpent's filth. And then he will attain receiving new Brains in the aspect of tefillin, the Tree of Life, which are the aspect of long life he will attain then. That is, then he will attain living such life forever, as at all times Life and Brains will be added to him, until the older he gets, the more he will attain beginning anew. Which this is the aspect of the Blind Elder, which this is the essence of everlasting life which whoever attains will attain in the future to come. For constant delight is no delight and is not called true life, but rather when one attains living new life at all times. And this is the aspect of long life, everlasting life, that the tzaddikim will attain in the future after revival of the dead, that is, the aforementioned aspect, as they will attain renewing their life at all times, which this is the aspect of tefillin as mentioned.

POINT #21

Dawidh had no vitality at all, for he ought to have been a *Nefel*/miscarriage/fallen-out. But Adam haRishon [*A"hR*] gave him seventy of his own years, as our Rabbis z"l have said. For, the life of *A"hR* was drawn from the aspect of *Arikh Anpin* [*A"A*, the Supernal "Long Face"], which is the aspect of *Arikhath Apayim*/Lengthening of Temper [or Face], the aspect of the aforementioned stories of *Shanim Qadhmoniyoth* [Ancient 'Years,' 'Faces'] etc. And as transmitted in the [Arizal's] writings, that the vitality of the first generations was from there, from the aspect of *A"A;* and therefore they would live very long lives. And all the stories that the Torah tells about the first generations, are all from the aspect of stories of *Shanim Qadhmoniyoth*, which are the aspect of *Hadhrath Panim*/Honoring the Face, as all the seventy faces of the Torah receive from it. And therefore the Torah began from these holy stories, before it explains the *mitzwoth* of the Torah. For, all the mitzwoth of the Torah, which consist of the aspect of the seventy faces of the Torah, need to receive from the aspect of *Hadhrath Panim*, the aspect of *shufreih de'Adam*/Man's beauty, the aspect of stories of *Shanim Qadhmoniyoth* and the essential holy vitality that is drawn from there. This renews his vitality at all times; each moment he begins living anew, which is the aspect of (Ps. 2), "*Ani hayom yelidhtikha*/ Today I have begotten you," that is said of the Mashiach [anointed to kingship] Dawidh. Namely, Dawidh Mashiach merited that it was reversed to good, from one opposite to the other. For, just as initially he had no vitality at all and really ought to have been a Nefel, the thing was reversed and he merited to live seventy years from *A"hR*'s years, and merited to live all the seventy years in the aspect of new life at all times, as if he had still never lived at all, but was just born today. And he, at all times was like a miscarriage that was born now, which has no life and has to receive, by Hashem's graces, new life; and so forth at every time and moment. And in this way he lived all his seventy years, which is the essence of life, as mentioned above. Until he merited through his devotion and effort in this aspect — trying and toiling all his days without sleeping his days away, but rather adding holiness and consciousness at all times — to renew his vitality at every hour. Until he merited thereby to live long, everlasting life for ever and ever, in the aspect of "*Dawidh Melekh Yisrael Chai Wekayam*/Dawidh, King of Yisrael, is Live and Lasting," as mentioned.

And this is the aspect of tefillin, as mentioned. For *teFiLYn* are a term for (Ex. 33:16), "*WeniFLiYnu ani we`amekha*/ and I and Your people are distinguished," which was said when Hashem Yithbarakh revealed to him [Moshe] the Thirteen Attributes of Mercy, which are the aspect of the light of the tefillin, which is the aspect of the "*We'raitha eth-achorai*/ and you shall see My back" stated there, which is the tefillin knot (*Berakhoth* 7), which is where the root of Dawidh-Mashiach's soul is, as mentioned, as he ought to have been *Nefel* as mentioned, but now he merited the thing being reversed to good and living new life at all times, as if he was born today, which is the aspect of tefillin, the aspect of "*Wenifliynu ani we`amekha*," for the thing becomes reversed, as mentioned, and is made from the aspect of *Nefel* into the aspect of *Wenifliynu*, which is the aspect of tefillin, which is the aspect of the aforementioned long life/longevity of Dawidh as mentioned. And therefore Mashiach is called "*Bar Nifli*/ My Distinguished Son" [*Sanh.* 96b on Amos 9:11] for Mashiach will attain that life, which is the aspect of the "*Ani hayom yelidhtikha*" that is said of Mashiach, and as mentioned above.

POINT #23

And this is the aspect of Rosh Hashanah. For Rosh Hashanah is the aspect of tefillin which are the aspect of renewal that we attain every day through sleep, when the brains are renewed in Emunah etc., which this is the aspect of Rosh Hashanah, as brought in the words of Rabbeinu z"l in the torah "*Ashrei Ha`am*" (*LM* #35), see there. For Rosh Hashanah is the aspect of the sanctity of Eretz Yisrael, as written, "Always the eyes of Hashem your God are on it from the year's heading until the year's ending" [Deut. 11:12], which this is the aspect of tefillin, which are the aspect of Eretz Yisrael's sanctity, the aspect of, "And it shall be, when He brings you" that is said in the tefillin's passages as mentioned. For the essence of Rosh Hashanah's sanctity is that we attain perfect Teshuvah/Return, for it is the first day of the Ten Days of Repentance. That is, that we attain renewing our days that passed in darkness, and from here onwards add additional sanctity and devotion anew, which this is the aspect of, "Renew upon us a good year," that we request on Rosh Hashanah. "Renew" specifically, that we attain a *new* year specifically. For every year is a particular facet of the seventy facets of the Torah as mentioned. Therefore every year we need to attain entirely new faces, living from now new life, which this is the aspect of long life as mentioned.

And this is the aspect of the much requesting and praying for life, on Rosh Hashanah, many, many times in each prayer; as we say, "Remember us for life... Inscribe us for life... Who compassionately remembers his formations for life..." and many of the sort. For the essence of the aspect of life is the aspect of long life, mentioned, of the **Blind Elder**, who attained the ultimate memory perfectly as mentioned, as from him is drawn the sanctity of Rosh Hashanah, which is the aspect of the sanctity of the tefillin, which are the aspect of, "and for remembrance between your eyes" as mentioned. And therefore Rosh Hashanah is called "Day of Remembrance." For the essence of its sanctity is from the aforementioned aspect of that Elder's remembrance. And all our request on Rosh Hashanah for life, the whole intention is for true and everlasting life, that is, the aforementioned aspect of long life. That is, to renew our life at all times, the aspect of, "Renew upon us a good year" — "renew" specifically, as mentioned.

POINT #34

And therefore it is necessary to write tefillin on the hide of a clean beast specifically (*SAOC* 32:12), for the hide is the aspect of the imagination, which is the exterior of the intellect, the aspect of the intellect's clothing...

For tefillin are such great "Brains" [intellectual faculties] that they have the power to clarify and repair the very Exterior of the Exterior, the Immaturity of Immaturity (*Qatnuth*) of the imagination, which is the main repair. For the greater the tzaddik, the more power that he has to clarify and rectify Qatnuth and Exteriority. And thereby all the worlds are repaired and all the Exteriorities and fallen souls have an ascent, by means of clarifying and purifying the utmost Qatnuth and Exteriority, which is where the main grip of the *Qelipoth*/Husks stems from. So now everything is clarified and nullified by this Tzaddiq, as mentioned. And this is the aspect of these tzaddiqim and elders, the least of whom remembers his umbilical cord being cut, which is the aspect of shrinking and cutting the umbilical, when one attains such perfect purity so as to remember what happened then. And this is the aspect of repair and purification of the skin, which is the connection between the mother and child, which is tied by the umbilical which is only skin. For the uncoiling of the all the worlds from world to world is only from the "Navel" downwards, as thoroughly explained in the `Etz Chayim in Sha`ar Hanequdim and in many places, that the beginning of the lower world in the upper world is from the aspect of the navel downwards, where the aspect of *NeHI* [Netzach-Hod-Yesod] begins, the aspect of the upper world's "legs," where the essence of the vitality of the world lower than it lies. And thus from world to world, from level to level. And therefore Hashem Yithbarakh created it such that the baby is also physically tied to its mother's navel, for the derivation from generation to generation, from father and mother to son and daughter, begins from the navel downwards. And therefore the main drawing of the Brains of these holy elders to us is by means of the least elder of them, who is the first elder from bottom to top, who related that he remembers the cutting of his umbilical, as mentioned. For from there is the essence of the revelation of the Brains and the unraveling of the worlds from navel downwards as mentioned, which this is the aspect of drawing the light of tefillin, which extend down to the navel, which are the aspect of the straps that extend down to the navel as mentioned. But really, even though we only receive the light from the aspect of the navel downwards, by means of the last elder among them from top to bottom, who remembers the cutting of his umbilical as mentioned, all the vitality of the Brains that we receive from there are drawn only from the highest elder, the first-ranking one of them, who is the aspect of this Blind One, who is this baby. For it is impossible to make vessels to receive the light below except by the power of the highest sanctity and the utmost supernal light.

POINT #36

And this is (Ex. 1), "And it came to pass, when the midwives feared God, that He made them houses." This is the aspect of the tefillin housings. For the midwives are the aspect of the children's mother, drawing the light of tefillin, which are the aspect of mother, upon the son, so they are the aspect of giving birth to the Brains, the aspect of (ibid. 13), "Sanctify to Me all the first-born, whatsoever opens any womb" as mentioned. And this is, "And it happened, when they feared" specifically. For tefillin are the aspect of fear, as written, "And all the people of the land shall see that Hashem's name is called upon you, and they will fear you" [Deut. 28:10]. And our Rabbis z"l explained that these are the head tefillin. For the midwives are Aharon and Moshe's mother, and Miriam their sister the other midwife, from whom royalty issued, as Rashi explained there. For Moshe and Aharon are the essence of the tefillin. Aharon the Kohen Gadol is the aspect of the Eight Tiqunei Diqna of the Kohen Gadol, which are the aspect of the eight elders, the aspect of the eight head and arm tefillin passages as mentioned.

Moshe Rabbeinu is the aspect of the Supernal Elder, who boasted that he is extremely old and yet is young and a suckling entirely etc. and the whole world does not amount to him so much as an eyeblink etc. This is the aspect of Moshe Rabbeinu a"h who is the aspect of (ibid. 2), "And behold, a crying youth," that even though he reached what he reached, the perfect aspect of the Elder in Holiness, still he was entirely in the aspect of youth and suckling, in the aspect of (Ps. 37), "I have been young and also old," that even though I have become so much an elder, still I am entirely young and a suckling, which this is the aspect of the boasting of the foremost elder who is the Blind One as mentioned.

And therefore Moshe attained that it was written of him (Deut. 34), "His eye was not dim and his natural force was not abated" — even after death, for no oldness jumped upon him at all, even when dying at 120 years of age. For he attained the ultimate elderliness, yet remained entirely a suckling, as if he still had not begin living at all, as written (ibid. 3:24), "You have *begun* to show" etc.; that is, he still did not grasp at all; Hashem Yithbarakh only *began* showing him His greatness etc. Which, all this is the above aspect, always beginning anew as mentioned. For Moshe is the aspect of "*MaN*/Manna," as is known, of which it says (Ex. 17:15), "For they did not know *MaH*/what it is." It is impossible to at all know what he is, that someone born of a woman should attain what he attained. And this is the letters of *MoSheH* being *Shin MaH* — Shin, the three fathers who are the entirety of the Brains, entirety of the tefillin; but everything is drawn from the aspect of MaH, the aspect of, "For they did not know what it is," which this is the essence of the aspect of Moshe, who is the aspect of the aforementioned elder, who was elder and a suckling etc. as mentioned, who is the root of everything and above everything as mentioned. As written (Num. 12), "And the man, Moshe, was extremely humble" etc., which is the aspect of (Ps. 131), "Like a weaned child with his mother; my soul is with me like a weaned child," which David said.

And this is that it is written in the Zohar, regarding Moshe, that amongst the *Sabas*/Supernal Elders he is the Elder, and amongst the sucklings he is the suckling, that is, as mentioned, that he is old and suckling etc. as mentioned. And this is his saying (Deut. 31:2), "I am one hundred and twenty years old today" — *today* my days and years are filled up, for he "can longer go," as our Rabbis z"l said (*Sotah* 13b), "this teaches that [the gates of wisdom] were closed to him." For he needed to live the aforementioned long life, going each time further and further, and when he could "go no further" he was forced to pass away, as discerned in the holy talks of Rabbeinu z"l. And therefore (ibid. 34), "And no man knew his burial-chamber," for they did not know what he is, as mentioned.

Hence Moshe is the aspect of the aforementioned Supernal Elder, who is the root of tefillin, which are the aspect of the face's skin beaming, which Moshe attained, which are the aspect of the light of tefillin, as Rabbeinu z"l said in the torah, "*Markevoth Par`oh..*" (*LM* #38), from the aspect of that Elder. And Aharon is the aspect of the eight Tiqunei Diqna, which are the aspect of the eight tefillin passages that are drawn from Moshe's aspect, from the aspect of that Elder.

And this is, "And He made them houses" — houses of priesthood and royalty (*Sh"R* 1). Houses of priesthood are the aspect of tefillin, which are the aspect of the priesthood's sanctity as

mentioned, the aspect of the sanctity of the firstborn, to give him
to the Kohen as mentioned. And houses of royalty are the aspect
of David Mashiach's kingship, the aspect of Emunah, which all
this is the aspect of tefillin as mentioned. And the essence of
tefillin's sanctity is the aspect of grasping Godliness, which the
true tzaddiqim, who are from the aspect of Moshe, draw upon us,
through many constrictions, which this is the main thing, that
they manage to attain such a high and enormous perception, that
they can constrict and clothe the perception in many constrictions
and vestments until we too can manage to grasp Godliness as
mentioned. And this is the aspect of tefillin housings, for it is impossible for us to receive the light of the passages themselves except by way of the housings and straps, which are the aspect of
limitations and vessels of ʿOlam haTiqqun, to receive the light by
degree and measure.

For they are able to enter the aspect of the Vacated Space and
reveal His Godliness there, and thereby make holy vessels.
For the essence of these vessels' genesis is by means of repair of
the Vacated Space which is the beginning of the limitation, which
is the root of all the vessels and masks generated from the coarsening of the light and its becoming distant from the Emanator.
For if there was no Vacated Space then the coarsening of the light
and its distancing would be irrelevant etc., as explained and discerned in the Writings. Hence the essence of the vessels' genesis
derives from the aspect of the Vacated Space. But by means of
Adam haRishon's failure he was seized in his vessels, the essence
of which is in the aspect of the skin, which is the ultimate vessel,
the exterior of the exterior; and that is where he was seized the
most as mentioned, which this is the aspect of the "Serpent's
bite," from whence is the grip of all the *Qelipoth*/Husks, God
spare us. And therefore the main repair is by means of purifying
and processing the hide in sanctity, which is the aspect of repair
of the imagination, repair of the Vacated Space, which the aforementioned great Tzaddiqim attain repairing, to the point that
from it, specifically, they make the aspect of holy vessels to receive the light in degree and measure. Which, this is the aspect
of the hide of a pure beast, insofar as the essence of writing the
Torah and tefillin is on their hide specifically, and as mentioned.

And this is the aspect of the housings made of hide. For we need to receive the light through limitations and vessels that are made by the repair of the Vacated Space which is the aspect of repairing the imagination, which is the aspect of hide, as mentioned. And this is the aspect of (Gen. 3), "And Hashem-God made Adam and his wife garments of skin and clothed them" — garments of skin specifically, for the main repair is repairing the skin etc. as mentioned. For, the garments of skin are the aspect of Tallith and Tefillin, which come from skin and from the hair that grows on the skin, as explained in the `Etz Chayim. Which, this is the aspect of (Ex. 22:26), "*ki hu kesutho levaddah*/that is his covering, only" — this is tzitzith; "*hi simlatho le`oro*/it is his garment for his skin" — this is tefillin (*Tiqqunim* #69), which are deeper and loftier than tzitzith, as written there. And all this is the aspect of repair of the imagination, which is repair of the Vacated Space, as the essence of the repair is by means of Emunah as mentioned. And this is, "And it came to pass, as the midwives feared God" — feared specifically. For holy piety is the aspect of repair of the constriction and stricture of the Vacated Space, which is sweetened at its root by means of holy piety, which is the aspect of a "holy decree," as is known. Therefore by the aspect of piety are made housings, which are the aspect of fixing the vessels and limitations to receive the tefillin's light by degree and measure as mentioned. And this is, "And it came to pass, as they feared... [God] made them housings" as mentioned.

Likutei Halakhoth Y"D Tola`im Halachah 4

The subject of worms [*tola`im*], which are forbidden specifically when they creep on the earth, that is, worms that grow on vegetation attached to earth, or on detached vegetation if [the worm] separates from it, in which case they are prohibited due to "teeming things that teem on the earth" [Lev. 11]; but [those that form] on detached vegetation and have not separated from it are permitted.

POINT #1

First we shall explain some of the sparks that flash in my mind, some hints in the awesome story of the Seven Beggars in its story of the Sixth Day when the handless one came and boasted of the enormous awesomeness of the power in his hands. See the whole story there, regarding the king's daughter that the [evil] king captured, and he saw in a dream that she will kill him, and he thought about what to with her etc., and thereby the love between them deteriorated and she fled from him into the Watery Castle that has ten walls of water; and he pursued her with his army and shot all the ten arrows at her and they hit her; and she fled inside the ten walls of water and remains faint; and the handless one heals her, for he has such power in his hands that he can extract all the ten kinds of arrows, and can enter inside all the walls of water etc., and knows all the ten kinds of pulsebeats, and can play all the ten kinds of melody that are her healing etc. (take a good look there at all this):

POINT #2

The utmost meaning of this story is hidden away from all the worlds, but nevertheless all of us are permitted to seek and request some allusions in it, whatever we can find, as I understood from his words mentioned above. And the concept is that the king's daughter is the aspect of the Israelite souls that are called "king's daughter," the aspect of "Hear, daughter, and see" [Ps. 45:11], the aspect of "all-glorious is the king's daughter, within" [Ps. 45:13]. And the king who captured her is the *Yetzer haRa`*/Evil Inclination, the aspect of the "old and foolish king." And he saw in a dream that she would kill him, for he himself sees and discerns that ultimately the souls of Yisrael will over-come him, kill him and expel him from the world, in the aspect of, "and the spirit of impurity I will drive away from the earth" [Zach. 13:2]. And this is the aspect of slaying the Angel of Death, who is the Yetzer haRa`, the aspect of "sacrificing the *To-dah*/Thanksgiving offering" [Ps. 50:23], which our Rabbis z"l ex-pounded (*Sanh. 43b*) is someone who sacrifices his Yetzer haRa` etc.

And he devised evil thoughts about her, what to do to her, and thereby the love between them deteriorated and she fled from him. That is, because the Yetzer haRa`, even when the Is-raelite lifeforce [*nefesh*] is subjugated under it, on account of see-ing she will ultimately defeat him etc. and thereby he begins to devise thoughts on the lifeforce, what to do to it — thereby the love between them deteriorates. For at first there was a little af-fection and tie between the Israelite soul and the Yetzer haRa`. For due to the enormity of her exile while captive to him, she for-got her eminence so much that she had a little affection and tie with him. But on account of her lifeforce seeing and discerning that he devises thoughts on her and wants to exterminate her en-tirely, God forbid, thereby she begins to bolster herself against him and devise thoughts against him, how to escape from him. So the love and connection between them spoils, until she escapes from him, in the aspect of, "Jacob fled" [Gen. 31:22], who is the generality of the Israelite lifeforce (as explained before else-where), the aspect of, "that the people had fled" [Ex. 14:5], and as Dawidh Hamelekh a"h said, "Who would give me a limb like a dove? ... I would haste me to a shelter" etc. [Ps. 55:7,9].

And the king took his whole army and pursued her. For the Yetzer haRa` collected all his forces and chased after the Is-raelite lifeforce, for when he sees the vitality wants to escape from him and she flees from him, then he collects all his forces and chases her. For the more her vitality fortifies itself against him, the more he fortifies himself against her; and as our Rabbis z"l said, "The greater the person, the greater his Yetzer" [*Suk.* 52a]. And he reached her at the Watery Castle that has ten walls of water etc., and she fled into this castle, and passed through and entered in all the ten walls of water, until she reached inside etc. Water is the aspect of the consciousness and the Torah which is called "water," as it says, "And the earth shall be full of knowledge of Hashem, as the waters cover the sea" [Isa. 11:8], and like it says, "Ho, everyone that thirsts, come for water" [ibid. 55:1]. And there, they are ten walls of water; this is the aspect of the Torah as a whole that is composed of the Ten Commandments which are the aspect of ten levels of prophecy (as explained in the torah "Tik`u", LM II #8:3).

And it is impossible to go in the waters of knowing Hashem, except through the Torah which is the aspect of walls and dividers within the waters of knowledge that wash like the sea, as whoever enters them drowns. For on account of Knowledge's vastness it cannot be received, and it is impossible to enter the knowledge of Hashem — on account of the aspect of *Ribui Or*/Overload of Light, for "too much oil causes the lamp to go out," as is known — except by the power of the Torah, the foundation of which is Emunah, the aspect of "All your mitzwoth are Emunah" [Ps. 119:86]. And Emunah is called a "Wall," as it says, "I am a wall" etc. [Song 8:10], and Rashi explains that Emunah is strong like a wall. And whoever is within the realm of accepting the Torah, who knows by himself, or has received from his rabbis the ways of the gates of these walls of water which are the ways of the Torah, he can enter in them, through all the ten walls, into the very interior. But whoever does not know the ways of the Torah and enters in the Sea of Wisdom and the Knowledge without the Torah, drowns and sinks there unto destruction, which is the aspect of all the naturalistic probing wise men, who are the aspect of the evil kingship, who entered the Sea of Knowledge without the Torah and sank in the apostasy and thereby lost out from both worlds.

But the Israelite soul fled inside all the ten walls, until she entered inside the interior. That is, she fled from the Yetzer haRa` into the Torah, as our Rabbis z"l said, "If this wretched one assails you, drag him to the Beith Midrash" etc. [Kid. 30a]. And he ordered to shoot her with all the ten kinds of arrows. This is the aspect of the enormity of the surge and the fight, as he most attacks Talmidei Chakhamim who delve in the Torah, for the depths of the sea surge upon them the most, as is known, as our Rabbis said, that he leaves the other nations in peace and just attacks Yisrael, and not only that, but he leaves all Yisrael in peace and only attacks Talmidei Chakhamim, as written, "For he has done great things" [Joel 2:20], as he extends his hand upon great figures [*Suk.* 52a].

And this is the aspect of all the ten kinds of arrows that he shot at the king's daughter who fled inside the walls of water. That is, he fired all the kinds of bad poison he has, and bolstered himself with all his powers, with all the aspect of the "Ten Crowns of Impurity" against the soul of the Talmid Chakham which fled into the Torah. And she fled inside all the ten walls of water, which is the Torah as mentioned, and remained faint on account of the bad poison arrows that he shot at her. And he, that is, the handless one who had wondrous power in his hand, heals her.

And the essence of her healing is by means of the ten kinds of melody which are the aspect of joy, as it says, "On the ten-stringed instrument, and with the psaltery... for You, Hashem, have made me glad through your work" [Ps. 92:4-5] (as our Rabbis z"l have said). For the essence of the arrows, which are the surge of the Sitra Achra, is by means of melancholy, the aspect of "and dust shall be the Serpent's food" [Isa. 65:25]; dust is the aspect of melancholy and sloth, as Rabbeinu z"l said (*LM* #189), that the essence of the Yetzer haRa`'s attack is in blemishing the Covenant, God forbid, for "the essence of the Yetzer haRa` is for forbidden relations" etc., as Rabbeinu z"l said. And the essence of sexual craving and blemish of the Covenant is by means of melancholy (as I heard from Rabbeinu z"l, and as brought in his words many times). And therefore the Qelipah that is strengthened in blemish of the Covenant is named "Lilith," after the *yelalah*/wailing and melancholy.

And therefore Rabbeinu z"l established ten psalm songs to repair the Covenant, which are the aspect of the ten kinds of melody, the aspect of joy. For the essence of Covenant blemish is by means of melancholy, the aspect of, "and it grieved Him at His heart" [Gen. 6:6] that is said of the generation of the Flood, who blemished the Covenant and "corrupted their way on the earth" [ibid :12]. And conversely the repair of the Covenant is by means of joy, the aspect of the ten kinds of melody. And thus Rabbeinu z"l wrote elsewhere (in *LM* #24), that the essence of the Shekhinah's exile is melancholy etc., and similarly in many places.

Therefore the essence of the king's daughter's healing, the aspect of the Israelite vitality, is ten kinds of melody, the aspect of joy as mentioned.

And it is necessary to know all the ten kinds of pulsebeats, and this person knows by having power in his hands to give wisdom to all the appointees in the world (as written there in the story; see there). For he needs to know the sicknesses and the descent of each person. And this is the aspect of knowing the pulsebeat of the king's daughter, the aspect of the Israelite vitality. And this is the aspect of, "Take unto you Yehoshu`a... a man in whom is spirit, and lay your hand upon him" [Num. 27:18]. Laying the hands is the aspect of this power of giving wisdom with his hands. And this is, "a man in whom is spirit," as he knows how to deal with every person's spirit, as he knows the pulse spirit of each one, as he knows the pulses, which are the aspect of spirit; all their lackings and illnesses, and how to go about their healing and draw unto them the repair of joy from the aspect of the ten kinds of melody.

POINT #3

And Rabbeinu z"l's words, especially this story, apply in general and in particular in every regard. For in general, the king's daughter is the aspect of the Holy Kingship, which is the root of all the souls, the root of all the worlds, as they all were created to reveal His Kingship through lowly mankind specifically. And the king who took her is the Evil Kingship that is drawn from the slag of the "Primordial Kings that died" and were broken and left behind 288 Sparks, and from them is the nursing of the Qelipoth, that aspect of the Wicked Kingship that always wants to overcome the Holy Kingship, to take the Holy Kingship, the aspect of the King's Daughter, to itself, to conceal His Blessed Kingship from the world.

And her fleeing into the water is the aspect of, "and the earth was astonishingly void, and darkness" etc. [Gen. 1], which this is the aspect of the destroyed worlds from which the Evil Kingship gets power, from which the ten kinds of arrow get power. And "the spirit of God" is the spirit of Mashiach; the Holy Kingship is the Mashiach's Kingship, which is when His Blessed Kingship will be revealed to everyone's eyes. "Hovering over the face of the water," is the aspect of the ten walls of water into which the Holy Kingship, Mashiach's Kingship, fled. And this is the "hovering" — like one who is become sickly, weak and nearly expired, God forbid, his spirit just hovering. And "water" is the secret of the new *MaH* light, which is the World of Repair, for water is the aspect of MaH in accord with the root of the four Elements, for it is known in the Arizal's writings that there is the aspect of *TaNT"A*   (*Ta`amim*/Cantillations,    *Nequdoth*/Vowel-spots, *Tagim*/Crowns, *Otiyoth*/Letters), and they are the aspect of *AB SaG MaH BaN*, and they are *ABY"A* (*Atziluth*/Emanation, *Beriyah*/Creation, *Yetzirah*/Formation, `*Asiyah*/Completion), and from them descend the Four Elements, Fire-Spirit-Water-Earth, which are the aspect of Inanimate-Botanic-Animal-Speaking. And the essence of the Breaking was in the aspect of BaN, so the repair is by the new MaH lights. Hence, the breaking was in the aspect of Dust, which is the aspect of Completion, where the main grip of the Qelipoth is, the aspect of, "and the Serpent's bread shall be dust." And the repair was by the aspect of Water which pertains to MaH.

For, the root of Fire-Spirit-Water-Dust is the aspect of *AB SaG MaH BaN*. Hence Dust is the aspect of BaN, as that is where the Breaking occurred, and Water is the aspect of MaH, as the repair is from there. And therefore waters purify from all impurities and one cannot enter any sanctity except by purification and immersion in water. The Kohanim at their service, the purification of a woman for her husband, the purification of all Yisrael entering the Covenant at the giving of the Torah, and the purification of the convert when he enters the Yisraelite religion — they are all purified by water. For Water is the aspect of the light of MaH, which is the aspect of the repair, as the essence of purity stems from there. But since the Evil Kingship prevailed against the Holy Kingship, even though it fled into the water — for it had shot all the ten kinds of arrows at it, for even after the repair it was still not perfectly repaired and there remained 288 Sparks among the Qelipoth, which the Qelipoth derive strength from, and from which are drawn the ten kinds of arrows, which are the aspect of "Ten Crowns of Impurity" which are all drawn from that slag, as they assail even after the beginning of the repair, by means of the Sparks that remained among them — thus on account of this, water is prone to impurity, for impurity stalks it exceedingly. For when some repair is begun, as long as it is not perfectly finished, they assail it and stalk it exceedingly, like two people fighting, when one sees the other winning and then he bolsters himself against him and assails him all the more (as explained elsewhere).

POINT #4

A nd this is the aspect of the parting of the Sea of Reeds, the aspect of, "and the waters, a wall to them" [Ex. 14:22] that is drawn from the aspect of those ten walls, for Yisrael as a whole are the aspect of the king's daughter, the Holy Kingship that is comprised of the souls of Yisrael. And the other king took her, the aspect of Par`oh king of Mitzrayim, and his power is from his angel the S"M, who is the minister of Mitzrayim as is brought. And this is the secret of Sarah being taken to Par`oh's house and to Avimelekh's house, as all this hints to the Mitzrayim exile, for all this is the aspect of the king's daughter's being taken unto that king. And the Evil Kingship saw she would ultimately rise up and kill him, the aspect of, "And Hashem plagued Par`oh and his house over Sarah's ordeal" etc., and the scripture, "And God came to Avimelekh in a night dream and said to him, Behold, you die because of the woman that you have taken" etc.

A nd similarly afterwards when he wanted to seize all of Yisrael in exile, it is written, "Come, let us deal wisely with them, lest they multiply... and fight against us, and go up from the land" [Ex. 1:10], for the Evil Kingship sees from afar that their end is to be cut off, therefore they devise thoughts what to do to the king's daughter, which are Yisrael as a whole, until finally she fled from him, the aspect of, "And it was told to the king of Mitzrayim that the people were fled" [Ex. 14:5]. So they came and told him that she is found by the Watery Castle, and the king and his forces went to capture her, the aspect of, "And Par`oh harnessed his chariot and took his people with him [v. 6] ... and overtook them encamped by the sea [v. 9]." So she fled into the water and entered inside all the ten walls, for all the walls of water opened for them, the aspect of, "and the water, a wall for them." And thereby she traversed the sea in peace, the aspect of, "and the Yisraelites went on dry land in the sea" [v. 29]. But Par`oh and his army who pursued them drowned in the sea.

A nd his firing all the ten arrows at her, this is the aspect of, "And the angel of God moved... and went behind them" [v. 19]. And Rashi explained that they received all of Mitzrayim's arrows and ballista projectiles, and even though the angel of God, which is the Shekhinah, absorbed the arrows and thereby Yisrael were saved and traversed the sea in peace. Nevertheless the poison of Mitzrayim's arrows reached Yisrael and harmed them, for the war was immense both above and below, spiritually and physically, as is brought. And as it says (v. 10), "and behold, Mitzrayim was advancing after them," as they saw the angel of Mitzrayim advancing after them to assist, and when the angel, which is the S"M, saw Yisrael fleeing into the sea and the sea splitting before them and the water a wall for them, then he fired the arrows at them, as he assaulted them and cast the arrows' poison at them, which are the foreign ideologies of apostasy and idolatry, which this is the aspect of, "but they were rebellious at the sea, at the sea of Reeds" [Ps. 106:7], as they said, "Just as we are going out from this side [Mitzrayim is going out of the sea from another side]," as it says, "and trouble shall pass through the sea" [Zech. 10:11], as even then there was some apostasy in Yisrael, as some bad mindsets were cast at them that were drawn from the aspect of the arrows shot at them.

A nd from this come all the trials wherewith our fathers tested Hakadosh Barukh Hu: with the Calf, the Spies etc. And they are Ten Trials that are drawn from the ten arrows that he fired at them into the ten walls of water; and still we are not healed from them. And from this come all the maladies of Kenesseth Yisrael in her exile, crying, "Sustain me with flagons/cakes, spread my bed with swollen fruit, for I am love-sick" [Song 2:5]. The aspect of "acquainted with disease" [Isa. 53:3], the aspect of, "From the sole of the foot even unto the head there is no soundness in it; but wounds, and bruises" etc. [ibid. 1:6], as all these illnesses are drawn from the ten kinds of arrows which are all the Qelipah's powers and the Yetzer Hara's armies as whole, which cast their arrows' poison at the souls of Yisrael, whence come all the apostasy, doubts, confusions, obstacles and bad cravings, and everything that masks, cuts off and obstructs from following Hashem

Yithbarakh; in regard to both individuals and the whole of Yisrael, the exile extending so long — everything is drawn from this aspect of the ten kinds of arrows, the aspect of, "Your arrows are gone deep into me" etc. [Ps. 38:3], cried by Dawidh Hamelekh a"h, who is the aspect of the Holy Kingship, the King's daughter, the aspect of the souls of Yisrael as a whole. And this is the aspect of (Lam. 3:12), "He has bent His bow, and set me as a mark for the arrow," which is said of Yisrael's exile as a whole. And this is the aspect of, "They have set their arrow on the bowstring, that they may shoot in darkness at the upright in heart" [Ps. 11:2].

And the king's daughter could not endure the pain of the poison of the arrows smeared in extremely bad and grievous poisons, especially for such a long time. But Hashem Yithbarakh "made the cure before the blow," for her, by helping her flee inside the ten walls of water, which are the Torah — for the Torah is the essence of Life and Healing, for "Hashem's Torah is perfect, the restorer of vitality" [Ps. 19:7] — from the paths of death to the ways of life, for Kenesseth Yisrael which fled into the waters of the Torah, thereby has power to endure the bitterness of the exile which is the aspect of the arrows' bitterness. And had she not fled into the Torah she would not have potential to endure at all. But by means of the Torah, even though the arrows have reached her even there, as mentioned, presently she has the potential to anyhow endure by the power of the Torah, which is the essence of vitality, the aspect of, "precisely it is your vitality" [Deut. 30:20] and Hashem Yithbarakh "gives strength to the weary" and gives her power to endure the arrows' bitterness by the Torah's power, until ultimately the True Healer comes, who is this handless one, and heals her perfectly, as mentioned.

This is the meaning of [Ex. 15], "Then Moshe will sing:" It says "will sing" rather than "sang." From here we learn that Moshe will sing in a future time to come. For even though they sang a jubilant song at that time, they still did not attain drawing all the ten types of melody perfectly, to finish the King's Daughter's healing perfectly. They only drew sanctity and emanation from the Ten Types of Melody, from which they attained the Song at the Sea. But the essential Song in its perfection will only be in the future, when Mashiach, who is Moshe himself, will come. For "that which was is that which will be" [Eccl. 1:9], as is known; the aspect of, "Then Moshe will sing" — "then" specifically, Moshe will perfectly sing all the ten types of melody [*Pesachim* 117a; *Zohar III*:101a; *LM I*:205; II:*92; Tikkun haKlali*], whereupon the healing of the King's Daughter, who is the aspect of the Shekhinah and Kenesseth Yisrael, will be complete. For then there will be aroused a New Song, the aspect of, "A song, Sing to Hashem a new song: something just wondrous He has done" [Ps. 98], which is the aspect of the "Song of Wonders," the Song that is Single, Double, Triple and Quadruple [*Y YH YHW YHWH*, v. *TZ* 51b], that will be "awoken" in the future.

And therefore they concluded, "Hashem will reign forever and ever" — a future tense — for, the revelation of His kingship, which is the aspect of the healing of the King's Daughter, who is the Dominion of Holiness, will be in the future, as His kingship will be revealed before the eyes of all; the aspect of, "And Hashem will be King over all the earth" [Zach. 14:9]. And then the joy and happiness will be perfect in all the worlds, through the ten types of melody being aroused, which are the aspect of joy as mentioned. And this is the aspect of [Ps. 99], "Hashem has reigned, the earth will rejoice," the aspect of (Ps. 96:11), "The heavens will be joyous, the earth will rejoice, and they will say among the nations, Hashem has reigned."

Then will be fulfilled the verse (Ps. 47:7-8), "Make music (*zammeru*) to God, make music; make music to our King, make music. For God is King of all the earth" etc. For the essential revelation of His Blessed kingship, the aspect of the King's Daughter's healing mentioned above, is through music and melody, the aspect of the ten types of melody mentioned, the aspect of "Acknowledge Hashem on the harp, play to Him on the ten-stringed psaltery. Sing to Him a new song," etc. (Ps. 33:2-3), and many such verses explaining the revelation of His Blessed kingship through song, music, and melody, which all of this is the aspect of the ten types of melody, which are the King's Daughter's healing, which is the aspect of the revelation of Holy Kingship, namely to know that the Kingship is Hashem's.

POINT #5

And behold, when you finely examine this story's words, you will find that Rabbeinu z"l spoke of four things, and each of the four are composed of ten. And they are:

1. Ten kinds of arrows
2. Ten kinds of walls of water, which are ten kinds of charity
3. Ten kinds of pulsebeats, which are ten measures of wisdom.
4. Ten kinds of melody, which are the aspect of [balancing the ten winds]

(see there, the whole story).

"And knowledge is easy to one who discerns" [Prob. 14:6]; they allude to the Four Worlds *ABY"A* (*Atziluth*/Emanation, *Beriyah*/Creation, *Yetzirah*/Formation, `*Asiyah*/Completion), and all the aspects of these four I related above, that they are the aspect of *TaNT"A*, which are *Ta`amim*/Cantillations, *Nequdoth*/Vowel-spots, *Tagim*/Crowns, *Otiyoth*/Letters), which are the aspect of the four Names *AB* etc., which are the root of the four worlds *ABY"A*, *Atziluth*/Emanation, *Beriyah*/Creation, *Yetzirah*/Formation, `*Asiyah*/Completion, which are the aspect of the Four Elementals, Fire, Spirit, Water, Earth, which are Inanimate, Botanic, Animal, Speaking (as brought in the Writings and as mentioned).

And this is known, that each of these four things are comprised of ten Sefiroth, as is known, for `*Asiyah* is the aspect of Letters, the aspect of *BaN*, whence is the elemental of Dust, corresponding to Inanimate, comprised of ten. And similarly *Yetzirah*, the aspect of *MaH*, Crowns etc. And similarly the rest. And this is the aspect of the four aspects of ten each, that are explained in the story. For ten arrows are the aspect of `*Asiyah*, for there in `*Asiyah* is the main grip of the Qelipoth and the Sitra Achra, as is known, whence are all the arrows that afflict the Shekhinah and Kenesseth Yisrael, the aspect of the Holy Kingship, the aspect of the king's daughter. Ten kinds of walls of water are the aspect of *Yetzirah*, which is the aspect of *MaH*, which is the aspect of the elemental Water etc. (as explained above). Ten kinds of pulsebeats are the aspect of *Beriyah* corresponding to *SaG*, the aspect of vowel spots etc. as mentioned, for the ten kinds of pulsebeats are the aspect of spots, as brought in the Tikkunim,

"Sometimes [the spirit] beats.. like a *tzere*.. and sometimes like a *sheva*, or *qamatz*" etc.; see there [*TZ* 108a]. Ten kinds of melody are the aspect of *Atziluth* corresponding to cantillations etc. as mentioned. For cantillations are the aspect of the ten kinds of melody, the aspect of playing the accents. Hence the four aspects in the story are the four aspects *TaNT"A*, the aspect of the four Names etc., that include all the worlds. And all the repairs included in all of them need to be drawn forth, all in order to heal the Queen's Daughter, to save her from that king etc., from the Evil Kingship. For the essence of the uncoiling of the worlds from head to bottom, was all for the sake of Malkhuth/Kingship, in order to reveal His Kingship, as is known.

Four Elements correspondences

Y-H-W-H	Y	H	W	H
TaNT"A	*Ta`amim/* Cantillations	*Nequdoth/* Vowel-spots	*Tagim/* Crowns	*Otiyoth/* Letters
Expansions	*AB*	*SaG*	*MaH*	*BaN*
ABY"A	*Atziluth/* Emanation	*Beriyah/* Creation	*Yetzirah /* Formation	*`Asiyah/* Completion
Elements	Fire	Spirit	Water	Earth
Kingdom	Speaking	Animal	Botanic	Inanimate
Seven Beggars: Sixth Day	Ten kinds of melody — [balancing the ten winds]	Ten pulse-beats/vowel spots — ten measures of wisdom	Ten walls of water — ten chari-ties	Ten arrows

POINT #6

Hence `Asiyah, the aspect of Dust, is where is the main grip of the arrows, which are the aspect of the Qeliphoth's and Sitra Achra's onslaughts. Therefore whatever is closer to the earth is more gripped by impurity. Therefore worms that creep on the earth, which are closer to the earth than all animals, as they creep and swarm right on the ground, are thus all forbidden, as no sort of them are permitted for consumption. For they are all forbidden due to "a creeping thing that creeps on the earth" — "creeps on the earth" specifically, for that is where the most grip of the Sitra Achra is, the aspect of "and dust shall be the serpent's food," the aspect of, "and dust you shall eat all the days of your life." And thus from there are all the ten kinds of arrows, as mentioned. Therefore they are all forbidden, but the worms in detached vegetation as long as they are not separated, which are not in the category of "creeping on the earth," are permitted. For the essence of the prohibition is on account of them creeping on the earth, where is the main grip of the Sitra Achra, the aspect of the arrows as mentioned.

POINT #7

And this is the aspect of the Parashah of the *Korban Tamid*/Continual Offering which we recite in the morning [Num. 28], which is for purifying and repairing the world of `Asiyah, as is known. And the essential thing is to subdue the Qelipah called *"TOLA`/Worm,"* through the aspect of *"`OLAT tamid/Continual Burnt-Up Offering"* (as brought in the Qawanoth). For, there, in `Asiyah, is the main grip of the aspect of TOLA`, which is an utterly hard Qelipah, as from it descend all the worms that swarm on the earth, which are the power of `Asiyah's impurity, which are subdued by the *Qorbanoth*/Offerings, the aspect of Korban Tamid, the aspect of `Olat Tamid as mentioned. For, the Qorbanoth are extremely lofty, and they have the power to purify the force of `Asiyah's impurity (as explained in the Ketavim).

For, explained in this story is that this person had such power in his hands, that when he shoots an arrow, he can bring it back etc. And thereby he has power in his hands to heal the Queen's Daughter etc.; see there. Now, seemingly it is puzzling why he mentioned in his boasting that he *shoots* an arrow and brings it back; shouldn't he just mention that he can bring back and take out the arrows, which is the essence of the story, as thereby he heals the Queen's Daughter, as he removes from her all the arrows that the king shot at her? So what is the benefit of shooting the arrows, as he mentions he can *shoot* the arrows and bring them back? Wouldn't it be better that he not shoot them at all? But, even the aspect of shooting the arrows is needed for the healing, and this is the secret of "sweetening the decrees at their root." And therefore it is impossible to remove the arrows that the king shot at her except by *him* shooting arrows at her and drawing them back, and thereby automatically extracting and nullifying all the bad arrows that the king shot at her. For the Wicked Kingship's arrows, which are the assault of the Qelipah, are all drawn from the power of the Strictures, as is known, and it is impossible to extract and nullify them except by sweetening the judgements, and the judgements are impossible to sweeten except at their root, as mentioned. And therefore this one with the power, who occupies himself in healing the King's daughter, cannot heal her except by shooting, at her, arrows that are the aspect of the root of the judgements. But these arrows, the aspect of strictures, are not harmful to her; just the opposite, thereby specifically he sweetens all the judgements at their root and removes from her all the arrows that were shot at her and he heals her.

And this is the aspect of slaughtering the Qorbanoth, which purify the `Asiyah*, which is where the grip of the ten kinds of bad arrows is. For, a sword or knife of slaughter is the aspect of the force of judgement, from which descends the grip of the Sitra Achra, as they are the aspect of the aforementioned arrows, as they are the aspect of `Esau's sword, the aspect of, "and you shall live by your sword" [Gen. 27:40]. And `ESau is named after `ASiyah, for he is the force of `Asiyah's impurity, for sword and arrows are one aspect, as it says (Prov. 25), "An axe, a sword, and a sharpened arrow." And similarly, in holiness, with Hashem Yithbarakh it is written, "If I have twofold [unleashed] My sword [like] lightning {i.e. as lightning flashes from one end of the sky across to the other end, against My people in retribution}, My hand will yet have hold on [strict] justice..." [Deut. 32:41], and Rashi explains, "Flesh and blood shoots an arrow and cannot retrieve it, but the Holy One, Blessed be He, shoots an arrow and does retrieve it." And Rabbeinu z"l brought this verse regarding this story; see there. Hence, sword and arrow are one facet; that is, through slaughtering the Qorbanoth with sword and knife — which are the aspect of arrows, the aspect of the force of judgement in holiness as mentioned — thereby are removed from the beast all the arrows of the Sitra Achra, which are the bad admixture, which is the force of beastly spirit in which it is gripped. And by the sword of slaughter, all the judgements are sweetened at their root and all the bad is removed from it, and human spirit is refined from beastly spirit, the good from the bad, by this aspect of shooting arrows and returning them, which this is the aspect of slaughter, as mentioned. And therefore the essence of slaughter is by to and fro motion, as our Rabbis z"l said: long enough to move to and fro, is the required length of a knife. For the essence of slaughter is in the aspect of to and fro motion, the aspect of the arrows being shot and brought back, which is the aspect of sweetening the judgements at their root as mentioned.

And this is the aspect of Rabbeinu z"l saying in the torah *"Tik`u Tokhachah"* (*LM II* #8) regarding the strong person who can, with proper intent, utter prayer in the aspect of judgement, that specifically through this he can extract from the Sitra Achra all that it swallowed in holiness, by prayer in the aspect of judgement, etc.; see there. This is as mentioned above, for when the prayer was in the aspect of judgement, by means of the compassion being spoiled and the sexual craving waxing strong etc., then the Sitra Achra swallows the prayer. And when the Sitra Achra grows strong, this is the aspect of the arrows shot at the Shekhinah, as it were. And then this one with the power needs to pray specifically prayer in the aspect of judgement, which is where the Sitra Achra nurses from, and therefore this prayer is also the aspect of arrows. But specifically through this strong person's prayer in the aspect of judgement, he removes all the arrows from the Shekhinah, from the King's Daughter. For specifically by this strong person's prayer, he subdues and nullifies the Sitra Achra and removes out of its mouth what it swallowed, whereby the arrows that it shot at the King's Daughter are nullified, which all this is the aspect of sweetening the judgements at their root, as also explained before. And see elsewhere where it is explained that this is the aspect of slaughter, which pertains to prayer, in the judgement aspect of the strong person, namely as mentioned (and see more about this below, if Hashem wills it).

POINT #8

And this is the aspect of fish and locust needing no slaughter. And our Rabbis z"l learned it out from the verse, "and of every living creature that moves in the waters, and of every creature that swarms" etc. [Lev. 11:46], that locust are like fish and so require no slaughter. For there is reason to say that the matter of the Watery Castle in the story alludes to secret of the wisdom and intelligence that exists in the *Chalal haPanui*/Vacated Space that was generated by the *Tzimtzum*/Constriction, as is known. But first you need to take a thorough look at the torah "Go to Par`oh" (*LM* #64). And further, look at what I found in the handwriting of Rabbeinu z"l himself, as he wrote that torah in his own holy words:

A nd this is the aspect of the Watery Castle, for it is explained there in that story in these words, "For there is a Watery Castle, and there they are ten walls one within the other, all of water, and even the floor they walk on there inside the castle is also of water. And likewise there are trees and fruits there, all of water. And the beauty and great marvel of this castle needs no telling, for it is definitely a most wondrous marvel, since it is a castle of water. To enter in this castle is impossible, for whoever would enter it would drown in the water, since it is entirely water. But the Queen's Daughter fled there" etc.; see there.

A nd there is reason to say that all this alludes to the secret of the Vacated Space from which He constricted His light, making it seem there is no light of wisdom and intellect there, therefore it is truly impossible to find His Godliness there through any wisdom or intellect. But in truth, even in the Vacated Space itself there is His Blessed light, which is wisdom and intelligence, except this intellect that is hidden and secret pertaining to the Vacated Space's constriction is impossible to reach and discern now until the future to come, when the Vacated Space will be revealed that it is [*B"R* 21:5], "like the locust [*qamtza*], whose vestment is part of itself" [lit. "whose clothing is of Him and in Him"], which this is the aspect of, "And my righteousness will testify for me at a future date" etc. [Gen. 30:33], the aspect of, "I donned righteousness" [Job. 29:14]. (Take a good look at all this there.)

H ence, even the constriction itself, which is the Vacated Space, with Wisdom becomes like all of Creation itself, as by Wisdom it becomes the aspect of, "With wisdom You have made them all" [Ps. 104:24], only it is impossible to discern it in this world with this intellect, how in truth even in the Vacated Space there is His Blessed light, which is the light of Wisdom.

But nevertheless it is vacated in order that there should be space for Creation. This is absolutely impossible to grasp presently with human intellect until the future to come (as thoroughly explained there; see there).

And this is the aspect of the ten walls of water, for water is the aspect of wisdom and intelligence, the aspect of, "And the earth will be filled with the knowledge of Hashem, as the waters cover the sea" [Isa. 11:9]. And there in the aspect of water, namely in the aspect of the true wisdom and intellect that will be revealed in the future, there is a Castle of Water which is ten walls of water etc., which are wondrous and awesome structures, and fruits etc., and it is all of water. And this is impossible at all to discern with our intellect, how structures are built of the water itself; but this itself is the aforementioned aspect, the aspect of the Vacated Space mentioned, that in truth it has intelligence, and everything is generated from His intelligence, which is the aspect of water. Namely, all of Creation and all the constriction of Creation which is the Vacated Space, is all generated by His Blessed charity, which is the aspect of water, only it is impossible to discern this. And this is the aspect of the Watery Castle that has ten walls etc., all of water, for water is the aforementioned aspect of intelligence.

And ten walls allude to all of Creation which was created with Ten Utterances, which are the aspect of Ten Repairs, the aspect of the Ten Sefiroth; and all these Ten Repairs, Ten Sefiroth, Ten Utterances, which are the entirety of Creation, would be impossible to extract and reveal except by the Vacated Space's Constriction, for otherwise there would be no space for Creation, as mentioned. But nevertheless in real truth there too in the Vacated Space itself there is intellect and awareness. Hence it is not vacated, except this is impossible to discern as mentioned. Hence, all of Creation in entirety and all the constriction of the Vacated Space, everything is generated from the water itself, which is the aspect of intelligence, only it is impossible to discern this through intellect. And therefore in truth this Castle of Water is a wondrous marvel and there is no man who can enter it because he would drown in the water, as it is boundless. For there is definitely no one who can enter in the Vacated Space to probe this intelligence, for he would drown there, for regarding this it says

[Prov. 2:19], "None who go to her return" (as explained there in that torah).

And therefore also in physical Creation, everything is created from water, for Hashem Yithbarakh created water first in all of Creation, as our Rabbis z"l said: First the world was water in water [*Y. Chagiga* 2:1], then He created all of creation in entirety from the water, as it says [Gen. 1], "Let the waters gather together... and let the dry land appear" etc. Hence Dust itself was generated from Water, and then He created from Dust all the earthly derivatives. Hence everything was generated from water, for the earth and the dust itself was generated from the water as mentioned, like it says, "Who spread out the earth over the water" [Ps. 136:6], and all this alludes that everything was generated and descended from the aspect of the aforementioned ten walls of water, which are the root of all Creation entirely that was generated by Wisdom within the Constriction, as He constricted the light of His Wisdom to the sides, and the Wisdom is the aspect of water, as mentioned. And in truth even the Constriction itself is from Water, for in the Constriction as well is hidden and concealed wisdom and intellect, only it is imperceptible. Hence everything is from water, as all the Constrictions, which are the entirety of Creation with all its constriction, are all from water, for all is from [His] wisdom and intellect, only this is incomprehensible, for it is forbidden to probe the aspect of the Vacated Space as mentioned.

And therefore in this physical world the main part of Creation is founded on physical dust, because Man — who has free will, who is the essence, as for him all was created — was created on the earth specifically, for it was necessary to constrict the water until there was earthly dust in order that man and all that was created could exist on it. For man cannot enter in water, for there it is the secret of the Constriction's intellect, mentioned above, that will not be revealed until the future when shall be fulfilled, "And the earth will be filled with the knowledge of Hashem as the waters cover the sea" — "as the waters cover the sea" specifically, namely the awareness will be tangibly shown like the waters that cover the sea, which have the aspect of the ten walls of water, which are drawn from the secret of the intellect of the Vacated Space's Constriction as mentioned.

And in the future this awareness will be revealed, for they will know Hashem with a wondrous intellect, that even though He constricted His light to the sides in order for there to be place for Creation, nevertheless "there is no place void of Him" and He fills all the worlds and pervades them etc. For they will attain the intellect of the Vacated Space, and the earth will be filled with all this awareness *"like the waters that cover the sea"* specifically, namely they will know that all this is like the waters that cover the sea, where there are ten walls that until now have not been revealed in the world; but then they will attain those ten walls. And like the perceptions of these ten walls, which are the aspect of the waters that cover the sea, so will they be aware of Hashem, for it is all one aspect as mentioned. For as long as the intellect of the Vacated Space is not revealed, it is impossible to be fully aware of Hashem. And therefore now the essence of our vitality is the Emunah that the True Tzaddiqim put in us, as they get revelation from there, from the intellect that will be revealed in the future; but in the future this awareness and intellect will be revealed how even in the Vacated Space His Blessed light is hidden; and then all the problems, doubts and confusions about Hashem Yithbarakh will be answered, even the problems that are drawn from the Vacated Space (as explained in that torah "Go to Par`oh;" take a good look there). So therefore finely examine the verse, "And the earth will be filled with the knowledge of Hashem, *as the waters cover the sea"* specifically, for the knowledge is really in the aspect of the water on the sea, which is the secret of the ten walls of water, which are the secret of the Vacated Space's intellect that will be revealed in the future as mentioned.

And all the ten kinds of arrows are drawn from the aspect of the Breaking of the Vessels, from which the Qelipoth were generated, which are the aspect of all the arrows. And the essence of the breaking was in the aspect of the name *BaN*, which is the aspect of Dust. And Water is the aspect of the new name *MaH*, where the repair is from, as mentioned. And therefore there are the ten walls of water which are the secret of the intellect of the Vacated Space that will be revealed in the future, which is the aspect of the repair. For the essence of the breaking was on account of the great concealment, as the secret of the Constriction's intelligence was hidden, as from this is the power of the harsh judgements, and thereby the strictures prevailed, which are the aspect of the slag that was in the vessels, and thereby they could not bear the light, for it exceeded their power, and thereby they broke, and from there were generated the Qelipoth. But in the future, as the intellect of the Vacated Space's intellect will be revealed, the Breaking will be completely repaired and all the Qelipoth will be nullified. Hence, even the problems drawn from Exceedence of Light, from the Breaking of the Vessels, they too have their main power and nursing from the aspect of the Vacated Space, namely from the problems drawn from the Vacated Space that are unanswerable. For the essential genesis of the Qelipoth that were made by the Breaking, their main genesis and power is from the beginning of the Constriction, which is the root of the stricture [*din*]. (Discern thoroughly, all this.)

And take a good look at the Arizal's writings and you will find these things explained, if you have intelligent eyes. And one can tangibly see as regards the problems, that they are all interdependent, as even the answerable problems that are drawn from the Qelipoth that were generated from the Breakage, they too are rooted in and are interdependent with the problems of the Vacated Space that are unanswerable, and therefore it is forbidden to enter in probing at all, for even the answerable problems, in an eyeblink one can enter from them into unanswerable problems, for it is all interdependent. For even the Qelipoth, which were generated from the Breakage, the essence of their root and power is from the beginning of the Vacated Space's constriction as mentioned. For if the secret of the constriction were not hidden, there would be no genesis of the Qelipoth at all, as mentioned.

And therefore in the future, when the secret of the constriction's intellect will be revealed in truth, all the Qelipoth will be nullified entirely, and "He will swallow up death forever" [Isa. 25:8] and "I will cause the spirit of impurity to pass out of the land" [Zach. 13:2] will be fulfilled, and as mentioned. And this is the aspect of the new name *MaH*, which is the aspect of the World of Repair, which is drawn from the aspect of `*Atiq*/the Ancient One, as the essence of the repair's perfection will be complete only in the future. But even though the repair was already begun at the time of Creation's genesis, as discerned in the Writings, which this is the aspect of the new name *MaH*'s secret, which He drew in order to repair the vessels, and from it is the genesis of all the Atziluth and all the Beriyah entirely — still, however, many sparks remained in the Qelipoth for the sake of free will, that they not be perfectly refined until Mashiach's coming.

And on account of these still unrefined sparks — which are the aspect of vessel fragments that are still unrepaired for the sake of free will, on account that the Vacated Space's intellect still has not shined in them perfectly, which this is the essence of the repair, as mentioned — there still remains the grip of the Qelipoth, which are the probers' problems and the apostasy, whence is the Yetzer Hara`'s power (as explained by us many times), and whence are all the ten kinds of arrows that are drawn from the breaking of the Vessels which are still not resolved, as mentioned. And therefore even though the king's daughter fled inside the ten walls of water, which are the aspect of the repair as mentioned, all the ten kinds of arrows reached her there, which have the power of the strictures that are still not refined, as mentioned.

And we are involved in this all our days, to refine the bad from the good, to refine and repair the rest of these sparks, in order to extract the arrows from the king's daughter and heal her. For, everyone, in accord with his transgressions, God forbid, thus gives power to the vessels' fragments, and the arrows prevail over the Shekhinah, as it were, God forbid, in the aspect of, "For Your arrows are gone deep into me" [Ps. 38:3], the aspect of, "He has bent His bow, and set me as a mark for the arrow" [Lam. 3:12] that was said during the Exile that happened through Yisrael's transgressions. And of this is said, "But he was wounded because of our transgressions, he was crushed because of our iniquities... a man of pains, and acquainted with disease" [Isa. 53:5,3], that is said of Mashiach's soul which suffers maladies and blows, who is the kingship of holiness, the aspect of the king's daughter, who suffers pains and afflictions etc. from the ten kinds of arrows.

And conversely, every one, in accord with his repentance and in accord with his good deeds, so does he add power to the Tzaddiq who involves himself in the king's daughter's healing, to extract all the arrows from her and heal her. And the whole time of the exile it is said of the Shekhinah and Kenesseth Yisrael

[Lam. 2:13], "For your breach is great like the sea; who can heal you?" and the scripture [Jer. 8:22], "Is there no balm in Gil`ad? Is there no physician there? Why then is not the health of the daughter of my people recovered?" and the scripture [Isa. 1:5-6], "The whole head is sick, and the whole heart faint; From the sole of the foot even unto the head there is no soundness in it, but wounds and bruises" etc., all from the arrows. But in the future will be fulfilled [Deut. 32:39], "I have wounded, and I heal:" He heals with that by which He wounds, in the aspect of, "My hand will yet have hold on [strict] justice..." [ibid. :41] that is said there about this matter, that his shooting an arrow and bringing it back, whereby he heals the king's daughter as mentioned, this is the aspect of sweetening the judgements at their root as mentioned.

POINT #9

And all the Torah the mitzwoth, everything is for the sake of refining the sparks left behind by the Breaking of the Vessels, as is known, whereby we extract the arrows from the king's daughter as mentioned. And this is the aspect of slaughter, which is the aspect of sweetening judgements at their root as mentioned, which this is the aspect of the one with the power shooting arrows and bringing them back as mentioned. And the essence of sweetening judgments at their root is by this aspect, namely by drawing revelation from the World of Repair, from the intellect of the constriction's secret that will be revealed in the future, whereby all the judgements are sweetened at their root. For the essence of all the judgments' root is from the start of the Constriction, as known, as from there descend and are generated all the strictures until sometimes they generate harsh judgements by means of the surge of the Qeliphoth that were generated the Vessels' breakages.

And when one wants to sweeten the judgements, it is impossible to sweeten them except at their root, namely one needs to go up to the root of the stricture that is drawn from the beginning of the Vacated Space's Constriction. And whoever can enter in there, for instance, those that are Tzaddik of the Era, that are of such great stature that they are in the aspect of Moshe, they can sweeten all the judgements at their root. For the essence of the judgements is from the intellect of the Vacated Space being hidden. For the essence of judgements is from hiding of the knowledge, for knowledge is the aspect of compassion, and concealment of knowledge is the aspect of judgements (as explained in Rabbeinu z"l's words many times). And the essence of concealment of knowledge in this world is drawn from concealment of the knowledge that is in the Vacated Space. So from thence is the grip of all the strictures, the Qelipoth, and the problems. And therefore whoever can enter the beginning of the Vacated Space's constriction and knows and perceives that there too Hashem Yithbarakh is hidden and concealed, and draws revelation from the knowledge and the repair that will be revealed in the future, thereby are automatically sweetened all the judgements from which all the constrictions and concealment were nursing, since it is revealed that Hashem Yithbarakh is found even there. And this is the aspect of sweetening the judgements at their root, namely by the beginning of the constriction, which is the root of all the judgements, by knowing that there too is Hashem Yithbarakh hidden, whereby everything is repaired, as mentioned.

POINT #10

Hence, the essence of the aspect of slaughter is the aspect of sweetening the judgments at their root, drawing and arousing the root of the judgment, which is the beginning of the constriction, which this is the aspect of the sword and knife of slaughter. And since we are fulfilling Hashem Yithbarakh's mitzwah with this sword and performing slaughter as he commanded us, hence we reveal that even in the grip of judgement, in the aspect of sword and knife, there too is hidden and concealed His wisdom and compassion. For in real truth, slaughter is a great compassion on the animal, as it is the essence of its eternal repair. And therefore through the mitzwah of slaughter we sweeten the judgements at their root and refine the good from the bad, human spirit from beastly spirit, which is the aspect of lack of knowledge, the aspect of the judgments' slag; we extract them and sweeten and repair them through the knife of slaughter, in the aspect of sweetening the judgements at their root as mentioned.

And therefore fish and locust need no slaughter, for the root of fish and locust is from the aspect of the repair that will be revealed in the future, therefore they need no slaughter. For fish grow in water, which is the aspect of the ten walls of water, which are the aspect of the repair that will be revealed in the future as mentioned. And therefore tzaddiqim are compared to fish, for tzaddiqim are the aspect of Mashiach (as Rabbeinu z"l explained elsewhere), the aspect of the World of Repair, as in each era they draw wondrous repairs from the aspect of the repair that will be revealed in the future, which is the aspect of the ten walls of water as mentioned. And the essence of maintaining the walls of water is in the merit and power of the mitzwah of charity (as explained in the story). And therefore the kosher indicators of fish are fins and scales; and the main thing is the scales, for whatever has scales has fins. For scales are the aspect of charity, the aspect of [Isa. 59:17], "And He donned righteousness like a coat of mail," the aspect of the armor of scales (as thoroughly explained before in *H' Dagim*; see there). For charity is the aspect of the Vacated Space's intellect that will be revealed in the future, "like the locust, whose garment is part of itself," the aspect of, "And my righteousness will testify for me" etc., the aspect of, "I donned righteousness," and as thoroughly explained in the torah "Go to Par`oh;" see there. And therefore charity pertains to the ten walls of water which are the aspect of the repair that will be revealed in the future, which this is the aspect of charity as mentioned. And thus it is explained above in *H' Dagim*, that charity is the aspect of water; take a good look there, for it relates to here, for charity is the aspect of the ten walls of water, the aspect of the World of Repair, which is the Vacated Space's intellect that will be revealed in the future, which is the aspect of charity, the aspect of "I donned righteousness" etc. as mentioned.

And therefore locust as well are likened to fish and are exempt from slaughter, for locust too are from the aspect of the repair that will be revealed in the future, as the constriction is "like the locust, whose garment is part of itself" (as explained in that torah "Go"), which this is the aspect of [Ex. 10:4], "Behold, tomorrow I bring locust in your borders." And therefore locust are juxtaposed to fish [Lev. 11:46, as mentioned] and are exempt from slaughter, for their root is from the aspect of the repair that will be revealed in the future; therefore they definitely need no slaughter, for the essence of slaughter pertains to sweetening judgements at their root to draw the repair from the intellect that will be revealed in the future at the beginning of the constriction etc. as mentioned. And since fish and locust are themselves drawn from this aspect, they require no slaughter.

POINT #11

And this is Rabbeinu z"l's writing there in that story that the walls of water are held up by the winds; see there. Accordingly, the king's daughter's healing is through the ten kinds of melody that are attained by this person who can cause all the ten kinds of wind to be balanced, see there, for the walls of water, which are the aspect of the Vacated Space's intellect, cannot be comprehended except through the aspect of melody (as thoroughly explained in the aforementioned torah "Go"), that the essence of the repair is through melody, which this is the aspect of, "Then Moshe will sing [yaShiR]" [Ex. 15:1], the aspect of, "Go, see/sing [taShuRi] from the head, faith" [Song 4:8] (take a good look there at all this).

For truthfully all the four aspects explained in this story, which are the four aspects TaNT"A (Ta`amim/Cantillations, Nequdoth/Vowel-spots, Tagim/Crowns, Otiyoth/Letters) etc., everything is interdependent, and each thing rises up and repairs the other, as discerned in the story, that she fled from the arrows into the walls of water, and the walls of water themselves are kept standing by the winds, which are the aspect of pulse-spirit and melody-spirit, for melody-spirit vitalitzes pulse-spirit (as explained in LM II). For the four aspects of TaNT"A as well are all interdependent and they draw from each other, and the essential ultimate perfection of the repair is by the aspect of Ta`amim, which is the aspect of playing the melody of the Ta`amim, which is the root of all, and it is the repair of all (as discerned in the Arizal's writings and in this story). Discern thoroughly, all this.

Likutei Halakhoth E"H Periah Urvia & Ishuth Hal. 3

POINT #10

And this is the aspect of Rosh Hashanah, Yom Kippur and the Ten Days of Repentance. For they are ten days, corresponding to the ten types of melody, which are the generality of joy, as mentioned. Therefore on Rosh Hashanah which is the first day of the Ten Days of Repentance, we arouse all kinds of melody through the mitzwah of sounding the shofar. For hearing the shofar's sound is the aspect of the ten types of melody, as written, "*Shiru-lo shir chadash, heitivu nagen bithru`ah*/Play well amid shouts of joy" (Ps. 33:3), and as we say before the blasts (Ps. 47:6-7), "God is gone up amidst the shouting sound (*teru`ah)*, Hashem amidst the sound of the shofar. Make music (*zammeru)* to God, make music; make music to our King, make music." For the shofar is the aspect of music (*zemiroth*) and melodies (*niggunim*), the aspect of the ten types of melody, to which corresponds the aspect of the ten soundings of the shofar, which are *TShR"T TSh"T TR"T* [*T=Teki`ah, Sh=Shevarim, R=teRu`ah*], which is blown during the ten *Malkhiyoth* (Kingships), ten *Zikhronoth* (Remembrances) and ten *Shofaroth*, which all this pertains to these ten types of melody, as discerned in the Tikkunim.

And therefore King David a"h ended the book of Psalms — which is composed of all the ten types of melody, which are the aspect of the ten lyrical styles in which the book of Psalms is composed; and as explained in Rabbeinu z"l's words (*LM II* #92) — with the psalm "Praise the Almighty in His Sanctity" [Ps. 150], which are ten *Hillul*s, which are the aspect of the ten types of song in which the Psalms are composed. So he ended with all the ten *Hillul*s as the conclusion of the book of Psalms. The final one of all these ten types of melody is "Praise him with the ringing of *Teru`ah*," for *Teru`ah*, which pertains to the shofar's sound, on Rosh Hashanah is comprised of all the ten types of melody as mentioned. For Rosh Hashanah is the first of the Ten Days of Repentance, and the essential repair of repentance is by the aspect of the ten types of melody, which are the entirety of joy, the aspect of reversing grief and sorrow to joy as mentioned. And as discerned in Rabbeinu z"l's words in many places, how much a man who is far from serving Hashem needs to rise up and make himself happy by any possible means of still finding in himself any good point. And this is the essence of his cure, for thereby he truly enters the scale of merit and can attain repentance, as is thoroughly explained on the verse, "I will make music to my God in my yet [being]" [*LM* 282 on Ps. 146:2].

Have a thorough look there, for this lesson, "I will make music to my God in my yet," needs to be reviewed a great deal and practiced, as Rabbeinu z"l heeded us a great deal to walk with this torah. For, every man, as long as he has pity on himself, and considers the eternal purpose, needs to very, very much enliven himself and to see, to seek, and to find in himself some good points, what he has ever done, some mitzwah or good things, in order to not be entirely downcast, and to accustom himself to make some joyful melody from time to time, especially on Shabbatoth and Yamim Tovim, when we need to be very, very happy in all sorts of joys from evening until morning, and make a great deal of joyous melody.

For the main way to follow Hashem Yithbarakh, especially for far people who need to return, is solely by means of the ten types of melody which are the aspect of the generality of joy as mentioned, and as discerned from the Rabbeinu z"l's words in the awesome and wondrous story which has never been heard in the history of the world: the awesome final story in the Seven Beggars, regarding which he said of himself that if he would know nothing but this story, he would still be an extremely great and wondrous marvel. For it is comprised of many torahs and many foremost tzaddiqim etc. etc.

And there at the end of this story, in the story of the Sixth Day, in which the handless beggar glorifies himself versus each and every one of them who boasted of the power in his hands etc. etc. — see there this whole wondrous and awesome matter — if you would have been amongst the *Machatzdei Chaqla* (Harvesters of the Field), or [even] if you have gotten a look from the holy books, especially the Tikkunim, the Zohar and the Saba, you would discern from afar, like one who "peers through a crack," the awesome "wonders of a perfect mind" [Job. 37:16]; but here is not the place to elaborate on this.

And at the end it explains that he boasts against all of them, because all of them, even though they were supreme on a most very exceedingly high level, and each one had a wondrous and awesome power in his hands that is not found even in one person per era, but only in singularly wondrous great tzaddikim that were one in many, many generations, for example the one boasting that he can remove the arrows with his hands even after the arrow has been shot and after the arrow has reached inside the one at whom they shot the arrow — "who has heard such a thing?" — who has heard such permutations of letters, a man boasting of such a novelty even in physicality, that in the place where an arrow was shot, a man can return and bring back the arrow after the arrow was dispatched and shot into the target person? For only Hashem Yithbarakh boasts of this, as our Rabbis z"l have said, "Flesh and blood shoots and arrow and cannot return it, but HK"BH shoots an arrow then returns it, as it says, "Yet my hand shall maintain hold of judgment" [Deut. 32:41 and Rashi there]. And especially since the matter of the arrows actually alludes to all the transgressions' damage to the Shekhinah, which are like arrows that are shot and which cause a great deal of damage to the Israelite soul, and to each and every man for every transgression and damage that he does, especially blemishing the Covenant; he really shoots an arrow at his soul, for the Covenant is called a "bow and arrow," as is known, in the aspect like our Rabbis z"l said, "Any sperm that is not shot like an arrow [cannot impregnate]," [*Chag.* 15a; *Nid.* 43a.]. And definitely the one who boasted that he can pull back the arrows after they have hit the target person was for sure a wondrous and awesome tzaddik and a wondrous novelty like no other in many generations, that he boasted that he can perform repair of the Covenant for one who has damaged it, which is the aspect of removing the arrows from where they were shot: Even though the one who boasted of this was such a wondrous and awesome novelty, still he was not regarded as such, in compare to this Handless Beggar.

For, the Handless One immediately asked him, "What kind of arrow can you pull back?" And he answered: such a kind. He spoke up and said, "You cannot heal the king's daughter;" see there. And even though I definitely do not attain knowing even one drop in the sea of the deepest meaning of the stories that

Rabbeinu z"l told that are brought in *Sipurei Ma'asiyoth* — and even more so, and all the more so, this story that is more awesome and holy that them all, as written there — nevertheless this matter is definitely hinted to in his words among all the rest of the awesome interests and secrets that he intended. But this interest is definitely also included in his holy words in this story. That is, this one asked him what kind of arrow can you remove, meaning what kind of Covenant damage can you repair, for there are many, many aspects of Covenant damage, millions and billions, for definitely not all damages and mistakes are equal, as everyone knows. He answered him, this kind (see there, what is written regarding the poisons that the arrows are smeared in, whereby the arrows injure etc., and everything alludes to this matter), in other words, this part of Covenant damage which is the aspect of this kind of arrow, he can pull back and repair. The Handless One replied: Still you cannot heal the king's daughter, since you can only pull back one kind of arrow.

And this is known, that the king's daughter there alludes to the Shekhinah, which is Kenesseth Yisrael, the entirety of the Israelite souls who are called "the King's Daughter," as it is written, "All-glorious is the King's daughter, within" [Ps. 45:13], and similarly in the Zohar and the Tikkunim it is called "the King's Daughter" in many, many places. And the Shekhinah in exile is downtrodden in afflictions and transgressions, as our Rabbis z"l said: when a human being suffers, what does the Shekhinah say? "Pain from my head, pain from my arm." As it says, "Rachel crying for her children, refusing to be comforted for her children" etc. [Jer. 31:14]; and regarding this it says, "He has bent His bow and set me as a target for the arrow. He has caused the arrows of His quiver to enter in my inward parts" [Lam. 3:12-13]. For, all the wicked arrows of Covenant damage are cast at the Shekhinah and Kenesseth Yisrael, as is known, and this is also the aspect of, "For Your arrows are gone deep into me, and Your hand is come down upon me" [Ps. 38:3].

And therefore even though this one boasted that he can remove an arrow, he still cannot heal the King's daughter, who is the Shekhinah, all the souls of Yisrael, since he can only remove one arrow. That is, he can only repair one kind of Covenant damage that he knows, but there are still wicked arrows that cause such great damage that even he cannot remove them and make repair.

B ut this Handless One boasted at the end that he can extract all the ten kinds of arrows that include all the kinds of mistakes, and all kinds of Covenant damage in the world, all the very greatest mistakes, transgressions and iniquities, God spare us; absolutely everything he can pull back and remove, and repair it all, for he can enter in all the ten types of walls of water wherein the King's daughter is lying, who fell down faint so many, many hundreds of years. And he can go in there in all the ten types of walls of water, and knows how to remove all the ten kinds of arrows. And he knows all the ten kinds of pulsebeats and knows how to heal her through all the ten types of melody. Hence the essence of the King's daughter's, the Shekhinah's, the entirety of the Yisraelite souls' healing, is through the ten types of melody making, which are the generality of joy. And this is Rabbeinu z"l writing in that torah that the essence of all physical and spiritual healing is through joy, which is the aspect of the ten types of melody making, for the ten types of melody making vitalize all the ten kinds of pulsebeats which are the man's vitality, and all the illnesses and all the healings depend on them, on the ten kinds of pulsebeats, as is known. So the essence of the vitality of the ten kinds of pulsebeats is through joy, which is the aspect of the ten types of melody making, therefore joy is an extremely great thing, and one needs to fortify himself in joy constantly with all his powers, for it is the essence of the body and the soul's healing, the aspect of the King's daughter's healing as mentioned.

H ence the essence of the repair of repentance — which is bodily and mental healing, as written, "Go and let us return to Hashem, for He has torn, and He will heal us" etc. [Hos. 6] — is by joy, which is the aspect of the ten types of melody making.

T herefore on Rosh Hashanah which is the first of the Ten Day of Repentance, all the ten types of melody are aroused through the mitzwah of hearing the shofar's sound which is comprised of ten types of melody. And this is what is brought in the Tikkunim many times, "Now the King's Daughter ascends with the ten types of melody making" etc.; see there.

Maps

Present-day maps indicating Breslev (presently Bratzlav), Uman
(Uman'), and other cities relevant to the Tales.

Abbreviations of Book Names

Abbrevia-tion	Description	Author
CM	Chayei Moharan, R' Nachman's Biography	R' Nathan of Nemyrev
Kethavim, Qawanoth	Writings of the Arizal	the Arizal
LM	Likutei Moharan, R' Nachman's Magnum Opus	R' Nach-man of Breslev
TZ, Tikkunim	*Tikkunei Zohar*, "Repairs of the Zohar," a special appendix to the Zohar. Its mission is the essential repair of the Shekhinah, namely in the lower worlds. *TZ* contains seventy commentaries on the first word of the Torah, *BERESHITH*, plus an additional eleven commentaries. R' Nachman extolled *TZ* as being entirely incomparable in sanctity and wisdom versus the rest of the Zohar (*CM* #359). He spent more time involved with *TZ* than with any other holy book.	R' Shim`on ben Yochai, aka Rashbi
Z"Ch	*Zohar Chadash*, parts of the Zohar published from manuscripts that were released after the publication of the Zohar and *TZ*, and containing material pertaining to both.	Rashbi and the *Chevraya Qadisha*, his Holy Friends

Transliterations Used

Hebrew	Transliterations	Comments
א Alef	'	
ב Beth	b v	
ג Gimel	g gh	
ד Daleth	d dh	
ה He	h	
ו Waw	o u w (more accurate)	v (more common)
ז Zain	z	
ח Cheith	ch	
ט Teth	t	
י Yodh	y i	
כ Khaf	k kh	
ל Lamedh	l	
מ Mem	m	
נ Nun	n	
ס Samekh	s	
ע `Ayin	`	
פ Pe	p f	
צ Tzaddi	tz ts	
ק Quf	q	k (more common)
ר Reish	r rh	
ש Shin, Sin	sh s	
ת Taw	t th	

Endnotes

1. An acrostic for NaChMaN found in Prov. 18:4; see Chayei Moharan #189

2. פוק חזי גבורתא דמריך, *puq chazi gevurta d'mareikh*, <u>Bava Bathra</u> 73a

3. *kayom hazeh*, Deut. 2:30, 4:20; I Kings 3:6, 8:24; Jer. 32:20, and many others

4. `Olam shekulo arokh*, "the day that is entirely (i.e. truly) long," <u>Chullin 142a</u>; <u>Mishneh Torah: Teshuvah 8</u>

5. <u>Ezra 9:9</u>

6. <u>Prov. 10:25</u>

7. Isa 42:9

8. Lam. 3:22

9. Isa. 12:3

10. דברים שהן כבשונו של עולם, <u>Chagiga 13a</u>

11. *qedoshei `elyon*

12. מחצדי חקלא, *mechatzdei chaqla*, Zohar

13. Num. 23:23

14. This is Eccl. 6:10, but with "*shehu*" instead of "*asher hu.*"

15. II Sam. 7:19

16. Eccl. 12:13, the end of the last verse of *Koheleth*

17. *ve'yismechu, ve'yesharim ya`alozu*, a phrase from Yamim Nora'im prayers

18. cf. Gen. 44

19. Ruth 4:7

20. Ps. 4:7

21. רחוק, מה-שהיה; ועמק עמק, מי ימצאנו, Eccl. 7:24

22. Isa. 33:18

23. Ps. 121:1

24. Isa. 33:14

25. Lam. 3:41

26. Ps. 31:5

27. Isa. 33:20

28. ibid :17

29. Isa. 23:18

30. אז במלאת ספק יפה כתרצה, הן אראלם ↑ צעקו חוצה, בן חלקיהו מארמון כיצא, אישה

31. יפת תואר מנוולת מצא, dirges of 9 Av; v. Jer. 15:9

31. Eccl. 3:11

32. Prov. 28:22

33. "In that year of [5]566/1806 after the child [his son Shelomoh Efrayim z"l] passed away, he went on the road to Medvedevka and its environs, and there he began to tell the first story in *Sipurei Ma`asiyoth*. And when he returned from the trip I was at his [place] and he repeated and told before us that story and he said, "On the way I told a story" etc., and then he said, "Now I'm going to start telling stories" etc. as printed there in *Sipurei Ma`asiyoth*." (*Yemey Moharnat* II #11)

34. a city on the Poland-Germany border

35. See *Midrash Tanchuma Vayetze* 16: that while Hashem retains to himself (in general; see *Taanith* 2a) the keys for rain, sustenance, revival of the dead and childbirth, He will grant these to tzaddikim. And *Midrash Tanchuma Va'eira* 22, *Bamidbar Rabbah* 14 and *Zohar* Vol. 1, 45b: "See how beloved tzaddikim are to Hashem, for whatever they do and decree, Hashem confirms it and fulfills it." And *Shabbath* 59b: "The tzaddik decrees, and Hakadosh Barukh Hu fulfills." And *Moed Katan* 16b: "I rule man. Who rules me? The tzaddik! For I make a decree and he can annul it." Et. al.

36. <u>36.0</u> <u>36.1</u> The word `etzem* was omitted here.

37. The big trip to Navritch, Zaslav, Ostroh, Dubna and Brod. See <u>*Chayei Moharan #160, 157, 68*</u>.

38. "*Shinei resha`im shibbarta*/ You have broken the teeth of the wicked" (Ps. 3:8); *Berakhot* 54b

39. do not pronounce the name: Samael, the accusing angel and the angelic prince of Esav

40. *mitzvah*: commandment or good deed, the root *tzaddi-vav* indicating a cleaving together of the commander, the performer, and the means.

41. do not pronounce the name: Samael, the accusing angel and the angelic prince of Esav.

42. This may refer to Leghorn/Livorno, the main port of Tuscany in central Italy, or perhaps Lugano, Switzerland. It is unclear since it says he travels into Italy from "Lagorna."

43. *chakham*; see *Sefer Hamidoth: Derekh* (Travel) II #4: By traveling, a person becomes discerning (*mevín*)

44. mazal: constellation; lit. "flow"; one's destiny or potential as provided by God via arrangement of the constellations

45. *Shabbath* 156

46. Crudely translated as "luck" or "fortune," *mazal* also denotes "constellation," and its root, *zal*, actually denotes drip or flow; thus *mazal* denotes the flow of providence and supervision from Hashem, down through the constellations and other devices.

47. *Chayei Moharan* #60 says that someone mentioned, in Rebbe Nachman's presence, a document written with golden letters, after which he told this story.

48. *groisser beryeh*

49. `*eved*, bondservant; "slave;" the bondmaid's husband

50. *la`akor,* here meaning to leave one's homeland

51. 51.0 51.1 a Talmudic expression introducing more than one alternative

52. Pl. *Behemoth*, sing. *behemah,* by root meaning "dumb beast" but usually denoting domestic quadrupeds of horned species e.g. cows and sheep; has connotations of animalistic traits.

53. Pl. *chayoth*, sing. *chayah,* the most general term in Hebrew for animals; it does not usually denote livestock, birds, fish or insects. Sometimes the author refers to *chayoth* and birds together, so that *chayoth* are land animals; and sometimes to *chayoth* and *behemoth* together, so that *chayoth* are wild animals.

54. 54.0 54.1 an Aramaic/ Talmudic expression

55. *keli,* meaning a tool, device, or vessel; not necessarily a musical instrument. A musical instrument is a *keli-zemer.*

56. 56.0 56.1 *Tsayt* with a *tzaddi* — an unusual spelling for "side" which is usually *zayt* as per Ger. *Seite.* Translator's note: there is a hint here.

57. 57.0 57.1 Yid. *der melekh vas er iz given,* Heb. *hamelekh shehayah*

58. *Se iz dart given oysgemalt a mensh.* It appears from the context that the depiction is a statue, but it also could also be a two-dimensional picture.

59. *me zal im arayn shtelin inveynik in der gartin arayn; veya`amidu oto lifnim betokh hagan hazeh*: both phrasings have extra expressions for "inside"

60. *gishlagineh vegin*, lit. "beaten paths"

61. *Zaytin* here is spelled normally, with a *zayin.* Heb. is still *tzad.*

62. כשהניחו הארון על הפרות התחילו לשורר

63. *Shab.* 63a

64. v. Isa 9:14; *Chayei Moharan* #272 et al.

65. See #114.

Made in the USA
Monee, IL
07 January 2026

37516127R00262